Foxfire 4

Foxfire 4

fiddle making, springhouses, horse trading,
sassafras tea, berry buckets, gardening, and
further affairs of plain living

edited with an introduction by
ELIOT WIGGINTON
Afterword by Richard M. Dorson

Anchor Books
Anchor Press / Doubleday
Garden City, New York

Eliot Wigginton, who started *Foxfire* magazine with his ninth- and tenth-grade English classes in 1966, still teaches high school in the Appalachian Mountains of North Georgia and, with his students, guides the activities of The Foxfire Fund, Inc. His students now are expanding their efforts to include not only the production of the *Foxfire* magazine and books, but also the creation of television shows for their community cable TV station, a series of record albums of traditional music, and a furniture-making business. Eliot Wigginton is also the editor of I WISH I COULD GIVE MY SON A WILD RACCOON.

Library of Congress Cataloging in Publication Data
Main entry under title:

Foxfire 4.

  "Portions of this book first appeared in Foxfire magazine."
  Bibliography: p. 490.
  Includes index.
  1. Country life—Georgia—Rabun Gap. 2. Handicraft—Georgia—Rabun Gap.
3. Rabun Gap. Ga. I. Wigginton, Eliot. II. Foxfire.
S521.5.G4F645   975.8'123
ISBN: 0-385-12087-7
Library of Congress Catalog Card Number 76–50803

The Anchor Press edition is the first publication of *Foxfire 4* in book form. It is published simultaneously in hard and paper covers.

Anchor Books edition: 1977

Jacket photo courtesy of John Hill
Jacket and Cover Designs by Jim McWilliams

CONTENTS

Introduction 7

Etta and Charlie Ross Hartley 15

Knife Making 51

Wood Carving 68

Fiddle Making 106

Thomas Campbell, Plow-stock Maker 126

Wooden Sleds 134

Gardening 150

Bird Traps, Deadfalls, and Rabbit Boxes 194

Annie Perry 202

Horse Trading 215

Making Tar 252

Logging 257

Aunt Lola Cannon 317

Water Systems 334

Berry Buckets 382

Cheese Making 385

Rev. A. Rufus Morgan 394

Update 442

Afterword by Richard M. Dorson 482

Index of People 486

A Selected Listing of Periodicals and Resource Material
  About the Appalachian Region 490

This book is dedicated to organizations like Patch in the Cabbagetown neighborhood of Atlanta, run by men and women who have consistently put the welfare of their neighborhoods ahead of personal gain—and to those blessed foundations that support them, year after year.

INTRODUCTION

There are several forces in the lives of teachers that seem to be universal. One of these forces, despite anything we can do to counteract it, sees to it that certain students will remain imbedded in our memories.

I've had my share, so far, of students like that. They are indelible. One of them, a kid named Ernest, is one of those extraordinary human beings who, while he was in our high school, set aside nearly every one of his weekends to help me build my log house. He raised logs into place, cut out the window and door holes with my chain saw, set rafters—he was everywhere on that structure, laughing and talking. Despite the fact that we were close then, I lost track of him temporarily after he left our school, but I never forgot him.

Several years later, during the September summer of 1976, I was in the parking lot of our school on one of those scorching afternoons that bring everything to a halt. I was leaning against the side of my green pickup truck talking to Lawton Brooks when I gradually became aware of another presence. I glanced backwards over the tailgate and saw there a skinny little four-and-a-half-foot-high kid looking up at me, grinning out through braces and from under a shock of blond hair, and wearing one of those yellow football jerseys with black stripes around the sleeves, jeans, and a pair of tennis shoes that must have been rescued from the trash at least twice.

He hesitated for a second, and then said, "Are you Wig? I'm Ernest's little brother. He told me to find you when I got here. I'm David Flanagan."

And instantly a wave crashed through me, and I looked into that apprehensive little face and saw, one after the other, each face replaced by another, an endless parade in which each student I had succeeded with, or failed with, was replaced by another in a never-ending line—each with new hopes and new needs and new expectations. And I felt things smashing around inside of me that I can never remember feeling before.

It was important that that happen then, for during the same summer, we at Foxfire celebrated our tenth birthday while the nation celebrated its two-hundredth. And I spent a lot of time doing—in regard to our organization —what I assumed others were supposed to be doing in regard to the nation: looking backward in order to see forward. I saw we had come a long way, and I noted, with gratitude, that we had passed through some choppy waters since I wrote the introduction to *Foxfire 3,* and we had come out on the other side relatively unscathed—strengthened instead of weakened.

At the time I wrote that introduction, quite frankly, I was frightened. The outside world had descended on us with such force that, from our perspective, we saw that world as the greatest single threat to our survival—a force that could consume us, and cause us to lose sight of our perspective, our main goals, and our main purposes.

And so we built a wall around ourselves and our kids. I'm convinced that that was an appropriate—even vital—reaction to all the strange fists beating on our door. It gave us time to breathe, time to regroup, time to get our priorities back in order and figure out how to keep them there. For several years we were more introspective than we had been in the past, and we experimented with our own educational formula in relative peace.

Large portions of that defense still stand, and appropriately so. They will be there for as long as our organization survives. But from where I stand now, I can see that other portions have been broken down, not from without but from within, as we've gone through the same kind of maturing process as an organization that we celebrate as we observe it in our kids. That maturing happened, and is happening, I think, for two reasons.

First was the growing realization of how much our success had depended on that very outside world we feared so greatly. When *Foxfire* magazine was young, most of the significant events affecting our little project were initiated in our behalf by others. Junius Eddy, for example, who was with the Office of Education when I hit Washington one day begging for money. He picked up a phone, called Herb McArthur at the National Endowment for the Humanities, and set up an appointment for me that resulted in our first significant grant.

Or Mike Kinney, a good friend and college fraternity brother turned editor who got us to put *The Foxfire Book* together and talked Anchor Press into taking a chance on it.

Or this: Shortly after our corporation was formed, I was in Washington again trying to recruit some men and women to serve on our advisory board. Someone suggested Sam Stanley of the Smithsonian's Center for the Study of Man, for at that time we were entertaining the notion that other students in other cultures might someday want to do the same sort of thing we were doing in Georgia, and since Sam was an expert in several Indian cultures, we thought he might be able to be helpful. Sam was visited several hours after I left his office by Brian Beun and Ann Vick of IDEAS, a private foundation in Washington that was exploring ways of assisting various Indian groups. Sam showed them the copies of *Foxfire* that I had left with him, they got in touch, and on my next visit to Washington came down and bailed me out of the jail I had been placed in because I didn't have enough cash with me to settle a traffic violation I made in northwest D.C. rush-hour traffic on the way to the five P.M. appointment I had with them; and that meeting led to our eventual collaboration as consultants for dozens of new *Foxfire*-type publications in high schools all over the country, and opened up a whole new series of educational opportunities for students of mine who were often invited by new projects to spend a summer on location helping them get their first issue of a magazine together. Mike Cook, for example, spent a summer in Ramah, New Mexico, helping to start the Navajo publication, *Tsa'Aszi'*, then majored in journalism at the University of Georgia, and is now on our staff running our entire videotape operation. Claude Rickman was able to spend a summer in Kennebunkport, Maine, helping Pam Wood and her kids start their magazine, *Salt;* they now have their first book out, and Ellen Massey's group in Lebanon, Missouri, that publishes *Bittersweet* will soon have one as well. Recently IDEAS sponsored the publication of two books designed to help teachers implement a *Foxfire*-type project in their own schools. One of the books, *Moments: The Foxfire Experience,* I wrote specifically for teachers. The other, *You and Aunt Arie: A Guide to Cultural Journalism,* was written for students not by me (and that's especially gratifying), but by Pam Wood and her kids at *Salt.*

And it was through IDEAS that I was introduced to the Highlander Center in New Market, Tennessee, where I met Myles Horton, its founder (a man I mention briefly in the introduction to *Foxfire 2*), and later Mike Clark, its present director, and Guy Carawan, its music director. Guy introduced us to George Reynolds, and George and his wife, Sharrod, are now on our staff helping our kids do fieldwork in traditional music.

Often, I wonder what would have happened had Brian and Ann not been able to come down to that police station and pay my fine for running that stop sign on S Street in Washington.

Linkages. Moments when lives intersect and combine to the eventual enrichment of both. We are not—and must not be—isolated if we are to grow. Then, as now, that strikes me as being a very profound notion, for those intersections in our lives, if welcomed, lead us on in ways we could never have mapped in advance. It's an old notion ("Knowing how way leads on to way . . .") ; no less valid then than now. As worth noting now as then. Again and again during those first ten years, new friends outside our region unselfishly opened doors, linked us up with friends of theirs, and so the network grew. And as this happened, so, too, came our growing realization that implicit in the selfish acceptance of that generosity was our obligation to take some of that energy and pass it on to others beyond ourselves in ways that we had never tried before. And down came a piece of the wall.

Second was a realization, growing with equal force, that we had been cheating our kids. Those who were not, at that point in their lives, able to get caught up in and excited and motivated by the processes involved in publishing *Foxfire* were cheated because that was all we had to offer. Those who did get caught up in what we had to offer got cheated later for the same reason—we could stretch them no further mentally or emotionally.

In addition, by being fiercely selfish in the examination of our own tiny piece of the globe to the exclusion of others, we ran the risk of isolating the students from the larger community of man that most of them would one day have to enter. I have learned through bitter experience, for example, that it is not enough for my kids to have an intimate understanding of their own past, roots, and heritage. That is immensely important, but to be truly effective citizens, they must next acquire an equally sophisticated knowledge of their culture's relationship to others. We are a multicultural world, and we are all linked one to another, for better or for worse.

In our rigorous self-examination, we ran the risk of making some of our students self-indulgent and defensive to the point where they could believe that only their own community had value; and so sometimes they, as students, erected the same kinds of walls that our organization had earlier erected. So down came another chunk of the wall.

Retaining as our basic educational tenet our conviction that true education must be more experiential than passive, we began slowly to add components to our program that we hoped would productively engage those kids who were not presently excited by print journalism, stretch those kids who were in ways they had never been stretched before by our program, and establish linkages that would move them more actively beyond their own community in terms of understanding and sensitivity.

One step at a time, we began to expand, strengthened and emboldened by a new perspective on our roles and responsibilities as an organization; adding each new component slowly, as it seemed appropriate and as it seemed possible for us to implement, each being a natural, organic extension of our educational philosophy rather than an artificially imposed new gimmick that could distract and fragment us.

We had always known, for example, that there is a larger Appalachia, beset with staggering problems to which we owe allegiance, for we are all fighting the same battles, facing the same foes. We are now actively working to build linkages with other Appalachian organizations, and assist them wherever possible in the same way we were once assisted. When Pam Porter showed up on our doorstep one day from Atlanta looking for a job with us, rather than hiring her for ourselves (since we reserve our staff openings primarily for people from this community as jobs are almost non-existent here), we sent her back to Atlanta to Cabbagetown, the desperately poor Southern Appalachian neighborhood there that grew up around the Fulton Bag and Cotton Mill at the turn of the century. Our kids then voted to give Patch, the community organization there, a small grant with which they could hire Pam, helped them get a second grant from the Georgia Arts Commission to keep her employed there working with their kids, and then rejoiced with them as they published a book of their own about Cabbagetown that is filled with interviews with elderly residents along with recipes and photographs. The book, *Cabbagetown Families, Cabbagetown Food*, is being marketed by Patch to bring additional operating income into that organization. Since it completely paid for itself in a matter of weeks after· publication, other books are being planned.

In addition, we've worked out a program whereby kids from Cabbagetown—many of whom have never been to the mountains where their grandparents were born and raised—can come and stay with our kids at our center for varying periods of time to learn more about what is meant by roots; and my kids visit Patch to find out what an Appalachian ghetto is like in the middle of a city.

We are also working closely with Patch to develop, in one of the abandoned mill buildings, a furniture industry that will turn out authentic hand reproductions of mountain primitive furniture. My students, assisted by kids from Cabbagetown, will scour our part of the mountains for patterns, record those patterns, produce a catalogue filled with photographs of the furniture we can offer; and, with the help of local men, they will hire, round up the necessary wood from local sawmills, cut out the pieces according to the patterns, and truck the pieces to Atlanta for assembly (with wooden pegs), finishing, and marketing by Cabbagetown residents on a co-operative basis. We will split the proceeds, and use the profits to provide additional jobs in both areas.

Using the royalties money that has come to us through the sale of the *Foxfire* books, we have added staff members here, each of whom has the responsibility of developing a whole new range of projects and opportunities and linkages for our kids:

Mike Cook, for example, has expanded our videotape program to the point where we are now broadcasting programs filmed and edited by kids on a weekly basis over our county cable TV system. The programs are not only *Foxfire* articles on videotape, but also such things as in-depth studies by students on such issues as clear-cutting on National Forest land, the advantages and disadvantages of consolidated schools (we are about to open one in our county) versus neighborhood schools, and interviews with candidates for regional political offices.

George and Sharrod Reynolds have, through new courses they are offering in our school, developed a file of musicians in the region, and have our students now building an archive of traditional music. Out of this work has now come a series of record albums recorded, edited, designed, and distributed by our students under our Foxfire label. The albums feature traditional musicians talking about and playing their music, mountain song writers who are creating new music out of their roots (some of them are from Cabbagetown), as well as mountain people talking about their lives, their aspirations, and their dreams—our "personality" articles on albums.

Paul Gillespie and Suzy Angier have begun our regional publishing company, the first offering from which was produced by Suzy and her kids and was titled, *Memories of a Mountain Shortline*. It is an oral history of the fifty-seven-mile-long Tallulah Falls Railroad that used to run through our county (and was so spectacular that Walt Disney used it as the site for his film, *The Great Locomotive Chase*) but is now defunct. Paul is working with students who are writing two more books: One is a sociological study of mountain religion that includes interviews with over fifty mountain preachers, each of whom was over eighty-five years of age; the other is an oral history of everyone of the log buildings that have been reconstructed at our educational center, along with a photographic record of their moving and reconstruction. Margie Bennett, in addition, is working with students who are interviewing black Appalachian residents for a forthcoming study of the black experience in the mountains.

Our students have also designed and built log playground structures for two elementary schools, have designed and equipped two woodworking shops at our center, and laid out one nature trail. By the time this book is published, we will have added a staff member who will be working with them on environmental studies, and will be building a greenhouse with them for use as a laboratory.

In every instance, these extensions are offered in the form of courses within our public high school, and the students who are involved in them receive full scholastic credit for the work they do with us. All this from a little high school magazine, the first issue of which was paid for by a community that believed in our potential.

And it is only in that growth—that welcoming of appropriate linkages in our lives and that receiving and giving of energy—that we live and mature. Cut off, like so many old people we have met, we shrivel and become dust. Cut off, like so many high school students we have met in classrooms around this nation, we atrophy.

As one teacher in one county—the entire population of which could be swallowed up in one corner of one suburb of any major city—I must constantly remind myself that it is only through rejoicing at the opportunities provided by these extensions of our original work that I and the staff I hire can build a network of experiences and opportunities for kids that will connect them to themselves, to their school, to their community, to their region, and to the world; and provide for each student an endless number of entrees *into* that world, and an endless measure of determination and belief in their capacity to act responsibly and sensitively and morally within it. This, rather than throwing them naked onto the world's streets with no more blessing than a half-remembered graduation speech.

All of us, as teachers, must have an infinite measure of hope for humanity on this rock as it whirls through space, and an infinite measure of determination to get better at this job each year and to correct the insane mistakes we make with such distressing frequency. For always, in lock step, one behind the other, constantly appearing behind the tailgates of our pickup trucks, fresh-faced, open, scared, hopeful, shuffling in tennis shoes, and grinning out through braces come the David Flanagans, asking where we stand.

BEW

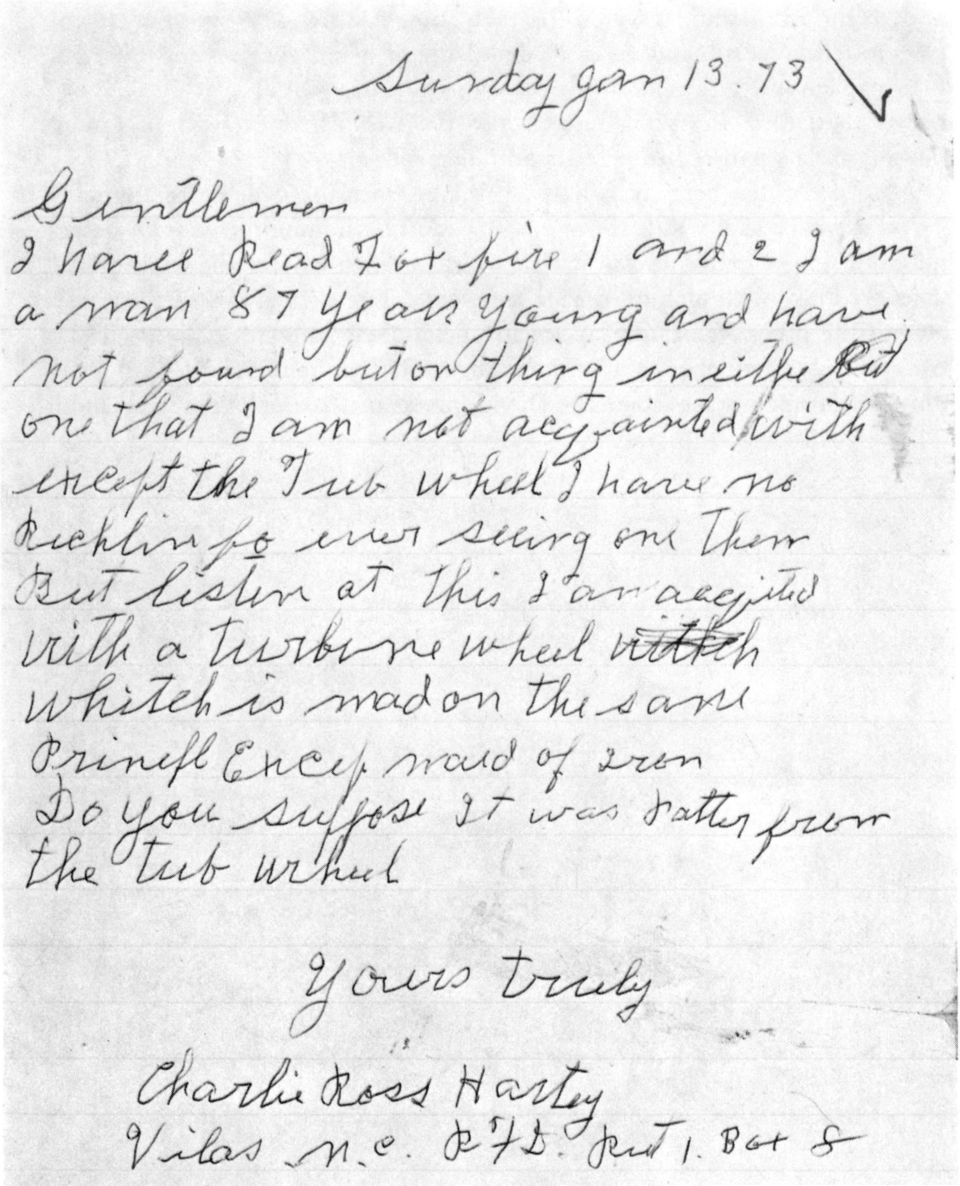

Sunday Jan 13. 73

Gentlemen
I have Read For fire 1 and 2 I am
a man 87 Years Young and have
not found but on thing in eithe But
one that I am not acquainted with
except the Tub wheel I have no
Ricklinfo ever seeing one Them
But listen at this I am acquited
with a turbine wheel which
whitch is made on the same
Prinufl Excep made of iron
Do you suppose it was datter from
the tub wheel

Yours truly

Charlie Ross Hartey
Vilas N.C. R.F.D. Rut 1. Box 8

PLATE 1   The letter Charlie sent us, which began our friendship.

ETTA AND CHARLIE ROSS HARTLEY

The letter on the opposite page arrived in our office one day, and sent us all in search of a map of North Carolina that could show us where Vilas was. Mr. Hartley sounded like someone we'd like to meet. We found, to our delight, that Vilas was near Sugar Grove, and we had already been in communication with a Tedra Harmon there who made banjos and had agreed to show us how (see *Foxfire 3*). We now had twice as much reason for a pilgrimage into that part of the mountains.

We wrote Mr. Hartley back immediately and asked permission to visit with him, received it, confirmed the dates with Tedra, and headed out only to be turned back by the gasoline shortage that had closed every gas station on our route. We returned home, tried it again two months later, and made it.

The greeting we received from Charlie and his wife was so warm and genuine that in the week we spent up there, their home became our base of operations. None of us really know how it happened. It just seems that we were constantly passing their little home on the way to another serendipitous interview, and we'd stop in for a moment only to find that they had anticipated us, and had a pot of coffee on the stove and pies on the table. We touched base with them several times a day.

Subsequent trips up that way have kept the friendship open—a friendship we are flattered by, and grateful for.

In the first part of this chapter, Charlie comments on the *Foxfire* books, and fills in the holes he's found as he read carefully through them. In the second part, we focus on Charlie's own life as a builder, mason, contractor, family man, and remarkable human being.

Article by Ray McBride, Steve Smith, Cheryl Stocky, and Louise Freeman. Photographs by Tom Carlton.

Part I

They's a lot of this stuff that began to slip my mind until I started reading these here *Foxfire* papers. But all that stuff is the truth. I bet they ain't a word in there from them old fellers what ain't the truth. There's so much of it I know. Now I've not done all of it, but they's a lot of it I have done. I've made every piece about a wagon at one time or another in my life. I've never built chimneys for log homes, but I've helped patch up one or two. I've been with a lot of different people. I've worked nearly everywhere.

Now all of these old buildings that you'll find—all these log buildings— was built before my day. I was born in a log house over here on Highway 105. And my brother was born there. Now we lived at what was known at that time as the old Moss place. And we lived in a log house. In fact, there was two log houses; and my wife's mother and daddy lived in one, and my dad and me lived in the other. Now I'm just going to tell you what I can remember. I don't think my daddy was ever as poor as I'm going to tell you about, but my daddy was a poor man.

The real poor people that I can remember used ash cakes. Now that's maybe something you don't know. If you happen to have a hearth, you rake your fire coals or your ashes out on it. If you have your dough ready, you

PLATE 2   Charlie Ross Hartley.

laid it down on that and you covered that with coals or ashes. When that got done, you'd take it up and shake the ashes off and eat it; and that's the fun that the old poor men like my dad got to do.

Now my dad was poor, and they was a few of them poor people right up and down the Watauga River and in Valle Crucis at the time. My dad was a renter. We moved from place to place around there for several years before we got our own place.

I'm going to tell about one feller now—he's dead now—that I've always had a lot of respect for. Back in the Beech Mountain country—I don't know how it happened—but they settled some Hicks in there. And why and where they come to get into the mountains, I don't know how it ever happened. But there was a set of Hicks. I built a house back there on that mountain for a feller by the name of Ben Hicks, and he took a great interest in telling me how they went along. But I built that house on the first lot that the first Hicks that ever come into that mountain come to. And he told me just what I told you'ns about ash pones. He said, "Mr. Hartley, you won't believe it, but my dad and us lived on ash pones."

And he told me just the same tale that my mother and daddy—in fact, my mother and daddy baked ash pones just to show us kids how to bake them. And the truth is, I helped bake them myself for the curiosity to see if I could bake them. And old man Hicks told me his poor little boy lived on ash cakes when he first come to this country. But now by the time I was in there, they had a good living—plenty of money. But they worked for it. I don't know, but his old daddy, he told me how much land the old Hicks had—I call them old Hicks because they was the first—and I believe it was about twelve hundred acres of land.

All right, now, you take the washing business. Now *Foxfire* starts it with a black washpot. Now they was absolutely no washpots at my knowing for quite a few years. We used a brass kettle. It would hold, I would say, about two bushels. Pretty good sized ones. Now that kettle was hung on two forked stakes. One set up on one side and one over there. One was sorta loose and you would pick up the crossbar on this end and carry it around—set it on the ground if you wanted to, or empty it. Now that kettle—with the whole community, that kettle was what they done all their washing in. They cooked in it. They done everything they wanted in that brass kettle.

And the washing, now, they always had to go to a branch or a creek—seems to me it was mostly a branch since it had more water at it. They got ready to wash them clothes and they'd boil them out in that kettle with lye soap. That's all we knowed in them days. I can't ever remember seeing a cake of store-bought soap. [Then they'd carry the clothes to the branch in tubs.] There must have been at that time some tub makers. In fact, my daddy could make tubs. He had all the tools, but I never saw him make but one. But we had a wood bucket. Now that's what we had at that time. You put your clothes in it and carried them out here now to the branch and tried to find a flat rock high enough for battling. Patty-cake with the battling stick, we called it. All them battling sticks—well, I guess I've seen a hundred of them—was made of red maple. Now you might wonder why red maple? Well, red maple is a fine grain, and in beating on them clothes, the grain stays smooth. Now you take oak, poplar or chestnut—it's got a coarse grain to it if you remember. If you beat with that kind, it gets so that it's rough and leaves streaks there and beats your clothes all to pieces.

Now that water, you can't rinse your clothes in a pond. You've got to have your water running. We always tried to catch a place where the water was running over the shoals or something—hold your clothes under that and rinse them. Sometimes, if you didn't have that, you could manage: get you a rock and roll him into the branch. Then when the water came rushing over it, you rinse there.

Then you get to the place next where you have water running through the heart of a log. Now the first log that I ever saw notched from the top to carry water, I made it. We got to a place that was too level to wash in, and we just absolutely had no place for water. My mother, she walked up to this little poplar tree—I'd say about eight inches in diameter—and she said, "Charlie, I believe you can cut this down and hew me out a log to run my water through so we can pour it off."

I said, "Ah, Mother, I can't."

She'd seen one somewheres, of course: "Yeah. Chop it down, square it off and leave the top on and I'll show you how it's done."

I chopped him down, squared him off, and I just started chopping along there—chopping with the axe. Chopped a little notch down into it—what they call a "V." Now that's the first one I ever saw, and I made 'it myself. But since that time, I've seen hundreds of feet of them.

Now that beating clothes on the rock, it does wear them; but them old-timers had to do something. When we come along, it was much the same way, and that's the way we done that.

Boil them, rinse them, beat them, go back and rinse them again to get the wrinkles out of them, and then dry them. Hang them on the fence. 'Course they wasn't no wire so they had to hang them on rail fences, bushes, poles—stuff like that.

Now then, that wasn't just my dad and I that had to live that way. It was all of them up and down the Watauga River. And all of them fellers outside of my dad owned their farms. 'Course the farms was handed down to them from their own forefathers.

I don't know what ever went with them brass kettles. I've no knowledge of them going. A part of the folks had a six-foot brass kettle three feet deep.

It was built up with rocks and mud—a wonderful job done with mud. You can take red clay and make a wonderful job of that. Old Daddy Beard—of course his daddy was sick; he'd been shot by a Yankee—now he had a six-foot washpot. And Captain Ben Beard had one which had been handed down to him by his daddy sitting back on the road. I've saw that several times. It used to sit up by the barn there, and there's a little old branch goes up the hill there on the right. It set there for years and years right at the edge of that branch. And all the old-timers that I can remember that had them six-foot brass kettles scalded their hogs in them.

Now then, I'm going to tell you a tale about black pots. I was a great big boy, now, when the black pots come around. And in fact, I never thought about where in the devil did them brass kettles get to until after I started [this interview]. What happened to these kettles—where they went—I'll never know. But now the first black pots my daddy ever had come from the Hagamans. They owned a sawmill up here. And they'd started going broke. A feller by the name of Moss owned it originally. Hagaman bought it, but finally he went broke on that place there and owed a lot of money. Finally he left there with his three or four boys. I've been told they left here in the night to get away. Well, naturally when they got away, and them broke, that big farm—something over four hundred acres in it but it wasn't worth over much of fifteen or twenty dollars—that was taken away from him [along with] what little stuff he had.

Now I can remember two items he had that my dad took care of for him. One was one of these black pots, and there was a tub. My daddy saved them until Tom, one of the boys, got sorta straightened out. They never did get this place back here back. There wasn't no use 'cause the people had already took all they had. You couldn't blame them for not coming back and paying off after all that they'd had had been took from them. But Tom come back to visit my daddy, and Daddy took him out there and showed him what he had saved for him. And he looked around and said, "Well, what good are they to me? I can't get them home." He said, "You just take care of them."

Now my dad, that's how he got his first black pot.

We used that pot until we burned one leg off—one leg off and a hole through it. Now that sounds like that pot was ruined don't it? But my daddy went to the blacksmith's shop and made him a piece of bar to fit down through there and put a bolt and a little washer on there and tightened her right up and we've used that thing for years and years now with a homemade leg on it.

Now then, we come to the skillet. I think that my dad had a skillet when I first remember, but I'm not positive of that. All of these folks now that I knowed at that time had a skillet that you baked your bread in. When I was a right small kid I can remember us baking pies in one—what we called beef pies. Now that was up till I was pretty much grown. I don't think that I ever had a biscuit to eat until after we bought a little farm. We finally, after all that moving around, got a little farm of our own. Then we raised our own wheat.

These old-timers, now, staying up and down Watauga River—beautiful country, good living in there—they was faring just like the rest of us. They were eating cornbread baked in the skillet. All of them done that. That's how hard we lived back then. It was just hard, and that's all there was to it.

There was no stores when I can first remember. The first one I can remember was a little store at Valle Crucis. It was right straight across from where Frank Taylor's is now. But he didn't sell very much. He didn't have nothing much. You might say he had the building. You didn't sell nothing much then 'cause nobody bought nothing much. Now they didn't buy coffee and shortening back in them days. You know what they used? Spicewood tea. And red sassafrak tea. Now that's what they used. I never did see any coffee till I was grown.

They didn't know what sugar was. They used molasses. When I first remember, they was a lot of maple trees, and they made lots of tree sugar, them old-timers did. Now I wouldn't be surprised when they wanted some sweetening that they didn't use that maple sugar. They made a lot of it. That's the first sweetening that I can ever remember myself was that maple sugar. Them old sages knowed more than both you and me put together. You got to give them credit for that. I wish you could go with me and see some of the stuff that they worked out.

I don't know why it is, but they's a lot of people in this country here—young people I'm talking about, educated folks—that wants some old-timey stuff. Just a world of them. I had so much of it that I wasn't interested in old-timey stuff. I never paid much attention [until recently]. [My wife] bought what books I got. Then we got that *Foxfire* and we'd set up there and we'd forget ourselves. Set up there and talk about old times. We'd set up and set up and talk three hours at a time about old times, and she loved to talk about them. And she gets a great kick out of me telling her about that old-time business because I know it. Take number one *Foxfire* there. I'm telling you the truth. That was so much word for word like I knowed— every word through thataway. Until number two. Just for fun I wanted to see how much [those kids had] missed [the truth]. But they didn't. If you put two rocks out here together you couldn't make it no clearer than that is. The board making was true. The log cabins was true, so truthful. Them old haint tales and snake lore, I went through all of them. Except I never have seen a blacksnake kill a poison snake. I've heard that talk all my life. I did talk to one man in Maryland, and I guess he told me the truth. He said he was out in one of them old fields, and he went into a fine blackberry field. And they was so nice and sweet he stopped in there to eat some berries and he heard something coming down through the briars. That's the way he told me now. He got to looking down to see what it was, and it was a rattle-snake running from a blacksnake. And he said not long after they got through the briars, the blacksnake caught the rattlesnake, and he had to stay for that fight till it killed it. I never have saw that happen, but I've heard lots of them tell they'd do that. And I believe there's one or two men in *Foxfire* that said they'd seen that happen. I'm not sure—I never saw that happen—but I'll tell you one thing. We lived near a copperhead den. We had hundreds of copperheads around. But you take a summer where we had a lot of blacksnakes and we didn't see but very little copperheads. Now that's a honest fact. But as far as seeing a blacksnake kill a poison snake, I've never done it.

Now medicine is a late thing. You know what *Foxfire* says about the way teeth was pulled? That's the truth as straight as you can go. It's going to take an older man than I am to show me something in that old book that I didn't know about. Everything's there that I know about. A lot of them old remedies we used. Let me tell you something. There was eleven children in our family. I'm the oldest one. A midwife took care of all of us but two. We had no doctors, and we absolutely had to depend on the old midwife. That old midwife would come out here and wait on you when you were sick or having a baby. They was wonderful women.

And they could always find tea. I've heard doctors argue that that tea wasn't worth a damn, but in my opinion, them midwives nine times out of ten were pretty well right with that tea stuff they had. I was raised when that's all the stuff we ever had. Made the tea myself. We had no doctors. It was live or die. You got pneumonia fever back in them days and most of them died. But a few old midwives lots of times would pull them through even with the pneumonia fever. Them old people deserve a lot of credit for what they done. The young doctors today, if they had to get out and do what the others did, they'd sure enough be up against a stump.

We lack a lot giving the old-timer credit for what he done. He done pretty doggone well. But one thing that I can't understand: what sort of home did them people from England and Germany have that [made them] come here to develop this country? Now my ancestors—the head of my name—come from England. What sort of home was in England [to make them leave] for this old rugged country? Two hundred years ago, and we can't imagine what a wilderness this was. At least I can't, even if I have been here eighty-seven years. It's a mystery to me. But another hundred years from now they'll be somebody along here wondering what *we* were doing. . . .

First old-timers that come here, they lived on game. They didn't have wheat and corn and stuff like we do today. That's what they lived on. I'm telling you, that old man that broke this river up, he deserves more credit than he ever got. How in the dickens that ever come about, that's just something to think about. I've been in log houses. In fact, I was raised in one that was two stories. Two-story log house, and them logs was just setting up there just as fine, and they had nothing else absolutely to work with but a pole axe and a broadaxe. That's all they had, and they knowed that was all they had, and then achieved the houses that they built—wonderful houses. And that's all they had, and they made them.

My dad was a good blacksmith, and I saw him lay a head on an axe. I never saw him make a broadaxe, but all them had homemade axes now that done the work. They were all homemade. And you could grind them axes and whittle them down where you could shave the hair off your legs, and how in the dickens them old-timers could ever temper so good. But they made them up in the country. There was blacksmithing. They kept their work going. It might be possible that up in one settlement they'd have one or two blacksmiths.

Now when it came to raising a house—old folks has told me this—when old folks got ready to build a house (a new man coming into the settlement or a new man got married)they'd pitch in there, get all them logs out, and get all them logs together enough to build the house. Then they would have a log rolling and get that house raised maybe in one day. I've talked to fellers who did them, so I guess I've got it pretty straight. I've heard one man say that he helped make a man a house out of poplar logs, and he said he split them, hewed them out, got every log ready up through the rafters, and then fifty men got in there and they laid that house up in one day. After the logs is split and cut out, there still is a lot of work to do 'cause you have to notch them. Them notches was cut with a axe, and that was particular work back then.

And I want to tell you something that I've had a dozen people ask me, I guess. How did them old-timers get their house level and square? You know there was no levels. How would you get that log level? It's very simple, now. Take a bucket of water and set it on there and stand and look at that water with your eye till it got practically the same all around and you had it level. It'll work just as good as my four-foot level. Now sure enough, that's the way they did it.

And a great many of them old log buildings [north of here] was actually covered with slate. In fact, I covered a barn that I built up there. Built a barn forty feet wide and eighty feet long and covered it with the slate that come off the old flint mill there. You ever read about that old flint mill that was in Maryland? Well, they said the old flint mill was a hundred years old when they took it down. A man that I was working for up there bought the slate roof for almost nothing. Twelve-inch wide and two-foot long slates, and it was pretty much accurate. And that slate roof, now, was held on with poles. Old-timers called it weight poles. Now that thing had stood on there a hundred years, son, with weight poles on it. And that man bought it, and the reason I know is that I'm the man that put it back on. Now that roof never had a nail hole in it. I cut the holes myself. First slate I ever put on. They got an old feller there—a regular slater—to come out there and show me how to put it on. The man I worked with tried to beg him to stay and help me do the job, but he wouldn't do it. He showed me how to put it on and then he left. I wouldn't say that all of them log buildings was covered with slate, but a great many of them was.

Now they was a great many weight poles used down here in North Carolina. That's all they had. But those weight poles held boards on. Had board roofs then. We never had no slate here. Every row of boards, you had to have a pole. I was a board man myself. My daddy was a board man. The first boards we ever began making was three-foot boards. And at that time they had old cut nails. My dad and me together decided it would be best to make a thirty-inch board, so we cut it to thirty. I'm the last man that was a board maker living in Watauga County. My dad learned me, and my dad was one of the best board makers here. I got pretty close to him [in skill], but taking white oak I never did get as good as he was. It ain't much fun making boards. But you take white oak or chestnut oak, you can split a board down pretty thin. I got to where I could split a half-inch board— make them all a half-inch thick. My dad was so good he could take that and divide it again. Make two boards out of a half-inch. But that, of course, was just to show you it could be done. You don't want a quarter-inch board for a roof. That's entirely too thin.

The half-inch board really worked the best of anything you could have. And that thirty-inch long board worked awful good. Later on they was a few got to making twenty-four-inch boards. Now that's not a bad board. Make them twenty-four inches long and put them on shingle fashion. Board fashion, you know, you lap it six inches. Shingle fashion you lap two-thirds the length of the board.

I've slept under them old board roofs. I'd just get up in the morning and throw snow off. Clean up the house so you could get breakfast.

And chimneys—they was several stick and mud chimneys here. Now that's a beautiful chimney. Lay your logs up and pack your mud in them. They actually had a fire in them. There was enough mud in there so you could build your fire down here and it went right on. There's a great many of them, and I don't know why it can't be done today.

And brick—the first brick that I ever remember being made in Watauga was made of mud, red clay. They had a machine made, they called it the mud machine. Throw that red clay in there, and add water in it. It had a hopper too, understand. Had a yoke of oxen hitched to it to pull that thing around and around. They got that mud mixed up and put it down here in square molds. Set it in the sunshine to dry. When that got thoroughly dried then, you had a pretty fair brick, but now it didn't last too many years. I sorta believe I have a recollection of something said about a straw brick too [with straw added to the mud for additional strength]. And they was a good many of them homemade bricks used in them old times. I seen a good many of them used in mud brick chimneys.

[Later, sawmills began to produce building lumber.] I can take you back to the first old-time mill there ever was around here. The first sawmill ever put in our county was what we called a sash saw. Went up and down. Now you've seen bandsaws. A bandsaw goes over a pulley and comes down around another pulley and cuts always going down. A sash saw goes up and cuts as it goes back down, but it goes up and down straight. Right up and down straight. And now then they had an overshot wheel. There was nothing but the overshot wheel in it for power. That belonged to Henry Taylor. He owned that first mill, and it set way up the road yonder down near the little old creek we call Crab Orchard Creek. And why it was called Crab Orchard Creek, it come down off the mountain and there must have been a space cleared by the Indians—a little space in there about two acres. That was the thickest place of crabapples I ever seen, and that's what give it the name.

They wasted a good bit of timber at those mills, but timber was millions and millions of feet. What did they care? Go out in the mountains and cut a poplar down to make something out of. Maybe it was two feet through. If it didn't suit them, go up and cut another and throw the other out.

But that's the first sawmill that to my knowledge was ever in our county. When the modern mills come out, Henry Taylor put him a modern mill right by the side of that one. That sash saw was powered with water though. The water came down in the flume and poured into the buckets on the overshot wheel. It was geared up with wooden cogs to pull your logs backwards and forwards. You didn't pull that. I don't much believe they cut a log over twelve feet long on them, but that's the way it was. And wood cogs made of hickory or black walnut. And for a drive shaft most of them tried to get red maple. I'd say the first one I ever saw was red maple. I saw some of oak once. In fact, [my wife's] grandpa on her mother's side had a mill that he run for years. That was with a turbine wheel. That's where I first saw the turbine wheel. It had a overshot wheel first. Well, when the time come and the water wheel give out—them old-time wheels would give out, understand; they didn't last a lifetime—somebody came

PLATE 3 Etta Hartley holding a coverlet woven by Charlie's grandmother.

along with such and all about this turbine wheel and he recommended it
and told him how it worked down in there, and grandpa put one in. Now I
didn't see him put it in, but I can tell you what I did see and know. We
moved over about two miles from the mill, and we made it a practice to go
to that mill. And when me and Walter, my brother, first started packing
corn over the mountain to it, we took a peck apiece. He was sorta grouchy,
and you'd think he was a old hellcat till you got used to him. But he was
friendly. That was just his way. I went up there one time with some corn
after his turbine wheel had been put in there, and he had overrun the thing
and he'd got some trash lodged right down in that wheel. And when I
walked up, there was grandpa down in there cleaning that wheel out. I set
my bushel down on the floor, walked down there, and I said, "Could I help
you some cleaning that out?"

He said, "Godamighty yes you could."

I said, "All right, where do you want me to work?"

He said, "You stand over there right close to the water there and I'll
hand all this stuff over to you and you pitch it over on the bank there, and
when it gets dry, we'll use it for wood.

Well, I helped him get it cleaned out good, and while we was cleaning it
out, he showed me it was steel, and how all the water and all went down.
He took a liking to me quick as I fell down to helping him. We got it good
and cleaned out, and he said, "Now Charlie, you stand right there until I
get the water turned on and let me see if it works."

He turned it on and see'd that it worked pretty good, and he said, "Come
on, Charlie. That's gonna be just fine."

We went up there and he said, "Charlie, you've been good to help me.
I'll grind you as much corn over a bushel as you can get back home." And
from that day till that old man died, he was a real friend to me. I could go
over and talk to him and he'd be just as nice as you please.

Now for payment he'd take, let's see. There's ten gallons in a bushel. He
took two toll dishes out of a bushel. That would be a gallon. If there was
just a half a bushel, he took one. If it was a peck, he didn't toll it. There
was a law for old-timey millers that you couldn't toll a peck. If it was less
than half a bushel, he didn't toll it. All of them done that way.

One time the county here raised wheat. I don't guess they raised more
than corn, but when they got to grinding wheat, that was when the farmers
were getting pretty well straightened out. First old thrashing machine I saw
was a wood thrashing machine.

Before that, what little they raised they used a frail [flail] on. That's
maybe something you don't know. Now they had to have a place to hold the
grain. They laid the grain down. Some of them laid it flat down on the floor.
And this frail was about, I'd say ten feet long. It was hinged at one end.

You had your handle back here, and you come up with it and then come over and down on the wheat with one whomp. The frails was usually a hickory withe wrung around and around [at the joint] so the end would flip. Beat the old stack of wheat with that end till you got it done. Then take a cloth and take your wheat up and clean it in the wind. That's what they first done I understand. But later on they got to be a small-like windmill that was made with wood and cogs. There was an old one that set up here. I don't know what ever went with it. But that was cranked by hand—had a fan in it—and you could run a bushel of wheat through that and clean it pretty quick. It had a hopper just like a mill hopper. You just pour your wheat right in and there you go. All of that now was handwork until the thrashing machine. Then take that wheat to the mill.

At one time before big mills come in, they was a right smart of hammer mills around North Carolina. You have to have water to flip that [hammer end] up and down. But you go to all that expense to have water to run through there to pull it up and down that way, why not have the wheel?

I believe I'll say this: I seriously doubt if they's a thing that they can ever write you about in the old-timey business that's actually never been here, but finding the man that knows about it . . . Now this old North Carolina's

PLATE 4 Charlie on the ramp he built leading from the porch of their home to the mailbox on the highway. Both he and Etta now have trouble negotiating steps.

been set up a long time. A lot of this stuff I'm telling you about tonight is way back yonder, and it's real survival.

Now they had turning lathes that were water-powered too. We had almost nothing back in them days only what was run by water. They was a few lathes turned by hand too—a big ten-foot wood wheel hooked to a spindle. Now I can't remember too much about that big wheel, but I can remember that grandpa run it until—have you heard talk of the '40 flood here in North Carolina? Well, he run it up till then. We' had a flood here in '40 that cleaned this whole country out. Water stood up on the porch within three inches of the floor, and us on a little creek, too. That flood cleaned everything out, now. Took everything.

Now all of that stuff come along up to where we hit *Foxfire 1* and *Foxfire 2*, which is just so accurate there's no use to talk about that.

Part II

In the second section of this chapter, we try to cover Charlie's career as a builder—a talent he learned not in school (he never went to college) but by experience alone. Many of the buildings he built are still used constantly today, though few of the people in his surrounding community could point them out to you. He did his work quietly and then stepped aside. Those buildings he is proudest of he supervised during WPA days, but his career spanned more than fifty years.

There are many things that make this couple noteworthy, not the least of which is the durability of their partnership (they've been married sixty-five years) and their large, close-knit family (they have four children, twelve grandchildren, and twenty-three great-grandchildren). When they married, Charlie was twenty-two and Etta was sixteen. They were introduced by Troy Danner, one of the knife makers featured in this book. "I robbed the cradle for her," says Charlie. "That's kind of a joke, but it's the truth. I did take her out at sixteen. I reckon that's the worst mistake she ever made—listening to me!"

Equally amazing is the amount that Charlie accomplished despite his lack of formal schooling; and more amazing still is the fact that he did all of his finest work after losing one leg in a logging accident fifty-five years ago. He gets around on a peg leg made by hand out of a two-by-six.

Etta warned us that if we encouraged him, he'd brag. We encouraged him, and I'm glad we did because their story is one that's worth telling. And though the pride is there, it is tempered by an almost childlike awe at what was accomplished, and a keen sense of disappointment now that the work is done. As Charlie said, "Sometimes I walk around, see buildings that I put up, and I say, 'Was I man enough to put that building up,' when I know darn well I put it up. I'm going to say something to you that I've never said to nobody else. I have went to the top, as I've told you, and been where I had to take the bull by the horns—swim or die. And she's been by me. Always been on the bank when I was in trouble. But that's what I've had to do. And I have never run onto a man that could out me in building, and even on this one leg I have never struck a man that could do as much work in a day as I could. I've learned to do the job fast when I had two legs, and when I thought I was knocked out, got to messing around with my brother taking jobs and began to work a little and found that I wasn't knocked out at all.

"And I've never been stalled. But I'm gone now. I ain't no good now. Nobody needs me now 'cause I ain't no good."

That's not true, Charlie. Your family needs you, and we need you, because the two of you give all of us a pattern to go by, and a ray of strong, clear light to rejoice over.

We began by asking Charlie to tell us what sort of education he had to prepare him for his career in construction. He began to laugh, and what follows is what he told us.

PLATE 5 Charlie and Tom Carlton looking at the Cove Creek School that Charlie built during WPA days (see Plates 6–8).

Let me tell you something. There was just a little school. We had school three months [out of the year]. It was supposed to be three months, but might' near always there would be window lights knocked out and they would have to fix that, and it would cut the schooling down to about near two and a half months. It was years and years before we ever got much of a school. But now I didn't go to school too much. After I got big enough to go to school, my dad used to say he would try to give us an education. Now my dad was wrong, but he did the best he could. When he would get hard up, he would come and take us out of school. So in a way, I got about two months schooling in a few years. That's the way it went.

We lived at Valle Crucis when the Episcopals come here and started their school up. They are great folks to try and help you get an education. The old fellow that started that talked Daddy into sending his four oldest children to that school for seven cents a month. So we went to school a part of a couple of years there. In fact, to be honest, the part of the education that I got, I got it through the Episcopals. Now I'm not an Episcopal, understand, but I will give them credit for what they done for me. Bigger part of my education come through them, but I ain't got much education. I doubt with all my experience that I could pass a fifth grade examination with arithmetic.

So I never got much school. I really started being a carpenter when I was a kid. My daddy was an old-time carpenter. One of the best that's ever been, and [he] could do the most work, but he didn't have much education [either]. I really started in messing with his tools and learning carpenter work—he says six years old. He had a box of fairly good tools, and they was kept locked up. He kept the key in his pocket most of the time. Once he was building a spring house, and he had about a mile to walk from home to that job, and he'd get lonesome. He got to taking me with him to sorta pass the time away. Well, when he got ready to put the roof on, I just couldn't behave my little self; I had to climb that ladder and carry shingles up to him. That's old-timey shingles, now. Then that didn't satisfy me and I had to get up and help him. On the last—getting away up—he didn't want to put the last scaffold on. He throwed him a two-by-four up and with one hand held that and laid the shingles with the other, and I got up there and nailed them—two nails to the shingle. That's the first work I can remember.

My father taught me a little. He taught me as far as he could go. We worked together lots. We were the first ones that ever started putting water pipes to a man's house. I guess you've read about the Mast Store in the papers? Now right across the road there is the first house he ever owned. He come to Valle Crucis a single man and he married there. Now away around up the hill there was a good spring and a little stream of water running into a little wood spout. He got it there and carried his water back to his house.

So Mr. Mast come back one day from dinner a little bit late. We was setting out on the porch of his store. He come walking up—and he has a by-word. "By gracious." He said, "By gracious, I had to go up to the spring and fix [the spout back] so my wife could get some water."

His brother-in-law was sitting there; he sorta looked up, "By junkies, well, why don't you go up there in the mountains at that good spring way up there in the hollow at those white pines and pipe that spring down here to the house? Save walking."

"By gracious, do you mean that?"

"By junkies, of course I do."

"Well, I believe I'll run it down there." Turned around to me. Said, "Charlie, how about you and Walter and your dad coming down here and digging the ditch up there and getting it ready? I'll try to get some piping up here from Johnson City [Tennessee]. I believe I could buy it and get it in here."

Well, I come home and told my dad what they wanted. Dad said, "Yeah, we'll go down there and we'll put that ditch up through there." It took about three days to get an order from Johnson City up here at that time, and by the time we got the ditch dug, the piping was in. Well, now the Episcopal School over there, they had a line of water off the top of that mountain, and they had a pipe wrench up there. Mr. Mast borrowed that one pipe wrench and we put all that pipe all together with that one pipe wrench, now. Covered it up, run it down here in the barn lot—still seventy-five feet from the kitchen—and set it up like that. We had nothing to cut pipe with, understand. We took that pipe—it's really hard for me to believe it could be done, but I done it and took a little handsaw file and filed around that pipe and cut it in two with that little file. Then we still had to bend it. We had two of us and we bent that pipe up and stuck it standing right up there in the barn lot—no sink, nothing. Water come up there. Of course it wasn't but a few days till it was muddy all around it.

Went down to the store one day. Mr. Mast was about half mad—water and mud all over him. He said, "Charlie, by gracious, I've just got a mudhole over there. Just look over there at what a place I've got. Would you and Walter, if I can borrow the Mission House tools, come down here and change that?"

"Yeah, we'll come do the best we can for it."

We went down there and we moved that pipe. Time had come that he could buy a sink, and so we run that water out there—bending the pipe by hand now, understand—and left the runout a'pouring there [into the sink]. "By gracious, how are you going to get that water away from the house?"

"Gosh, Mr. Mast. I don't know. All I know is just dig a ditch and just let the water run out down through there."

Well, that didn't make it much better. You still had the same water running down except you had water in the kitchen now. Went back down a few days after that.

"Charlie, I want that pipe changed someway. The Mission says they'll loan me the wrenches."

I said, "All right. We can cut and twist that around." We went over there and fixed that. Then that's where I stopped [working] with him. But from then on, I eventually got to where I could buy one pipe wrench. The first job that I done after that, I done it with a pipe wrench and a little file. Didn't even know a hacksaw then. Probably they was made somewheres, [but we didn't know about them]. But now that's the way I started my first plumbing.

After Mr. Mast had water pumped in, it got to be a great thing; and now right over there in Mrs. Henson's house is the first bathroom and tub that was ever put up in Watauga County. She got the first bathtub that was ever put in Watauga County, and it's still there. At Valle Crucis, Harley Taylor put in the second one, and I was the helper on it. When we got that job done, the plumber in charge walked over and said, "Charlie, I'll give you the same price as I'm getting to go with me to Johnson City as a helper."

I said, "I ain't got no use in Johnson City. I've got a home up here. I ain't interested in going down there and help you plumb." I stayed at home. I didn't go. And from that [time] on till I've got so I can't plumb, off and on I've been plumbing. And these plumbers up here that I patronize now, they're a little better than me on copper tubing and such as that; but so far as knowing plumbing, they don't know it a bit better than I know it because I come right on up. I concreted the first spring that was ever concreted here, and that's quite a job—bringing the water around, make your cement box—it's a right smart job. I run one one time twelve hundred feet. That's a right smart distance, but I've done that.

And so far as a plumber, if I was able to do my own plumbing [now] I wouldn't let them put in my plumbing for a dime. I wouldn't let them have a dime because I've never seen a plumber do the work exactly the way I want it done. I *have* to patronize them now. I've had them down here two or three times in the last five years. When I go in there (they're Republican and I'm a Democrat) I go in at the door and say, "Hello there. Old Democrat's in trouble today. You gonna help me?"

They might near always say, "Why, yeah, we're gonna help you. We ain't gonna turn you down."

But now the time's come when I can't do nothing. But I could boss. My old head ain't so crazy yet that I don't know how the job's done!

Now up till I was seventeen, my dad was the boss absolutely. The way he said it was what went. I was under him. Next thing I was doing, I was on my own going out here maybe three miles or five miles. Take charge of a house and build it with one or two hands. Build it myself without even a blueprint. Now we didn't know blueprints when we first started. Those nice big catalogues come out with all the beautiful homes—just pictures. Folks would pick out a picture of a certain house, "I want one built like this." No blueprint or anything. I built that house by looks just identical to the way they wanted it. Somebody'd come along: "Where's your blueprint?"

"Right up here" [pointing to his head].

I always got just what they wanted. I'm not a natural-born carpenter, understand. They say my father was a natural-born carpenter. I don't know. I don't think anybody's ever natural-born for any trade. He may be born with a sense of following in his daddy's tracks, but he's got to learn it is the way I see it. Up till I was seventeen, I was practically on my own because my father couldn't see the newer ways. And he absolutely couldn't stand for one of his children to tell him anything, and the time come that me and him quit. Then I was on my own absolutely myself. It might be farm work today, and tomorrow it might be carpenter work.

After I went on my own, I soon got to the point where I didn't have to go and ask for a job. They asked me. When I was eighteen years old, I was far enough along in the carpenter business that I could go out on my own hook and build a house, and it was considered good. And repair work—there was about six or eight women in Valle Crucis who wouldn't let nobody else do their work but me, so I didn't have to go out and ask for work at that time. And then I went to Tennessee, and made three trips to Maryland to build dairy barns. I was my boss and done the work too with maybe one hand.

Same way here. I'd go out in the mountains—some asked me to build a home. In them days, you'd go out and stay with them—board with them. Go out, build a house and stay with them till it was done. Stay with the people I was working for. That was customary then. But since World War II, there ain't no such thing as that. A man comes and wants you to do him a day's work, or build him a house, and you look after your own board. That's all done away with. But now that's kindly the way I worked. And in most cases, they had a hand in the community that would be able to help—not a carpenter, understand. I hardly ever had a carpenter. I'd go out there and pick up a laborer—anybody that could help me. I done the bossing and part of the work, and we both went together that way. I have never built a whole house by myself because you can't put the rafters up by yourself. And it's mighty hard to raise your frame—one man.

And now about the only tools I had were a hand saw, a hand axe, and a drawing knife. The first few houses, now, I built were not storm sheeted—

weatherboarded. When they began storm sheeting, it went up and down at a forty-five [degree angle]. We cut all that by hand. And a few jobs that I've done, now, was old hard wood that was taken from the sawmill. The culls that wouldn't pass for market would pass on into subflooring and storm sheeting, and it all cut on a forty-five, and with a hand saw for the first few years.

And on a lot of them buildings I've put up, that lumber was not surfaced, and you had worlds and worlds of maple and oak to cut on a forty-five. Now let me tell you the difference. Twelve-inch boards cut straight across is just exactly a twelve-inch cut. But when you start at a forty-five, it takes nineteen inches to cut that forty-five. That's the difference in doing it. I even built one or two that I had to put a forty-five on the roof, which I think was foolishness. Lumber going crossways on the rafters!

[So I was a boss on those jobs, but] when that WPA started, I had no say-so. I had to show them what I could do. That's the way I started. I started *under* the courthouse. I went over there and I excavated under that courthouse—one of the hardest jobs that you can think of—to build a foundation under it. I had sixty-five men. I had forty-seven the first morning I went in there. For forty-seven men, I had ten shovels. The bossman came in and said, "Well, here's your crew, Charlie. You got ten shovels. Can you handle them?"

I said, "I'll divide them—work one man awhile and work another one awhile."

Now there was men standing right there hungry. That's the first big job I ever started. And all these hands that came to me to work was what we called "certified." They had to have a card that come from headquarters showing me that I had the right to work them—all of them. And I had to train them men to help me. When I started on WPA, I did not have anybody but raw laborers and people that needed a job. Come in with overalls double-patched and not enough to eat. I had to take care of them men and work some too. All these big rock buildings I done with WPA during the Depression were done with laborers that had to have a job. A fellow that had a farm, they would hardly ever let him on 'cause they figured he could live without it. Let's say it was a starvation job. A man on WPA was hungry and naked and that's why he was put there. It was up to me to take care of them. And it didn't make a damn bit of difference to them whether I made him work or not work. I took care of him and kept him on the payroll. If he was a good stout fellow and could work pretty well, let him work. If he was sorta knocked out and not too stout, give him a light job. Let him work awhile and play around. Now you may wonder how did I do all that work—get these big buildings [put up] with that type of people. Well, I had to have a little bit of know-how; and they is nobody—even you—that is

PLATE 6   The plaque on the
Cove Creek School.

so dumb that he can't do something for me somewheres. If you've got patience, you can take anybody and train them for something. If he couldn't use a pick, he could use a shovel; and if he wasn't stout enough to do much, put him to carrying water. I got some criticizing along, but it was from fellows who didn't know.

Now the Valle Crucis School is the first WPA job I bossed. I'm the man that built that absolutely with common labor except laying the rocks. Now I had a few men later on that were on the WPA that were good rock men, but the County hired most of the rock men because they wanted a good job. So that building standing over there will be a monument to my grave when I'm gone from here. The first one I ever put up on WPA. It's still a beautiful building. It's been there for about forty years now. Mr. Wigginton [*Foxfire* advisor] went over there to look at that and stood there and looked at it and said, "Mr. Hartley, I want to know how in the world you done such a pretty a job as that is." Well, now, on that job, I had good rock men.

Then I built a big rock building at Boone. And Blowing Rock has a big rock gymnasium that I built. I'm proud of all of them, but the Cove Creek School is my pride. That's the last one I built. You've been there and seen it. That's worth being interested in. I think more of that job than any I've ever done, but I had men there that was hungry.

During World War II, I was riding to town with two men. Driver slapped the one in the middle to wake him up. Said, "Wake up. I've got something lined up here I want to show you in a few minutes."

PLATE 7   Charlie in front of the Cove Creek School.

Well, I was wondering what he was going to show that man. Got up, said, "Look over there. You see that rock building?"

"Why sure."

Said, "Don't you think that's something fine?"

He answered him, said, "That's the finest thing I ever seen."

Reach over and slapped me on that old wooden leg; says, "Mister, don't you think that's a nice building over there?"

I said, "Naturally I'd think it was a nice building. I'm the man that built it."

He looked at it and looked straight back at me. Says, "I don't give a damn who built it. That's the prettiest thing I ever saw."

That was a great surprise to them that I was the little old peg-legged fellow that built it. I wonder lots of times, "*Did* I do this?" But there's the building to show. I guess I could pick out a hundred buildings around Boone that I was the boss on. But Cove Creek is my pride. [The building took two years to build. The architect was Mr. Coffee whose offices were in

PLATE 8   Charlie watches with a smile as students who attend his Cove Creek School race by on their way to recess.

Lenoir, North Carolina. Charlie was the supervisor and was over 106 men for most of the time the building was under construction. Working with him was an assistant superintendent, three building foremen, and a fourth foreman at the rock quarry.

The walls of the building are twelve inches thick. The inside studding is all two-by-six hemlock, and the floor joists are two-by-twelve hemlock. There are wood floors and plaster walls. All the concrete pieces were precast at the site.

The Federal Government paid for the major labor except for the three Lyons brothers—Leslie, Clarence, and Earl—who were the main rock men and were paid by the County. The County also paid for the materials. Three other rock men, Ben Brewer, Guy Carlton, and Willard Watson were paid by WPA.]

So I didn't have much education, but I fooled the public and a lot of fellows. I'm going to tell you one. That Cove Creek School that I bossed—I went walking around with a fellow who was the checker. That's the man watching to see that nothing was stolen. And he was with the engineers and he knew well and good who was running that job up there. He knew that I was buying all that material which was [the engineers' job]. The engineers there should have made every one of them bills, but they did not do it. I made all the bills and everything. And so I'm awalking around one morning checking my building and my men, and he was always kidding, and he said, "Charlie, where did you go to college at?"

I said, "Good God, man, I ain't never been inside of a college."

And he turned around and said, "Don't be telling me a darn lie."

I said, "I am telling you the truth," and I like to have never convinced him.

He said, "I want you to tell me how in the world—I know you are making the bills for this job—how in the world are you carrying this job if you never went to college?"

I said, "I got mine the hard way." And I did. I got mine through experience. I went to the top. At one time, I was the highest paid carpenter in the County. At one time, I had as much as three calls a week. Right there is the woman setting there [his wife, Etta] that can tell you that.

Now let me tell you something. We were supposed to work twenty-eight days a month. Twenty-eight days is a working month. I took that Valle Crucis School. I quarried the rocks out, hauled them in, done the ditches, built that school up to the foundation—basement and all—at fifty-six dollars a month. Now you study about that. What was I getting a day? I was pretty near working on starvation wages too wasn't I? Finally the big white-collar man come in. "What are you getting?"

And I said, "Fifty-six dollars."

"Chicken feed." And he walked off.

The next check come in and it was seventy dollars. In a few more weeks, eighty dollars. By the time I got that building done, I was up at a hundred dollars a month. And when I got through with that building, the WPA white collars began to say, "Well, we got a man up there that knows what he's doing." And when I finished the Cove Creek job, I had the white collars coming to me asking me, "How we gonna work this? What we gonna do?" That's the way I've come up.

ETTA: You're bragging now, Charlie.

CHARLIE: That's what I told you I was going to brag some! Even on defense jobs when I was the little boss—the third man down, the one that always gets the beating and all the dirty work—they'd come around, "Charlie, how we going to do this? How we going to do that?" And me fool enough to tell them how and let them get the credit for it. You ought to know what I mean. If you don't know, I can tell you: On all jobs anywhere, whenever you get to the point that you can go into any offices around and be the best secretary there is there, there'll be a white collar appear over you telling you what to do. That's the way it'll be when you get there, now.

But I guess I'd be safe to say I've built twelve or fifteen hundred houses in my fifty years [as a carpenter]. And I always loved the work. Nowadays, right now, they're storm sheeting with plywood, and some of them put only four-foot pieces to each corner. Well, I don't know but that's all right, but it certainly ain't as stout as what I had to build. I never had plywood to sheet the side with. It wouldn't be quite as stout, but I guess it would hold if it were put on right. Now plywood, you don't want to make just a straight joint. Now that's what a lot of them do. Say you put in two sheets right over each other. It's quick, and I reckon it'll hold. It's a lot quicker done.

It'll be all right till one or two of them blows away. Then you'll find out one way or the other!

Back when you were making fifty-six dollars a month, what was Etta doing?

CHARLIE: She was at home looking after the family. She has never worked away from home. She stays at home and has been a real wife and bossed the family, and we've got four wonderful children—but she's the one that made them, not me.

ETTA: No, no, that's not true!

CHARLIE: I've worked away from home. Sent the money when I had some. She stayed in those old rough mountains, steeper than anything. She worked up there till her heart knocked her out. She's been there many a day and worked.

Do you feel that a wife should stay at home and work?

CHARLIE [laughing]: I don't much want to answer that because I've been an old fogey myself. I'd love to just turn everything entirely different from what I done it then. If I could go back, I'd be an entirely different boy and a man from what I've ever been. I believe I'd change two or three things. One way I'd love to change would to be more friendly and polite. My back life has been an old crabby life, mostly. If I could go back, I wouldn't want that at all. I'd want it entirely different. That's about all the way I know to answer that.

ETTA: I'd just wish to keep good health, I suppose, so I could work. If I was young back again, I'd like to go into nurse's training. I love that work. I took some, but I'd love to be able to work at that now, but my health won't permit it. Back then my children were small and I couldn't leave them and do what I wanted to do because I felt my duty was to my children.

CHARLIE: There's two sides to look at. When I was raising a family, the truth is there wasn't too much else for the women to do [away from the home]. Back then, we considered the woman's place at home tending to the babies—taking care of them. And she didn't only take care of the babies—she went out in the mountains and worked. I'd send money when I had some, and she done the best she could.

ETTA: I did the farming, in other words.

CHARLIE: And that's why I call her the boss [laughing again]. She bossed so much she still can't help but boss a little!

ETTA: We had a twenty-six-acre farm. I'm still a little bit fogey now that a woman should be at home with her kids. But the way times has got, living is so high I don't see much chance only to let the wife work when she can. Sometimes the wife can get a job when the husband can't. I think after the children leave home, it's all right for the wife to get a job, but I'd rather be at home to see that my children are taken care of up till they can go to school.

CHARLIE: Mothers are working today letting their kids be carried and tended to almost any way and sort of drug up by the hair of their heads. [That's the cause] for a lot of this devilment.

ETTA: I'd like to see some of this here crime and racket done away with. There's getting to be too much of it. Now that's one thing that I would love to see changed. I'll tell you one thing, and I'm going to be frank with you. I've thought this ever since the second World War. The mothers went to work on these here defense plants and things in place of staying at home and taking care of the children. Of course, [the country] needed some help, and everybody pitched in and helped all they could during the War. 'Course that's something that you kids don't know nothing about. Well, it left the children by theirselves. I think they just didn't have enough discipline in other words, and they felt they weren't taken care of like they should have been. Now I'd love to see more mothers stay at home. I think it could be managed. I stayed at home and raised my children, and I know I had a hard time, but I'd rather do with less and know that my children were taken care of properly than left in anybody else's hands and just left to take care of theirselves. Do you understand me? Now you're going to have to work as best you can and try to improve things. Now I may be wrong in what I think and what other people thinks, but I think that your children comes first unless you absolutely have to get out and work for a living.

[Of course, the lessons parents try to teach kids now aren't so different from what they were back then. They just don't seem to be taking hold as well now.] My parents, and so did his, always taught us to be honest and truthful about everything, and I suppose most parents do now. At least I did to my children, and I know parents that do teach their children that now. And I think friendship and kindness goes a long ways. I tell you girls, I was reading the other night on that, and on if you spoke kind words to somebody, why, how it helped them more, so to speak, even if you didn't like them. Maybe it made them feel better if you spoke to them kindly. And it made you feel better. I think it does. Try to be kind to anybody, even if they don't appreciate it or nothing about it, because you'll feel better about it yourself.

And we taught our children to be honest and to be truthful. That it didn't pay in the long run not to be truthful. That usually it was caught up with and it went against them. And another thing that I stressed on my children was to never, never when they went to school to come home with tattling tales of what the other students done or anything. I wouldn't allow it at all. I'd punish them if they did. And they understood I would punish them if they did. [Charlie] was away at work—maybe in Maryland or in Durham or Asheville—and I had to look after them, and I just simply told them that I wouldn't allow it, because it didn't concern me and it didn't concern them. They did wrong to come in home with great big tales about how they got punished at school thinking I'd take up for them, because I knew the teacher wouldn't have punished them if they hadn't done wrong.

And another rule I laid down up till they was sixteen or eighteen years old was that if they wasn't back by a certain time when they went out at night, I'd come after them. And I did. But they usually marched in. Up till they were sixteen, they had to be in by 9:30, and not later either. I guess I was a little too strict on them. I always tried to be kind to them, and understanding, but I had certain hours for them to get in.

[Now I didn't force things on them like religion, though.] My parents didn't force it on us to go to church, but they took us to church. I know we never missed church, but we went willingly because we liked to go with them. I don't think anything should be forced on anybody because in time they will get tired of it and rebel against it. When I was raising my own children, we took them to church and they never rebelled against it. They never said anything against it. But I didn't push it on them. They just naturally went.

CHARLIE: I don't think that it's a good idea to force a kid or a man or a woman to do certain things. In fact, we had one college teacher over here that expressed it to me once in a way that suited me: if a [student] is not interested enough in getting an education, turn him loose. Let him do as he absolutely pleases. If he don't want an education, let him go. Don't force him. I still feel like he did.

And I don't think religion should be forced on anybody because that is the main thing that caused them to leave the old country on account of they could be free here. Now we have a tendency—you and I and her and all of us—to feel the church you belong to, that's all the church there is. We have a tendency to feel that way, but it's the wrong idea. Let me tell you something that is really funny to me now. My daddy and mammy were Democrats and Baptists. They raised me with the idea that nobody went to heaven but a Democrat or a Baptist. That's how strong I was raised. But now I'm a Methodist and she is a Methodist. Now when I got up and got out in the world, I had to throw all of that away. Now you just remember this: I don't believe there is any kind of religious organization that tries to be good but what there's good people in it, be it a Catholic, Methodist, Presbyterian, or whatever. You'll find good men and good women in all of them. So I think it should be on his own hook. When she joined the Methodist church, I went with her. Now I don't believe in being a Democrat

PLATE 9   Charlie remembered meeting Tedra Harmon when he was working on the church in Tedra's community. When he found we were going to visit Tedra to see some of the knives he made (see knife-making chapter in this book), Charlie asked if he could come along. We welcomed him, and had one of the best interviews of the trip.

today and tomorrow a Republican, and I don't believe in being a Methodist today and tomorrow a Baptist. But I'm a Methodist now and I'm glad
we stayed there. If the time was to ever come to go to forcing us like before,
I think we'd have a regular war right between us. I don't believe in forcing
for anything.

[And that's the way we raised our children. Now we've criticized the
young people today some. Thinking about it, though, and about all you all
have to deal with], I just don't know but what the younger generation is
doing a pretty good job of it. We have a lot of jack-leg preachers that get
up—what I mean by jack-leg is ones that's just about ready to start out.
They've got to criticizing that all the kids are going to the bow-wows and
they're going to the devil and all such stuff as that. Now according to the
number [of bad ones] we had when I was a boy, you could almost pick out
the worst gang [of young people] we've got now and it would be a credit to
us older ones. I'd just like to see it keep on like it is and keep getting a little
better.

ETTA: I think the young people are fine now. I think they're more sincere.
That's what I think about it.

CHARLIE: I'm of the opinion that the younger generation's got just as
much sense as us old fellers had.

ETTA: More.

CHARLIE: That's what I feel about it. 'Course, everyone has their faults.
[When I was out working around], one man had his faults and it would
be one thing, and another man had his. Practically all people has got a
fault. I've got one. You've got one. But people can overcome their faults. I
think Etta will agree with me in that I've done away with a lot of my faults.
I've always been a high-strung fellow, and the truth is, in the community I
was raised in, that made a difference. They was always hard on us. Whenever they got too tough with me, I could back-cuss just as big as they could.
I'd go right back on it. That's the faults I had. I sort of broke myself of
that. WPA days had a great deal to do with it. But these big construction
jobs that I had to go on—(I say I had to go on them. I reckon I did. I had
to go somewheres to get a job.) I learned a great deal there. I learned that
if you had a lot of men, more than you had jobs for, keep them moving, just
keep them moving around, and there was no fuss about it. I don't
remember on the defense jobs—I never fired a man. I had the authority to
part of the time when I was a foreman, but I never fired a man on all them
big jobs when I had hundreds of men scattered over the area. I was on the
defense job out in the open for four years and then I went into the factory.
I got along with all of them and *mostly* quit the cussing. [Etta] I think will
agree with me—a lot of the faults that I had when I was young are not

there now; maybe some new ones though. It might be something worse. I don't think there would be any fault that what if you tried hard enough, you could overcome it.

ETTA: Like my granddaughter said the other night. She thought an acquaintance of ours felt that the other side had all the faults and they stuck out like a sore thumb, but that person has faults that were just as bad, or worse, but they didn't see them. They see them in the other person. You have to realize your faults before you can get rid of them.

CHARLIE: People now are quite different than what they used to be. In a way, some are better and some are worse. Young people are just about like they used to be when I grew up 'cept they're more frank about things, I think. I think the average-run young people are fine now. At least I hope they are and I know some fine young people and I'm proud of them. We didn't have too many people when we was being raised up. We've got thousands and thousands now where we didn't have a hundred then. But the younger generation in most ways is far different than when I was coming up. The boys and girls (we'll put it that way, because you've got to be a boy first or a girl first), they are more outspoken; they are more plain. In other words, if you do something that we thought back then was wrong, it's open. But back when I was coming up, the young folks and the old folks, too, was the same way. They was more sneaky then than the generation is now. You can go along out here with a crowd of girls and boys, and they get into something that they oughtn't to but you could line them all up and ask, "How many was into that?" and there wouldn't be a one of them that would lie. There might be some of them that would keep their mouth shut until they had to talk, but they're praying. You ain't going out here and do something that you oughtn't to, be sneaking about it. You own up to it. In fact, you want to try to be plain spoken and do just what you think's right. You might do something wrong, but you don't do it intentionally. But now, when I was agrowing up, us boys (and our fathers and mothers were just as sneaking as we was) was more sneaking than they are now. But back them days, you didn't know when you got the truth. If something come up wrong, you just didn't know when you got the truth. I think there's a difference. Now we have the drugs—that's the greatest fight we've got now. But so far as otherwise, you young folks is a credit to us old sages back there. But now you can't get nobody else to tell you that—"Oh, I didn't do that back then." They were meaner than I was. It's not been too many years since the preachers would get up, "All the young folks are going to the 'bow-wows,' going to the 'bow-wows.' "

ETTA: In other words, going to the dogs.

CHARLIE: I heared that when I wasn't six years old. And you still hear it yet from some of the preachers. Maybe I expect too much. Maybe we're not giving the young folks a chance.

What is your most valuable possession?

CHARLIE: You want me to answer that honest? Right there [pointing to Mrs. Hartley] is the most valuable thing of anything in my whole married life.

ETTA: Charlie, you consider your children valuable. I do.

CHARLIE: If I didn't have you, how would I manage the children? Don't try to tell me that.

Is there something you could have done without in your lifetime?

CHARLIE: I could have done without everything but her, if I'd had to. In fact, there've been times I've had to do without. For instance, you take money—there's a great many times I had to do without money and work it some other way.

When we first started out, me and her, there was a part of the time when we had to make it without much money and part of the time without any, but now listen, there would be people we'd work for who couldn't pay you the money—they'd give an order to the store. We made it that way. I'm twice or three times old as you. They's no family, no one human being, I don't think, on this earth that can live without some money—money is the backbone *but* the Bible says it's the root of all evil and it is. Money enough would hire you somebody to go out here and burn your house down; go out here and shoot you. Enough money, I mean. So money *is* the root of all evil and yet we've got to have it. Can't live without it.

Now I lived for years with orders for the store and go and buy stuff with orders, but suppose when taxes paying come, then you had to have money. I can remember when the old people were so hard up—such a little money —now not [only] my daddy, I'm atalking about all the people. They were so hard up for a little money that they would even save the pennies. Put them back in a certain place to pay taxes with. Now that's how scarce and how hard money was. I said folks my father's age, but also for a while after me and Etta was married, we practically had to save the money and if we had something on the farm we could sell, sell that, or if I could get a day's work and take an order at the store, I had to do it. But your orders to the store (there's nobody takes them anymore) at that time, they was always cheated and [the storeowner] took enough off of it where you was hurt. In other words, if you took an order to the store for a dollar, you got about seventy-five or eighty cents in goods for that order. If you go in with a dollar in money, they lay the stuff out and you could say, "Well, I ain't gonna give you that much. I've got the money to pay for it." They couldn't stick you then because you had the money in your pocket and you could do like the little boy told his mother, "Do as you damn please then."

ETTA: Well, when we lived on a farm, we raised everything and he worked away. I raised chickens and had a cow, sometimes two cows, and hogs and things like that. We raised practically everything we ate. We raised chickens and I had enough eggs to sell and buy a lot of groceries with. That's the way we lived over there during the Depression. We were some of the only people that didn't go on relief on account of (well, there were several in our neighborhood that didn't) I sold enough eggs and butter to buy a big part of our groceries and then I raised a large garden and done all our canning and we had chickens to kill and sell if we needed to. I raised chickens to sell, so we made a pretty good living on the farm over there even if it was a little rough farming. We raised crops. Had corn and things like that. Of course, we had to buy flour and sugar and coffee and all our groceries with the money we got from eggs and chickens. After the children got older, they helped me with the work. They would go to school, and then come home and help me.

CHARLIE: They'd come home from school and usually they'd have to have a snack; the kids were always starving to death when they'd come home from school. Get a little snack and then they'd have to get out and help mother work. Some of them would feed the chickens and some the hogs.

ETTA: I'd usually do the milking.

CHARLIE: She was usually home with the kids and I was off somewheres, especially after I lost my leg. I was up somewhere where I could get a money job and she was at home being the boss. She made it a rule and I don't suppose that she ever refused them a snack when they come home. Then they got out and worked a little unless something else happened.

ETTA: They helped in the garden, and if the school work was finished, they helped with the canning. We canned six to eight hundred cans, sometimes quarters and sometimes half gallons, of food. It took all that food for four children going to school. It had to do all winter till it come spring and garden time again. I enjoyed it and I sometimes think that was the best living. I was well enough to work and I didn't have to buy everything like we do now.

CHARLIE: Now you see a lot of divorces. Well, I don't like it. It's hard to explain. I think that in some cases probably it's all right, but the average I think that on each side they should come to an understanding about things, and then they wouldn't be so many divorces. I'll be honest with you. I absolutely hate divorcing, but we've got two kids that's divorced. But if you can't get along together without trouble, then that's the only thing you can do. I don't believe in it, but there's a lot of it being done. There's a lot of divorces and I know of a great many cases where there's been marriage and divorce, and both sides afterwards got along just fine and made a good living. So I guess maybe there's a little ol' fogeyness there in me.

You've been married for sixty-six years and some people would find that impossible. How have you made it?

ETTA: Remember in this time that it hasn't been all smooth sailing. Oh, there's never been a couple yet that didn't disagree, but you can work these disagreements out.

CHARLIE: What in the devil is the trouble with these folks when they raise a family and grandchildren [and then part]? Whatever in the devil would be wrong with me and Etta if we were to divorce today at this old age? If we could live together and raise a family, what's got wrong with us in our old age? That's a question I can't see through. Now I think it's the most foolish thing to happen. To think about living together, raising a family, after the family's gone, then have to get a divorce and start out hunting another man and another woman, but we have that happen. Is so-and-so a little crazy or something? That's the only thing I can figure about it. His mind must have went off, or his woman one. But you can't—no one person can run the world. Not even the President can run it by himself. And still you can't put two Presidents in 'cause you can take where you put two bosses on the same job and look what'll happen. I've even tried that. Two bosses can't run a job; two bosses can't run the Presidency.

ETTA: Two bosses can't run a marriage.

CHARLIE: I guess it's not hardly fair for a fellow like me to—maybe it ain't fair for me to be atalking about it, because I went through all of it except the divorce business. We've never even studied about a divorce. We've had a spat a time or two. [Both he and Mrs. Hartley laugh.] Quarreled a little, but I guess, I don't believe that we've ever had a quarrel that more than six or eight words passed but what one or the other cooled down. I have never slapped her through madness. She has never slapped me. When we was young, we played together slapping one another. But she said if I was to ever hit her, she'd kill me. [Laughter.] And I was crazy enough to believe her.

ETTA: You'd have to knock me cold and then you'd better be outside when I come to.

CHARLIE: But it has never been a time me and her has felt like fighting. We've scolded one another and I doubt if there's anybody that's ever lived sixty-six years together but what's had a few cross words.

ETTA: We've talked things over.

CHARLIE: I believe I'll tell you the worst spat—the worst feelings I've ever had with her. The worst spat we ever had—during the WPA days. I was so miserable hardup, but I had got money enough and got ahead enough till I was able to buy a car. I had a good '39 car. [Our son] was the restless type and you can tell I'm restless, even and me crippled up—I'm never still. [He] just absolutely could not be still at home.

ETTA: That's our youngest son.

CHARLIE: Part of that time, I took care of Etta in the daytime and at night he wanted the car to go acourtin' or somewheres. Well, I felt like I was too hardup to let him go out and burn gas, but he couldn't see it that way. Well, one morning I got up and I said, "Etta, don't let [our son] have the car tonight to run around and burn gas."

When I come in, the car was gone. I said, "Etta, you let the boy take the car and go off."

She said, "Charlie, he begged so pitiful that I just didn't have the nerve to tell him he couldn't have it."

[Laughter.] I let myself fly off five or six words, sorta scolding. In a little bit, I missed Etta and her mother was there with me, too. I said to Granny, "Where did Etta get to?"

She says, "I don't know. She went out the door. I believe she went up to the old toilet."

I said, "Go up there and tell her to come to the house." Like I couldn't of went myself. She went up there and come back and says, "She won't come."

Then I realized it was my time to go. [Laughter.] I walked up there. She was settin' there acryin' so badly hurt. And I was just about as bad as she was, but I hadn't known it. I said, "Darlin', come on and let's go to the house. You'll take pneumonia fever and die."

She said, "I'm hurt so bad, I don't give a dern if I do take it and die."

I put my arms around her and hugged her up and petted her and said, "Come on. We'll not fuss about an old car. The damned old car ain't worth what I've already done to hurt your feelings. Come on, let's go to the house." I think that's about the worst one we ever had. I've never since that told her not to let the boy have the car.

Now that's the way I look at it and you kids, when you get married, you can look at it that way. A little ol' car—you can buy another car. But you hurt your wife's feelings—you'll never get over that. She'll never get over it and I'll never get over it. 'Cause I was so dirty to scold her. I'll always remember that. Now we've scolded one another—one or two words—since, but we've never had that big a scrap. Now you see how it goes? And we're still here together.

Before concluding the interview, we asked Charlie and Etta if they would talk to us briefly about what they saw happening with land in the mountains, prices, and so on.

CHARLIE: I can remember when land was five cents an acre. That's nothing. But on the other hand, what was that land worth? There was four hundred acres in the old Moss farm, and it sold to one man for an old-timey Ward rifle and a hound dog. And he wasn't as big a fool as you might think. He didn't have nothing to do *with,* so he couldn't live off that land. But he *could* take the rifle and dog along and kill game and have stuff to live on.

Now, of course, land is worth money, and you'd have to pay a thousand dollars for a little lot around here. Now it's going for summer homes. Right up there's a beautiful hill cut out for a man's home. I hated to see that hill tore up, but that man bought it and paid for it and the law is you can do as you please with it. When we moved here, there was three or four homes here. Now it's covered up. I bet we got a million people where we had fifteen or sixteen then.

And we're throwing money away fast as we get it. I know where there's a brick house a man built where he went broke building it. It cost too much. That house went into the hands of the ones that put the money up. Somebody else is living there now, and they're trying to sell it for sixty thousand dollars. In my day, I expect I could have built it for ten thousand. But now all the stuff is so high. Now I wouldn't know how to figure out a building today to tell you the cost. Money comes in and some people go crazy.

ETTA: I don't approve of these here developers taking a lot of these mountains and hills and just bulldozing them off. I don't approve of that. I think they're ruining a lot of places from what God intended them to be. You take for instance as you go toward Blowing Rock, they have bulldozed that hill off and that's an ugly sight. Oh, it's ugly. And that was a beautiful place. I hate to see these places done that way. I think it should be left like Nature intended it to be.

CHARLIE: Everybody from away from here wants a place in the mountains now. I could just walk out here and stick a little note up for sale and sell [this place] maybe that day. But there's a lot of us don't want to do that. Others, whenever stuff goes to getting up in value, we all get excited. We [want to] bore with a bigger auger. But me and Etta, we're not going to do that. We never have. In place of looking for more expensive things, we educated our children.

But now almost everybody's got to where it's dog eat dog. That's the one trouble we have now. If a man's got a dollar's worth of stuff to sell, he ought to sell it for a dollar instead of asking five dollars for it. Now you're having to pay out so much money for nothing that I don't hardly see how we can fix it. People have just gone crazy. We've got a situation that's got to get worse or better one. Way back yonder when I was a young man, we had an old fellow over there on Cove Creek by the name of Bingham. Pretty good old-fashion doctor. He had a neighbor woman, and one morning she sent word over to him. "Doctor, won't you come over and see me? I'm kindly sick this morning."

He walked in, said, "What in the world's wrong with you this morning, lady?"

She said, "Oh, doctor, I'm asuffering and hurting so bad that I'll have to get better before I can even die!"

Now that's the way we are now in this country. Prices are so high that the poor man just can't come out. And now they've even taken farming away from him [as a way of making a living.]

ETTA: I think they need to improve the conditions that make farming more attractive. The farmer doesn't get enough for the produce he sells to have a living and pay for fertilizer and seeds too. He doesn't come out with enough, and he gets disheartened.

CHARLIE: That's why our young people are all leaving. Our family—the boys and all had to scatter out to get a job. There was absolutely nothing to do here but to go away and hunt a job or starve one. And they had too much of their daddy and mammy in them to sit down and starve. Now one's in Rhode Island, one's in California, one's in Florida, and one's down in North Carolina. He's been over in England and back. There's just nothing for them to do here to make a go of it.

I don't know what we can do, but I guess we'll have to have something like the WPA for a short time, at least, or let the people that want to stay here starve to death one. And of course, the more we have to help them, the more it hits us [through taxes]. But if we have to put him on relief and pay, it hits us just the same. Whatever way, we're going to have to carry them through for a while [until we get things fixed]. We've got to try to help him. You won't sit in your home and see your neighbor over there by you starve to death will you? Just as long as you've got something, you'll help him won't you? Well, that's what we've got to do. We've all got to do a little extra. People will say, "We're spending too much money. We're spending too much money." But what's the money for if we don't use it? We've got to stick out a helping hand.

I admit that I can't help much. I'm broke down. I can't hardly walk through the house. But if there's a way I can help, I'll do it.

Somehow, we've got to get things fixed.

KNIFE MAKING

I really became interested in making knives after I had made one of my own. After completing it, I set out for ideas for designs by which I could make others. After going to stores and making copies of some that were in the windows, I began to wonder how they were made before modern machinery and blacksmithing equipment was invented.

So I went out and tried to find some people that still knew how to make knives as they were made fifty years or more ago. By searching, a lot of luck, and help from good friends like Charlie Ross Hartley in Vilas, North Carolina, I found two people who still made them the old way.

By interviewing Troy Danner and Tedra Harmon, I collected much information. In the following interviews, I will show the different ways that these two men make knives. Tedra Harmon had an extraordinary way of making a kitchen knife: He used sections of the spring from an old windup phonograph for the blades. Troy Danner, on the other hand, used one of the oldest methods of all: knife blades broken off from old crosscut saw blades.

Both ways of making knives were really something to see, and I will try to show you both in this chapter.

Article, diagrams, and photographs by Tom Carlton.

THE TEDRA HARMON VARIETY

Tedra Harmon has become a good friend since we interviewed him about the banjos he makes. Since then, we have found that he knows how to make lots of other things besides banjos. When we found out that he makes knives, we jumped at the chance to interview him again.

When we started off that morning, it was pretty cold. We went by Charlie Ross Hartley's house and picked him up to go along on the interview with us. He wanted to go as he remembered working with a man by

PLATE 10 Tedra places a piece of steel from a phonograph spring in a vice, clamping it at a point that allows the proper length for the knife blade.

PLATE 11 He then scores it on each side with an awl, and, with a sharp tug, snaps it off.

that name once when he was helping to build a church for their community, and he wanted to see if it was the same man he had known a long time ago.

When we drove up into Tedra's yard, he and Charlie remembered each other right away, and they had as good a time visiting together as we did being there.

Tedra told us that he had made knives since he was a kid. His father never made them. It was just a skill that he picked up on his own. He started out just using whatever metal he could find. If he had to temper it, he would heat it cherry red and then dunk it into water. He has made knives out of saw blades before, and he showed us a couple of hunting knives to prove it. The day we were there, however, he was using a long thin strip of metal that he had gotten out of an old phonograph. He was breaking it into pieces to make the blades for a set of eight kitchen knives. He had taken the pattern for the knives from an old kitchen knife like the ones that were used years and years ago.

PLATE 12 Now, using a ball peen hammer, he pecks the steel until the curve is removed and it lies flat.

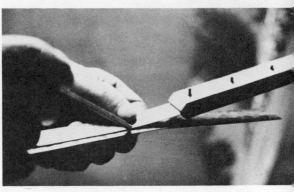

PLATE 13 Then, using another knife blade as a pattern, he marks the width of the blade on the new stock.

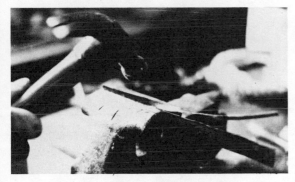

PLATE 14 He again clamps the blade in the vice and breaks it off by striking it with a hammer so that it is the proper width.

PLATE 15 Then he files the ragged edge smooth.

For handles, he uses black walnut because it doesn't split and it looks so good. He also told us that he thinks that using copper wire to brad the handles together is better than using rivets because it's easier to work, and when it's hammered into the handle it swells into the wood and holds better. He said he had seen a knife once that was held together with wooden pegs, but he hadn't tried that.

When he makes a knife out of a saw blade, he cuts the saw blade out with a saber saw, but when he makes one out of a crosscut saw blade, he breaks it out with a cold chisel just as they used to do, and then shapes it with a file.

He claims that, like the old knives, the ones he makes will last a lifetime. The photos and diagrams show you the method he used for the kitchen knives he made while we were there.

PLATE 16 Now Tedra marks the steel where the holes will be cut for the rivets that hold the handle to the blade.

PLATES 17–18 A punch is driven through the blade into the hole provided by a nut placed at the right point under the steel. He hammers the punch through the steel into the nut.

PLATE 19 Now he saws a slot in the wooden handle for the blade to slip into.

PLATE 20 He then places the blade, holes punched, over the handle to mark the points where holes must be drilled in the handle for the rivets.

PLATE 21 After marking the handle, the holes are drilled.

PLATE 22 He slides the blade's base into place in the handle, matches up the holes, pushes pieces of copper wire through the holes, and then flattens the ends to bind the handle and blade firmly together.

PLATE 23 Now he smooths off the rough corners of the handle with a file.

PLATE 24 Final sanding completes the job. Traditionally, the handles were not waxed. They were just left natural, and, through time, kitchen grease soaked in and darkened them.

PLATE 25 The knife at the top has a handle made from a deer's foot. The other three knives show various stages of construction of the knife we just saw Tedra make.

THE STEEL— HARMON

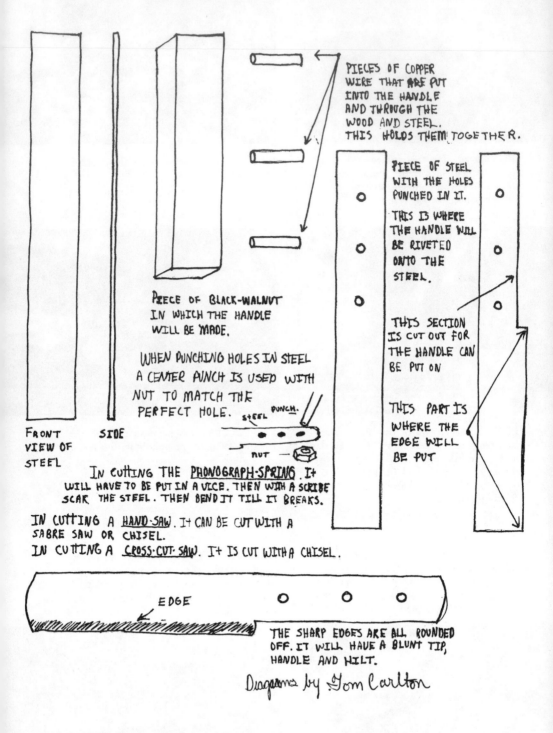

PIECES OF COPPER WIRE THAT ARE PUT INTO THE HANDLE AND THROUGH THE WOOD AND STEEL. THIS HOLDS THEM TOGETHER.

PIECE OF BLACK-WALNUT IN WHICH THE HANDLE WILL BE MADE.

WHEN PUNCHING HOLES IN STEEL A CENTER PUNCH IS USED WITH NUT TO MATCH THE PERFECT HOLE.

STEEL   PUNCH.

NUT →

FRONT VIEW OF STEEL

SIDE

PIECE OF STEEL WITH THE HOLES PUNCHED IN IT.

THIS IS WHERE THE HANDLE WILL BE RIVETED ONTO THE STEEL.

THIS SECTION IS CUT OUT FOR THE HANDLE CAN BE PUT ON

THIS PART IS WHERE THE EDGE WILL BE PUT

IN CUTTING THE PHONOGRAPH-SPRING. It WILL HAVE TO BE PUT IN A VICE. THEN WITH A SCRIBE SCAR THE STEEL. THEN BEND IT TILL IT BREAKS.

IN CUTTING A HAND-SAW. It CAN BE CUT WITH A SABRE SAW OR CHISEL.

IN CUTTING A CROSS-CUT-SAW. It IS CUT WITH A CHISEL.

EDGE

THE SHARP EDGES ARE ALL ROUNDED OFF. IT WILL HAVE A BLUNT TIP, HANDLE AND HILT.

Diagrams by Tom Carlton

PLATE 26

THE HANDLE — HARMON

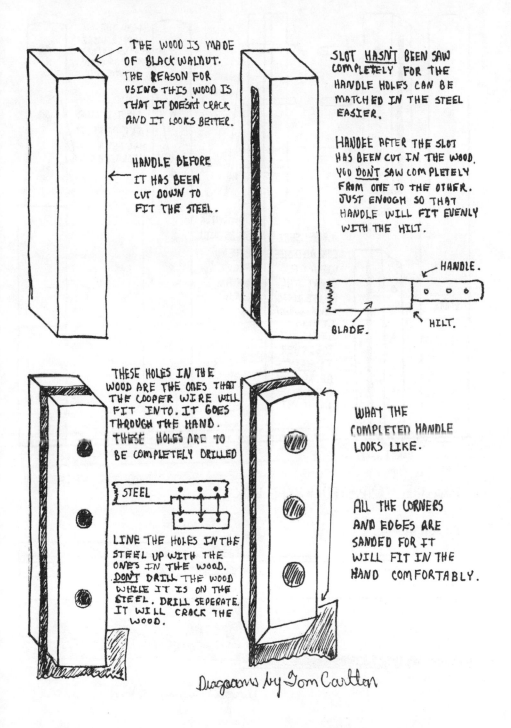

THE WOOD IS MADE OF BLACK WALNUT. THE REASON FOR USING THIS WOOD IS THAT IT DOESN'T CRACK AND IT LOOKS BETTER.

HANDLE BEFORE IT HAS BEEN CUT DOWN TO FIT THE STEEL.

SLOT HASN'T BEEN SAW COMPLETELY FOR THE HANDLE HOLES CAN BE MATCHED IN THE STEEL EASIER.

HANDLE AFTER THE SLOT HAS BEEN CUT IN THE WOOD. YOU DON'T SAW COMPLETELY FROM ONE TO THE OTHER. JUST ENOUGH SO THAT HANDLE WILL FIT EVENLY WITH THE HILT.

HANDLE.

BLADE.

HILT.

THESE HOLES IN THE WOOD ARE THE ONES THAT THE COOPER WIRE WILL FIT INTO. IT GOES THROUGH THE HAND. THESE HOLES ARE TO BE COMPLETELY DRILLED

STEEL

LINE THE HOLES IN THE STEEL UP WITH THE ONES IN THE WOOD. DON'T DRILL THE WOOD WHILE IT IS ON THE STEEL. DRILL SEPERATE. IT WILL CRACK THE WOOD.

WHAT THE COMPLETED HANDLE LOOKS LIKE.

ALL THE CORNERS AND EDGES ARE SANDED FOR IT WILL FIT IN THE HAND COMFORTABLY.

Diagrams by Tom Carlton

PLATE 27

THE ASSEMBLY AND COMPLETION — HARMON

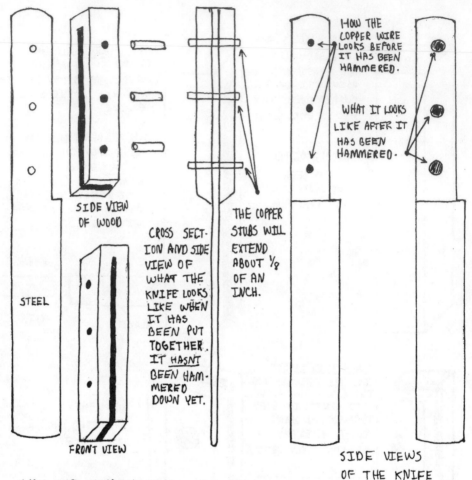

SIDE VIEW OF WOOD

STEEL

FRONT VIEW

CROSS SECTION AND SIDE VIEW OF WHAT THE KNIFE LOOKS LIKE WHEN IT HAS BEEN PUT TOGETHER. IT HASN'T BEEN HAMMERED DOWN YET.

THE COPPER STUBS WILL EXTEND ABOUT ⅛ OF AN INCH.

HOW THE COPPER WIRE LOOKS BEFORE IT HAS BEEN HAMMERED.

WHAT IT LOOKS LIKE AFTER IT HAS BEEN HAMMERED.

SIDE VIEWS OF THE KNIFE

HOW THE COMPLETED KNIFE LOOKS.

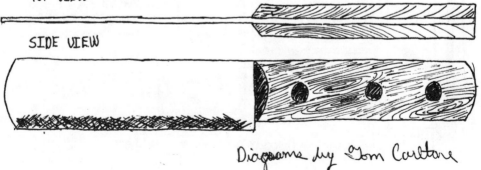

TOP VIEW

SIDE VIEW

Diagrams by Tom Carltone

PLATE 28

OTHER VARIETIES

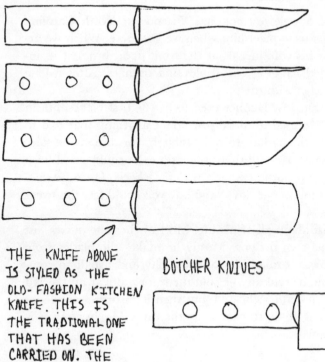

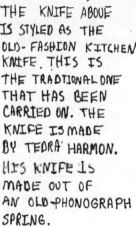

PEELING - KNIVES

Most of THESE KNIVES DO NOT HAVE HILTS ON THEM. THESE ARE THE KIND THAT TROY DANNER MAKES FOR HOME USE. THESE ARE ALSO MADE FROM CROSS- CUT SAW BLADES.

Most of THESE ARE FOR CARVING AND SLICING MEATS AND VEGETABLES

THE KNIFE ABOVE IS STYLED AS THE OLD- FASHION KITCHEN KNIFE. THIS IS THE TRADTIONAL ONE THAT HAS BEEN CARRIED ON. THE KNIFE IS MADE BY TEDRA HARMON. HIS KNIFE IS MADE OUT OF AN OLD-PHONOGRAPH SPRING.

BOTCHER KNIVES

THESE LARGE KNIVES ARE MADE FOR CUTTING MEATS AND BUTCHERING. ALL OF THESE ARE MADE OUT OF CROSS- CUT SAW BLADES.

Diagrams by Tom Carlton

PLATE 29

THE TROY DANNER VARIETY

Troy Danner is one of our newest contacts. Friends in North Carolina told us about him and took us to meet him when we got there. When we arrived at his home, he and his wife met us at the front door, brought us inside by the fire, and started handing out apples and oranges. After a long day, it was really nice to relax with them.

Several people told us that Mr. Danner used to be the best blacksmith in that part of the country. He used to make just about anything that had to do with blacksmithing. He finally had to quit, though, because, as he said, "I just got old and wore out." He said that at one time, he could stand for a whole day shoeing horses and putting wagon tires on wheels. Once he shod sixteen horses at his little shop in one day, "and boy you could feel the sweat run out of you too!"

He has made knives just about all of his life. Most of them he makes just for his own use and to his own designs. Mostly he makes the blades from crosscut saws and handsaws. It takes him about a day and a half to complete one, and the last time he sold any he sold them for a dollar and a half apiece. He says, "Guess I'm getting cheated, but then it's worth a whole lot to me just to have something to do to pass away the time. Making knives is just a gift given to me, I guess."

PLATE 30 Troy makes his large kitchen knives from pieces of crosscut saw blades. He breaks out a blade-sized chunk of the saw by striking it a number of times with a cold chisel and hammer. It takes hours to break it out.

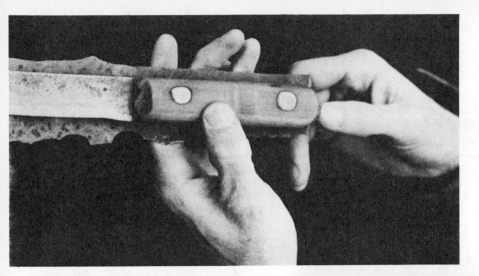

PLATE 31 Here Troy holds a finished knife over the top of a piece of a cross-cut saw he has just broken out for a new knife blade.

PLATE 32 He trims off some of the jagged edges with his hammer and cold chisel.

PLATES 33–34 For punching the holes in the blade's base, Troy has fashioned a homemade clamp. The clamp holds the blade tightly while he drives an awl through the blade using the holes in the clamp as a guide. Then he attaches the handle and shapes the blade with a grindstone.

THE STEEL — DANNER

CROSS-CUT SAW BLADE

HAND SAW

STEEL IS ABOOT AN 1/8" THICK.

1 THIS IS A SECTION OF THE CROSS-CUT SAW BLADE. THIS IS WHAT KNIFE BLADE WILL BE MADE OF. THE STEEL WILL BE CUT WITH A COLD CHISE AND A HAMMER.

2 THE STEEL IS MARKED OFF WITH CHAIR. THEN WITH THE COLD CHISEL BEGIN TO CUT YOUR STEEL. GO AROUND ONCE AND THE SECOND TIME IT SHOULD BREAK CLEAN.

WHEN YOU HAVE FINISHED CUTTING THE STEEL OUT IT WILL LOOK SOMETHING LIKE THIS.

3 WHEN YOU HAVE CUT IT OUT THE EDGES WILL BE VERY SHARP AND JAGGED THEY WILL HAVE TO BE ALL FILED DOWN.

4 WHEN YOU HAVE FILED ALL THE SHARP EDGES OFF THE STEEL IT SHOULD LOOK LIKE A RECTANGLE. IT IS NOW READY FOR THE BLADE TO BE MARKED OFF ON IT.

5 BLADE MARK IT OFF IN THE SHAPE AND CUT IT ON THE LINE THIS WILL GIVE A ROUGH OUT LINE.

THE EDGES WILL BE JAGGED AFTER IT HAS BEEN CUT WITH THE CHISEL.

6 BLADE

THE BLADE WILL BE OFF TILL ALL THE EDGES ARE SMOOTH.

7 BLADE

Diagrams by Tom Carlton

PLATE 35

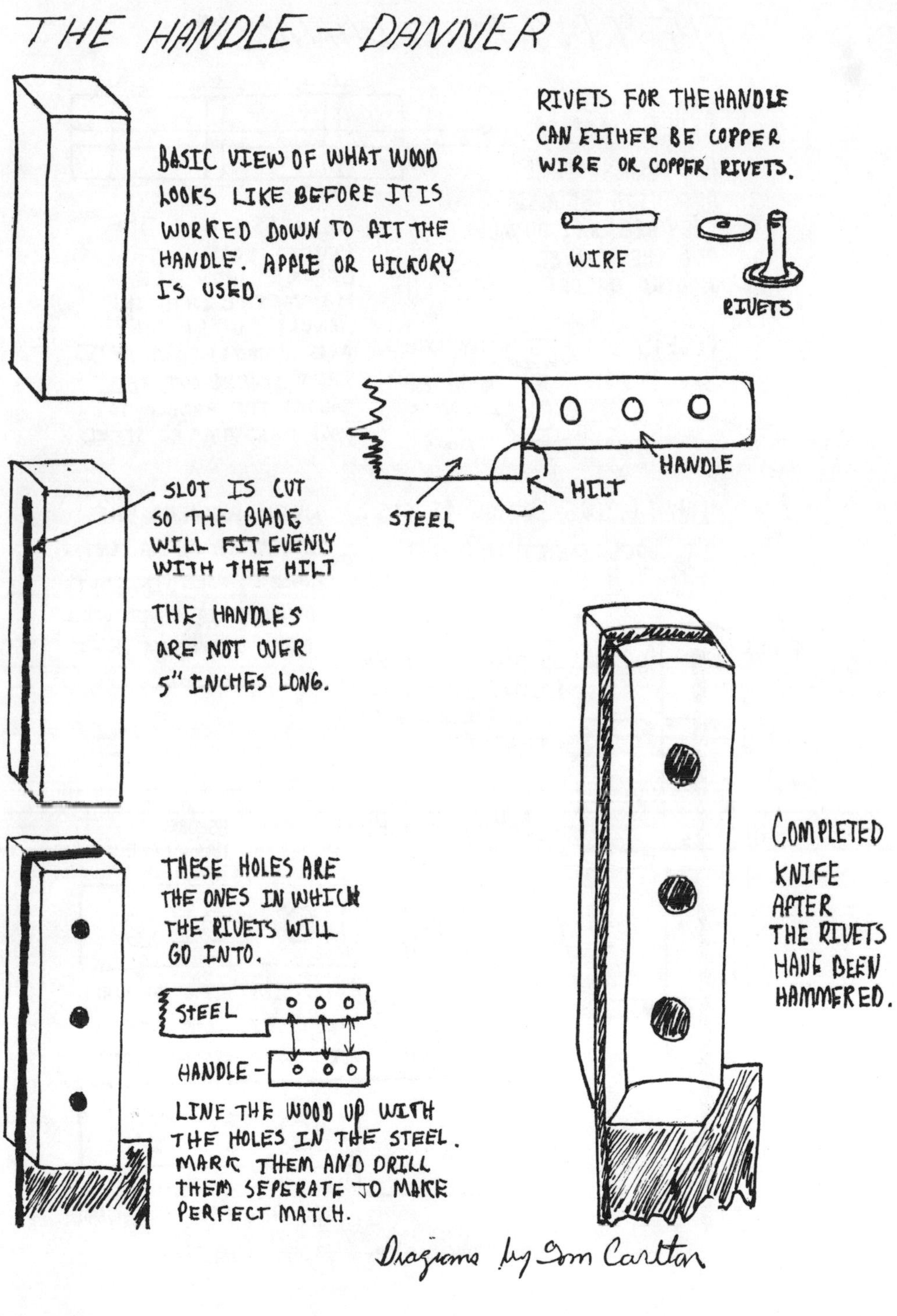

THE HANDLE — DANNER

BASIC VIEW OF WHAT WOOD LOOKS LIKE BEFORE IT IS WORKED DOWN TO FIT THE HANDLE. APPLE OR HICKORY IS USED.

RIVETS FOR THE HANDLE CAN EITHER BE COPPER WIRE OR COPPER RIVETS.

WIRE

RIVETS

STEEL

HILT

HANDLE

— SLOT IS CUT SO THE BLADE WILL FIT EVENLY WITH THE HILT

THE HANDLES ARE NOT OVER 5" INCHES LONG.

THESE HOLES ARE THE ONES IN WHICH THE RIVETS WILL GO INTO.

STEEL

HANDLE —

LINE THE WOOD UP WITH THE HOLES IN THE STEEL. MARK THEM AND DRILL THEM SEPERATE TO MAKE PERFECT MATCH.

COMPLETED KNIFE AFTER THE RIVETS HAVE BEEN HAMMERED.

Diagrams by Tom Carlton

PLATE 36

THE RIVETS – DANNER

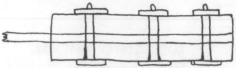

RIVET = COPPER
AND BRASS. THEY
ARE USED BECAUSE
THEY ARE SOFT METAL
AND THEY CAN BE
WORKED EASIER.

RIVETS –

← Top Washer

Bottom Bolt
← Washer.
OR
Rivets.

THIS . IS WHAT THE
RIVETS LOOK LIKE
BEFORE THEY ARE
HAMMERED INTO THE
HANDLE. WHEN THEY
ARE HAMMERED IT MAKES
THEM SPREAD OUT. THIS
CAUSES THE HANDLE TO
HOLD FAST TO THE STEEL.

WHEN PUTTING IN THE RIVETS
IT LOOKS SOMETHING LIKE
THIS.

WHEN PUNCHING HOLES
IN THE STEEL . A CENTER
PUNCH IS USED WITH A NUT
BEHIND IT. THIS WILL
PUNCH a PERFECT HOLE
IN YOOR STEEL.

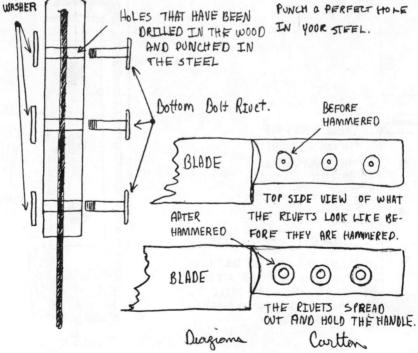

Top
WASHER

HOLES THAT HAVE BEEN
DRILLED IN THE WOOD
AND PUNCHED IN
THE STEEL

Bottom Bolt Rivet.

BEFORE
HAMMERED

BLADE

TOP SIDE VIEW OF WHAT
THE RIVETS LOOK LIKE BE-
FORE THEY ARE HAMMERED.

AFTER
HAMMERED

BLADE

THE RIVETS SPREAD
OUT AND HOLD THE HANDLE.

Diagrams   Carlton

PLATE 37

THE COMPLETION - DANNER

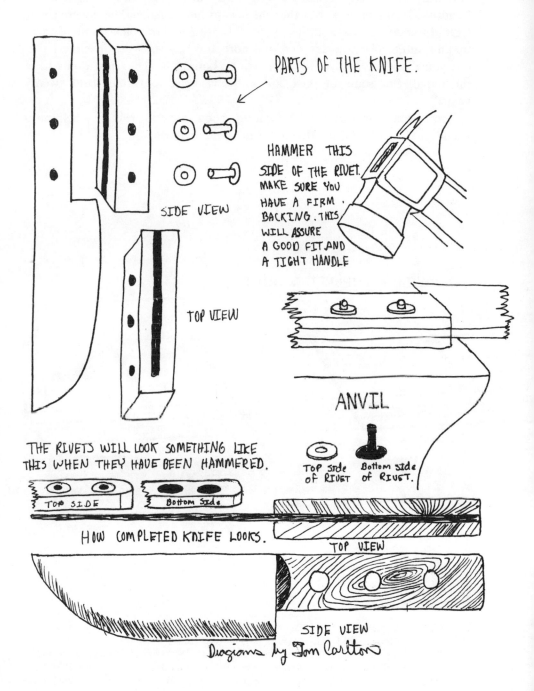

PARTS OF THE KNIFE.

SIDE VIEW

TOP VIEW

HAMMER THIS SIDE OF THE RIVET. MAKE SURE YOU HAVE A FIRM BACKING. THIS WILL ASSURE A GOOD FIT AND A TIGHT HANDLE

ANVIL

THE RIVETS WILL LOOK SOMETHING LIKE THIS WHEN THEY HAVE BEEN HAMMERED.

Top Side of RIVET.   Bottom Side of RIVET.

TOP SIDE   Bottom Side

HOW COMPLETED KNIFE LOOKS.

TOP VIEW

SIDE VIEW

Diagrams by Tom Carlton

PLATE 38

At this point, his wife interrupted and said, "I wish you could see all the knives he *has* made." Then she went into the kitchen and brought out a handful of some of his knives that she uses in her cooking. There were six or eight different designs, and they were all beautiful. Troy picked one of them up and said, "Now you can go to the store and buy yourself a peeling knife, but you don't have anything after you've bought it. They just don't have the metal. But some of these knives we've used for fifteen and twenty years."

Troy Danner was born on March 29, 1892. He still feels that helping a friend out is the best thing that a person could ever do.

THE WILL CAMPBELL VARIETY

PLATE 39   A butcher knife made by Will Campbell, who died several years ago. He cut the steel using a cold chisel and a hammer. If those tools weren't available, he would warm the steel slightly and scribe a line on it. With the steel hanging over the edge of the anvil, the line on the edge, he would hammer along the line until the excess steel broke off. Like Troy Danner, he usually used old crosscut saw blades for his supply of knife blades.

PLATE 40   Here Tom Campbell, Will's younger brother, explains to Tom Carlton, the student who wrote this article, how the knife was made. Tom, who lives near Bakersville, North Carolina, still carries on the craftsman tradition, making plow stocks (see chapter in this book), hoes, and tool handles.

WOOD CARVING

O n the four-by-eight sheet of
plywood that serves as a desk
in my log house, there sits a
tiny, inch-and-a-half-high wooden rabbit carved out of poplar by some
whittler I never met who scratched his initials, JAM, into its base. It's a
wonderful rabbit; it was given to me here in the mountains when I was very
young by a warm, generous woman named Violet Winterfield, and it is one
of the very few things I have brought with me into my adulthood from
those early days on Betty's Creek.

That rabbit is as appropriate a way as any to begin a section on wood
carving—a craft that has been around for as long as there have been trees
and hands to shape them with. Some of the items fashioned in the mountains were made expressly as gifts. A coon dog whittled by the fire on a
winter night might find itself in a young son's Christmas stocking, for example.

Others carve gift or collector items as a means of making a little extra income: wooden bowls, animal figures, mountain characters, or even whole
farmyard scenes complete with miniature barns and farm animals, or man-
ger scenes complete with wise men and sheep and buildings, or mountain
home scenes complete with furniture, fireplaces, and pots and pans. Such
carving was one of the early industries in the Southern Appalachians. Many
of the groups have been written about by Allen H. Eaton in *Handicrafts of
the Southern Highlands,* a tremendous study originally supported and published by the Russell Sage Foundation in 1937 and reissued in 1973 by
Dover. On page 180 of the Dover edition, for example, Eaton writes about
the work done at the John C. Campbell Folk School in Brasstown, North
Carolina—a school still in existence: "The IXL brand of pocketknife, familiar to many of us of an earlier generation, has never been put to happier
use than by the farm workers, students, and neighbors of the John C.
Campbell Folk School . . . Mrs. Campbell believed that anyone who with
his pocketknife could cut a fence rail in two in a short time or cover a board

surface with sharply incised mountain hieroglyphics without interrupting his own or anybody else's conversation might, with practice, put that skill and energy to more satisfactory use . . . (Now) no scene about the Folk School is more pleasant or characteristic than the young people resting at lunch time or around the fireplace in the evening whittling away at their different figures in all stages from the rough wood to the finished object. A small block from which a mule, a rabbit, a goose, or a rooster is being whittled fits conveniently and safely in the shirt pocket, and a sharp knife in another pocket awaits the free moment when whittling can be resumed."

Then, of course, there is the carving or shaping that is either totally practical (tool handles, spindles for spinning wheels, crow calls, turkey calls, wooden door latches and hinges, triggers for rabbit boxes), or practical with decorative touches (toys, butter molds that leave an attractive design in a pat of butter, ornamentation in some furniture such as church pulpits and fireboards, inlay in gunstocks, scrolls on the pegheads of a fiddle or dulcimer, walking sticks where the imprint of a honeysuckle vine has been taken advantage of to produce a serpent crawling toward the handle).

Beyond that, there are even such things as religious wall hangings carved in relief out of two-inch-thick slabs of wood, some fully colored and amazingly detailed. The variety is just astonishing. In this section, we hint at some of it, but a book twice this size couldn't show the work of all those who work in wood just in our state. There are hundreds and hundreds of such people, each taking delight in seeing a recognizable shape take form through his own hands, and each celebrating the fact that he can express his own vigor, individuality, and craftsmanship in this fashion.

BEW

CHARLES EARNHARDT, CARVER OF SCENES

Charles Earnhardt whittles both for a living and for pleasure. He started eleven years ago when a man he met showed him a few tricks of the art and some good tools to use. He learned the rest by trial and error, and began selling pieces about seven years ago. The money goes for a good cause; for years Charles and his wife have been trying to buy back the family farm in North Carolina. When we first met him, Mr. Jim Hagan, the industrial arts teacher at Highlands, North Carolina High School, had asked him to visit his classes for a week to teach his students some of the same tricks he had been taught. The afternoon that we visited Charles at the high school auditorium, he was surrounded by about twenty-five pairs of hands holding pocketknives and blocks of wood.

The tools he uses consist of two knives and two small chisels. The blades of his knives are made from a straight razor and a pair of barber scissors.

PLATE 41

PLATE 42   These are Charles' favorite tools—the knife blades are made from a straight razor blade and a pair of barber's scissors.

PLATE 43   Charles holds a block that he has marked according to his pattern and is now roughing out into the figure of an old woman with a rolling pin.

Charles' favorite wood is white pine because it is easily accessible and is easy to work with. White pine should be set aside and cured for at least four to five months—a year is preferable.

Some of Charles' carvings are shown on the next pages. It took him a little over one hundred hours to complete the scene with the man and the deer. The shop took close to one hundred hours and the kitchen scene about two hundred hours. He spends five or six hours on each figure that he reproduces to sell. When he creates a new figure, it takes longer.

Some of the larger, more intricate scenes are not for sale. The dulcimer maker, for example, is one that Charles wants to keep himself. The other, smaller figures, however, Charles makes specifically to sell. As the photographs show, he is incredibly talented.

RAY MCBRIDE

Photographs by Ray and Ken Kistner.

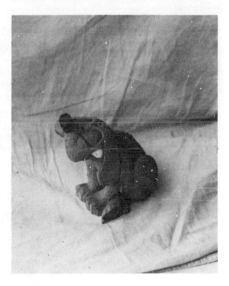

PLATE 44 Many of his works are comical or satirical in nature. He creates a new figure or grouping and, using it as a pattern, turns out a series for sale. This wife yelling to her husband through an ear trumpet is one such example.

PLATE 45 This little hound scratching behind his ear is another example of the more humorous works Charles produces.

PLATES 46–47   Other typical Earnhardt scenes are those two boys playing marbles, and an old man leaning on his banjo, a jug of moonshine behind him.

PLATES 48–51   Others of his scenes are one-of-a-kind, breathtakingly exact replicas of scenes from years ago. Here, for example, is an early living room/dining room scene complete to the tiniest pair of scissors and child's rocking horse—all carved out of wood. In this scene, the sideboard is 10¼″ tall, the long table is 10⅝″ long, and the chair is 5″ high.

PLATE 49

PLATE 50   PLATE 51

PLATE 52

PLATE 53

PLATE 54

PLATE 55

PLATES 52–55 Another scene shows an old man in his mountain dulcimer shop. Even the tiny saw blade, spittoon, pegs for the dulcimer strings, and the knobs of the drawers are painstakingly carved out of tiny slivers and blocks of wood.

PLATES 56–57   In this more comical scene, immaculate in detail (complete to shot-gun and shells and tiny squashed cans), a hunter is caught cleaning his gun just as a deer walks past. The look of surprise and pain on the man's stubbled face tells the story. Most of these more intricate works wind up in private collections.

DOUG SHEPPARD, BIRD CARVER

Imagine a place where the only sounds are a creek in the distance tum-bling over rocks and birds of all kinds singing around a peaceful three-room cottage. It seems that someone would be able to carve birds effortlessly in such surroundings. And thirty-two-year-old Doug Sheppard does make it look easy. He talked to us about how he started carving birds and what his dreams and plans are as he shaped a wren from a chunk of basswood.

Doug carves his birds of basswood (or linden, another name for the tree). Other woods used by carvers are white pine and buckeye. Doug's fa-ther prefers basswood, and that is what Doug feels has influenced his choice.

Doug paints his birds with water colors. He paints the basic colors on and after these dry, he "blends" in the other markings, like the red on the robin's breast and the yellow on the quail's feathers. Finally, he adds mark-ings like the white around a robin's eyes, or the mask on the cardinal, or the brown spots on the quail.

Asked why he prefers water colors over oils or acrylics, he said that water colors are easy to work with, mix well, blend with one another easily, and look more like the natural colors of the birds. He feels that oils and acrylics are too shiny to be natural looking. The water colors give a flat, soft appearance.

Article and photographs by Bit Carver, Shelley Pace, and Susie Nichols.

PLATE 58   Doug Sheppard's studio in Franklin, North Carolina.

PLATE 59

PLATE 60   Doug paints most of his birds with water colors.

I've been carving birds like this about five years, but I've been around it all my life. I carved back there when I was a kid—pick up a block of wood and carve something out. And one time, years ago, I carved a bird out and that was a pretty good bird—it wasn't bad at all for shape. I painted it, didn't do a very good job on painting, but my mother got that bird and kept it. I believe she's still got that bird somewhere. I looked at it not too long ago and I wasn't at all ashamed of it.

My dad showed me ways to do things when I started carving. I really didn't learn much from him. He'd tell me something and I wouldn't listen to him. I was determined to do it my way. A wood carver's going to do it their own way—no matter what, everybody's going to be different.

When I started out I wasn't any good at all, but they were good enough to sell. I feel now like they really looked bad, but here lately I'm getting into it where I really change something every time I carve one and paint it. I can put something different on it that makes it look better all the time. I keep learning more about it. As small as it is, there's a whole lot to learn, believe it or not. When you really get down to carving, you can work on this one bird right here all day if you wanted to, if you wanted to study it, keep adding to it, go right on down and cut every feather on it. I haven't had a chance or the time to do that.

A friend and I have just opened up a shop in Franklin, North Carolina. It is situated near the square. There are a lot of people who come through here in the summer who never see stuff like this. And the good thing about our shop is that they can see me carving like I'm doing before you, and I can really sell them.

We are calling the shop "Cardinal Crafts." We are just selling our birds mostly. People seem to think we'll be a success, that this is something people will want to come see us do and they'll want to buy the birds. If it goes well, we'll probably keep it open this winter. If I'm down there at the shop, I'll be carving birds.

I can sell birds. I hope to continue to keep my buyers supplied as well as selling in my own shop. If there's anything that's any better in my shop, I'll get more money for it because I'll be putting more time into it. If my buyers still want my birds and I can make enough for them, I will make them because they've treated me nice. I'll try to keep my prices the same as they are now. I'll not go up sky-high on them.

People come to the door and they think if they come in, they've got to buy something. And I wouldn't drag them in. I don't care if they do or don't buy something. If they come in and just say that they like it, that's fine with me. They're welcome to come in and stand here and look.

To tell me just that my stuff is priced too low [would be okay with me]. Most people don't realize it, but a lot of our stuff is priced too cheap. I get

PLATE 61   Doug carefully   PLATE 62
carves the wing feathers
of a wren.

PLATE 63

mad when they come in and say that [our prices are] too much. I know
that's not true. I got into it with one lady. She came in here and there was a
bird sitting over there on the shelf, and she said, "How much is that one?"

I said, "Ten dollars."

She said, "Oh, that's too much!"

I just said, "Too bad."

She came back the next day and she was still kind of nipped about it, but
I just told her that that was a good price and she finally did buy it.

I do watch the birds when I can, and I feed them through the winter.
There are so many different kinds flying in here. There's a family of Eastern
bluebirds nesting out there right now [in a little birdhouse on the fence].
Can you hear those catbirds? And I've seen a hummingbird twice already.
There's a family of little phoebes nesting over my bandsaw in that little
workshop out there.

I've seen some indigo buntings here this year—there's lots of them. Last

PLATE 64

PLATE 65

PLATE 66   The knife Doug uses for much of his work.

year I saw cedar waxwings and rose-breasted grosbeaks; I'd never seen a rose-breasted grosbeak before in my life.

I've got a good pair of binoculars and I have several good books on bird identification and use them for reference and as models sometimes for my carvings.

I'm starting to really understand paint now. I understand how to mix the colors and the blending and what you've got to do to make it look good. I don't know about distance and dimensions. I've had no art training whatsoever, other than what I've just taught myself. It's starting to come to me— different shadings and paints and how to carve the feathers. There's probably a lot of terms in art that I don't know. I'm thinking about going to Western Carolina University this fall and taking a year of art. I'm not interested in the credit. I just want to go there and learn. I want to be able to talk to people about the birds when they come into my shop. I'll have a little knowledge of art to be able to discuss the birds' features with the customers.

I mount my birds on driftwood, because it's about the best thing you could find. You could go in the woods and cut off stumps and things— pretty stuff I guess, but you can find driftwood at Fontana that's the prettiest stuff you ever looked at. A person could pick up enough driftwood to make a living around these lakes and sell it. In fact, there's people coming in here and wanting to buy it.

I'm going to start upping my prices if I'm gonna take time to find real select pieces of driftwood and carve a hawk, and spend three or four days on one piece of work. But that's the only reason I'll up my prices, because I'd have so much into it. That is, if I can find the time and I'm going to take time. I don't care if people are waiting for me to carve one bird at a time. I'm just going to take time and do that 'cause I've got to.

I want to carve one to where it's like a real bird of some kind and be just as good as these [famous] wildlife artists. They're real good. They paint every hair or every feather on them. I want to do work like that, and I believe I can if I can find time. I know it can be done because I've seen it—out of basswood, too. This guy in Asheville carves them. He does it for a hobby and he gets ninety dollars for one little bird and I do it for a living. But I'd sorta like to do it like he does—take my time and really detail one and carve every feather on it. I've practiced that and I've studied that and I know I can do it now, or think I can. I can do real fine work.

Having freedom is my idea of being rich. A man spends eighty thousand dollars on the interior of a building and he keeps going on and on, and I don't understand that. I mean, why have all that money? What are you going to do with it? You could get what you want and then quit. Being rich, to me, is not having to work and getting to sleep late every morning and not having any bills and not owing anybody anything and having your own place.

I'm not really interested in making lots of money. I do want enough to buy me a little piece of land back in the woods, maybe backing up to some national forest land somewhere, and building me a house like the one described in *The Foxfire Book*. I had always wondered how a house like that was built, and then that book came out with the plans in it. I could have figured it out probably, but this way I know what to do and I'm going to build me a house like that someday. [I want a cabin built] out of logs. I'm going to build one one of these days if I ever get a place to build it.

Then I could just sit and carve, because I hope to really get better and better, where my birds look real. I have a dream of becoming a famous wildlife artist—who knows?

C. P. LIGON, FOLK ARTIST

One day out of the clear blue sky, Mr. C. P. Ligon of Toccoa brought some of his carvings to Foxfire *for the students at our school to enjoy. This was the first time he had brought any of his figures up our way as most of his work is on display closer to his home in Stephens County.*

A couple of months later when it was time to return the carvings, several of us decided to go along and find out more about Mr. Ligon and his hobby. We drove into his backyard and knew immediately we'd come to the right place. His garage and shop area were filled with logs, stumps, and sticks of all shapes and sizes. There were carved figures resembling totem poles, rabbits, a seven-foot-tall Ichabod Crane, a small penguin—all kinds of figures that can be made from odd-shaped pieces of wood.

When we began to talk with him, we found out that he was seventy-five years old and had begun carving in 1967 after retiring from a roofing business. He had never done anything like this before in his life until then. It all began, he said, one rainy day when he went to town to get some enamel paint and began painting a picture. He had never had an artist's brush in his hand before and said he even did a lousy job of painting a house. But he enjoyed the feeling, and he soon had picked up a hatchet, a handsaw, a power saw, and some chisels and started on a piece of wood. Soon a rough figure emerged and he was hooked. Now a steady stream of one-of-a-kind

PLATE 67 Mr. Ligon in the parking lot of the Rabun Gap-Nacoochee School with two of the figures he brought along to share with our students.

PLATE 68 The totem pole standing in place at the Campfire Girls' Camp in Toccoa. Both sides of the pole are covered with carvings.

figures comes from his shop created out of wood he has picked up in the surrounding woods and knots and odd-shaped chunks people have given to him. That day he showed us some cypress knots he was going to make something out of eventually.

The carvings he makes are never sanded down. He doesn't believe in going to all that trouble. All the things carved by him he describes as, "Junk for the school children." He feels they enjoy his rough work more than things that are finished and can't "be touched and played with." In line with his desire to make things for kids, he refuses to ever sell a piece of his work. It is made exclusively for donation to, or display by, local groups that work with young people. Collectors are sent away empty-handed.

I felt as though we had been to a wonderful and peaceful place. Nobody wanted to leave. We were now beginning to understand why Mr. Ligon carves the things he does and wants no money for them: He likes what he's doing and he loves kids—money can't buy those things.

Article by Sid Jones. Interviews and photographs by Sid, Al Oakes, Robert McLanahan, Melissa McGee, and Alison Rutherford.

The first thing I carved after I quit work was an old Indian. I cut down some apple trees out there, and I said, "I'm going to make me an Indian out of this thing." I got my power saw and cut them grooves out in his head. Took a little old handsaw and sawed around the chin, the ears, and everything. It just come natural. Do you know what's the matter with people today? They don't use the talents they've got. And lots of them don't have the time to. Just like I was. I wanted to educate my children. I never took a vacation until it was almost time that I quit work. I quit work at sixty-seven.

I think kids ought to get involved with things like this early. I was working on that totem pole I put up at the Campfire Girls' Camp in Toccoa, and one of my grandsons said, "That just don't look right to me."

And I said, "Well, just go ahead and finish it like you want it." That was Walter's boy, Matt. So he just finished it off. Then the others came—Mark and Perry and Bryan—and they all worked on it some too. I told them, "Go to it, boys. You can't make it any rougher than I'm doing."

That totem pole was from a white pine tree that had been in my yard. I planted that tree. I got it from down here on Lake Rabun from a fellow. We was up there covering his house. I looked there and saw that little white pine and I dug it up and took it home. It was planted before 1950 and was about twenty-five years old. One day there wasn't a cloud in the sky, but the wind came up and started blowing awful hard. It was on a Thursday, and I was fixing to go in the house and that tree started giving away and

PLATE 69   Mr. Ligon replacing the bow in the arms of the Indian that now stands in the cafeteria of the Stephens County High School.

fell over. I've made a few other little pieces out of it besides the pole. I've about used it up now.

And the eagle on top of it is made of oak. It came from a tree that was out in my yard close to the well. I decided to put that eagle on it, and I made it up at the house while we had the pole lying down. Then when they wanted to take the pole down to the lake and set it up, they brought a big truck down there with a lift on it. That's where it's been ever since.

Then I made an Indian for the Stephens County High School and took it down there and set it out in the hall. They didn't ask me to. I just wanted to do that. They're the Stephens County Indians, you know.

It sat out there in the hall. The boys came along and wanted souvenirs. They took the arms and everything off that thing; just left the main body. That's all they left. So then it was set back in the book stacks or the storage area. I kept telling them if they'd bring it to me, I'd remodel it. Then you people from *Foxfire* came down and brought it home for me. I appreciated that. Then I remodeled it to what it was when you saw it the other day in

PLATE 70 A figure of Lester Maddox riding on a donkey. The donkey holds an apple in its mouth, and there is a peg in its back under Lester so he can also be turned to face forward. As in the two standing figures in Plate 67, the arms are connected to a stick that passes through the figure's body enabling the arms to rotate.

the dining room at the school. I carried it over there and told them I was bringing him home. I asked where we should put it, and the lady over there suggested that it be put in the cafeteria, and that's where it's standing now. The principal over there is a fine man. He's a wonderful person. The students respect him all right.

I also made a doll house once. A little girl we know had an older brother die of leukemia. Her mother asked me, "How about building us a doll house for her for her birthday?"

I said, "All right. The case like it is, I'll make it." And I got it done on time. All I charged them for was the material that I had to buy to go in there—the walls and the ceiling. I made a little bit of furniture to go in there. And I made little shakes for the roof myself. I worked with it about a week. I'd go home and think about the next step. It didn't take me long to make those shingles. I had a two-inch chisel. I got some little two-by-four blocks from the lumber company. The fellows over there give them to me. I've done a lot of work for them. I took the little chisel and tapped the little shakes out of the blocks. If it's a good two-by-four, I can get about twenty-two shingles out of it, but I usually get about eighteen out of each one.

The little church I made and gave to Young Harris College had little shingles on it, too. I gave a little church to Reinhardt College, too. Those are both little log buildings. The first contact I had with Reinhardt was in 1939 when I went up there and covered the girls' dormitory while I was in the roofing business. Our preacher's wife went to Reinhardt, and I told her not too long ago that I was going to make her something for her old alma mater. Me and the preacher took that little church up there. They were so tickled with it up there. They said, "I'll tell you what we're going to do. We're building a museum, and that's the first thing that's going in it." You know, that was a pretty good send-off.

I had about seventeen little children come over to the house from one of the schools about a week or two ago. They asked if it would be all right to come. They asked me when they got through looking at all the stuff I've carved around here, "Can we have a picnic here in the yard?"

I said, "Go right ahead." They got out there and had a big time. They seen that tree house out there that my grandchildren play in. They played in there. I have a lot of fun with the children that way. It's great. What I'm doing it mostly for is to bring it back like this country used to be. Children didn't used to have anything to make anything with. No tools. The kids always made their own things—country children did. We'd make wheels out of most anything. We've had a right smart of little fun with stuff like that. We like to hunt and fiddle around with the dogs and have a good time. We really didn't have toys. The first thing I bought for myself was a little old

PLATE 71 Woman churning. The arms rotate pulling the churn dasher up and down.

PLATE 72 Mr. Ligon standing beneath his bearded man in a top hat. The figure was carved on an inverted tree trunk.

knife for a dime when I was a boy. I would have liked to carve then, but that knife wouldn't even cut. I just had it just to have a knife.

But now that I'm retired, I do all this stuff for the school children, and try to get them interested in things like this. If I can get one of them to try something, they'll understand and maybe enjoy it. I don't try to make nothing fancy like it was out of a store—finished. I make it rough. And they can understand that. If they go to the store and get something, it's all dolled up. But this is an incentive for them to do something. They'll try to do something like this. Something rough like this, they're not afraid to do it. Painting's the same way.

I've worked with all three grammar schools in Stephens County, and two in Habersham County so far. I do them just like I done you all. I come driving up and say, "This is what I've got."

Like the other day. I went up to a little school up there in Habersham County back in the country there. They never had had anything much. I

PLATE 73

drove up there and I asked for the principal. He told me to walk on in his office. I told him what I had. "Would you like to see what I brought?"

He said, "Are you going to charge me anything for them?"

I said, "No, they don't have to pay me nothing to see the stuff. I'm making it for the good of them. Not to make money."

We drove around behind the building there and they took it right on in, and he said, "We're going to have a break in ten minutes. We'll let all the children see it."

They brought the first grade in right on up to the sixth grade, and when they all got through, they brought the little fellows back in which I appreciated. That did me a lot of good for the little fellows to see it.

They had one kid there who had to sit down. He didn't seem to feel so good. I had the little covered wagon with me, and he got down there and looked at that, and looked over there at me, and studied that wagon some more. It was well worth that trip up there for him, even if I'd got throwed out. He was enjoying it. All those little kids crowded around. They wanted to know this and that. They wanted to know what it was all about.

My wife has seen what I'm doing for the children and the interest they have in this stuff, and she likes that. The grandchildren like for me to make stuff. They take an interest in it. One morning when I was in California on our trip recently, my granddaughters out there were looking through this scrapbook of pictures I've got and clippings and stories that have been written about my stuff. I told them to take out anything they wanted, and they about cleaned it out. I didn't care. I wanted them to have those things.

My mother died when I was ten years old, and I loved her greatly. And my father got hurt about three or four years later at the cotton gin. He was knocked out of a wagon by a bale of cotton and then run over by the wagon and hurt. After that, I stayed with my father. He wanted me to wait on him. He didn't care about the other kids waiting on him because I done the things just like he wanted them. I learned a lot. I didn't get to go to school, but I learned a whole lot of what I needed to know. I didn't really have a childhood like some children do, but I can't complain. The others went to school. My father took up a lot of my time, and I never regretted a day of it. That's one reason today I have a whole lot of respect for old people and kids, too. I enjoy the kids and I enjoy the old people.

LON REID, TOY FURNITURE MAKER

Lon Reid was one of the most exciting chairmakers we ever found. As such, we featured him in *The Foxfire Book*. One aspect of his life that we did not mention at that time, however, is that he was also a fine whittler. Not wanting to waste anything at all, he took all the scrap wood and white oak splits left over after making one of his large chairs, and, with his pocket-knife, turned those scraps into what he called "toy" chairs that were just as popular as the larger ones. We bought boxes full of them and gave them away to people who still treasure them today. Many of them went to children, and the thought that people he had never met had received his work pleased Lon enormously.

Though he is dead now, the hundreds of tiny chairs he made in his lifetime survive, and carry his name forward.

RICHARD PAGE

PLATE 74 Lon, seated behind his shaving horse, carves out the rocker for one of his toy chairs with his pocketknife.

PLATE 75 Two holes are drilled into the top of each rocker, and the rockers are tapped into place.

PLATE 76 Lon's granddaughter watches as he works.

PLATE 77 Lon and *Foxfire*'s Richard Page with three of his chairs.

WILLIAM FLOWERS, RELIEF SCULPTOR

William Flowers was born and raised in Copper Hill, Tennessee. He now lives with his wife and three children in College Park, Georgia, outside Atlanta, where he works the day shift on the assembly line at the Ford Motor Company. In his spare time, he carves in wood, and, most recently, in marble. For his woodwork, he says, "I use hand tools: pocket knives, carpenters' chisels, hammers, mallets—a little bit of everything according to what size piece I'm carving. I've got a few handmade tools—a few little sharp blades and things I use. You know, you can't hardly buy them. I haven't had a day's training, but I could always draw about anything I wanted to when I was a kid. I never tried any woodwork until about ten years ago. The first thing I ever did, I was just playing around. I just mainly wanted to see if I could do it."

The most ambitious works he does are large religious scenes which he carves in relief out of solid blocks of wood, the figures in almost three-quarter round, and colors with paints and stains of various shades and mixtures. Occasionally, he sells a piece, and buys more materials to work with. His wife, Cathy, for example, is a mechanic at Curley's Speed Shop—a garage in College Park that both fixes private automobiles and sponsors dirt track racers; the owner saw some of Flowers' work and purchased both a crucifixion and a Garden of Gethsemane.

Although pictures of several of his pieces follow, he has also carved many things that we don't have pictures of. "I made a tomahawk for my next-door neighbor. I gave it to him. It's a great big old piece of a hedge bush I got there beside where I live. I cut it down and carved a snake around it with its mouth open, and I did some hand painting on the snake and split a big rock, and split the stick and drove my rock down in it and bound it with leather. It looks pretty good."

We, however, do have a photograph of work he's doing in his latest passion: marble. If anything, he enjoys working in it even more than in wood as he feels he can get more lifelike figures. Recently, for example, he carried the Garden of Gethsemane in a four-inch-thick slab of marble and placed it on his father's grave. He hammered it out at home, working on top of a chest freezer they have on the porch. His next project is so large he's going to have to do it away from home, however, at the Cowart Monument Shop just outside College Park. It's subject? A life-size crucifixion in full round carved out of one solid piece of Alabama marble. "Can't afford to make much mistakes with a piece of rock like that," he laughs.

If he could establish his work enough to make a living, he would, "Come

PLATE 78 William Flowers with his wife, Cathy, and his three sons, Dennie, Andy, and Billy, after one of their frequent camping trips to our mountains.

PLATE 79 This crucifixion is one of four Flowers has carved. It measures 26½″×32½″×1½″ deep. It is carved out of white poplar, and colored with acrylic paints and wood stains. He made up the design for this piece himself.

PLATE 80 This Garden of Gethsemane scene is carved out of hard maple and measures 26½″×32½″× 1½″ deep. It was copied from a painting by the German artist, Heinrich Hoffman. It is colored with acrylic paints and wood stains, and is the second one he has carved.

PLATE 81 An unfinished Garden of Gethsemane that Flowers is doing in solid marble.

up in the mountains somewhere and set up a carving shop and an antique shop, all combined with natural things." His love for the mountains is demonstrated partly by the frequent camping trips he makes to our county with his family.

It was on one of these trips that he met Buck Carver, one of our favorite contacts, who introduced him to us.

Article and photos by Wendy Guyaux, Sharon Pope, Juel Butler, and John Pope. Photos of the religious reliefs were contributed by Anna Wadsworth of the Georgia Council for the Arts and Humanities.

PLATE 82 Flowers has only carved one Last Supper out of wood, and he got the design for it from the World Book Encyclopedia. It is carved out of white poplar and measures $44\frac{1}{2}'' \times 29\frac{1}{2}'' \times \frac{3}{4}''$ deep. It is colored in the same manner as the others, with the addition of pokeberry juice for the deep reds.

PLATE 83 This frog was carved out of ash, and won a jury credit at the Atlanta Artist's Club. The award entitles the artist to leave his work at the Club for thirty days to be viewed by prospective buyers.

PLATE 84 A gazelle carved out of walnut.

PLATE 85 This relief scene was carved into a discarded chair seat.

PLATE 86 Flowers has carved many gunstocks for collectors and enthusiasts. This is one he is especially proud of.

DICK HARRISON, WOODWORKER

"I don't like to cut a dogwood unless it *will* make a good stick and *won't* make a good tree. You see, I shake that tree, and it'll shake this way and it'll come over this way, but it won't go back that way because of this big main root here. Well, a tree with one big root, it'll never support a good tree [but it will make a good cane]. If the tree shakes the same on all sides, that shows you it has a good bunch of brace roots, so I don't cut it—let it make a good tree."

Trees were important to Dick Harrison. He was a fountain of information on wood and things that could be made from wood. He knew how to make splits, shingles, ax handles, wooden bowls (or bread trays), walking sticks, wooden planes, and stools. Making things with wood had always been part of his life. He was born more than eighty-nine years ago, in a house built in 1852 by his grandfather. The house was covered with poplar shingles put on with nails handmade by a blacksmith. Mr. Harrison told us about a pit saw used by his grandfather for cutting planks. His father had a shingle mill on their home place and made shingles of oak, poplar, and pine. He made many of the tools and instruments used on their farm.

When we arrived one day to talk to Mr. Harrison, he had the outline of a wooden bread tray drawn on top of the stock. He talked to us as he worked. As he hewed out the inside of the bowl, he was so accurate he split the guideline in half with his small adze. These bowls were one of his favorite projects. He made them of birch, butternut, maple, black gum, chestnut, serviceberry, poplar, sassafras, cherry, dogwood, and apple—the last four were his favorite for looks. Applewood came out spotted and was beautiful. He called this "appaloosa."

When he finished a bowl, he painted on a couple of thick coats of a mixture of one-third spirits of turpentine, and two-thirds boiled linseed oil. He saturated the bowls with it. After that dried, he would sand and wax the bowl. As far as he knew, not one of his bowls had ever cracked.

Mr. Harrison was known for the unique walking sticks he made and gave to friends and special guests of the Rotary Club of Highlands, North Carolina. He had been a Rotarian there since 1954, and never missed a meeting. For these special sticks, he used small trees, vines, and limbs of trees that seemed to him would make straight, strong canes. When he was a boy, he noticed that a tender vine such as honeysuckle would grow from right to left around a tree. He assumed this was due to the rotation of the earth. He found that certain vines as they wrapped around limbs and small trunks helped shape interesting spirals in the wood that gave some of his walking sticks a special character.

All of Mr. Harrison's tools were neatly racked and well-sharpened. He had made boxlike sheaths for the blades of his adzes. He said that "A sharp tongue is the only edge that grows keener with constant use."

As he hewed out the bread tray with the carpenter's adze, he told us some things about scarifying knives, buttons, woodworking, and preachers quoting him.

"Back during the Civil War, my grandmother used to tell me about using persimmons for buttons. Buttons were scarce, and they'd take one of those awls and punch two holes in persimmon seeds and use them for buttons.

"They used the inner bark of dogwood for quinine. All those plantation owners had to have something for medicine.

"They had what they called a scarifying knife. It was a little bitty machine. There's a thing up there on the tool rack that reminds me of it. They had eight little blades in there in a section with the blades about a quarter of an inch apart, and you pulled this back and you'd cock it just like a gun.

You put it down on a fellow's shoulder where you'd want to scarify him, and trip that trigger, and those eight little blades would come down there so deep to get the blood and make him bleed. They used to think bleeding was the answer to all ills. My daddy had scars up on his shoulders; I've seen them many times.

"I've had a lot of people quote me. My preacher quoted me from the pulpit one time. I had carried him in the woods to get some sticks. I'd get one up [and] it looked like a bunch of roots to him; and I'd say, 'That's a nice one to have a good handle.' He talked about me seeing the potentiality of something. Woodwork is when you see something, and see what you can make out of it, and have enough imagination to see how it will look before [you make it].

"Take those stools there; every piece has to fit individually, and in each one I try to get different curves. In fact, I don't feel there's any straight line. Nature doesn't deal with straight lines. The only thing that I can recall that's straight is the prisms on crystal rocks like amethyst and things like that. That's the only thing I know of that's got a few straight lines—everything [else] is a curve. You can't find two leaves on the ground that are close enough to be exactly alike; they might be similar, but they won't be identical."

He also told us how to make a wood kiln and how to use it [see *Foxfire 3*, pages 366–68]. We learned the mistakes that could be made, the work involved, and the fun.

He left all his tools and work bench to us when he died about two years ago. He left bowls and canes not finished, and took a lot of knowledge with him. But he also left the friends he had made, and some of the things he had learned.

The instructions for making a tray like the ones he made follow. Don't be afraid to try—he wasn't. Make mistakes, and try again.

Article by Don MacNeil, Tom Carlton, Ray McBride, Scott McKay, Beverly Justus, and Bit Carver.

Select a good piece of wood at least four or five inches longer than you want the tray to be. Mr. Harrison uses poplar, maple, cherry, walnut, black gum, or pine—anything that will split easily. Starting with a froe and mallet and ending with a wedge and glut (wooden wedge), split the log into two pieces through the heart as shown in Plate 87. Don't use the glut unless you can see all the way through the split.

"Now the ol'timers, we always used the wooden maul to drive our wedges with. The wedges were iron, but they always used a wooden maul to drive 'em with because it protected the metal tools we had."

With a hand axe hew off the inside surface of one of the halves. (See *The*

Foxfire Book, "Tools and Skills," for a description of the maul and glut, and the proper way to hew a piece of wood.) The half must be hewn so the top and bottom will have parallel surfaces. In Plate 88, Mr. Harrison measures down 3¾" from the top of the tray and marks for the bottom. "See, now that three and three-fourths inches doesn't mean anything except in this particular block. Sometimes it'll be nine or ten inches [when] I'll be working on a big block."

With the froe, he splits the wood on the line marked. It will run out and the hewing will have to be finished with an axe. Mr. Harrison says you could also use a planer if you wished. You might want to tack cleats on the end of the block and clamp the wood down as shown in Plate 89 to make it easier to hew.

Mr. Harrison works the top of the block to a uniform width, then hews the two surfaces. Once that is done, you are ready to mark off the pattern for the tray, as shown in Plate 90. Mr. Harrison does this mostly by feel for how the tray will look. In this case, the actual tray had to be shortened because of the crack visible in the lower right part of Plate 91. You can check your progress with this photo as you mark out the tray. The distance between the ⚹7 lines is not important, but it *must* be uniform.

First, mark a lengthwise center line (⚹1) running the entire length of the block. In this case the block was 11½" wide, so Mr. Harrison came in from the edge 5¾" for the center line.

From one end of the block, measure in about 2" and mark a line (⚹2) perpendicular to the center line. The 2" are for the handle of the tray. You can leave more or less depending on how far you wish the handles to extend. The handles won't extend the full 2", naturally, as they will be worked down.

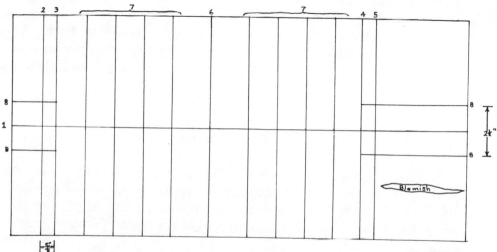

PLATE 90

PLATE 91

PLATE 92

Now measure in another ⅝″ and draw another line (⚹3) parallel to the one you just drew. This line will indicate the thickness of the tray.

From this line, measure down the block whatever length you wish the inside of the tray to be (in this case 16″), and draw a line (⚹4) perpendicular to the center line. Measure out another ⅝″ and mark again (⚹5).

Mark a center-width line (⚹6—the one with the circle on it in Plate 91). In this case, you would measure 8″ in from either of the *inner* lines. Transfer this line to the bottom by the method shown in Plate 92.

Go back to the center line you drew down the length of the block. You are about to mark out the width of the handle. The lines you see in Plate 93 are marked 1¼″ on each side of the center line for a total width of 2½″. Extend the center line down over the edge of the block on both ends so you can draw a center line on the bottom.

The other lines on the block are what Mr. Harrison uses to develop his own theory about making the trays. They help him keep up with what he is doing when he marks the curvature and begins to dig out the bowl. He laid these off by the width of his square.

On the circled line in Plate 91 you will notice a short mark near the edge of the block. The mark is ⅝″ in from the edge of the block. It is marked in with dividers (Plate 94) using the point at which lines ⚹1 and ⚹6 intersect as the center.

In Plate 95, Mr. Harrison uses the dividers to begin to mark the arc of the tray. He tries several radii until he gets one that "pans out," being careful not to mark the wood which will become the handle. Mark with the dividers until the curve begins to turn toward the center. Finish the curve

PLATE 93   PLATE 94   PLATE 95

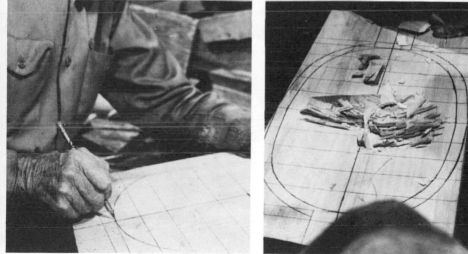

PLATE 96   PLATE 97

with a "French rule," as shown in Plate 91. "I call this my French rule 'cause I get so many curves out of it. There's some more up there I made. I just bent this piece of green pine and it holds." Mr. Harrison then goes over the final outline of the bowl with a lead pencil (Plate 96).

You are now ready to begin digging out the bowl of the tray. Mr. Harrison uses a small adze called a cooper's adze to do this. Start from the middle and work slowly outward (Plate 97). Be very careful not to go too deep.

If a chip sticks to the blade of your adze, stop and take it off. If you don't, the chip might make your adze bounce and ruin the tray or cut you. You must be guided by your feel in this step, so work slowly until the bowl is roughed out to the point shown in Plate 98. Mr. Harrison then scrapes the bowl with tools he has made for this purpose; then sands it.

To make the scrapers, use a piece of steel that will hold a temper well, and flare one end. Bend the flared end down at an angle slightly better than 90° and put an edge on it. After scraping and sanding, put the bowl aside to dry for two to three weeks.

Now mark the bottom of the tray in the same way you marked the curvature of the top. Mr. Harrison says a 10″ (length) bottom was about right for a 16″ tray. Mark 5″ from each side of the short center line, and as much as you want on each side of the long center line. After doing this, turn the tray over and mark it as shown in Plate 99. The areas marked with an "X" are to be cut out with a saw. These new outer lines are drawn so they will

PLATE 98

PLATE 99

run parallel to the arc of the tray as far as possible from the intersection of the bowl arc and one of the ⌗8 lines. If these lines do not intersect one of the ⌗7 lines and the edge of the tray at the same point, draw another line parallel to the ⌗7 lines from the point where the slanting outer line intersects the edge, and carry this to the other side of the bowl so that the two new lines have the same angle. The inner lines are drawn tangent to the bowl arc at its intersection with the first ⌗7 line. Continue the outer lines down the edge, to give you a better idea of the shape, and cut the sections out with a handsaw. Saw in toward the handle along the angle you've just marked on the sides of the tray, stopping a little before you reach the handle lines (⌗8). Then split off these pieces of wood. Cut along the inner lines perpendicular to the top of the tray.

You can now begin to shape the outside of the tray with a chisel. Work the blocks left at the handles down with the chisels until they are about 1⅛″ thick. Once the tray is roughly shaped, coat it with linseed oil and set it aside to dry. This may take from two to six weeks, depending on the weather and the wood, so test it from time to time by feeling to see if the wood is thoroughly dry.

Plate 100 shows Mr. Harrison marking off the handles. The innermost line connects the intersections of the arc of the outside of the bowl and the two lines already drawn for the width of the handle. Drop back from that line 1¼″ for the outer line of the handle. Measure in from the width lines ³⁄₁₆″ and make a mark. Then draw lines as shown in Plate 100. Saw the handle off at the outer line, leaving the handle 1¼″ long.

PLATE 100   PLATE 101

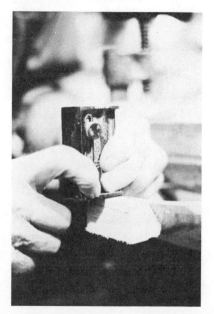

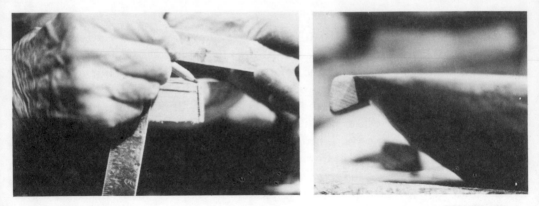

PLATE 102   PLATE 103

Measure down from the top of handle about ¼" and make a mark as shown in Plate 101. The scratch gauge you see shown here makes this an easy job. Using a rasp, curve the wood from the top of the handle to this point. Continue the width lines of the handle down the end of the block (Plate 102). Using a chisel, form the sides of the handle into these lines. You may want to slope the underside of the handle up as shown in Plate 103. Use a rasp to finish the curves, then sand the handle.

The finish for the tray is your choice. Mr. Harrison used a mixture of linseed oil and turpentine (two parts to one). If you intend to make bread in it, Mr. Harrison recommends that you rub lard or vegetable oil into the wood to avoid giving the bread a bad taste.

ALEX MARTIN, WOODEN BOWL MAKER

We went to see Alex Martin after a friend informed us that he made wooden dough trays, spoons, and rolling pins. We found his house at the end of a rutted dirt road far back in the hills. Alex was on the back porch of his little house working on one of the trays when we arrived.

He lives alone, surrounded by a good supply of wood for his work. In his hard-packed clay yard, we could see large halved logs and wood chips cluttered around. The porch was filled with the tools he uses. A well stood in the yard across from the porch, and in back of the house we could see his corn patch and his beehives. There was even a combination sawmill/gristmill run by an abandoned six-cylinder Chevrolet motor.

Alex is an interesting person. He has done many different things during his life. He has operated gristmills (one he overhauled during World War II was so efficient that it could grind a bushel of meal in two and a half minutes flat); he has filed saws, and made knives out of broken saw blades;

once he even had a syrup mill that he hauled around to make sorghum for neighbors in the fall (he got a third of the syrup as payment). He has made ox yokes, and he has made split-rail fences and strung them out across mountainsides.

And he is full of knowledge of life in the mountains. He knows, for example, that the best time to castrate a hog is when the signs are in the knees and going down; and that to keep rabbits out of a garden, you can set some glass jars out with the lids off. The wind blowing over the tops of the jars makes a sound that scares them off. And he warns you that the best way to plant is not by putting fertilizer into the rows with the seed, but by putting the seed in and covering it and then putting the fertilizer on top. That way birds won't try to go through the fertilizer to get at the seeds.

He's also full of stories. As he worked, he told us many. One of his favorites was the story of a white man who owned a dog with a short tail, and an Indian who had a long-tailed dog. The short-tailed dog was always outrunning the other, and one day the Indian asked why his dog was always being outrun. The white man told him that his dog's long tail slowed it down, and he offered to cut it off. The Indian agreed, so he put the dog's tail on a stump and cut it off—but too short. The Indian, in alarm, cried, "*Too* fast, *too* fast, by damn!"

The main reason that we went to see him, however, was that we were interested in finding out how to make the bread trays he is famous for (he sells all he can make through the Georgia Mountain Arts Craft Cooperative in Tallulah Falls, Georgia). The wood he usually uses is yellow poplar, but he also likes walnut. He carves the bowls while the wood is still green, and if the wood starts to crack as it dries out (which rarely happens) he advises painting a coat of linseed oil on the bowl.

The directions for making one follow. Before we left, we all tried our hand at it, and profited in that that is one more thing we now know how to do.

ROY DICKERSON

PLATE 104 Alex does much of his work on his back porch and in his backyard.

PLATE 105 When making bowls, Alex first halves a block of wood, traces an oval pattern on the flat surface, and, with a chain saw, makes a few cuts down into the block to make the hewing go a little faster. Of course, before chain saws, he had to leave out this short cut.

PLATE 106 Next he prepares to hack out the center of the bowl with his cooper's adze.

PLATE 107 Despite his more casual technique (when compared to the methodical approach of Dick Harrison), Alex is actually very careful to stay within the penciled oval he has marked on the top surface.

PLATE 108 He also shapes the bowl by using a hammer and chisel as he begins to get closer and closer to the critical points. Here, Roy Dickerson, the author of this chapter, tries his hand at it.

PLATE 109 Finally, using the hammer and chisel, Alex hews out the outside surfaces, and then does the final shaping and smoothing with a wood rasp and sandpaper.

When we started the research on banjo makers that was published in *Foxfire 3*, one thing naturally led to another, and we soon found that we had a list of fiddle makers as well. We interviewed three of them, and the results of those interviews make up this chapter.

One of the men, Harley Thomas, turned up in our own backyard. Though we had known him and worked with him for years (spinning wheels, caskets, furniture, mill wheels), we never suspected he made instruments as well. I guess we never asked him. Or he never thought to tell us. That happens a lot here.

Harvey J. Miller of Greenmountain, North Carolina, found the other two men for us. One lives near Harvey in the Pigeon Roost Community; the other lives outside Bakersville.

To introduce this chapter, we all thought that an appropriate beginning might be the following fine piece of material from a Lawton Brooks interview that we never found an appropriate spot for until now.

They was lots of people I used t'play with. Oh, I have played with Bill Lamb. Sure have. Me an' Bill played right out here at th'York House. An' that old man out at Mountain City—his wife an' me always used t'dance—Hilliard Taylor. They had a little place built, a little dance hall. It's still there. They had'em on Saturday nights. Sometimes they'd have'em through the week when big crowds was up. I got t'going out there to'em—we had some awful good times. We just danced, had some of the best dancin' you ever seen. Now back at home, we had to have our dances in the houses. Back then they'd give us a dance, some of th'people would. Some of'em didn't believe in it, didn't want t'have no dances, some of'em. It tickled most old folks t'give a dance. Well, they'd give us their biggest room in the house—they'd clean it all out. Us boys would all go out, y'know, and get up wood an' stuff ahead of time for the folks t'have good firewood. We did that, so the old folks could set an' enjoy themselves, so they'd give us an-other dance. When they gave us one, we'd git up enough wood t'do'em a month'r'two. Haul it in, put it right where they could get it. They'd just clear ever'thing out of the way, an' set those old kerosene lights in the corner, y'know, so we could see—seemed like then I could see as good by them as I can by electric lights now. An' so we'd have the awfullest dance you ever seen. An' we'd dance sometimes away long after midnight. Us boys, we'd get busy for them dances, whether we wanted to work or not. We'd all go work like the devil t'get t'go play. We'd move everything out of the room—used whichever room was the biggest. Most times it was th'dinin' room. The music makers, they'd git right up in one corner. An' they'd come right around by us, y'see. We had t'bow right up in the corner. It always fell my luck t'help make the music, an' I didn't git t'dance too much them days. An' then me an' old Arthur Young—we used t'make *lots* of music. We'd go t'hotels down there at Hayesville [North Carolina], big hotels, the Herbert—they had some big'uns! But just around in the commu-nity, oh, we'd have two'r'three a week all th'time. We never missed a week of not having a dance, Saturday especially. An' sometimes two'r'three dur-ing th'week. We didn't git no pay for that now, without it was—well, what you'd call a big shot now, he might pitch in fifty cents. They'd set a hat down if anybody wanted t'donate anything. Lots of'em maybe would put in a nickel, some of'em a dime, some of'em didn't put in nothin'. Some days we'd get up a pretty good hatful. Pretty good payday. I have made as high as fifteen dollars in a night. Back in them days, that was lots of money. That'd took me fifteen hard days t'work that out, when I made it there just in a little while.

Me an' Florence lived on that for a long, long time after we was married. If it hadn't been for that, I don't know what we'd 'a'done. You couldn't git work then. Back in what they called "Hoover Days." Always said, "He come in as President, a dollar a day an' a pair of overalls is enough for a workin' man."

An' that's all they got. An' they's s'many people wanted work, you couldn't find nobody had any money. People who had money just set down on it'r'somethin'. They didn't circulate it. So all the way we had any money in our pockets a'tall was t'go t'them dances an' we'd git a few nickels'r'dol-lars'r'something. Outside of that, you'd go work for a man—he'd pay you in corn'r'meat'r'something you could eat. They could pay me in that, but they didn't have no money t'turn loose.

We had some of the awfullest times you ever seen. And when we broke up the dance then, we stayed, by gosh, till ever'thing was put back in the room an' all cleaned up. 'Cause see, it was in a community—we knowed'em all an' they all knowed us. The women an' men stayed right around there till we got ever'thing fixed back in the room like they had it. An' then we'd all go home. It wadn't no time then till they asked if we wanted another one.

Oh, the old folks did dance! They danced just the same as th'young-uns. They shore did. They had just as much fun as we had out of it.

You didn't see no little'uns. That's th'reason we had s'much better dances. They'd just sit back. They didn't git in there t'bother nothin'. They'd go t'th'house; might be a gang of'em, but they wadn't in there in th'way. It was a all grown folks' dance. It was nice. I'm a'tellin' you, it was s'nice, I'd just like for it t'be back an' get t'go to another one'r two like that.

Sometimes they had food cooked t'eat if anybody wanted t'eat anything. Always kept somethin' in there for'em t'eat on, but they didn't take time t'eat much; ever'body was too much interested in that dancin'.

We had such a good sober time. You didn't see no drunks, nothin' that went on out of th'way. Never did see no trouble in a dance in my life till after I moved here an' got t'going t'these dance halls. Then I seen a fight'r'two. But back where I was, it was as rough a country as you ever seen, but ever'thing was sober. They come sober an' they left sober. Because they knowed if they went wrong, that'd be th'last one that they'd git t'go to, 'cause they knowed them folks wouldn't have nary another one around'em. They'd say, "Well, if you can't beat that, never be another one at my house."

They knowed what was comin' up. We all knowed what was comin' up, so we all stayed straight.

Oh, I do remember the names of some of the songs! We had that old "Cripple Creek," an' "Free a Little Bird," an' "Down th'Road," an' "Shout Lou"—that's one they always wanted us t'play. Oh, we had lots of'em, sister. I just don't remember how many they was, but we had lots of'em. Used t'be a man could just pick up a fiddle; I could pick anything he played. I still b'lieve I could. But I just can't do nothing myself, I just can't git it in m'mind just right, like it oughta be.

The women, they was awful good t'stay an' clean up. Oh, they'd sweep, sometimes even mop th'house before we left. But anyway, we had a whole lot nicer times than they have at dances now. I know that. *Lots* better. You could take your girl to a dance then, dance all night, then take her home.

When we got married, I had t'make th'music and Florence'd do the dancin'. She couldn't dance with me. Wadn't no point in her just sittin' there, so she danced. I got hooked to th'music all th'time. We just played square dance music. I used t'know all the steps. They were all the same as they have now.

They had the "grapevine twist." Boy, that'd kill you! And the Georgia "rang tang." We had the same thing they have now. Shore did. Sometimes somebody'd jump out there an' buck dance a little, anybody who could buck dance.

Now they have so many more of these cloggers an' things, they've changed the dancin' around. That cloggin' business is different from a square dance. They kindly of buck dance around, and call it cloggin'. We used to just kindly skip our feet. The way we done, we played the figgers [figures], we didn't care about the dancin'. Just do every figger when it was called, do it like it was supposed t'be done. Then y'never messed up with your partner.

They always had t'have a extra man t'call [not the fiddler or banjo picker] all th'time. Earl Anderson was the best man I ever heard t'call. He run a hardware there in Hayesville. We played the same figgers they do now, but we done it s'much better than they do now, you ought t'just see th'difference. I'd just like t'have me about sixteen on the floor like we used to back then when we used t'dance, an' let you see. We could just play one whole outfit by ourselves, an' just show you the difference.

We didn't have no special name for our music, but the people didn't want nothin' but a fiddle an' a banjo. They didn't have no guitars nor nothin' like that. They said they could dance as good again with just that. And I'll still argue that with'em. It's a whole lot better—take a man who can play a banjo an' a fiddle right there, an' you get out there, an' you can do as good again dancin' as you can with these ol' guitars an' these ol' pianers an' things. All that damn noise agoin'—half th'time you can't hear your figgers—the man a'callin' the music. You take a fiddle an' a banjo, an' you kin hear ever'thing that man says. Me an' Florence quit when they started up with all them bands an' things.

THE HARLEY THOMAS VARIETY

Harley Thomas has been one of our favorite contacts for a long time. During the early years of *Foxfire,* Harley vitally contributed to our issue on log cabin building, as he was one of only two people who could show us how to notch the logs. His demonstration included the detailed intricacies of the difficult dovetail notch (see *The Foxfire Book,* pages 66–73). Harley also showed us how to make a spinning wheel, and his expertise in its construction was something to see (see *Foxfire 2,* pages 194–95). Harley agreed to show us how to make a fiddle, but before we relate these instructions, we would like to tell you a little bit about Harley Thomas.

Harley was born on December 2, 1892, in the Skeener community of Macon County, North Carolina. Except for a period of eight years during which he lived in Alto, Georgia, Harley has always made his home in Macon County. He married Fannie Bradley on September 2, 1912.

Harley has made fiddles since the early twenties and he learned how to make them by observing "old Man Gurley," who lived in Baldwin, Georgia. Harley has made a total of twelve fiddles during his lifetime and each one was perfectly crafted. He surprised us all, however, by saying that he could complete a fiddle from scratch in one week. He has his own sawmill and carefully selects and cuts his wood for his fiddles. He also uses his sawmill to cut other wood since he is a skilled woodworker. Harley makes gun cabinets, shelves, and other furniture as well as spinning wheels and fiddles. He also used to make caskets when there was a demand.

Several older fiddles that Harley has collected over the years hang in his shop. One he treasures in particular was given to him by Fate Long of the Betty's Creek community. He clearly remembers how he obtained this fiddle, and we thought it only proper to give you Harley's account of this story:

"I bought Fate Long's timber up there on his place and moved a sawmill in there and I boarded with him. He had that fiddle back there and he found out I could play a fiddle. He had me playing the fiddle about every night till bedtime! I didn't have a fiddle at that time and they wanted me to play down here at a party, and I borrowed his fiddle. I told him I wanted to borrow it and play it. He said, 'You take that fiddle and you keep it till I call for it.' He died out and never did call for it and I still got it. His folks just told me to keep it because he told me to."

ROBBIE MOORE AND RANDALL HARDY

PLATE 110   Harley Thomas with one of his fiddles.

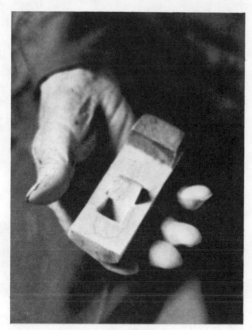

PLATE 111 Harley used a homemade plane to shape the top and back of the fiddle.

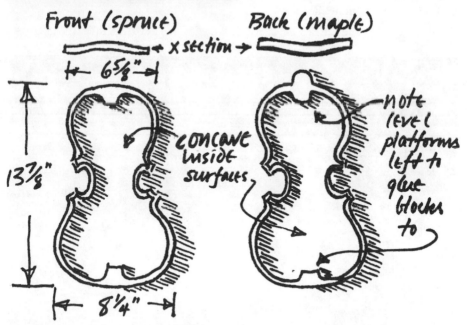

Front (spruce)   Back (maple)

← x section →

6⅝"

13⅞"

8¼"

concave inside surfaces

note level platforms left to glue blocks to

PLATE 112 The patterns used for the fiddle's top and back. These are each made of two pieces of wood ⅝"×15"×4¼" that are glued side by side lengthwise with Elmer's Glue. (The fiddle is held together only by glue.) The top is made of spruce to produce the best sound. All other parts are made of maple (curly maple is best) except the finger board, which is ebony. The diagrams indicate how the top and back should be shaped, and the areas to be "dug out."

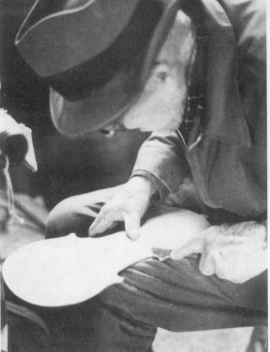

PLATE 113 With the plane, Harley shapes out the top and the back of the fiddle until they are about ⅛″ thick.

PLATE 114 Harley smoothes the sides with a rattail file.

PLATE 115 The "ribs" or sides of the fiddle are thin strips of maple 1¼″ wide, and are soaked in hot water until pliable and then placed in wooden forms to harden in the correct shape. Blocks of maple—1¼″-high—are placed at each end of the top to hold the ribs secure (see Plate 120).

PLATE 116 Double linings, indicated by the arrows, provide strength for the sides. Pins hold these in place until the glue is dry (see white arrow on Plate 120).

PLATE 117 The neck of the fiddle has been cut out of a block of maple $9'' \times 2\frac{1}{4}'' \times 2\frac{1}{4}''$. It is shaped with a pocketknife and sandpaper. The end may have any design you want. Pegs are tapered so they will tighten in their holes.

PLATE 118 The neck is "dovetailed" into a $1\frac{1}{4}''$-high block of maple (see Plate 119).

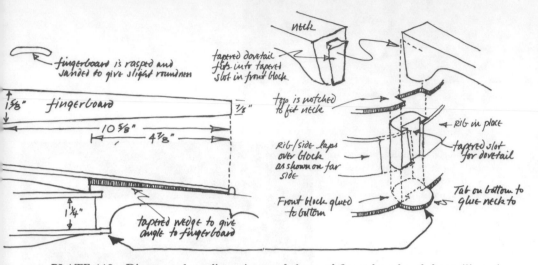

PLATE 119   Diagrams show dimensions and shape of finger board and dovetailing of neck.

PLATE 120 Overall view of completed top. Note bass bar (dark arrow) which is 7″ to 8″ long and ¼″ square tapered at the ends. Also note pin holding the lining, as mentioned in Plate 116.

PLATE 121   The finger board is made of ebony and stained with black ink. Arrow denotes tapered wedge that gives slight angle to the finger board (see Plate 119 for diagram of finger board).

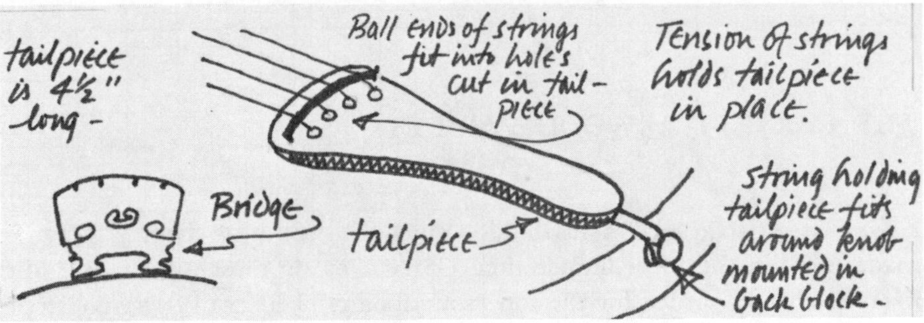

tailpiece is 4½" long –

Ball ends of strings fit into holes cut in tail-piece

Tension of strings holds tailpiece in place.

Bridge

tailpiece

string holding tailpiece fits around knob mounted in back block.

PLATE 122   Diagram of tailpiece and bridge.

PLATE 123   After a sound post (a small dowel ¼" in diameter connected to the top and back on the inside of the fiddle—see Plate 143 in Clarence Rathbone's variety) is inserted and a tailpiece and bridge (see arrows) are added, Harley demonstrates the final product.

THE GARRETT ARWOOD VARIETY

Garrett Arwood makes his fiddles much the same as Harley Thomas made those in the preceding section. Garrett, as do most mountain fiddle makers, chooses spruce for the top (soundboard) because of its good tone quality. The rest of his instrument is shaped from curly maple which is selected for its beauty. As soon as the tree is chosen, cut, planed to a ¾″ thickness, and cured, he begins shaping the top and back using tools and gauges he manufactures in his shop. Both the top and back are cut from solid ¾″ planks, unless wood is scarce and large enough pieces can't be found, in which case Garrett will join two pieces together side by side with Elmer's Glue (Plates 125–31). The effect in sound is no different, and he has made fiddles both ways. The strips that Garrett uses for the sides are cut from curly maple approximately ⅟₁₆″ thick, and must be cured for at least a year. He must be careful not to cut them against the grain for they would most likely split. When properly cured, they are shortened to the correct length and boiled in water until saturated and thoroughly pliable. Then he presses the wet strips into shape using his homemade forms as illustrated in Plates 133–34. The maple must be left to dry for at least twenty-four hours while in these molds.

Using such tools as a saber saw, rasp, chisel, and knife, Garrett carves the neck and scroll, and rasps the edges smooth (Plates 135–36). Because of the precision required, he drills the holes for the tuning pegs.

The remainder of the job is, for the most part, assembly. With all the pieces laid out, Garrett begins gluing the neck and back together, and then concentrates on attaching the dried sides. This must all be clamped and set to dry overnight. The lining strips and reinforcing blocks are added next, and everything is sanded to accommodate the top. When snugly fitted, the top is glued and clamped, as is the finger board (Plates 137–38). The setting of the sound post comes next and must be handled delicately (Plate 139). The bridge, tailpiece, and pegs are the only remaining items to be attached before the final step of either varnishing or staining (Plate 140). Garrett's fiddles have a tone and feeling all their own. He takes a lot of pride and enjoyment in the instruments he makes, and many a friend and neighbor has enjoyed the spirit of Garrett Arwood's fiddles.

DOUG CORNELL

Photographs by Ken Cronic.

PLATE 124   Garrett Arwood, playing his fiddle.

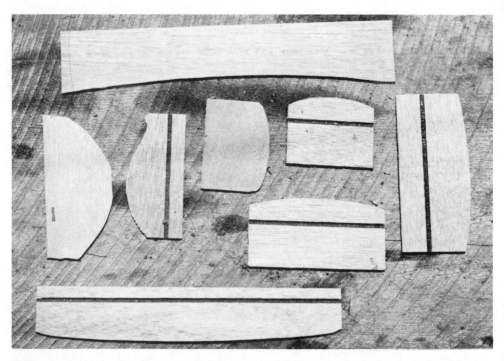

PLATE 125   The patterns Garrett uses to check the slopes and shapes of the fiddle pieces.

PLATE 126   His set of homemade chisels, many made of old files.

PLATE 127   The homemade clamps Garrett uses.

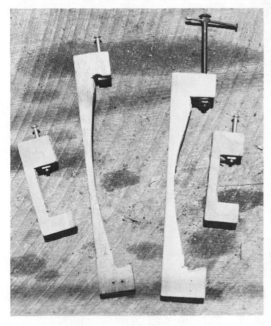

PLATE 128 Garrett's home-made vises.

PLATE 129 Garrett shapes the inside concave surfaces and the outside convex surfaces of the top and back with his chisels.

PLATES 130–131   He checks the slopes and depths with his patterns.

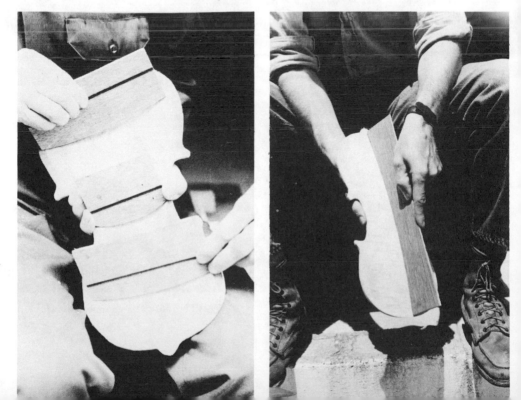

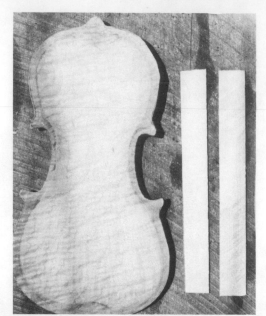

PLATE 132 The back and two strips used for the long curves on one side of the fiddle.

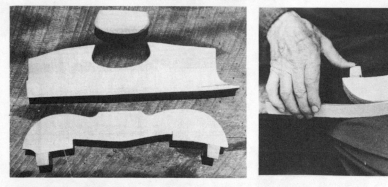

PLATES 133–134 The sides are clamped into forms as shown.

PLATE 135 Carving the scroll of the neck.

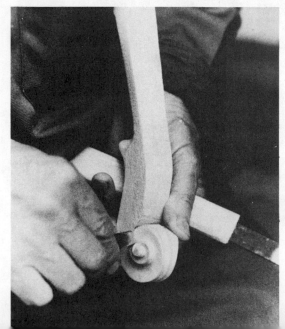

PLATE 136 The completed neck.

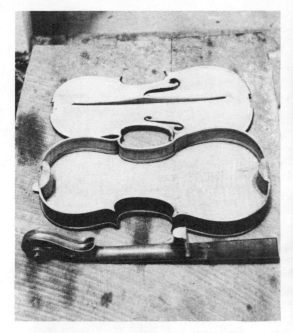

PLATE 137 The top is ready to be glued to the back and sides. Note the blocks at either end of the back to which the sides are glued, the double lining, and the triangular support blocks where the sides come together in the middle.

PLATE 138 The neck is now glued onto the body of the fiddle.

PLATE 139 Garrett adds the sound post with the help of a curved, sharpened wire. He slips it into the middle of the instrument and wedges the post into place, then pulls the wire out.

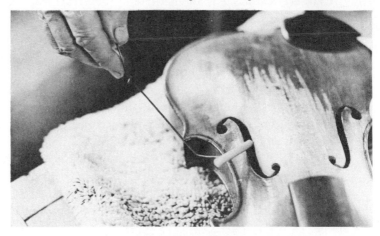

PLATE 140 Then he adds the tail-piece, strings, and bridge.

PLATE 141 Garrett Arwood shows us the finished fiddle.

THE CLARENCE RATHBONE VARIETY

Clarence Rathbone is another one of the great people that Harvey Miller introduced us to. He and his family live at the end of a narrow gravel road near the top of a mountain miles from the closest town, Bakersville. He made his first fiddle in 1961, and gave it to his son as a present. It's not for sale. He may make some in the future for sale, but he hasn't decided yet.

For this particular fiddle, the top is made from a ¾"-thick solid piece of white spruce (the longer seasoned, the better). The back is a ¾" "fiddle-back" or curly maple, chiseled out and seasoned. The top and back are both inlaid with white hickory strips. The groove for the strips was cut out with a pocketknife. The strips were placed into boiling water to soften, then placed into the groove. The sides, he called "ribs," are of cured curly maple ¹⁄₁₆" thick. He put them into boiling water, then placed them into the forms until they dried. Once dried, they could be removed and would not lose shape.

The neck/head is one solid piece of curly maple and was carved out with a pocketknife. The bridge is made of curly maple. The pegs, finger board, and tailpiece are all made of boxwood, then painted with a coat of black enamel. Both pegs and tailpiece are inlaid with mother-of-pearl.

To assemble, he glued a 6″-long bass bar on the underside of the top so that it runs directly under the bass string. Next, he glued the ribs together and held them with "C" clamps. After that, he put in triangular posts for added bracing in the corners. Then he glued the lining in and added the top, back, and neck at the same time and clamped it together.

After he had it set up, Clarence added the sound post under the first string and directly under the bridge (see Plate 143). He then stained it with fiddle stain, rubbed it in with a rag, and put on two coats of clear lacquer. Then he added the tailpiece and strings.

JEFF LANE

Photographs by Ken Cronic.

PLATE 142   Clarence Rathbone with the fiddle he made.

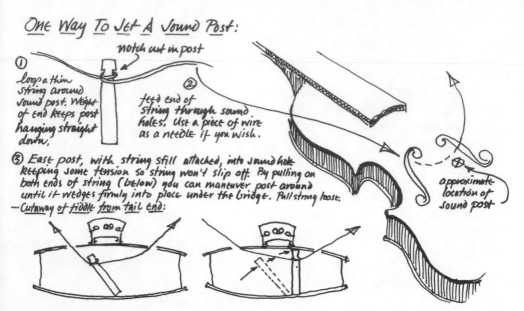

One Way To Set A Sound Post:

notch cut in post

① loop a thin string around sound post. Weight of end keeps post hanging straight down.

② feed end of string through sound holes. Use a piece of wire as a needle if you wish.

③ Ease post, with string still attached, into sound hole keeping some tension so string won't slip off. By pulling on both ends of string (below) you can maneuver post around until it wedges firmly into place under the bridge. Pull string loose.

—Cutaway of fiddle from tail end:

approximate location of sound post

PLATE 143

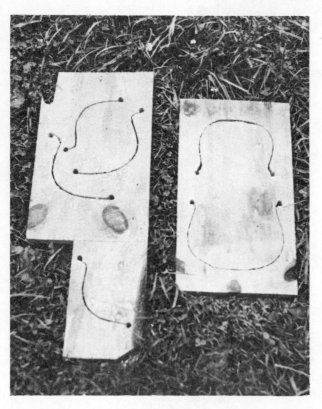

PLATE 144 The forms that Clarence uses to shape the sides or "ribs."

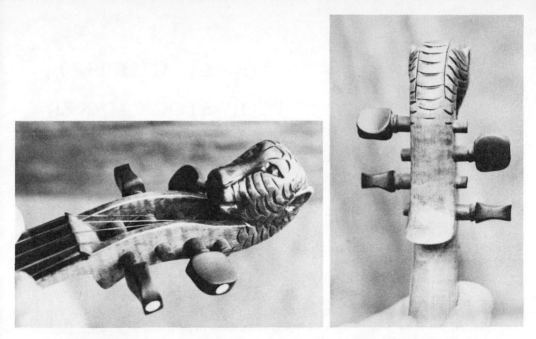

PLATES 145–146 Views of the head of his fiddle. The idea for the lion's head came from a fiddle his father owned. Clarence remembers seeing the lion's head as a boy, and with his Case knife, carved the head on his own fiddle.

PLATE 147 The back of Clarence's fiddle.

PLATE 148 The top of his fiddle is inlaid with a white hickory strip (arrow).

THOMAS CAMPBELL,

PLOW-STOCK MAKER

We met Tom Campbell through Harvey Miller's generosity, and we're genuinely grateful to Harvey for introducing us. Tom was born in 1879. Although he doesn't plow with a horse anymore, he still farms using a push plow. He raised forty bushels of potatoes this year.

Members of his large family live nearby and are in constant touch, but he still prefers to live alone, do his own housework, and let his shop keep him busy. Out of that tiny shop comes a flood of hand-shaped handles for every tool imaginable, apple-butter stirrers in two sizes, hoes (he rivets a piece of a crosscut saw blade to the old shank and adds a new handle: "They don't never wear out."), and plow stocks. He's slowed down a little—he used to make banjos too (he made them from a solid poplar or white spruce rim, a groundhog or house-cat hide tacked on for a head, and strings made of cat gut).

His brother had a blacksmith shop out of which came knives, rifles, grain cradles, fiddles—and just about anything else.

Tom still doesn't use glasses. "I read the Bible without them. And I read newspapers, letters, see there [pointing to two twelve-inch high stacks of mail]. I don't get many! Any that ain't just *literature*. That's real letters. From *people*. Relation people."

Tom Campbell's energy humbles us.

Article and photographs by Tom Carlton and Gena McHugh.

"My daddy was seven year old in the Civil War. That's what he always told us. He lived a hundred years, eleven months, and ten days. They's just two of us brothers living. The rest are dead. I was the first born.

"We had a log house. My daddy built it. He was a pretty good carpenter. He'd build weatherboard houses and work every speck of the timber [by hand]. Just rough lumber, you know. That was before there were saw-

PLATE 149 Thomas Campbell

mills. They'd rive boards out of water oak for doors, shutters, and to cover the house with. My granddaddy did it the same way. They'd block [the tree trunk] out as wide as you wanted the boards [see *The Foxfire Book*, page 46]. The old style was three feet long; they'd lap them over six inches. All that lumber was to hand dress. Then it was to joint—had to gauge it and joint it—and then all these facings and trimmings to cut; two edges and a face, you know, to nail up. Had our tools to tongue and groove with, all that.

"[When they built a log house] they only used a broadaxe and a chopping axe. That's all they had. And a froe to rive boards with. There was no locks on the doors. No windows—just holes. They'd cut out [windows] beside the chimney to give light to the fireplace room. Cooked on the fireplace.

"Families made it hard. It was hard living back then. They was no money, no jobs, no work, you see. Only just clearing and building fence and making corn and taters and stuff like that back in these mountains.

"Mother wove blankets. Old Bill Grindstaff used to make looms back over here where I was born—Greasy Creek. [We had one he made.] And my grandmother wove cloth to make pants out of and stuff like that. And Daddy made shoes; got leather and made us shoes. Only got one pair a winter. He made'em in the fall, you see, and we had to wear them all winter. If we wore'em out, we went barefooted. I've seen a lot of kids barefooted and it as cold as whiz. Go to school thataway. Big heavy frosts and they hadn't got no shoes. One man lived right at us and his children—half of them—never had a shoe to their foot all winter. They'd go outdoors, though, and paddle around in the snow. And didn't have no outhouses then. They wasn't even thought of. People just went to the woods.

"I remember when they wadn't a speck of lamp oil. They had no lamp oil when I was a boy. Not a match. Had to kindle a fire with a flint. Take one of these flints, and they was a maple that has what you call the 'punk' in it. You take that flint and your knife and lay this punk down and you [strike the back of the closed knife blade against the flint] till it'll spark, you know. And that punk'll catch the spark and then you blow it and keep ablowin' it till it flames, and then you add shavings and build you a fire. It'd just spread right out and burn like whiz, you know. Blow it a little and get a blaze and pick it up and put it in a fireplace and put you some shavings on it and first thing you know you had a fire. I see'd my daddy a many a time get down on his knees and kindle a fire when I was a little boy.

"[For light] he'd go over here in Limestone Cove and take him a sack and his axe, and he'd hew out these rich pine knots and split'em up into splinters. Then he'd light one and stick it in the chimney someplace for light.

"And then another way—Mother would put hog's lard in a pint cup and twist her a piece of cloth into a wick and push it down in there and light that wick, and that fire would draw that lard oil right up in that wick. She'd set that on the table and we'd eat breakfast before daylight.

"Mother's first stove was a number six-step stove. Then they come a number seven—a bigger one, you know. It's an iron stove up on four legs—a little flat feller. They's two caps [eyes] down here, and then it raises up a little and they's two caps up here. They're a good cook stove. They come in about seventy-five years ago.

"Big Charles Hughes up here, he got him one when they first come in, you know. And he built a fire in it—had good dry wood—and it got red hot on top! And his wife was named Till. He said, 'Till, that stove is going to blow up! Get a bucket of water to throw on it to cool it down.' And he threw that water on there and busted that stove all to pieces. I know right where the house was. Been in it a many of a time. Big old log house. That was before I was married. It ruined his stove. Had to buy him another one.

"I went to school. Had to walk three mile back up on the mountain. Had that blue back spelling book. But I never learnt to figger none. I didn't know a thing about arithmetic. But I've learnt someway. You can't figger [cheat] me out of nothing. I can figger with any of'em. I've got it up here [tapping head]. Went to school two years off and on, but the school only went three months [a year] during the winter time. Had to set way back in the cold. Had a big old log house with a big chimney in one end of it. When you'd get cold, you'd get up and go to the fire and get warm and go back and study your lessons. It was so cold you just didn't learn much, that's all. Couldn't. And we didn't have no teachers back then to amount to anything.

"And my daddy didn't get no learning neither, but he learnt to read his Bible, and he preached for about forty years.

"[It was hard to make a living.] I've plowed oxens a many a day when I was a boy. Hoed corn for twenty-five cents a day. That's the biggest thing there was [for work] in my younger days. And clearing and building fence —seven and eight rail fences. See, stock run out at that time in the woods. You had to fence your fields up where you made your corn and taters and stuff like that. Had to fence that all up. After they done away with that, then, you had to turn around and fence your stock in [because of the new range laws].

"I had thirty to forty head of hogs in the woods after I married. My mark was a swallow fork in each ear and an underbit in the right. My neighbor had his marked the same way except the underbit in the left [see *Foxfire 3*, page 85]. Had them registered at Bakersville.

"After I married, I built some rock culverts over streams for the railroad. Then I sawmilled for twenty-five years. They wasn't no mills in this country till I was a great big boy. First sawmill that ever come here was right down here in this bottom here. Steam powered. They was lots of women come to where we'd move into a new section, you know. Why, they'd come and stand there and watch that engine run an hour at a time. Three or four or six of'em. They'd never seen one, you know. They'd get a kick out of that! I worked my way up in the mill. I set block first, then I fired [the boiler], then I sawed. When the steam would get down—we've had to shut down many a time to build up steam in the boilers.

"We went from Laurel Forks to Hampton, Tennessee, to Cane River to Limestone Cove in the Unaka Mountains for seven years to Ripshin County for two years. I cut thirty-two thousand feet in there one day. We never fell under twenty-five thousand feet a day. That was a regular day's work. A man stood there with a rule—a log stick—and measured every one that went on the carriage. That's all he done.

"The sawing then was big hemlock. Fifteen to sixteen thousand feet in a log. Had a double rig [so they could take the whole trunk without quartering it]. Had a gang edger, equalizer, cutoff saw, and all that stuff. When some of those big ones went through the edger, there'd be four two-by-fours there to pick up and get out of the way. Had to trim'em, too. Turn'em around and throw'em on that trimmer.

"I run a big saw. Put twenty-five years in on that. Never done nothing else, hardly. I'd work a few days on the farm of a fall—come in and pick off apples and put'em away. We generally put up three or four hundred bushels of apples every fall. And kept a lot of cattle. My wife and kids tended to them.

"When we were sawing, we had sawmill camps—boarding houses we called'em. About a month at a time is the longest I stayed off from home. I generally went home every weekend. I'd cross those Unakas—I've crossed that walking a many a night way in the dark. Then after I got across, I still had three mile down the creek to get home.

"They logged with yokes of cattle. Move the mill up into the mountains and log to it. Then they got trucks. They'd skid'em, load'em on trucks, and bring'em to the mill and dump'em off.

"But back then they had no trucks, you know. Didn't know nothing about'em. No gasoline. We just roughed it."

Thomas Campbell learned how to make plows from his father, who had a pattern that Simon Harrell, an old Civil War veteran, had given him. Simon was Tom's father's uncle, and after he returned from the war he made his living making plows. Those he made, however, were for oxen, and so they had a shorter foot (see Plate 152 for names of parts) than those Tom makes. Tom lengthened the foot because when plows made for oxen were hitched to horses the height of the horse would cause the beam to be tilted up too high to make it effective.

It takes him two days to make one plow stock. He uses nothing but hand tools, including a shaving horse. For holes that have to be square, he bores the holes first with a brace and bit, and then chisels out the remainder and dresses up the sides with a hammer and chisel. The pegs and crosspieces are all made of hickory that he air-seasoned for a year or more, but the pieces they are driven into are always green. As with chair rounds, this is the most effective means of keeping them from coming loose, because as the green wood seasons, it shrinks; wherever there is a peg, it shrinks around the peg, thus gripping it more tightly than would probably be possible otherwise.

The woods he uses are oak for the beam, yellow locust for the foot and

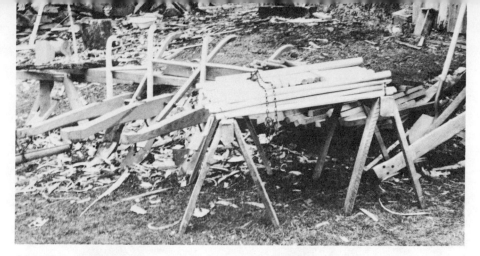

PLATE 150   Tom's work area, with axe handles and hammer handles in the foreground.

handle, and hickory for the crosspieces and any pegs (recently he has been trying metal bolts in place of pegs to see how they will work). He makes the foot first, then the beam, sloping the surfaces by random with his drawknife and block plane. Then he makes the remaining parts and pins it all together. The false coulter is always made of metal. "You see, be a big stout horse pulling that, you see, and [if you] hit a stone or anything, you'd break your foot out. Tear it right out. Thisaway, it can't move."

His brother, George, agreed. "I've tore them all to *pieces.* Have a mule going pretty pert and hit a root . . ."

The plow point goes on last, completing the job.

Tom is constantly tinkering with the construction to make it a better plow. The present use of bolts instead of pegs is one example. "I work everything that I know how or can think about. [Add] something new to get it to move, you know. And I'm making them to *last.* These plows someday will bring a hundred dollars. They'll be in the antique places, you know."

Though Tom has made them for years ("I made about every plow stock on Pigeon Roost"), he has not become rich. For years he sold them for three dollars apiece. Now he gets a little more, but probably not what they're worth. He doesn't seem to require much money, though, and so it doesn't seem to bother him greatly. Being rooted in the past, his attitude toward most modern conveniences is casual at best. While we were visiting, for example, one of the relatives who was there noticed that his refrigerator was unplugged. She pointed it out to him, saying, "If you don't keep your Frigidaire hooked up now, Thomas, it'll die!"

"I don't care if it does die," he replied. "I don't use it in the winter noway."

He has, however, been able to save *some* money. "I got a bank account," he says proudly. "I got seven hundred dollars in there!"

One of the relatives who was there heard him, laughed, and then said to us within clear earshot, "Well! He'll have to get us an awful nice Christmas present then!"

The following photographs and diagram show how his plows are put together.

PLATE 151   Tom shapes a piece of raw stock. Note the hickory "spring" (see arrow) that pulls the head of the clamp back when the foot pedal of the shaving horse is not depressed.

PLATE 152

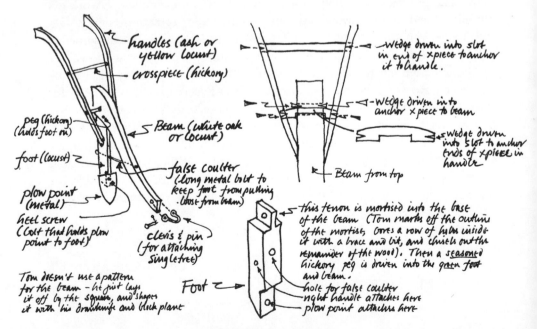

PLATE 153 'This shot, from underneath the plow, shows how the foot is mortised into the underside of the oak beam. Note also the crosspiece that goes through the beam (and thus through the foot's tenon) and through each of the handles.

PLATE 154 The plow from the side, finished except for the addition of the plow point.

PLATE 155 Here Tom attaches the metal plow point to the foot with a bolt.

PLATE 156 Tom with another finished plow, ready for a local farmer.

PLATE 157 Tom also does some repair work. Here, he shows Tom Carlton how he salvaged a hoe by riveting a piece of an old crosscut saw blade to the original shank and adding a new handle.

WOODEN SLEDS

In the Appalachians long before I was born, mountain farmers made sleds to use where their wagons wouldn't go. Low to the ground, the sleds wouldn't tip over nearly as easily as wagons; and being narrow, they would fit through tighter places between trees in the woods. Bob Bennett, our school's work supervisor, found one of these old sleds rotting away in the woods where someone had abandoned it. He brought it back to his house and called us over to look at it.

I talked to Tommy Lee Norton and Lake Stiles about the sled, and this is what they told me:

In our area of the mountains, the runners for such sleds were usually made out of sourwood (a soft wood that often has a curved place in the trunk that makes it ideally shaped), the standards out of locust or hickory, and the benches (the horizontal pieces that go across the runners to hold the body of the sled up off the ground) out of oak.

There were three kinds of sleds, but they were of basically the same design, and built of the same materials.

One type was the sled that had four- to five-foot standards drilled into the runners but no sides or ends. It was used for dragging split-up acid wood, firewood, fence rails, poles, or long strips of tan bark out of the woods.

A second variety had lower standards with side pieces nailed to them and no ends. These were used for dragging heavier loads such as rocks for a chimney, sand, or dirt. Sometimes a sled of this sort was fixed so that ends could be slid into place if needed.

Third was the type that had high sideboards and ends and was used for hauling lighter loads that would slide easily such as corn, fodder, hay, wheat, grain, etc. Without the sides and ends, the farmer might leave a trail of corn behind him.

If the sleds were to be used in the woods, the benches were usually mounted high up so that the body of the sled was well off the ground and

PLATE 158

PLATE 159

PLATE 161

PLATE 160

PLATES 158–161 Park and Conway Hughes are brothers who run a self-sufficient farm in the mountains of North Carolina. They have always used a sled of the type Tedra Harmon built for us, and they still favor it over a tractor and wagon which might overturn on land as steep as theirs is. In the photos, they bring a load of hay into their barn.

could be pulled over rocks and stumps without tearing out the bottom. Sleds used in fields, on the other hand, were lower, their benches resting directly on the tops of the runners since there was no need to worry about rocks and stumps.

The sleds would be pulled by a horse, mule, or steer by means of a pulling bar running between the runners at the front. The bar would have a clevis for a singletree, or a hole drilled in it for a chain or rope.

If the sled was used frequently, the runners might have to be changed as often as every six or seven months. New ones would be cut and their sides and tops hewn off square, but the bottoms would be left rounded as they would wear down anyway through use. A sled that wasn't being used was turned upside down so the runners could not soak up ground moisture and would face the sun so they would harden.

Mr. Stiles said, "When a sled is new, if it's been well made, it can sure be a pretty thing." I can imagine it would be.

Stanley Hicks, one of the banjo makers featured in *Foxfire 3,* is someone that we also talked to about sleds. In his section of the mountains, several hours to the north of us near Sugar Grove, North Carolina, sleds were sometimes half-soled (a process described later in this chapter) to keep them from wearing out so quickly. He describes the sleds he remembers from their farm as follows: "Dad made all of his sleds. And I've made many of a one. We had one we called a log sled that we logged on, and then we had a rock sled. And then we had the one that we hauled our hay and corn and stuff like that. The rock sled, it was down low on the ground and solid floored across. The log sled only had two crosspieces on it—log pieces back here and in the front. And the other sled, it was slatted the other way.

"Made the runners out of sourwood mostly. Or, if we couldn't get sourwood, we got ash. Got them where they'd be crooked up, and then we'd hew them, you know. We didn't half-sole them at the first. That was later. And we bored them to put the standards in and put crosspieces and that.

"The rock sled would have a solid bed on it, and it was built real low down so we could roll rocks up off of the ground on it. And it had sides on it and a front end. Hardly ever had any back end on it so we could roll rocks on from the back.

"And the other sled was made up higher so we could get it over rocks. Sometimes have to take a prize, you know, if it got down too low with a load on it and got on a rock, and prize it off, or lay something under it and pull it off.

"If you kept it in the dry, it would last. Then sometimes we'd half-sole them. If the runner got wore down too much, we'd half-sole them. But they'd last about half of the summer without half-soling.

"Then when we'd half-sole them, Dad would take and split white oak—cut a white oak bush and split it open. Then we took a bent piece of metal and put it over the end of the runner and ran this white oak piece through it, and then we bent it down to the back of it and then attached it with pegs. Bore a hole with a bit and drive pegs in it."

We begin this chapter in the book with Tedra Harmon (see *Foxfire 3*, pages 61–64 and 134–39), who showed us how to make the variety of sled that is most common in his part of the mountains around Sugar Grove, North Carolina. Many of the sleds in that section have runners that are half-soled to prevent the runners having to be replaced so frequently.

We then conclude the chapter with descriptions of several other varieties of sleds we were fortunate enough to find. We soon realized, however, that it would be impossible to document all the variations, for sleds, it seems, come in as many shapes and sizes as the farmers who made them.

LOY SMITH

THE TEDRA HARMON SLED

Tedra Harmon, one of the banjo makers we featured in *Foxfire 3*, also knows how to make sleds. When he found we were interested, he offered to make us a sled so we could get a series of photographs of the entire process. It turned out to be a longer job than we had counted on, and we had to drive the several hundred miles between our school and his home twice before we finally finished it, but we made it, as you can see from the following photographs.

I'd like to tell you a little bit more about our visit before we get to the making of the sled. Once while the other guys were working on the sled, I took a walk around his land and in his shop. His shop fascinated me. It is like a small house with a heating stove unit and a kitchen in it. Upstairs were bedrooms, but I didn't want to bother something I shouldn't. I later found out he and his wife actually *did* live there until they built their new house about a hundred yards away. A huge deer hide and deer skin cover one of the walls of the shop. On another, he has letters ordering banjos, as well as tools, saw blades, banjos, and pictures. Also he has a rack with deer hooves turned at a 90° angle holding up some knives he made, and a hat with a fox head on it. The fox hat is a dark shade of gold and is thick and fluffy. I found a box of groundhog hides cut in circles ready to put in banjos. All I could say while looking at his furs, banjos, knives, and things was, "I wish I had some money." I had some, but not enough to buy all I wanted. He later sold me a knife he made with the handle made from a deer hoof.

During the middle of our interview, Mrs. Harmon came out and said, "Have you all had any lunch?" Since we hadn't had any, we told her no. A little while later she came outside and said, "Tedra, bring'em on in." We stopped what we were doing and went in and our eyes almost popped out. There on the table was a whole lot of good food. Of the food I remember, we had eggs, sausages, fried chicken, fresh creases, bacon mixed with green beans, homemade biscuits, honey, cake, fresh plums, corn-on-the-cob, milk, and coffee. While we were eating, Mrs. Harmon kept apologizing for not having enough. When we told her how much we liked the creases, she gave us about three hundred seeds to plant for ourselves.

When we got through eating, we just talked for a while before going back to the sled. Tedra started talking about the old-timers: "It's unbelievable to know how well the old people *did* get along [with almost nothing]. Lots of people might laugh at them, but they wasn't nothing to laugh at. I've had a lot of folks come by here in the summertime when I was cutting oats with a cradle or mowing grass with a scythe, and they'd stand and look at that and say, 'Why, anybody can do that.' Well, I'd hand it to them and they couldn't do one thing. They thought it was easy, but when they took ahold, they found out different. I have a few times thought that I could do something the best of anybody and come to find out that another man could just skin me alive. I learnt to just keep my mouth shut unless I know what I'm talking about.

"Now sometimes people get so educated they can't see obvious things. That's another thing that gets me. I was talking to a man once—had a little toolbox and a handsaw that was too big to go in it. And he says, 'I'll give some man a five-dollar bill to tell me how to put that saw in that box.'

"I said, 'Gimme a screwdriver and hand me your saw and I'll put it in for you.' He handed me the saw and a screwdriver, and a crowd just went to boohooing and laughing. I took the screws out of the handle and throwed it down there and throwed his saw down in there and said, 'Gimme your five-dollar bill.' And [since] he was so smart—like I didn't know what I was talking about—I *kept* the five dollars. I *would* have give it back to him if he hadn't acted so smart. But why he couldn't see that always buffaloed me. When I took that off, he looked like a fool."

When Tedra asked Cheryl if she had one wish, what would it be, Wig turned around and asked Tedra that same question, and he said, "If I had just one wish, I'd wish to have my health back when I was eighteen years old. Then the other things that I want so bad I'd be able to go on and work and get them. A lot of people you ask about a wish ask for absolute foolishness and stuff that don't make sense. I'll bet not four in a hundred wishes for a home in heaven. I wish for good health, and then I can go ahead and gct the rest: a home in heaven when I die, a nice home here, and just a common living. Wouldn't want to be no rich person—I'm honest about it, wouldn't want it. Live like I am now. I'm satisfied with my life. I don't want no earthly things much. Lot of people, they want a big fine home stuck away up in the air. I don't want that.

"If I had the health that I had when I was eighteen, and knew what I know now, there's lots of stupid things I've done that I wouldn't repeat. If I had it to go back over, I could correct that and live a better life—a cleaner life. I've done a lot of stupid, mean things that if I had my life to live over, you couldn't get me to do at all. I've even abused my body drinking and stuff like that. And you know yourself they's a lot of people doing that right now. And this acid, marijuana, dope. Well, you know they're ruining their body. Just a ruination of it. And God, he didn't make our body to just be bruised and beat around every way. I think we should take care of it. Be as particular about taking care of your health as you can. For when you've lost your health, you've lost it all. And you don't realize that until you come to that point and see that you haven't got none and can't do nothing. I think that's the happiest thing that a young person can have is health. If you'd a'went through the suffering that I did when I went through that operation, you'd know exactly what I'm talking about. [Tedra had a diseased section of the main artery in his leg cut out and replaced with a patch.] I wanted to die and get out of there. Such pain, my mercy. It was awful. But God tells in His book that He won't put no more pain on you than you can bear. But, brother, I had a load of it. Now the doctor explained, said, 'Mr. Harmon, now I'm gonna tell you the facts. Now you're old enough to realize and not get excited now.'

"I said, 'You needn't worry about exciting me.'

"He says, 'I can't tell you how long you'll live, but,' he says, 'I'm hoping you'll live a long time. But,' he says, 'whenever that artery *does* come loose from that patch on either end where I cut it, if I had you on the operating table I couldn't save you.' Said, 'You're gone.' Said, 'You might live to breathe two or three breaths.' But said when it come apart, my heart'd just throw all the blood out on the inside and stop it. He says, 'It'll be an easy death. I can assure you that. Now don't let that scare you.'

"I said, 'It ain't scared me,' and it ain't. If a doctor would sit right there and say, 'Tedra, you're gonna die in fifteen minutes,' I'd never even shake my hand for I'm ready to go. You won't be afraid with the power of God almighty. He's your protector.

"Now I've seen the time that I guess I'd a'been like a lot of other people. When I seen death on me, I'd start a'hollering and a'screaming. I've been in hospitals with people real sick, and someone come in and say, 'Are you ready to die?' and they'd go to bawling. Well, something's wrong. They're afraid. They ain't got the faith to stand up and say, 'I'm not afraid to die.' I don't *want* to die, but I ain't afraid to!"

Then we got up from the table and went out into the yard and worked on the sled until dark.

DWAYNE SKENES

Photographs and research by Dwayne, Cheryl Stocky, Louise Freeman, Ken Cronic, Loy Smith, and Claire Bender.

PLATES 162–163 Tedra begins his sleds with the runners which, in this case, are made of cucumber. Here, Cheryl Stocky cuts the notches that the front crosspiece will fit into.

PLATE 164 Tedra fits the front crosspiece (made of seasoned locust since it has to take so much strain) into the notches on the runners. He will peg it into place later.

PLATE 165   Cheryl and Dwayne Skenes toenail three chestnut blocks onto each runner. The sills will fit on top of these blocks.

PLATE 166   The last block goes on. The wooden strip in front of Tedra's left hand has been nailed on temporarily to hold the runners the correct distance apart.

PLATE 167   Now the hemlock sills are tacked into place. They will be set permanently later. They hold the floor of the sled up off the ground so that it can be pulled over rocks and stumps without hanging up.

PLATE 168 A hole is drilled through each end of the cross-piece into the runners below, and pegs inserted. Here, Louise Freeman saws the yellow locust. pegs off flush.

PLATE 169 After the bottoms of the pegs are sawed off flush, Tedra splits the bottom of each peg. Then he drives a wedge into the split to make the peg bind firmly in the hole.

PLATE 170 When the wedge is in place, as shown here, again a saw is used to cut it off flush with the bottom of the runner.

PLATE 171 With the sled up-right again, the seasoned oak crosspieces are placed. Tedra first drills holes for the nails to keep them from bending in the hard wood. Then Dwayne drives one nail in each end of the crosspieces and places them *off center* so they won't interfere with the 1″ auger used next.

PLATE 172 With the 1″ auger, Dwayne drills down through the oak crosspieces, the sills, blocks, and well into the runners. Long dowels driven into each of the six holes hold the sled together and keep such loads as logs from rolling off.

PLATE 173 On our second visit, we added the half soles to the runners. Here, Ken Cronic hews two green poplar poles so each has a flat side. Normally the half soles would be of white hickory for longer life.

PLATE 174 Now Tedra removes the dowels/standards, turns the sled over, sets a pole in place, and marks where it will have to bend to fit the bend of the runner.

PLATE 175   Then he shows Ken how to cut a series of slots at the spot the pole must bend.

PLATES 176–177   Tedra nails a metal strip to the front of each runner, then he fits the front end of the half sole into it and bends it over to fit the runner's curve.

PLATE 178   Wig holds the half sole down while Tedra ties it temporarily with twine.

PLATE 179   Ken drills holes at regular intervals (four holes per half sole, in this case) for the pegs that will pin the half sole into place.

PLATE 180   Then Tedra carves a seasoned half-inch yellow locust peg for each hole (the holes go through the half sole and completely through the runner) and drives them in. As the green half sole seasons, it grips the peg. The excess peg length is cut off with a hatchet or saw.

PLATE 181   One half sole in place and the other ready to be set. The half soles wear out with use, of course, but are easily replaced. Meanwhile, the runner itself remains unworn. If kept dry when not in use, the sled should last for years.

PLATE 182 After the other half sole is set the sled is righted and an oak floor is added. With the standards replaced, it's ready to use. Some farmers also make a long wood box with high sides that will fit down between the standards and rest on the floor. This is set on the sled when hauling small rocks, corn, and the like, and is removed when not needed.

Tedra calls his sled a "bench" sled. There is also a "Yankee" variety held together with metal rods. He thinks it got this name when someone from outside the community introduced it (see Plate 183).

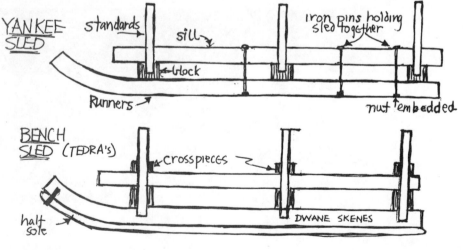

YANKEE SLED — standards — sill — iron pins holding sled together — block — Runners — nut embedded

BENCH SLED (TEDRA'S) — crosspieces — half sole — DWANE SKENES

PLATE 183

PLATES 184–187 (Variation ✳ 1) This sled, made by Tedra years ago, displays some notable differences from the one he made for our article. Both the runners and the half soles are in two pieces, the crosspieces on top of the sills are inset, the front of the sills extends to the runners and are bolted to them, and the standards run beside the blocks rather than through them.

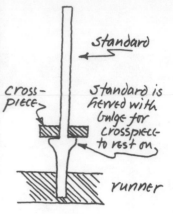

standard

cross-
piece

standard is
hewed with
bulge for
crosspiece
to rest on.

runner

PLATES 188–190 (Variation #2) This sled, made by a man outside Bakersville, North Carolina, is a very simple but very common variety. The outstanding features are the crosspiece in front of the sled which is actually set into the fronts of the runners in almost mortise and tenon fashion, and the four one-piece standards (see diagram). There are no half soles on the runners. These runners, like those on so many mountain sleds, are simply curved sections from the trunks of young sourwood trees.

PLATES 191–192 (Variation #3) This sled was made in Rabun County, Georgia, and found abandoned in the woods by Bob Bennett. It, like variation #2, has sourwood runners without half soles, a crosspiece mortised into the runners, and one-piece standards. Other variations show up in the diagram (Plate 192).

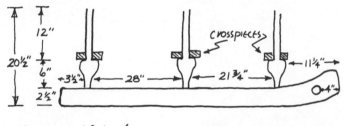

12"

20½"

6"

2½"

Crosspieces

3½" 28" 21¾" 11¼"

4"

diameter of holes for
standards = 1¾"

1½ O ← 26" → O 1½ 6"

Crosspiece

Runners
Length = 71"
height = 5" (at front)
width = 4"

Sideboards
Length = 66½"
height = 8½"
width = 1" (thickness)

floor
Length = 66½"
width = 8¼"
thickness = 1"

width of sled from
outside edge of runner
to outside edge = 33¼"

Below: Stephanie
Shuptrine drawing
sled for Foxfire.

PLATE 192

PLATES 193–194   (Variation ⚹4) This sled was made by Harv Reid in Blairsville, Georgia. It has curved sourwood runners and a mortised crosspiece, but the box is nailed to the standards and rests on crosspieces that are nailed to the tops of the runners. In Plate 194, Harv shows where the clevis goes.

GARDENING

All my life I had heard talk of, and even watched my family make, a garden. But because I was younger and the grocery store was just down the road, I never felt that I should go out in the hot sun and hoe the garden. Suddenly last year the fact that I was going to have to plant a garden dawned on me. The first thing that came to my mind was, "I don't know anything about a garden." That's when I started working on this article.

My first question was why did they plant a garden? Esco Pitts, one of our contacts, said, "Then you couldn't just go to the store and buy much stuff, 'cause they wasn't much stuff to buy. And the people just made their living, just got the practice of making their living at home."

And that's just what they did. The women would take care of the vegetable garden. Mr. Pitts recalled, "My mother would always put one row of flowers in the middle of the garden. She took care of them just like she did the vegetables."

What did the men do? They took care of the field crops—things like two acres of corn or wheat. The corn was saved to take to the mill for their cornmeal and the wheat was made into flour. Sometimes they grew cane for cane syrup, which could be used in the place of sugar.

Yes! People really did get out and work in the field. And if you got sick and couldn't work, you didn't worry about it much because some of the folks that lived near would come over and help. Aunt Arie said, "People wasn't a'scared of each other, like they are now." All the people far and near would gather at one house. They would have a barnraisin' or beanstringin' or cornshuckin'. The families would all bring food and after the work was done, all would eat and talk. Lawton Brooks said, "We had a many a cornshuckin' way back yonder, but no more."

After getting the land ready and planting the seeds came watching it grow and keeping the animals out and the bugs off. Finally came the harvest. That was the time when everybody worked. They worked not only

PLATE 195   Ednie Buchanan's vegetable garden.

to gather it, but to store it for use during the winter. The mother would can the vegetables and dry the fruit. The father had to bury the things like potatoes and cabbage. He buried them to keep them from freezing. Florence Brooks said, "You could go back in the dead of the winter and dig out a cabbage and it would be just as good as the day you cut it."

The people raised their pork and beef, so they didn't have to buy much. They only bought what they couldn't grow, going to market about twice a year. A family would raise enough vegetables to have some left to sell after putting up what they needed for the family. Kenny Runion remembered, "We loaded up the wagon and it was so far [to market] that we would have to camp on the way there or back."

When they sold the vegetables, they would buy their supplies consisting of pepper, salt, some seeds, and coffee beans. Mr. Pitts commented, "I've woke up many a'morning to the smell of coffee beans roasting on the fireplace."

After about ten or fifteen interviews I found that I had not only learned how to plant a garden, but I had gained a small amount of understanding of what life was like thirty or forty years ago.

MARY THOMAS

Interviews and transcriptions by Bit Carver, Mary Chastain, Vicki Chastain, Susie Nichols, Cheryl Stocky, Mary Thomas, and Terese Turpin.

Organization and editing by Mary Thomas and Lynnette Williams. Photography by Brenda Carpenter, Myra Queen, Annette Reems, Barbara Taylor, Mary Thomas, and Lynnette Williams.

CLEARING THE LAND

Families in the mountains generally settled on land that had not been previously homesteaded. They, therefore, had to build their homes and clear their land for farming using only simple tools, manpower, and oxpower. To cut the trees, many of them two and three feet in diameter, they had only large two-man crosscut saws and axes. They chose the levelest, richest-looking land, and cleared that for their crops. This was very important, because those mountaineers were not gardening casually; they were, of necessity, farming for their survival.

R. M. DICKERSON: All this country, this bottom land here where we see it now, in my father's and mother's day and my grandfather's day, was in a swamp. It was growed up in woods. And the first settlers here settled around the foot of the hills above the swamp. The swamp was full of water and you couldn't do any good down there until it was drained out, so they first settled around the edge of the mountains and up on the mountains. They cleared the land there and got the logs and built log houses; that's the kind of house I was raised in—a log cabin. They built those log cabins out of logs that they took off the land they was going to cultivate. They took those logs and used this kind of tractor [a horse and sled] and skidded them up to where they was going to build a house.

They [sawed] the trees down on th'place and cut'em up. The ones that they was going to use, they rolled them over to the side. But they rolled the old rough logs and the stuff that was too big for a house log, they rolled that up and built'em a fire and burned'em all up in the brush. Sometimes it would take two or three days to burn all the logs. They'd just keep rollin' the logs together till they got'em burnt up.

Never thought anything about getting them stumps out. You'd just plow around the stump. In the middle there might be some little stumps or rocks in the way. Come time to take a big stump, they might lay some loose rocks up on it to get them out of the way of the plow or the hoes or maybe a stump that wasn't burnt up quite in the pile they would lay it up on the stump and let it rot.

MARY CARPENTER: You've seen them big bottoms in the valley. That was all in timber once, and that was all cut down. [In order to clear the land], they'd go out with their crosscut saw and an axe, and they'd chop down the trees and they'd work them into logs if they wanted to build a house. If not, they worked them into firewood; saw it and bust it up. Then they take the mattock and the shovel and dig the stumps up. It took a long time to dig a stump up, but that's [what they had to do]. Sometimes they

PLATE 196 It took a tremendous amount of work years ago to completely clear this fertile bottomland.

dig down to a tap root. That was a root that went straight down, [the others spread out] and sometimes they'd be so big that they couldn't hardly roll the stump out of the hole. So they'd hitch a mule to it with a chain and pull the stump out. Then they'd fill the hole back up.

People would sled rocks off a field. Why, we used to have an old mare and we made a sled, and put rocks on it. We'd load that old sled with rocks —every one we could put on it, and Oshie Holt would drive the old mare. She was a big and mean horse, too, if she wanted to be. And we'd take them down in between Grandpa's place and Bleckley's and add them to one side of the rock fence. Mr. Bleckley would haul and pack the *other* side of the rock fence. It was down in the valley, just old loose rock out of the field; we'd just take a sled load, place them in there, and keep filling the wall up. We didn't need any wooden fence; see, there wasn't no cattle grazin' in there then, but it was a line marker between their place and Grandpa's.

PREPARING THE SOIL

A man couldn't walk into the general store and buy his fertilizer and lime —no such things existed. The people had to provide for the enrichment of the soil from what was available on their farms. Every scrap of chicken and animal manure that could be collected was put back in the soil. Some folks made compost piles, and many spread ashes on the ground to sweeten and enrich it. They were true organic farmers.

ANNA HOWARD: We'd terrace if we had a really steep place. Sometimes you'd have t'do that. You know, the way they'd do that [was to] make a ridge right through here, an' they'd put some sage'r'somethin' through there, and it'd stay there all th'time, an' th'sage'd hold the edge of the ridge.

LON DOVER: Now that new ground with natural soil that's not been disturbed maybe for a hundred years or longer, see it's got everything in there it needs. Until you tended it an' got nutrients out of the soil, why we didn't have nothin't'do but plant it. When we'd grow stuff till the ground wouldn't make any more, we'd sow grass for th'horses on those bald places.

HARRY BROWN: We took the manure out of the barn and put it in a pen as big as this room. We'd clean out the stalls of the mules, cows, hogs, and chickens in the early part of the fall. And then we'd go to the woods and get a load of leaves to throw in there. From time to time during the winter, we'd mix it up and keep addin' to it till it was time to use it. We

PLATE 197   Belle Dryman's father built this pen for composting organic matter, and Belle still uses it.

had big sacks we made into big aprons, and we'd go to th'pile and some-body would fill up our apron and we'd go scatter it around the gardens.

I was raised at Scaley, back in th'mountains, and you'll find that nearly ever'body has a different way of farmin'. Our garden, we kep' it special. We'd clear it in the spring of th'year, cleared off every little briar, an' took a rake an' raked it; then broadcast it with stable manure—tried t'broadcast it ever'year. Now farmin' is different—like a broomsage field, we'd burn that off, where if we'd had somethin' t'turn it under, see, that'd be just like good fertilizer. We didn't know that back then. Land was cheap back then and people cleared up new ground nearly ever'year or we'd just leave. 'Course, that'uz hard—plowin' with those stumps all around. An' we'd tend that every year till it got where it wouldn't make nothin' and then we let it grow up. That's th'reason s'much of this mountain land washed away.

We'd try t'plow it th'first year—we'd just go along an' it'd hang up, an' we'd take it out and go again an' hang it [the plow] up again—it'uz kinda aggravatin'. Some folks just dug holes and planted in the hills th'first year. Y'know those sprouts an' briars in that rich dirt'd grow some times six inches in one night. You could buy two, three acres of land back then cheaper than you could buy a two-hundred-pound sack of fertilizer. My daddy bought three hundred acres for less than a dollar an acre!

MARY CARPENTER: We'd cut those weeds and things all down, then we'd rake them to the middle of the garden. Just put them all into rows; one at one end, and one at the other end, and one in the middle, then light a fire to them. We'd light a cornstalk and keep stickin' it along—it don't make a big fire. Just let it burn a little at a time. You know, if it had been burning from one end to another it would have made a fairly big fire. It'll just burn up so high and go out—just stir around with a fork and make certain it's all out. Then we went to plowing with a horse or a mule.

LAWTON BROOKS: They'd let the old cornstalks and vines and ever'thing rot on the ground, and that fall, they'd plow'em under. They usually plowed in th'fall or through th'winter, because the freezin'an'-thawin' would break up that dirt an'make it s'fine. Made your ground bet-ter. It don't have clods'r'nothin' in it. You plow it in th'spring of th'year an' it happens t'be a little bit damp, you'll have clods in there all year you couldn't bust with a durn hoe. I've hoed old cloddy ground when you couldn't do nothin', only roll the clods. I despise that—just like gettin' in a rock pile. [They used ashes for fertilizer.] I've hauled many a'wheelbarrow load of them. They used'em kinda like they use lime to sweeten th'soil. An' that's where they get their potash. They put that mainly in their vegetable garden, not in th'cornfields. Put'em down through th'winter. Every time y'clean out th'fireplace, get your ashes and fill up your wheelbarrow and go spread it on th'garden.

WILLIE UNDERWOOD: Before we planted, we'd have to plow it; back then we'd have to plow it with a mule, 'cause we didn't have any heavy equipment—like big harrows and things like that. We used a low gopher plow and what we call a single-foot mule and plowed through those things. We didn't tear it up too much the first year after it was cleared. We worked it then through the summer, and the next year it would be a lot easier, and we could do a lot better job plowing because we could break those roots up; they died out and started to rot out. And that helps your soil, too. When I was growin' up it didn't take too many years for the soil to stop producing a good crop; we'd let it grow up in stubble one year and the next year we'd plant it in rye and the next year we'd plant it in corn. We rotated then. Now a lot of times, we run year after year with the same thing. We put a lot more stuff back into the soil than we used to. You grow a lot more in soil if you put back in it. Soil builders, you know. They rot in there and make better soil.

PLATE 198   Gay McClain uses an old push plow to lay off his rows for planting.

TOOLS

The tools available for farming in this area fifty to one hundred years ago were relatively simple and non-mechanized, except for the wood-burning, steam powered grain thresher which people hired out on a shares basis to thresh their rye, wheat, and oats. It seems almost every family had a plow, shovels, hoes, spades, rakes, and mattocks; but some families had several kinds of plows, harrows, a corn planter, and a grain cradle. And then some people just made do with what was on hand—Florence Brooks told us that since her father didn't have a harrow, he took a big old pile of brush and hitched it to the mule and dragged it over the field until it was smooth.

R. M. DICKERSON: Well, people used about the same tools—hoes, rakes, mattocks, and a plow—that's about it.

My grandfather used to have a braid hoe. When they come out here to a pretty good-sized sprout or grub that they wanted to dig up, they'd use this hoe as a mattock and dig it up. And as th'sprouts come out on a stump, they could take this old braid hoe and go around th'stump and knock'em off. But these ol' light hoes we got now, you'd break the handles out of

PLATE 199 Kenny Runion has used this hoe for over sixty years.

them. This one had a good, big, strong handle in it and it was what people called a grubbin' hoe. I don't know how come them to be called "braid" unless [someone named] Braid invented them.

Now you've seen these single-foot plow stocks that people would lay off a row at a time with just one mule to it. Now that was the only kind of a plow they had to get the land prepared. After they got the land prepared and the rows laid off, they'd have what they called a double-foot that would have two feet on it—one plow in front of the other. The front plow would be next to the row and a little ahead and this one would come along and go along like that and get some of the dirt to the row sort of, and then they'd turn around and come back down that row and throw the dirt to the other row. Now that'uz what they called a double-foot plow. And that'uz the only kind of a plow that they had to cultivate corn with. They had this single-foot plow that they plowed up the land with and laid off the furrows, and then they used this double-foot to cultivate the corn with and to plow up the weeds. Then along behind that the children would hoe. Lots of times one of those harrows would belong to three or four families. Every family didn't have one—couldn't afford it. So they'd work together and when they got the land ready, they'd go somewhere to a good neighbor's over there and they'd get his harrow maybe and they'd go in together and all [work together].

HARRY BROWN: We didn't have nothin' but a little bull-tongue or single-foot plow t'plow it with—didn't have tenners back then. They call'em

PLATE 200   A homemade drag harrow with wooden teeth. Drawn behind a horse, this harrow would break up clumps of earth in a garden before planting.

single-foots now, but back sixty years ago they called'em a bull-tongue, because most everybody plowed with a steer. I can remember seein' one fellow plowin' with a plow he made out of a locust tree—just a stick hangin' down t'dig up th'ground.

For a long time, hand wooden plows were all we had. Then people began t'learn how t'work with iron; they made the plow-shoe out of that. Later they had turnin' plows, an' shover or [a] lay-off plow for layin' off rows, an' twister plows for hilling your dirt.

MARY CARPENTER: They had a drag harrow that was a big old iron thing with bars across it and sharp teeth. They'd put a big rock on there and a log and sometimes they'd stand on it, when they'd get in a place that was pretty clotty, you know. That'd help to mash it down. And you could harrow it when the ground was damp. Why, it'd be as smooth as a lettuce bed.

FAYE LONG: Well, they used a horse in those days. We didn't have a tractor and we hoed the corn. We planted big fields of corn, and we plowed the corn about three or four times. Every time we plowed, we had to hoe it, but now we just spray the corn instead of having to hoe it. That was a lot of work, having to hoe the corn every time it was plowed. But you had to keep the weeds down. We used a single-foot to lay off with, and a cultivator to plow with. We used one horse, and hooked it to the cultivator. That turned the soil real good and if you could plow it, if your corn was big enough, you plowed close to it, throw the fresh dirt from the far side of the

PLATE 201   Robbie Letson holds another homemade drag harrow, this one with metal spikes for teeth.

row over to the next. That would cover up a lot of the little weeds that were coming, but you still had to cut the big weeds that were in there, and if it was a dry season that would kill'em. But if it was rainy, they'd grow right back.

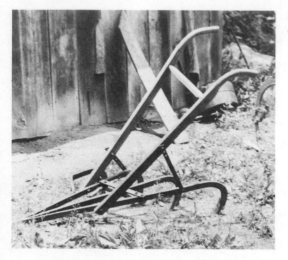

PLATE 202   Horse- (or mule-) drawn cultivators such as this one are still in use.

SEEDS

Everyone saved almost all of their seed, but many people did buy some; lettuce and cabbage seed, for example. Gathering and storing seed for next year's crops was serious business. A supply of healthy seed assured a family that, barring great misfortune, they would be able to make it through the next year as they had made it through the last. Precautions were taken to insure that the seed would remain safe and dry, as next year's food supply depended on that.

ESCO PITTS: I don't reckon there's not much of anything a fellow can plant but what he can save th'seed off of. Let'em get ripe on th'stalk or vine, get'em up, shell'em out, dry'em, save'em in little pokes or jars. Pepper seed, tomato seed, cucumber seed, all kind of bean seeds, all kinds of seeds. People used t'never buy seeds. An' people used t'save their onion seeds, too. Had th'multiplyin' onions—red button onions—that'd run up an' make their buttons on th'stalk. Save th'buttons. We never did save no cabbage seed, but you could save your cabbage through the winter, and then set'em out in th'spring of th'year. And they'll make you cabbage seed. Beets, the same way—save them through the winter, put them out in a row in th'spring of th'year, and they'll run up an' make seed. If you leave'em in th'ground, they'll make seed th'next spring. [My daddy] picked him out some purty potatoes, and he'd take some hay or somethin', maybe leaves, put that in a hole in the ground and put his potatoes on that and put hay over them. And rake dirt over it and put a piece of tin over that to keep the water out. That was the seed. Now sweet potatoes he couldn't save. He just had to buy them.

LON DOVER: You get your seeds from pretty ripe vegetables, put them on something and let them dry. Then you take them up and put'em in jars. They have to be dried, or you can't keep them through the winter. We'd put th'seeds in a jar or a tin can back then. When th'bugs got t'gettin' in, people would store their bean seed in a snuff can an' kept enough snuff in there t'cover'em up. For tomato seeds, you'd just squeeze the seeds out on a cloth, then lay them down somewhere to dry. Then put the cloth up somewhere to save for the next year. The seeds stuck to the cloth. You do the same thing for cucumbers, squash, and pumpkin, but you had to let the seeds dry before you packed them away. People were more anxious in savin' seeds then than we are now, freezing things. That was a big thing.

MARY CARPENTER: There was nowhere to buy seeds, so we saved them. Once we got'em, we kept'em. We'd leave a row of beans in the garden to seed for next year, then we'd shell them out when they dried up, and put them in a can and put a spoonful of soda in'em and shake it real good. And that's your seed for next year. It's the same way with peas.

For corn, when we were shucking it out after it was dried on the ear, whenever we found a big pretty ear, we'd throw it in a separate pile to save for seed. Even mustard—we'd let one or two grow up and make seed, and they'd leave one cabbage stalk to grow up and make seeds. Same way with spinach. The pea and bean seeds are the only ones I put soda in—the rest I'd just put them up in a cloth bag in a dry place and hang it on a nail somewhere.

PLATE 203 Belle Dryman hung these bean plants in her barn to dry in the fall, and will use the seed next spring.

BELLE DRYMAN: We growed our own seed. For sweet potatoes, we'd save some from the last year and, in the spring, bed them down. Fix up a seed bed, ever how big y'want, and put manure in it. Cover that with dirt —don't mix it in, then put your potatoes pretty close together on top of that, and cover'em up with some more dirt. When they start t'sprout, watch'em and let those slips get six, eight inches tall, and pull'em off and plant'em where y'want your sweet'taters.

SIGNS

It appears that many more people used to plant by the signs of the moon than do now. Some may call this practice silly or superstitious, but many swear by it. They would no more plant corn under the wrong sign than farmers now would plan to cut hay during a rainy spell. We don't know if any carefully controlled scientific experiments have been done on planting by the signs, but several people have told us that they have conducted their own simple experiments and found that the seed planted under the proper sign did much, much better than the same kind of seed planted under the wrong sign.

LON DOVER: I wouldn't plant nothin' only by th'signs. Now they's lots of people that don't believe in that, but I do. I'uz raised that way, and I go by it yet. Don't you plant anything till th'moon gets full. Don't plant nothin' on th'new moon for it'll grow up high and it won't make nearly as much t'eat. Now roastin' ears planted on th'new moon grow small ears right up at th'top of th'stalk. An' planted on th'old moon, it makes a bigger ear an' kinda falls over. I plant by th'signs or I won't plant at all. Irish potatoes, plant them on th'new moon and they'll grow that [three feet] high and they won't make a total failure, but they won't make half as many. The old moon [is] any time from the time the moon fulls till it gets its smallest. You can plant all the way to the new moon. Plant everything on th'old moon. Now mustard or greens, if you plant on the new moon, they'll run way up an' won't have much leaves on'em an' they'll go to seed.

I don't know what causes the signs to do what they do. I just plant mine like I told you, and I don't know much about how it works. I plant by th'signs an' gather when it gets ripe. I learned it from the old folks. If you want to make a good yield, you better go by th'signs, I'll tell you that now.

The dark nights is when th'moon is going down, last quarter before it news, there's three dark nights before the new moon. My daddy [planted by the moon]. I don't know what the signs were, but it was th'moon, a certain time he planted his corn, a certain time he planted his watermelon patch. Whenever th'signs are in th'arms is the best time t'plant your beans. An' you shouldn't plant corn when th'signs is in the heart—y'get black spots in your grain. There's certain times as th'moon goes down that I won't plant. Sometimes as they go down, they'll be maybe in th'bowels an' get in th'legs an' feet is a real good time to plant. An old friend of mine—the best potato raiser I ever saw—said t'plant your taters when th'signs is in the feet even if it's on the new moon. The best time in the world t'make Irish potatoes is when th'signs are in the feet. The signs are good from the head down to th'heart, then from just below th'bowels on down to th'feet. The signs get t'every part of th'body ever'month. They go from the feet back to th'head all over again.

HARRIET ECHOLS: [There are certain signs to plant under], and that is on the new of the moon when you have dark nights. When you plant your cabbage, plant when the signs are in the head. Now the dark nights is for onions and potatoes. The new moon, I believe, is for corn where it won't grow so tall—if it's planted on a full moon, see, it grows straight up. You sow your plants at different signs, and when you plant your beans the best time is to plant'em in the arms. When you set out plants, start with the signs in the thighs and you'll have good luck. That's the old-time rule, now, and we still go by it. 'Course, I'm old timey myself, you know. My parents went by this and I found [usually] the old timer's go by the zodiac signs. When the sign is in the bowels, you don't plant because your seed rots.

ETHEL CORN: An' if you plant beans on th'new of the moon, if y'ever like t'raise any, they'll rot an' speck. They'll make good vines, but they'll rot and speck. I didn't b'lieve that at one time—then I tried it once.

PAULINE HENSON: If you want a lot of cucumbers, plant [the seeds] when the signs are in the twins.

R. M. DICKERSON: Well, some people'd plant by the signs, 'specially beans, but we never did take much stock in plantin' by the signs. A lot of people believed in'em and sometimes it worked out and it'd look like they's right; then again maybe it won't. But what most ever'body had to do back then when they got their land ready and the time come, they'd plant signs or no signs. It's kinda' like Uncle Bob, that lived in this two-story house over here. Somebody was asking him one day about plantin' by the moon. He said he always planted his down here 'cause it was so far to go to the moon to work it that he'd never get it worked.

LIZZIE LOVIN: Mamma planted beans when the signs was in the arms. They'd never plant corn when the signs was on the new of the moon; it would grow so high you couldn't reach the ears. They planted corn on the full moon, and it'd grow short and the ears would be full. And potatoes the same way—if you plant them on the new of the moon, they'd make all vines and no potatoes. So we'd plant potatoes on dark nights in March or

April. My mamma used to say the moon was just like a man. It changes every eight days. She'd plant things that grow leafy on the new of the moon.

ESCO PITTS: You want'a put onions out in March. You can put them out earlier, but they do better to put them out on a dark moon, for they make under the ground.

COMMON VEGETABLES

The different kinds of vegetables grown here years ago are still prevalent today, with some variations in particular varieties. The Jerusalem artichoke, which many people used to cultivate, appears to be the main exception, as it isn't grown very widely here now.

Corn was one of the most important crops—it was a staple for both people and all their animals. They ate it fresh on or off the cob; in fresh corn cornbread; used it dried to make cornmeal, popcorn, parched corn, grits, and hominy; and sprouted it to make moonshine. The fodder (leaves) was used dried to feed the animals, and the shucks were made into mats, scrub brushes, hats, and various other things.

The vegetables are listed in the general order in which people said they planted them, starting with the cool-weather ones in the early spring, and going to the warm-weather ones in late spring and through the summer.

Potatoes

R. M. DICKERSON: Usually the first thing they would plant was Irish potatoes 'cause they'd stand the cold. We used to plant'em back in February. 'Course they never came up maybe until sometime in March. Then you'd have some to eat because more'n'likely you'd eaten up all your potatoes that you'd made last fall by that time.

EDNIE BUCHANAN: We always planted potatoes on a dark moon in April, but some folk'd plant'em in March or even February. We'd cut the potatoes from last year that we saved for seed into a couple pieces each. Had to be sure there was two good eyes in each piece. Well, we'd already have our rows ready and fertilized with manure, and just plant those pieces.

LON DOVER: You can plant potatoes real deep. We used to always take th'turnin'plow an' lay off for our potatoes an' then cover'em with a ten-nin'plow, an' that'd ridge'em up.

ADA KELLY: After we planted the potatoes, we'd work'em and ridge the soil up some as the vines grew. We found that if we made a small ridge, we'd get big potatoes. We always put ashes on our potatoes, and it made them grow really well. We'd dig new potatoes around the time the vines were blooming, but wouldn't dig the whole patch until all the vines had died down. We'd plow them out—that plow'd run along under the potatoes and run'em out on top of the ground. But I guess some people would dig them out.

LAWTON BROOKS: [To store] potatoes, we'd dig out a round hole, not too far. Then we'd take us a big sack of leaves, put right in th'bottom of that hole, pile th'potatoes up. You can pile them up over the level of th'ground, then you put some leaves over th'top of them, or straw, an' cover that with dirt. You end up with a sort of mound, then when you want some potatoes, scratch you out a little hole right down at th'bottom an' them potatoes keep a'walkin' right to you. You can do apples th'same way.

Onions

AUNT ARIE CARPENTER: [The onions were] planted early. We put them out in March if it got dry enough. The earlier you get thcm out, the better they do. We always bought onion buttons, and Mommy had some of those multiplying onions. A big onion made little onions and a little onion made a big one. And we had these little white shallots, as they call'cm. Set out one and thcy'd just make a whole big bunch.

PLATE 204 Aunt Arie Carpenter getting some help digging hcr potatoes from *Foxfire* students.

LON DOVER: If I don't get onions out in March, I might just as well not plant. Seems like they never would do no good [if they were put out any later]. They do best in a pretty loose, rich dirt, and they need lots of sunshine. Sometime along in August when the tops dies down, we'll pick'em and spread'em out till th'dirt gets dried off, and they get cured good. You can't store them till they've dried and cured. Then we'd put'em in a box'r'somethin' and not let'em freeze. Lots of people'ud tie'em in bunches an' hang'em up in a dry, cool place.

BELLE DRYMAN: We always raised our own onions. We had what they called th'multiplyin' onion back then. [They were biennial because] the first year, a little onion would grow into a big onion. Save that big onion till next spring, plant it, an' it'd grow into a whole bunch of little onions [each of which, when planted next year, would grow into another big onion, and so on]. An' we had some that made what we called buttons on the top o'th'stalk, where them blooms grow. You save those buttons till next spring and pull'em apart and plant'em. Now if you planted the buttons or the little multiplyin' onions in the late summer, they wouldn't make too big of onions, just green onions.

Lettuce

FLORENCE BROOKS: They did have leaf lettuce; you didn't never see a head lettuce. We planted it early, and when it give up, we planted it late. It needs cooler weather—we didn't try t'grow it in th'middle of th'summer.

PLATE 205   Onions and lettuce may be planted in February or March.

Plant it around March if the ground's dry enough. Our seeds—we bought'em in th'store.

ESCO PITTS: My mother grew it every year. She had two kinds—leaf lettuce and some that made heads. She planted it very early in the spring, even before th'frost quit, because lettuce is a hardy plant. She had a corner of th'garden where it seemed t'grow better than any other place. Then she had lettuce along in her onion rows.

EDNIE BUCHANAN: I just sow my lettuce in sort of a bed. It loves cool weather, and once it gets up some, even a freeze don't kill it. It does real good where the ground is rich, but now it's something you have to use when it's ready, or it will ruin.

Peas

R. M. DICKERSON: [Plant] five or six rows of garden peas. You know nothing but a hard freeze'll hurt garden peas. The frost don't bother them, and then in May we'll be gettin' peas from th'garden.

LON DOVER: You plant a row of peas on th'new moon, an' cover'em up good with dirt, they'll just crawl right on top of that dirt. I go by th'calendar; you can see what phase th'moon is in, and where th'signs are. I go by th'moon and th'signs.

We had what we call English peas—that's all they called'em back then. We'd let th'peas dry an' save'em for seed from year to year.

HARRIET ECHOLS: We'd plant garden peas, also called them English peas. You have to plant them early, February or March, because they like cool weather. They don't need a real rich soil like, say, corn does, but a pretty good soil. They do best if you can stake them up, but you don't have to. They're harder to pick if you don't, though.

We also planted crowder peas and black-eyed peas, which are really more like a bean in the way they grow. Now they like the warmer weather, and you can plant'em in your corn, and they'll climb the corn and you pick'em after they're mature and all dry.

Turnips

FLORENCE BROOKS: We raised great big turnips—people don't raise turnips like they did then. Old people had great large turnips back then, and they had'em all the winter. Lot of times they'd have t'plow those old turnips up and push them aside to plant again in the spring. And my father went to th'field with a big basket [to gather the cast-aside turnips], and we'd put on pots of'em t'cook for the hogs. We used the same turnips for greens that we used for the turnips themselves.

HARRIET ECHOLS: The turnips, you saw them early in the spring, 'bout like peas or lettuce. We usually sowed them in late summer, too, to have the greens through the fall and winter. Turnips'll grow in a fair soil— now if you want the turnips instead of the greens, you have to thin'em out some so they'll have room to grow. People used to bury turnips to keep over the winter just like they buried potatoes.

ESCO PITTS: The turnips [we grew] was the purple-topped gold. And I've seen them get as big as six inches through.

Carrots

EDNIE BUCHANAN: I plant carrots just about the same time I do beets, early spring. I dig a little ridge, then sow the seed along in that ridge. They do the best in a loose kind of dirt, but it doesn't have to be too rich.

HARRIET ECHOLS: Carrots like the cool weather—you can plant'em in early spring and you can plant'em again in the summer for fall carrots. Now y'can't plant'em too deep, because they'll not come up too well, and you have t'cover [the seeds] with fine dirt. You have to thin'em good and keep'em weeded, too, in order to get big carrots.

Beets

AUNT ARIE: Now I'll tell you when to plant beets . . . the twenty-sixth, twenty-seventh, and twenty-eighth of March. If you plant beets on them three days, you'll sure have beets. But you have to keep right after them. If you let the weeds get a little bit ahead of you, they're hard to raise.

HARRIET ECHOLS: Beets should be planted in February—if they're planted later and along comes a dry spell in late spring, they may die if they're still real small. They like th'cool weather, and want a fairly rich dirt, but nothin' like corn. Sometimes they're bad to not germinate, so it's good to sow'em pretty thick. You have to thin them out if they're real thick though, or they won't make much beet. You can store'em, but they taste the sweetest right out of th'garden.

Mustard

FLORENCE BROOKS: We planted mustard [in March] · about the same time as turnip greens. We mixed th'seed together most of th'time. Then we'd plant'em both again along in August an' have late greens.

ESCO PITTS: You plant your mustard early in th'spring—it can stand frost an' it's th'first greens that come in th'spring.

MARINDA BROWN: My mother used to sow mustard from early spring, all through the summer. It likes cool weather, but it did all right through the summer. We'd eat it into the late fall. It likes a good rich garden soil.

Cabbage

LIZZIE LOVIN: My mother always planted her cabbage seeds in between the onions, in certain intervals—she didn't put'em thick, but she put'em where there'd be skips in the onions or where she'd pulled out the onions to eat. Then she'd have a row of cabbage where the onions was. [Onions, having a strong smell, can help in repelling the cabbage moth, which lays eggs on the leaves, which turn into cabbage worms which eat the leaves—Ed.]

ESCO PITTS: Seems to me we grew a Flat Dutch [cabbage] back then. The head would get as big as a half a bushel. Cabbage likes a pretty rich dirt to grow in, and they need cool weather t'do their best growing—the best times are spring and fall, but here in some of these mountains we can grow them all summer long. We'd usually plant'em in March. Some folks'd plant seeds right in the rows, and some would start'em in a small seed bed and then transplant'em into th'rows when they got up about four to six inches. Now the early cabbage we'd eat or make into kraut, but the late cabbage, we'd dig down a ditch, pull the [mature] cabbage up by the roots, and bury them [head down] in the ditch—instead of putting them straight up and down, they was slanted up at an angle. We'd cover the heads, and leave the roots sticking out. That was the best cabbage you ever eat. Any time of the winter you could go out and dig some out.

LON DOVER: At that time we grew what we called late Flat Dutch [cabbage]. I don't believe I've seen any of that lately; it had a big old head. And another smaller-headed one called Copenhagen Market. We had t'buy our cabbage seed. But if y'take a cabbage that's been buried all winter, and set it out again in the spring, it'll put up a stalk and make seed. You've got t'go th'second year t'get cabbage seed.

PLATE 206 Cabbage just beginning to head.

Corn

LIZZIE LOVIN: Back several years ago, people grew yellow prolific and white prolific and Indian corn. The Indian corn, sometimes Dad would take it down yonder to the mill [and have it ground] and us kids wouldn't eat it because it was too red. We didn't have any sweet corn back then, though.

Corn likes a really rich soil, and most of the time, people would put it on the newly cleared ground, and plant it there for a couple of years until it didn't make good corn anymore.

To harvest the corn we just hitched the mules to the sled and went through there and pulled the ears off and leave the stalk standing. But then they'd usually fall over before Dad plowed and he'd plow them under. Then we'd take the corn and put it in the crib.

R. M. DICKERSON: Our old rule for planting corn back then was the last week in April and the first week in May. That was when the ground began to get warm enough for the corn to come up. That was as late as you could plant that old field corn and it mature in the fall.

LON DOVER: Up in June, we'd plant a patch of corn, and it'd be in good roastin' ears till frost. We'd cut th'stalks off before th'first frost, stick'em down in th'ground and shock it. Th'frost wouldn't hurt it and you could pull roastin' ears a good while after th'frost. Stick th'stalks down in th'ground, y'know, and just shock it up. Make a big year of corn—y'get it in roastin' ears what y'want now, but what you don't use for feed or for

PLATE 207   Margaret and Richard Norton planting corn.

bread, you wait till after it comes two'r'three good frosts in th'fall of th'year and then y'gather your corn and put it up. They say [the frost] helps t'dry th'sap out of th'shuck. I plant corn in March and harvest in fall.

In plantin' corn, you want to cover it, early corn, about that [two inches] deep. But now if th'ground's gettin' warm, it's gettin' late, you don't cover it deeper than three-quarters inch an' it'll come up quicker. But if you plant it too deep, it won't come up.

KENNY RUNION: They've changed from th'old way, and th'best corn I ever raised was when I planted it in March and it'd get up an' get frostbit, and then it'd come back out. Of course, if it's barely picked up out of th'ground, if it bites it down into th'bud, why it won't come out. As long as it don't bite it plumb down t'th'ground into that bud, your corn'll come out. It'll come out and make th'heavy corn earlier.

HARRY BROWN: To harvest the corn we were going to keep over the winter, we waited way late, till after several frosts. That's so the corn would

PLATE 208   This corn has matured and dried and is ready to bring in and store for the winter.

get good and dry. If it didn't, when you gathered it, it would rot. We'd go in an' pick the corn and heap it up, and then somebody would come through with a wagon, loading up and carrying it to the barn. Sometimes we'd pile it out in the yard, and have a corn-shuckin' with twenty-five to thirty men and have a great big dinner.

Sweet potatoes

LAWTON BROOKS: You take y'potatoes for seed, an' you got to fix you a good bed, an' keep it where it won't rain in it—keep it covered—and use good, rich soil. Plant your seed potatoes, lay'em in there whole, bury em side by side till you get your bed full. When they come up, you just slip one [sprout] off, an' another'll just come on. Tater'll just be covered up with slips. Y'start your bed in th'spring, an' you have t'keep it warm. You plant your slips along in June. We always just grew them in a corner of th'corn patch close to th'house. You want clay land, not rich soil. Them roots have to have hard soil t'push to or they won't make. They'll get real long an' not be any bigger than my thumb. You harvest them long about frost. Sometimes a frost'll hit'em, an' you cut your vines off. If it rains on'em after a frost, they claim th'frost goes in'em, an' causes th'taters t'rot. We plowed'em up—they're hard t'dig up without you cuttin' a lot of'em diggin'em.

ESCO PITTS: My father always, when he dug his sweet potatoes, let 'em dry in th'sunshine. Then he'd bring'em in th'kitchen an' put'em back of th'stove. He'd sort out all th'small, long, stringy potatoes that weren't big enough to try t'eat, [and he'd save them for seed]. He stored th'sweet potatoes over the winter in the smokehouse. Early in the spring of th'year, he'd take those little ones and make him a cold frame with a cover to start his plants.

Tomatoes

HARRY BROWN: To make seed beds for our tomatoes, we'd burn [organic] trash in a pile. Then just took a shovel and hoe, and just turned it all up, and mixed it all in the ground. Then we'd sow the seeds, and when they got up several inches, we'd set'em out in rows.

EDNIE BUCHANAN: I sow the seeds in April and sometimes I sow them the first of March, but you can't set them out without keeping them covered until the middle of May.

LAWTON BROOKS: People didn't always stake up their t'maters, but they do just so much better than when they just crawl over th'ground. Now, t'maters is a thing that does best in the new ground—even if you put lots of manure or fertilize to [the old] ground, there's still somethin' about th'new ground—they do best in it. The dirt needn't be too rich, but it can't be poor neither. And, sun—t'maters need sun or they'll grow taller and taller lookin' for light, and not make many t'maters.

ESCO PITTS: I never saw a tomato till I was ten or twelve years old. My daddy wouldn't hardly go to the table if there was a tomato on there. He said they wasn't a hog would eat'em and he wasn't going to eat'em. Tomato was something we never saw in our young days.

Peppers

ESCO PITTS: Mother used to grow a lot of hot pepper—we didn't have any bell pepper in those days—none of these big sweet peppers. She sowed th'seeds right in th'garden usually, but sometimes she'd plant'em in a box an' set'em in th'kitchen, an' they'd get up an' then she'd transplant'em. Y'got t'wait till frost is over t'plant or set'em out—latter part of April. It takes quite a while. They don't start making peppers till July or August. She used pepper in her sausage; rubbed pepper on th'cured meat t'keep th'flies away. She used it in her relishes, too.

FLORENCE BROOKS: [The peppers were] just like they have now—all but th'banana pepper. We had bell pepper and hot pepper. We planted them early, about April, I guess. Planted th'seeds right in th'row—didn't ever thin'em out because pepper'll make pretty thick.

Okra

ESCO PITTS: We planted okra just as quick as warm weather gets here after th'last frost. It can't stand cold weather. Mother sowed'em in th'row; then thinned them if they was too thick. She had th'green kind of okra.

FLORENCE BROOKS: You don't put any in till after frost—I guess May. We always put th'seeds in a cup of warm water one night, let'em sprout, an' take'em out an' plant'em th'next day. We always made sure we put chicken manure around—chicken manure will really make okra. Th'okra was just like th'one we have now, an' we used t'have a white okra —it's just so pretty and smooth, an' it was good too. Okra takes a while before it starts bearin', but once it *starts* bearin', it just keeps growin' taller, and *keeps* bearin' till frost. It's best t'pick it ever'day, when th'pods are around four inches long. It gets tougher the longer it grows.

Squash

ESCO PITTS: I don't remember seeing these yellow crookneck squash when I was a boy. [My mother] planted hubbard and butternut squash, [the kind that can be stored over the winter]. My daddy had a smokehouse where he put his meat, and that's where he stored the squash. He'd pile them in there and cover them with shucks or sacks to keep them from freezing. Squash likes any good garden soil and pretty much sun. It's not a hard thing to grow. We'd just plant them in hills, several feet apart, and give them room to crawl.

HARRY BROWN: Old people always—any vine, th'tenth day of May they called Vine Day—that's when they always planted them—squash, Kershaws, and hubbard. Kershaws are pulp-filled an' grow great long, an' they're white, have a neck to'em kind of like crookneck squash, only great big. They were really good t'fry like sweet potatoes, or slice up an' put butter an' sugar on'em, an' put'em in th'stove an' bake'em.

Cucumbers

ETHEL CORN: You put cucumbers out just as quick as th'danger of frost gets over—frost kills'em—along in May, unless you just put out a few that you can cover from the frost. Plant'em in hills an' give'em plenty of room to crawl.

EDNIE BUCHANAN: We usually plant cucumbers around the tenth of May, Vine Day. I just plant them in hills, several seeds to a hill, and they just run out on a vine on the ground, and the cucumbers come on the vine. Like most everything else, they like a good soil.

Melons

LON DOVER: We'd plant watermelon an' mushmelon—y'always planted them th'tenth day of May—Vine Day. I've known that as far back as I can remember. Poppy always'd step off about a half a acre that we'd put in watermelons.

EDNIE BUCHANAN: We used to grow whole patches of melons, but we didn't have a certain time to plant them, just early enough in the late spring or early summer so they'd have enough time to grow. We'd have watermelon and cantalopes, and the whole family would come over to eat watermelons. We never did sell them, but I think we sold a few cantalopes. My husband just loved to raise'em, I don't know why.

MARINDA BROWN: We grew watermelon and mushmelon, which they call cantalope, now. We grew them in the field, in good bottom land, because they like a more sandy soil, not in the garden. We'd plant them in hills, and work'em until [the vines] started to run out, then we couldn't weed'em any more.

Pumpkins

ESCO PITTS: We had pumpkins all in th'cornfield. We'd plant it by hand, and plant a pumpkin hill here, another one there, another one yonder.

FLORENCE BROOKS: We'd put'em in th'corn planter an' plant it with th'corn. An' just let them drop out whenever they wanted to. An' boy, did we have pumpkins! Never did plant'em till 'bout th'time blackberries go t'bloomin'—that's th'best time. We had a old mule that got scared of a pumpkin vine one time, an' tore down 'bout half a field of corn! We raised some great big'uns, an' we ate'em in pies, and cooked and fried in grease.

MARINDA BROWN: Pumpkins like a good rich soil, and they seem to grow best in cornfields, possibly because of the shade the corn gives them. I've planted them just out by themselves, and they don't seem to do as well. My parents used to grow the big field pumpkins—we'd store them in the shuck pen, buried under the shucks to keep them from freezing. We'd also peel, slice, and dry some of them. Those we didn't eat, we'd feed to the cattle and hogs.

Beans

FAYE LONG: We like to plant our first beans on Good Friday, which is just before Easter. Some of the time they'll get frostbit, and part of the time not. I can keep going with fresh beans all summer, as long as I keep planting them two weeks apart, until I don't think there'll be enough time for them to mature by the first frost in the fall.

FLORENCE BROOKS: There's altogether a difference—people ain't got none of th'old-fashioned bean seed they used t'have. The beans ain't near as good as they used t'be. We had what we called greasy-black beans—I've not seen any of'em in years—little white beans in a white pole bean. Th'greasy-black bean, you can either eat the green bean or a dried bean. For a dried bean, after they get dry on th'vine, y'pick'em an' put'em in a sack an' beat'em out with a stick. The beans fall out of th'pod.

We planted green beans and cornfield beans. We always planted th'cornfield full of them, so we'd have beans that'd dry up an' we'd have our own soup beans. When they got dried up, we picked'em an' shelled'em out. They're th'same as green beans, only we let'em dry.

HARRY BROWN: We didn't have any half-runners back in those days; we had cornfield beans. We'd pick'em after they got large enough. We'd take'em and break'em like we were going to cook them, and set down with a big needle and string'em on a thread—[called them] leather britches. People didn't can so much like they do now.

PLATE 209   Everyone helps when beans come in.

ESCO PITTS: When I was a boy we didn't have bunch beans—they's all cornfield beans or running beans. Around the edge of the garden my mother planted her butterbeans and what we called October beans, those big old red striped beans. And they'd run up those garden palings, and they'd be nothin' to bother'em and they'd make all kinds of beans. And out in the cornfield we'd plant field beans and they'd run up on the corn and they'd just be bushels and bushels of beans out there. We ate [the cornfield beans] green as long as the season was open, and what we didn't pick before the frost, we let dry on the vine.

Fall garden

It was a common practice to take advantage of the cooler weather in late summer and fall to grow more cool-weather vegetables. People planted the same kinds of things they planted in the early spring, but not as big a variety. Collards are included only in this section because they really don't taste good until they've been hit by frost, but everything else mentioned here was also grown in the spring.

ESCO PITTS: For a fall crop, we planted turnips in September and cabbage. Sometimes we'd put out late-multiplying onions in the fall [around September] and have onions all winter. We buried th'turnips along with th'cabbage t'keep'em through th'winter. Usually, my mother planted [collards] in th'fall of th'year. Latter part of July, first of August, she'd sow a collard bed an' when they come up good size t'transplant, she'd have a row in th'garden. Collards are not much good till th'frost bites'em—makes'em better t'eat.

FLORENCE BROOKS: They planted mustard an' turnip greens; that's about all except for late cabbage which they planted before August. They'd dig a hole an' store those cabbage. Didn't plant late potatoes—they wouldn't make.

Collards you grow like y'grow late cabbage. They taste th'best if it frosts on'em before you pick'em—they just have a sweeter taste that way. If you grow'em like early cabbage, they don't taste right. You can sow your seeds [in July] in your rows, or in a bed an' then transplant'em into rows. Come the first frosts in October, you can start pickin' the leaves and cookin' 'em. Y'don't pull the whole plant up at one time, just keep pickin' the leaves, and they like cooler weather, so for a time they'll just keep growin' more leaves.

HARRY BROWN: My father would take the collards after they got so high, and push them over, and put a piece of pine bark and then dirt over them. That'd protect the collards and keep them through the winter.

Other farm crops

In addition to the garden vegetables mentioned, people grew other things, either for themselves, or for their livestock. These crops occupy a separate section because they are not garden vegetables per se, but were very important to the overall functioning of the farm as a nearly self-contained unit.

Perennials, herbs, and spices

It was common for a corner or edge of the vegetable garden to be set aside for perennials. The herbs and spices (many of which are perennials) were often dug from fallow or wooded areas and transplanted into the garden so they'd be close at hand. Plants such as Jerusalem artichokes and rhubarb were commonly grown (as vegetables) with the herbs and spices. The Jerusalem artichokes form edible tubers under the ground, and if a few are left each year, they will sprout and grow up again in the spring. Rhubarb grows back each year from the same stock. (We have not included another well-known perennial, asparagus, here, because no one we spoke to used to grow it.)

MARINDA BROWN: My mother had her herbs and spices set aside on one edge of the garden. She grew horseradish for putting in pickles, sage for seasoning sausage, garlic for flavoring different things, dill for dill pickles, and peppermint for flavoring tea. None of these things took much pampering—all but the dill would come back from the same roots, and that would self-sow, and they didn't take a really rich soil. Of course, you had to weed them and keep them from spreading too far, especially the garlic.

She also grew rhubarb and Jerusalem artichokes along the edge of the garden. The rhubarb she got when a neighbor divided hers. They like a rich, well-drained soil, and [the roots] need to be divided every couple of years. The Jerusalem artichokes grew in rich soil, too. We liked to eat them raw.

FLORENCE BROOKS: Oh, we had [Jerusalem] artichokes. I don't know when they planted'em; they was just there when I was. They kept coming back, an' we'd just dig'em an' *eat,* Lord mercy! They were planted outside of th'fence—it was good rich soil right below th'garden.

Ever'body had rhubarb. We always set it out by th'garden fence an' let it go. Didn't dig it up, just let it grow, year after year. It gets in big bunches. Set'em inside th'garden.

ESCO PITTS: My mother had all kinds of [herbs]—rhubarb, rue, comfrey, Jerusalem oak, mallards, sage, parsley, and catnip. She had in one corner of her garden all her medicinal plants, and that corner never was plowed up—she was very careful of that. They'd just come up ever'spring. The rue she made tea of, and I ain't seen a stock of rue in many a day. She used Jerusalem oak to make candy out of for worm medicine. And th'mallard leaf was to put on a burn—wilt it in front of th'fire an' slap it on a burn an' it would draw th'fire out. The comfrey she used for poultices for sores.

ADA KELLY: My mother [had a corner of the garden] where she grew dill and sage, catnip, ground ivy—the babies had to have that for tea. And she grew tansy and peppermint. Most of them came back year after year, but a few, like dill, she had to plant from seed.

Fruit

Many people cultivated fruit in the mountains years ago, with apples, peaches, and grapes being the most common. But it appears to us that people relied very heavily on the wild fruit which grew in abundance. Some examples are blackberries, strawberries, huckleberries, persimmons, cherries, mulberries, mayapples, and elderberries.

KENNY RUNION: People grew apples, peaches, grapes, plums, and pears. And they were delicious. At that time there was no such thing as sprayin'. The people in my young life pruned their trees and grape vines in

February, and that was all that was done. And it was delicious fruit. You don't get fruit now'days that tastes like that fruit. Now some people had a cellar t'put stuff in, but most people just dug holes in th'ground.

MARINDA BROWN: While I was growing up on Middle Creek, my father had all kinds of fruit, and there was no problem with bugs. There were several apple trees all around the house and barnyard. He always fertilized them with stable manure every year. The kinds I can remember that he grew were Shockley, Ben Davis, and Limbertwig. I guess he pruned them, but I really can't remember.

He also set out some cherry trees around, but as far as I can recall he never pampered them. They just bore every year. There were also some currant and some gooseberry bushes that were on the place when Dad bought it. He never did anything with them, either. They just bore fruit.

There was a man who used some of our land to start seedlings [to sell] on—all kinds of fruit trees. Many of those seeds were carried around by the birds, I guess, and we also had self-sowed plum and peach trees all around from that. And no one ever took care of them—all we did was pick the fruit.

ADA KELLY: We had a nice apple orchard and a peach orchard. We called'em Indian peaches, and they were small and about as red as a pickled beet. And then we had a small peach we called an openstone, because the peach didn't cling to the seed. We had to take care of the orchard— mainly, we pruned and fertilized them during the cold months. We'd store the apples in a hole dug in the ground. First, we'd put in some hay or straw or dry leaves, and pour the apples in. Then, we covered it over with more hay or leaves, then heavy soil. They kept all winter.

LON DOVER: We grew grapes and had wild grapes, too. Grapes don't take a whole lot of work, and they'll grow in a lot o'different places. We always gave them a trellis t'grow on, and we'd prune them and put stable manure on them every fall or winter. Nothin' much used to bother'em, but the Japanese beetles [we have now] are bad to eat the leaves. I've heard old folks say about pruning, that if you saw an apple tree limb off on the new moon it's guaranteed t'heal—just grows over like skin grows back. If y'saw a limb off on th'old moon, th'wood'll generally rot. So, if I have *any* prunin' to do, I'll do it on th'new moon if I can.

Cane

LON DOVER: Many people grew cane. Y'sow your cane and when it grows up, it's like corn. When th'seed turns brown, it's ripe. Some people cut their cane green an' make syrup from green cane. If it's not good an' sweet, it'll have a kind of bitter whang. But you let the seeds get good an' ripe on your cane, cut it down, strip th'fodder off it and bring it to a cane mill t'make syrup. That's what old people baked their sweet bread out of. Th'people who grew it sold it t'people who didn't have it. They wasn't too many people had mills. They'd take it t'other people's mills an' make it. Sorghum makes an awful black syrup. We thought it was good then. Black soil like we had won't make clear syrup—you have t'have a red clay t'make clear syrup.

BURNETT BROOKS: There's not a whole lot to growing cane. The work starts when it ripens. You just plant it and forget about it for sixty to sixty-five days. You don't even put much fertilizer on it. It's really an easy crop grown. You can plow and hoe it about twice. You don't have to spray it [for bugs]. Then you take it up about this time of year [the middle of October]. This [year's crop] wasn't planted until July fourth because of the weather, but usually we try to get it in around the beginning of June.

LAWTON BROOKS: Cane is something that takes a soil that's not too rich—a good clay soil's the best. Sow it in rows so it can be worked a time or two during the summer—it's best to sow it in early June. It won't take too much wet weather, 'cause it's bad to blow over during bad weather, and that ruins it.

You've got t'try t'get it stripped, cut down, and made into syrup when it's ripe; if y'wait too long it could come a frost on it in the field and that ruins the taste of the syrup. If y'think it's gonna soon come a frost, and it's still in the field, y'can strip it, cut it down, and stack and cover it for a few days, and the frost won't hurt it that way, but y'can't leave it stacked too long because it won't make as good syrup.

HARRIET ECHOLS: My father grew cane. All those mountain folk made their own syrup. You plant it in the spring. Syrup was cheap and it

PLATE 210 The cane tops Myrtle McMahon is holding are fully ripe.

was hard work. We couldn't sell it. I used to sell it for twenty-five cents a gallon. My father just made hundreds and hundreds of gallons. He cooked syrup for all the neighbors. He had his own equipment, his own furnace and cooking vat and everything. Everybody couldn't own a vat to cook syrup 'cause it was too expensive. One person in the neighborhood like would start the operation. They paid'em so much, I don't remember the prices now, but we always had a big cane patch. I had to hoe it, and that was a job. Plum up until after I married, we had cane.

Tobacco

HARRIET ECHOLS: You get the seed and prepare your bed. First you put your fertilize or barnyard litter in it. Frame it in with planks and put a screen over it. Dig the dirt up and make it soft. Then, in the early spring, sow the seed, just pat them in. They are little seeds and you don't want them very deep. When they come up then you put a screen over them; or wire; then a plastic cover. You plant them on the east side so the morning sun will hit them. You let your plants get up six to eight inches high, at least six. Maybe eight. The bigger the better.

Then you set them out in your tobacco patch. You have to work the soil carefully to keep the weeds down. Plow it, but you can't plow close to the plants; you have to go around and be careful not to bruise them. When it starts to ripen, it goes to seed; it has a bloom and a seed on top. Then you top it. They have little suckers on them, little plants that come out on the stalk at the leaves. You have to pinch those little suckers off to make good tobacco, and all that strength goes to the leaves. Then when it ripens enough all the leaves go together.

They cured the tobacco back then. They didn't have curing houses just for a small farm. They would just hang it in the barn.

ESCO PITTS: My grandfather grew tobacco for his own use, a patch about as big as this room [12′×14′]. When those leaves began to turn— now that was his job, we couldn't do that—he'd go through the field when those bottom leaves began to turn and very carefully pick one off at a time and put them in a basket. He'd go over his little patch two to three times a week. He'd take those big tobacco leaves, tie a bunch together, take'em and hang'em up in the barn till they got good and dry. He'd put'em where we couldn't get to it. It was hard to grow; seems like every three to four days checking those leaves, looking for worms. I always wanted to work with him in his tobacco, but no, that was apart.

When he got ready to twist his tobacco, he would make a sweetened water with homemade syrup and he'd put a big wagon sheet down, put his nice leaves down on that sheet, and take that sweetened water and sprinkle

PLATE 211 When the tobacco is cut, the curing process is begun by tying it in bundles and hanging it in the field.

PLATE 212 Tobacco curing in the sun on Conway and Park Hughes's farm.

it on the tobacco. When it got pretty damp, why, he'd twist it. He'd keep on until he got it done. Some parts he'd have for chewin', and some for smokin'. I'm pretty sure he saved his seed. Some people had big old tobacco patches. They didn't sell it. They made their tobacco and they divided it with people who didn't have any.

Hay

LAWTON BROOKS: Lots of people grew hay. They could sow it along in August in their corn. After I laid by my corn, I'd go in th'corn an' sow it. Then when y'gather your corn, you go back in there, cut th'stalks, rake them off, an' you'll have you a clear meadow. An' then when your hay gets up big enough t'cut, you cut it sometime in th'spring. They'd get an old mule mowing machine [pulled with mules or horses]. Then they had an old rake driven with horses, an' it'd rake up an' when it got full, you'd trip it an' it'd dump th'hay. Then after it cured, y'had t'stack it. Didn't have no balers then.

You could get three cuttings out of a meadow. You won't get too much th'third time. It keeps comin' up by itself each time. Then you could plow it under and put it in something else, like corn.

HARRIET ECHOLS: Hay is a crop raised in most every area now. All the work is done with tractors and big machinery today, but used to be, it was all done by hand. Lot of times people would plant grass on worn out

PLATE 213   Belle Dryman and her son Foy put up these haystacks. Her cows have nibbled away some of the hay from the bottom portions.

cornfields, where the land wasn't good enough to grow other crops any-more.

When the hay got up tall enough and there was a good stretch of dry weather, people'd go out with their scythe and cut it. Now some folks had horse-drawn moving machines, but we didn't. How long it takes to cure depends on the temperature, how long the sun is out, and the humidity. They'd turn it a time or two with rakes while it was curing, till it was ready. Then they'd rake it up and haul it in the wagon where they were going to put their stacks. We didn't know what a *bale* of hay was. I didn't see one until I was full grown, 'cause they didn't have the machinery to work with like they do now.

BELLE DRYMAN: We stack our hay yet. [My son] Foy bales some, but we don't have enough cover for it all. We put up a tall pole t'stack the hay around it, then lay some brush on the ground [around the pole] so it doesn't set on th'ground. Then we just go to stackin' it around the pole. Y'have t'try t'make the top of the stack bigger than th'bottom, and you have t'lay th'hay on the top so the water'll run off. It'll keep right on— just a little on the outside'll get moldy.

Rye, wheat, and oats

ESCO PITTS: You can plant wheat in December, and harvest it late next spring. Back then people had t'harvest it with a cradle, an' th'same thing with rye and oats. I've followed my father many a time and banded it, picked it up and tied it in bundles, an' put eight bundles to th'shock. Let that cure, an' th'thrashing machine'd come around after a while an' thrash it. You grow all three 'bout th'same way, except y'sow your rye when you lay by your corn in June. We never grew many oats, but I think we sowed them in th'spring. They'd just cut th'oats in th'green stage, and feed it whole to th'animals—grain and hay and all.

LAWTON BROOKS: You can sow rye in August in your corn—it likes cooler weather. I'uz always proud t'see th'old thrasher come in there— pulled by oxen—after we cut it with a old-time cradle. M'daddy'd cradle it an' me an' m'brother'd tie it in pretty good-sized bundles. Then we'd go back an' shock it—several bundles in a shock an' two bundles spread out on th'top for a kind of roof. Stayed dry till we got ready t'stack it in th'field. We'd stack it when th'old iron thrasher could be brought in by th'oxen. When they got done thrashin' at my house, he'd go to yours. We had to haul wood for the thrasher—it had a old steam boiler. We'd stack the straw t'use for bed ticks. Ever'year we got new straw for our bed ticks.

We grew our wheat and oats. At harvest time, you cut your wheat and had a thrasher thrash that wheat out, sack it up, take it to the mill and get your flour. The oats was for the animals.

HARRY BROWN: Well, th'way we thrashed th'rye, we laid a bunch of poles over a hole in th'ground, and laid a wagon sheet in th'hole. We laid th'rye on top of th'poles [over the hole] an' beat it with a pole. You get as much as you would out of a thrashing machine, just took longer. Th'rye falls down into th'wagon sheet—then you take that wagon sheet out, and put it in sacks. Then y'had a lot of chaff in it. Well, on a windy day, you get out and pick up a handful of rye an' pour it over into another sack, and th'wind blows th'chaff out of it.

HARRIET ECHOLS: Rye, wheat, and oats, it's all planted the same way. Except rye, they'd plant it earlier in August or September. The rye will make without being plowed. Wheat and oats, they had to prepare the ground. It's the same way they did hay. They didn't have to sow the ground as thick as they did hay, because it spreads as it comes up. They planted wheat and oats about the same time. If they had winter oats, they'd plant

PLATE 214   Louin Cabe shows us how a grain cradle is used.

them in the fall, the spring oats in February or March. The winter oats will stand the hard freezes, but the spring oats they had to put in when the hard freezes were over.

They had to prepare the ground the same way, put in the fertilizer or the barnyard litter, whatever they had. Broadcast it over the land, then plowed it under, then sowed their grain. A lot of people used to sow it in rows. They had this machinery to sow it. One little grain will come up and make dozens of stalks. Then they had to harvest it. They'd cut it with grain cradles, and put it in bundles and shock it. It was hard labor all together. They called it cradling the grain. The grain cradle was as sharp as a razor blade —it had to be to cut the grain. When the shock cured, they'd haul it to the barn where the thrasher could go, and thrash it out. It took four or five to operate the thrasher.

Pests

Interestingly enough, all the people we talked to said the insect problem used to be very small. Some felt it had to do with the fact that people often burned off their gardens and fields before planting, and that the mountains were burned over every year. We were assured that there would have been little need for chemical insecticides even if they had already been developed. It must have been quite a blow to people who had for years grown healthy, relatively bug-free vegetables and crops, to witness the ever-growing insect population and watch them lower their gardens' productivity.

Animals, however, both wild and domestic, presented a greater problem to people's gardens years ago. For this reason almost everyone fenced their vegetable gardens, and while cattle, etc., were still on open range, most people fenced their fields. Following we present a general quote from Anna Howard about pests; after that we'll give suggestions on dealing with individual pests, and finally, we'll present a small piece on fencing.

ANNA HOWARD: [There are so many insects now] 'cause they ain't no cattle nor hogs nor nothin' in th'woods is my idea. An' people don't burn like they used to—burn off fields and big brush piles, kill all them insects.

I remember we had rats. They'd get in th'garden once in a while and eat a little in the garden. We didn't do anything about them. Now crows would eat up your corn crop if you didn't keep them scared out. We'd make scarecrows and put around the edge of th'field—that'd scare'em out. Sometimes they would get so bad, people would get out in th'edge of th'woods and shoot at'em.

Now we had rabbits. They was worse than anything else. We kids would have a couple of rabbit boxes set out in the edge of th'field, and every morning or two, we'd bring in a couple a'rabbits and Mama'd cook'em. Th'rabbits could get through a fence like that, but they had s'much stuff t'eat back then, they didn't bother gardens like they do now. We had moles, an' used to, one of us'd sit around through th'day with a hoe t'kill it, but then we got a mole trap. Th'ground squirrels got in a lot and we'd shoot [them] an' eat'em. See, we kept dogs, and that was our pastime.

Well, now, 'coons, they'd eat corn in th'field after it got hard an' dried up. But th'rabbits, they'd eat stuff some, but you could put up scare-boogers an' keep'em out, an' nearly everybody kept dogs to keep'em run out of their garden. People'ud make scare-boogers t'look like a man an' put a hat an' clothes on'em.

Ants:

- plow the garden up good
- sprinkle fireplace ashes, soot, or snuff over the anthills
- pour hot water over the anthills
- pour gasoline over them and light it
- place cucumber peelings in the garden; the ants will avoid them

Bean Beetles:

- plant marigolds in the beans
- pick them off and put them in kerosene oil

Cabbage Worms:

- pour warm water that's had a red pepper soaked in it over the cabbage
- dust with soot or ashes from the fireplace
- sprinkle dry dirt on the cabbage
- pinch off a leaf from the bottom of the plant, lay it on top of the cabbage—in the morning it will be covered with worms

Cut Worms:

- dig down to them and kill them

Flea Beetles:

- dust them with soot or ashes from the fireplace

Potato Bugs:

- sprinkle plants with sulfur or ashes
- boil tobacco stems in water and sprinkle over the bugs
- plant petunias in the patch

Tobacco Worms:

- dust with ashes or soot
- pick them off and kill them

Blackbirds:

- shoot them
- use a scarecrow
- keep a cat in the garden
- run out to the garden and make a lot of noise

Crows:

- put up a scarecrow
- shoot them
- hang tin foil or aluminum pie pans in nearby trees and on the plants; they'll rattle in the wind and reflect the sun intermittently and scare them off
- shoot one crow and hang it up in the garden—it will keep others away
- put an old hat high on a pole
- hang a white sheet up in the garden—it will flap in the wind and scare them

Deer:

- watch for them to enter the field or garden and shoot them
- put up a *tall* fence around the garden

Groundhogs:

- keep a good groundhog dog
- stick a sock soaked in gasoline in his hole
- fill his hole with tin cans
- set a trap in front of his hole
- sit around the garden in a concealed spot and shoot him

PLATE 215 Jake Waldroop demonstrates one way of keeping pesky animals out of his garden.

Moles:

- watch for them from 10:00 A.M. to 11:00 A.M., and dig them out and kill them
- put kitchen matches in the mole run—they will eat the heads and the sulfur will poison them
- set a mole trap in the run
- put mothballs in the run
- stick rose stems in the sides of the runs—they'll scratch themselves on the thorns and bleed to death
- teach your dogs and cats to kill them
- soak corn in lye or arsenic and put some in the run, and poison them
- put very salty cornmeal dough or biscuit dough in the run—if they eat it, it'll kill them
- plant mole plants (also called castor beans) around your garden
- put small windmills in the garden—the vibrations will drive the moles off
- whenever you kill a mole, put him in another mole run and his body will scare off other moles
- get a long metal pipe, fill one end with strong tobacco, light it, and force the smoke into the run by blowing on the other end of the pipe
- sprinkle salt in the runs

PLATE 216 Esco Pitts has used this mole trap for years and years. He told us it has killed numerous moles.

Owls:

- set a steel trap baited with a piece of chicken on top of a pole

Rabbits:

- get a good rabbit dog
- sit around out of sight and shoot one when you see it and then make rabbit stew
- set up stakes around the garden and run a string about six inches off the ground around the garden—they won't cross the string
- set out rabbit boxes (traps)
- sow lettuce in your squash—it'll put the rabbits to sleep
- put up a fence
- plant marigolds in your beans, or petunias in your potatoes—the smell will keep them away
- set an old shoe out in the row
- feed them all they can eat, and they won't eat up your garden
- set glass jars around in your garden roughly twenty feet apart. The sound of the wind blowing over their tops will scare them away.
- fill a gallon jug with water, add one tablespoon of kerosene, and sprinkle it on and around the plants the rabbits will eat; the smell will keep them away for several days
- take a piece of paper like the Atlanta *Constitution*, two or three folds of it (it has to be this big because it won't rattle if you don't) and fold the paper down over the stake at the top. Tie a string big enough to fit around the stake so the paper won't blow off. It looks just like somebody's head and arms flapping. When the wind blows, the paper rattles and flaps and scares them something awful.
- string some aluminum pans on wire. Be sure you string them over whatever the animal is eating. You can tie the wire to two stakes, trees, or anything that's near around. Don't put on too many—just enough so when the wind blows, they'll rattle. And they shine in the dark, so that helps.

Raccoons:

- keep a good 'coon dog and hunt raccoons regular during gardening season
- set a trap for them

Rats:

- set mothballs around where you last saw them
- set a rat trap in a mole run, as rats often use mole runs
- teach your cats to hunt and kill them

Squirrels:

- get a squirrel dog
- shoot and eat them
- poison corn with lye or arsenic

The following people contributed information on how to deal with garden pests:
Joe Arrowood, Ednie Buchanan, Mrs. Cecil Cannon, Carl Carpenter, Leana T. Carver, Doc Chastain, Mrs. Norman Coleman, Imogene Dailey, Fred Darnell, Mimmie Dickerson, Barnard Dillard, Bobbie Dills, Harriet Echols, Tom Grist, Lonnie Harkins, Mrs. Earl Holt, Mrs. L. D. Hopper, Mrs. Ray Kelly, Ted Lanich, Aunt Faye Long, Pearl Martin, Jim McCoy, Ulysses McCoy, Belzora Moore, Mrs. George Nix, Mrs. J. D. Quinn, Kenny Runion, Will Seagle, Vina Speed, B. J. Stiles, Lake Stiles, Mrs. Oren Swanson, Gladys Swanson, Gladys Teague, Cal Thomas, Nell Thomas, Mrs. Birdie Mae Vinson, Ralph Vinson, T. F. Vinson, Pearl Watts, Grover Webb, Naomi Whitmire, Mrs. Ben Williams, Mrs. Grace Williams, Lee Williams, Will Zoellner.

Fences

Most people put up a paling fence around their vegetable gardens. A paling fence is sort of a rough picket fence made of hand-split boards, pointed on top so the chickens wouldn't fly up on it and then into the garden. Many people fenced in their farm crops, too, but there they used split rails put together in a zigzag pattern for that. These fences kept out larger domestic and wild animals which would eat the vegetables and/or farm crops.

ESCO PITTS: You had to enclose your garden so my daddy split chestnut palings in those days. Chestnut trees was mostly what he built his house out of. Chestnut trees would be sixty feet to the first limb and long straight trees. And they would split awful easy and he would just split palings about six to eight feet long. They're thin slats about three quarters of an inch thick, about four to six inches wide, and as long as you want to make them. Then he put his locust posts in every eight feet and made his railings one at the bottom and one at the top to nail his palings to. The palings went up and down; they were sharp on the ends.

PLATE 217   This old paling fence surrounds Aunt Arie Carpenter's vegetable garden.

PLATE 218   The rail fence in front of Thomas Stubbs's cabin is very much like the ones people used to put up around their fields.

R. M. DICKERSON: Ever'body had to fence their own fields. You had fence logs and you were supposed to take care of your own cow yourself. But back when I was out here, they had what y'called an open range and anybody could turn their cattle out, and if you had a cornfield; you had to keep it fenced up to keep the cattle out. But after we voted out the free range and voted in the fencin', ever'body that had cattle had to put them up and keep'em in their own pasture. After that we didn't have to fence our cornfields so much.

DIFFERENCES IN THE OLD AND NEW

Many people we spoke to felt that the vegetables they used to grow tasted better than those they grow today. The differences were attributed to the facts that they used to grow non-hybrids, whereas today most seeds are hybrids; that they used to grow vegetables totally organically, but don't now; and that age may have hindered their sense of taste.

ANNA HOWARD: I think the fertilizers make a difference. I think that makes th'difference in the taste of the plants we eat. You take people that use stable manure for their garden; I think that makes a difference in the flavor of the food—it grows off better. Now I garden with store-bought fertilizer, and I don't like it either. I can't get a good pretty garden like I want to. I think about back when I was a kid and my father used t'have those pretty gardens. And now I can't get one like that, and I'm sure it's that stable manure. It's really good for a garden.

ADA KELLY: I really believe that some of them had a richer flavor. They were grown just from the soil with no additions at all, and it just seems that they had a better flavor.

LAWTON BROOKS: They have a lot of difference—in th'beans an' in th'tomatoes and things like that. Th'beans taste altogether different from th'kind they used to grow then.

HARRIET ECHOLS: There is a difference in the taste of vegetables now and then. I don't know whether it's that we people have grown older and our taste buds are getting away from us, dimming, like our eyes, but it doesn't seem like the vegetables here taste as good now as they used to. You know, I used to love fruits and I ate them all the time. I still do, but I have to force myself. I don't care for them like I used to, I don't know why.

BIRD TRAPS, DEADFALLS,
AND RABBIT BOXES

BIRD TRAPS

Lawton Brooks, one of our most informative contacts (*Foxfire 3*, pages 221–44, for example), amazed us again by showing us how to do something that we hadn't seen before. Lawton, who stops by our office occasionally, revealed on one particular afternoon that he could make a bird trap—a trap that not only caught other small game as well as birds, but one that also left the animal alive. Since we were interested in other methods and devices that snared animals such as rabbit boxes and deadfalls, we asked Lawton to show two of the students who work with us, Robbie Moore and David Hopkins, how he made one. As Lawton made it, he told us a little bit about them, as well as a funny story about his brother:

"Back when I first learned to make bird traps, my brother Neil and I would use our father's boards. He always kept a stack of boards around for patching the roof with—everything was covered with old-time boards. Well, we'd slip those boards and split'em up and make the trap out of them. We didn't have no nails. We knew that if we got his nails, he'd raise cain. You *could* use nails, though. But we had to learn to do it the way we had to do it. We didn't have no nails to nail'em together with, so we put a bow on'em to hold'em together.

"We used to catch a lot of quails, or any kind of little bird that would come and get in it. 'Course you take an ol' hog or something big, they'd tear it up pretty easily, but just common game won't. I've caught rabbits in it before. You can bait it with corn or anything. You just make the trigger and put a nubbin of corn, a piece of bread, or anything you want to put on it, and the animal or bird will come."

As Lawton showed us how to make the trap, he told us a little about his childhood. There were six children, four boys and two girls. His oldest brother was Ernest, then after him was Wayne, then came Neil, and Lawton was the youngest boy. Neil died as a result of the flu in the flu epidemic about the time of World War One. He was twenty-one, and was working as a brakeman on a train. "He took the flu, but got better and thought he had to go back to work. The doctor told him to stay in, but he went to work anyway. He took a backset and never got over it. He hadn't been married but a month or two when he died."

As he talked about his brother Neil, Lawton remembered something the two of them had done when they were younger.

"Neil was about the size of this one here [Robbie, age sixteen] when he jumped out of the barn loft. He thought he was going to make him a kite and fly, and he liked to have got killed.

"We had big doors at either end of the hayloft up in the barn. We'd push the hay out into the cow lot from there. We didn't have much hay up there at the time. My daddy and mother had gone to town and left Neil and me alone. They'd always tell Neil to take care of me. My mother and daddy had one of these big ol' canvas umbrellas. You'd set in the buggy and it'd cover the whole buggy.

"So Neil got to studying about making a parachute. He said, 'Tell you what let's do. Let's take this umbrella, take a run to go, and jump out that lower door [of the barn]. Just as you jump, open it. And you'll float down to the ground easy.'

"He tried to get me to do it. Well, I started to. I ran to the door, but when I looked down, I stopped. I couldn't do it. And he commenced to hollerin', 'You're a chicken, you're a chicken. I'll show you how to do it.'

"So he just backed in there and he took a run to go, and when he opened the umbrella, it just went wrong side out. He hit the ground like a log. He didn't move for a long time, knocked the breath out of him. I thought he was gone, too. I looked down there. I went down the stair-steps and out in the lot and rolled him over three or four times before he ever got his breath. I was just sure that it had killed him. But he was all right. He was just sore. My daddy asked him, 'What's the matter with you, Neil?'

"And he said, 'Well, I'm just kind of sore like I been lifting or something.'

"And I was afraid to tell my father anything. I knowed that if I did, me and Neil would have a fight."

Interviews and photographs by Robbie Moore and David Hopkins.

PLATE 219   Lawton begins the trap by laying two boards ($24'' \times \frac{3}{4}'' \times 1\frac{1}{2}''$) parallel about 22" apart. He then lays two more boards across these to form a square.

PLATE 220 Lawton adds on boards alternately going straight up on two sides and sloping the other two sides until the trap is eight to ten boards high.

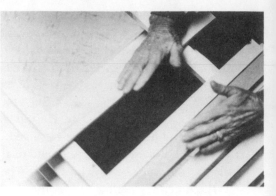

PLATE 221 He then "tops off" the trap with several more boards so the birds cannot fly out the top. Lawton says, "You can top off the trap anytime you want to. Make the spacing in the boards so the bird [or animal] can see and they ain't in the dark."

PLATE 222 The trap with all the boards in place.

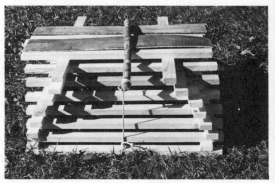

PLATE 223 Lawton does not use nails in making his traps, but holds them together with a bow—a green stick about 2′ long that he pulls taut over the top and ties with rope to the bottom board on either side.

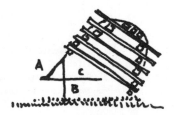

PLATE 224 Diagram shows scale of the sticks used to make the trigger. Stick "A" is 9″ long, "B" is 9½″, and "C" is 20″. The sticks are the same as those used for the deadfall trap (see PLATE 229).

PLATE 225 The trigger is made of small green sticks of hickory or other hardwood. Lawton carves out the notches while the wood is green and pliable, then lets it dry before putting any stress on it. The set trigger is baited on the right end of the horizontal section with bread or corn or other bait.

PLATE 226 The trigger assembly is made of three sticks. When set up, they make the numeral four. When set, they hold together only because of the weight of the trap pushing down on the vertical stick. It is so delicately set and balanced that the slightest movement by the animal or bird against the horizontal piece will collapse the trigger assembly and bring the trap down. The base of the vertical stick is not stuck into the ground, but sits on top of the ground so that it will fall over easily and not keep the trap from falling.

PLATE 227 The set trap. As the bird or animal nibbles at the bait, the trap falls, holding the victim unharmed inside the trap.

DEADFALLS

A deadfall trap works on exactly the same principle, and uses the same triggering device, as the bird trap Lawton Brooks showed us how to make. By definition, however, a deadfall kills the animal when the trigger is released.

Tedra Harmon explained that when he sets up a deadfall trap, he finds a large flat rock that is heavy enough to crush any animal unlucky enough to be under it when it falls. He then raises one end and sets the trigger. As with a bird trap, the bait is placed on the pointed end of the horizontal stick. In order to keep the bait on the stick more securely, Tedra pushes it past the pointed end, splits the end, and drives a wedge into the split to spread the end and anchor the bait in place. For rabbits and possums, he uses apples, beets, or cabbage for bait. For raccoons, he uses sardines. For minks, foxes, possums, or skunks, Tedra baits the trap with one third of a gray squirrel or a whole bird.

To insure that the animal enters the trap only from the front, wood, rocks, and brush are placed at both sides of the trap.

Article and photographs by Robbie Moore.

PLATE 228   Millard Buchanan and Wig construct a deadfall trap.

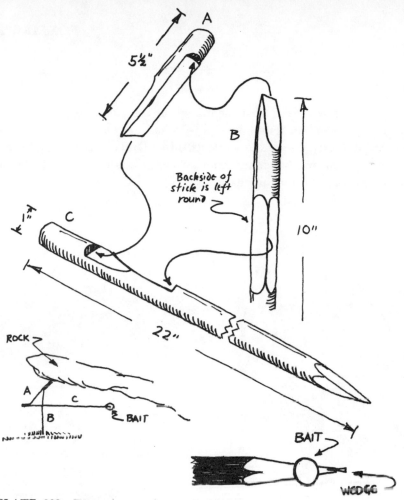

A

5½"

B

Backside of
stick is left
round

10"

C

1"

ROCK

A

C

B

BAIT

22"

BAIT

WEDGE

PLATE 229   Dimensions and
mechanism of the deadfall.

PLATE 230   The set trap.

RABBIT BOXES

Though rabbit boxes have been mentioned in the past [see *The Foxfire Book*, page 257], we never found anyone who had more complete information on them. Recently, two of our students, Mike Drake and Bob Sjostrom, found an old one at an abandoned home place in our county and photographed and measured it for this chapter.

PLATE 232 The bait is placed behind the notched triggering stick. When the rabbit pushes against this, it is released . . .

PLATE 231 The rabbit box—set and ready.

PLATE 233 . . . and the door slams shut.

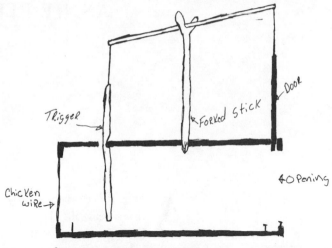

PLATE 234 Diagram illustrates the trap mechanism.

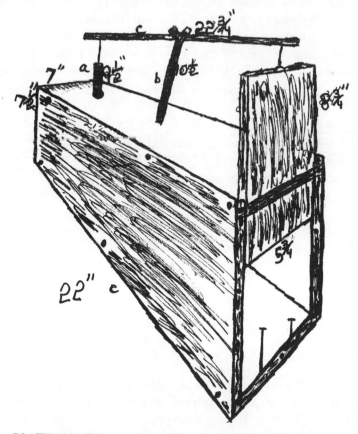

PLATE 235 Diagram shows dimensions of the rabbit box.

ANNIE PERRY

Annie Perry is a lively eighty-three-year-old lady who lives in a home that her ancestors built before the Civil War. The one thing that really amazed me about Annie when I first met her was her remarkable memory. She can remember things that I can't remember from one day to the next. For example, she can remember how to measure a room to see how many bushels of corn it will hold; she remembers how to figure out the interest on borrowed money; but I think the most important thing she remembers is that we are all in this world together and that we have to love and help each other.

Annie also has a great love for animals. The first time we met her, she had a newborn pig whose mother had died and she was feeding it on a bottle until it got big enough to eat.

She has the gift of making anybody feel at home with her. She told us that one thing she loves to do is talk, especially when there are people there to listen. Annie talks a lot about her hair and how it used to be so long and beautiful. She has told us many times that she thinks a person's hair is their beat feature, and she told us that she wished her hair was still long and thick.

But Annie doesn't have to worry about her hair or her outer appearance. I know that inside Annie is the most beautiful person I've ever known, and that means more to me than any outer beauty anywhere.

KAYE CARVER

Interviews by Kaye Carver, Maybelle Carpenter, Jan Brown, and Laurie Brunson.
Photos by Jan, Kaye, Maybelle, Roy Dickerson, and Beverly Justus.

I've lived here all my life, 'round and about. This house was started about July 1864, and in August it was finished with a top on it. My grandfather and his neighbors built it. It didn't have any chimney and Grandmother

PLATE 236 Annie Perry stringing and breaking beans in the shade of her back porch.

cooked outdoors under a brush arbor. In the fall, they sealed the cracks with boards, three-foot pieces split out of timber. The house was first covered with logs and built like a bird trap at the end. It was tapered up with logs for the gable and logs put across from the long ways of the house [poles running the length of the building acting as both rafters and lathing].

They put the chimney on that fall. It lasted about a hundred years. We tore it down about fifteen years ago because it looked like it was going to fall on us.

The first floor was a puncheon floor; it wasn't plank but made of split logs that were about two inches thick. Then they were smoothed off. There have been three extra floors [since then].

We had store-bought furniture. We had a little iron bedstead and its head and foot weren't no bigger than my little finger. Then we had one homemade bedstead that was a great big old thing. It had great big posts, big railings, and slats. It didn't have any cords—it wasn't a corded bedstead, never did have one of those. We had straw mattresses and cleaned them out every year. We'd burn the old and get some new. I'll tell you what, they lay just as good after you get them fixed and leveled up. They lay good with a big, heavy quilt over the top of that straw mattress, just as good a bed as anyone wants to lie on. Mother had a feather bed.

PLATE 237 Annie greeting two *Foxfire* editors from the front porch of her log home.

My mother, my aunt, and my uncle all grew up in this house. My mother and father lived here till I was born, and then they built them a house up on a hill from here, and we lived up there till my grandmother died in 1925, and then we moved back down here. We moved down here on account of the spring. Papa thought the spring was the greatest thing that ever has been. I've been here ever since.

I don't want no city life because I don't like it. I lived in a city in South Carolina for two months, and I didn't like it. I lived there long enough to know I don't like it, because I like neighbors, but they were just too close there.

When you live in the country, you can have a garden and you can go pick fresh vegetables when you want'em, and they don't cost you so much. God gives you the strength and if you use what He gave you, you might not make a bountiful crop, but you can make some. If you've lived long enough and nobody won't hire you and you're able to work, you can make you something to eat, and you can eat it.

I like to be close to people, but I don't like them to live in my door! I like to be where, if I take a notion to fuss, I can fuss.

Oh, I'd be like a bird in a cage. Catch a bird and put it in a cage—living in town—that'd be like a bird in a cage.

I think children have freedom [in the country] that they don't have in the city or a town. Now you can't turn a child loose in town; you can turn one loose in the country. I just know that a child in the country has freedom, but they don't have as many advantages. They do have advantages enough. They won't be near as mean. They can have their minds occupied with something else besides badness.

[Out in the country] you breathe more oxygen, and more pure oxygen. The oxygen that we gather from the air is more pure than it is when you're in a city or town. It's not been breathed.

They's some difference in people in the country and people in the city, but there's no real difference in people. People's people.

My father farmed around here near the creek. He'd gather up a load of apples. He'd have apples and cabbages and potatoes, and carried them to Anderson, South Carolina. He'd buy us shoes out of the money and pay his taxes.

One time I was with him, and something happened that wasn't funny. My feet caught afire. We had a tent and we had a spread on the ground. We built a fire in front of the tent and for some reason the quilts caught afire at my feet and I woke up. I said, "Daddy, get up from here. We're afire." That's my last time camping out. I don't want to camp out any more.

When I was a little girl, my parents didn't buy too much. Mama made our stockings and dresses and sweaters. We had to buy coffee, sugar, and salt. We never did buy any flavoring because if we wanted apple pie, we wanted apple pie, and if we wanted peach pie, we wanted peach pie. We didn't add extra flavorings. I guess during my daddy's and mother's life, they didn't buy five dollars' worth of flavorings.

My parents grew all kinds of things—beans, potatoes, peas, onions, lettuce, corn, beets, and lots more—one time, Mama raised some celery. We'd use this to feed ourselves and the stock. And we raised cane to make syrup —used to have plenty of syrup. We planted by the signs—I still do. Plant corn on the new of the moon, it grows tall, but plant it on the full of the moon and it won't grow so tall. But now the signs of the zodiac—you can plant potatoes when the signs are on the bowels and they'll rot. And beans, you can plant'em on the signs of the bowels and they'll be covered with little black snakes. Plant your beans when the sign's in the feet and in the thighs, because they'll bear next to the ground. And when the sign's in the

PLATE 238 Annie in her garden. She's had the garden in the same spot since she was a little girl, and it still grows corn ten feet tall. She does not use fertilizer, and plants only by the signs.

arms, you plant your cucumbers. Your root crops, you plant when the sign's in the legs and feet. Now as for other things, we'd make jelly on the new of the moon, and get a whole lot more jelly and the juice would jell quicker than making it on the full of the moon.

My grandmother'd make her own soap. And she'd always make the soap on the new of the moon. That's when you just see it jelling the best.

When we'd kill hogs, we'd always try t'kill'em on the decrease of the moon—when it gets smaller. And then your meat won't puff up and be big old thick pieces, and it's easier to render. [See the chapter on planting by the signs in *The Foxfire Book*.]

We had a lot of animals—oxen, mules, a horse, hogs, cows, chickens, ducks, sheep, dogs, and cats. The hogs and cows went wherever they pleased all over the mountains.

We've had bees ever since I could remember. There weren't no grandchildren for a long time except Suzie and me, and I begged Grandpa for some bees. He gave me one stand and he said the first time that one swarms, it belongs to Suzie. The next thing, it swarmed and that one was

Suzie's. We had "this one's mine and that one's yours" a long time. Each one knew his beehive.

The most important thing I had, what I liked best, were my sheep. Yes. Because they were gentle and they were pretty when they were little. I also liked cattle and hogs. I liked all animals. That's why I said I wasn't no housekeeper. It's because I was always helpin' take care of the hogs and sheep, and I've milked since I was twelve years old. That's the reason I like outdoor life. All that I did was outdoor work. I never did do any indoor work. I just helped my daddy. I was the only "boy" he had for sixteen years. I was sixteen when Dennis was born, and they treated us the same.

I think everybody should work. We're all put here to work. We are all put here to make a living by the sweat of our brows. And some people are more fortunate than others. You *can* abuse the body by overworking. I mean working in a way that hurts you.

Work keeps people's minds occupied and keeps'em from doing things they're nor supposed to do. If they got their minds on their work, they'll be successful.

I had a lot of chores to do before I went to school. And I had chores to do when I got back from school. We had no special time to play. We played when we got the time.

We didn't work for fun; we worked to have something to live on. Papa'd make his axe handles of a night by the fire, and his mauls that he used, and singletrees he'd use on the plowstock. We had pine knot lights to see by at night for a *long* time. I was already grown when Mama first bought her kerosene lamp, and it was little bitty lamp that'd hold about a pint—it made a good light. It was a curiosity, and kerosene oil cost five cents a gallon.

We worked all the time. Even in the winter, we fixed the fence around the farm, and done clearing around, and when the ground was dry enough we'd plow in the winter. I had to feed the chickens, ducks, hogs, sheep, but I went to school every minute that we had school. My daddy never kept us out a minute from going to school, no matter how much work he had to do that we could help him do. He said he didn't want us to grow up like he did.

We had a hard time washing the clothes. We had a big old pot (I've still got that washpot) of iron, and you gather up your dirty clothes, take'em down to the branch, fill up your tubs with water, fill up th'pot, heat it good and have it warm, and have homemade lye soap, and a big stick about so long, trimmed off like a bat. You'd have a big stump, piece of wood settin' up that way, and put your clothes on there and beat'em with that stick, and then put'em in the pot and put a fire around the pot, and some soap in the pot, parboil'em, and then boil'em. Then you rinse your clothes and get all the soap out. You didn't have a wringer; you wrung this way [Annie makes a wringing motion] with your hands. And then hang'em out on the line and let'em dry and they'd be pretty and white. We'd hang'em on the grapevine, and go to the woods and get long, slim poles, and get one with a fork and set it in there and hang your clothes on that. The clothes were real strong then, not like what we got now. [The clothes today wouldn't] last long, would they? You get after'em with a battlin' stick like I used to have to get after Dad's old britches—it would get'em clean.

I didn't have very many toys. I'll tell you what toys we had—we had two dogs and two cats and a rag doll. My grandma made me a rag doll about three feet long one time. Yes, she took a one-pound flour sack to make the front of it. Stuffed it with cotton. Me and Suzie, that's my sister, we'd take care of our cats. We had two old cats, Sandy and Coachie. And Bouncing Ring was the dog. He'd go as far as from here to the top of the hill and stay all day. We'd play with our dogs and cats. We didn't have toys like children do now. We climbed trees, too. I fell out one time and like to broke my neck. And I'll tell you another thing. Down below where we went to play, there was a branch—and a white oak right on the edge, and a limb sticking out. We'd catch ahold of that limb, swing way out over that branch. We'd a'killed ourselves if we'd a'fallen. Papa came along and found us hanging on that limb. He cut it off. That ended the fun. He cut it down.

We'd play ball and drop-the-handkerchief and ring-them-a-rosie. We also played grape-vine twist. It's a dance. We didn't have any music. They's two sides to everything, you know. Each fella had a partner. Ring up around us and we'd break and swing backwards. It's lots of fun. Now that was a game we used to play at school. They didn't allow us to do that either, and we'd slip off down the road, halfway to the top of the hill, that's where we'd all go. Just have a partner apiece and we'd just have a big time.

We played big ring. It ain't nothing but square dancing and there's nothing that's any more interesting. If nobody gets lost!! The teachers didn't allow it. They didn't think it was right. There's no harm in dancing, surely, if it's carried out right. There's not a bit no more harm in square dancing than there is in eating.

My parents were strict, and they wasn't only strict at the house, but if they let us off by ourselves, my daddy would say, "Now, you'd better not do this what I'm telling you not to do. I get ahold of it, and I'll whip you." Well, we didn't do it, because my daddy was a truthful man and he'd whip me. He wouldn't have let us get by with it. When he let us go to the neighbors' house to play with the children, he'd say, "If they're going somewhere, you come back. I want to know where you are." If they were going somewhere, we came back home. He kept a real close eye—well, he just wanted

to know where we were. He said he didn't want to turn us loose and let us be from here to the Chatooga River and not know where we were.

We didn't have much freedom. Sometimes I thought we didn't have enough, but that was his way of thinking, and if there was one thing we were not allowed to do—we were not allowed to talk back. Daddy gave me one whipping—*one whipping*. Mama gave me many whippings—I didn't keep count. But Daddy whipped me one time for telling him I'd not do it; if he wanted it done to do it himself. He made me come to him, made me come between his legs and sit on one leg and he set on a woodpile and talked to me. He said, "Now, Annie, I'm your daddy and you're not going to talk to me like this and you're going to respect me. I'm your daddy. When you are grown, you may talk to me like that but not as long as you stay under my roof."

He taught me to be truthful, honest, and kind to everybody and not to speak ugly to a grown person and not to touch a thing that belonged to the other person without asking. When we first started to school, the path went by this little bridge where Mrs. Bleckley had an apple tree and apples would fall in the road, and we didn't have any apples. Daddy said, "Now, Annie, Mrs. Bleckley has an apple tree right there on the side of the road and don't you go picking up her apples."

I went to school about two miles and a half from here, toward the east. I went for thirteen years. One of my nieces said, "Why, Annie, I wouldn't a'went that long!" I went till I was twenty-two years old. Yes, and I didn't get farther than the seventh grade. But that was all right, I went to school. I wasn't so dumb, but there wasn't nothing else to do from July to December. We'd help my daddy in the fields. Then we'd have nothing to do, and the teacher would say, "If you've got nothing to do, well come on then, maybe you'll learn something." I never went a year but what I learned something. I was seven when I started. The schoolhouse was a good building. It was built in plank. The first school building I ever went to was about a mile from here. I went there till I was ten or twelve years old. And then they consolidated the schools together, there was two schools. One couldn't get along through the winter by itself, so they put'em both together. Then I went from this side of the Baptist Church to a slab-block building with a roof on it. When it rained, it leaked at the top of the door. We'd go start up to class, go up right through that water. We went in about eight-thirty, supposed to get there by then, and you'd have an hour and a half of recreation. An hour at lunch and fifteen minutes in the morning and fifteen minutes in the afternoon. We done some tall playing at that hour; run ourselves to death playing ball!

We studied history, geography, English, arithmetic, and spelling. I wish I could find me a United States history book. I started out at three [months in the school year] and quit at six months. The county provided that. I don't know, I guess the state paid in some taxes, too. But the teachers didn't get but thirty-five dollars a month, and that was the one that got the most. From twenty to thirty-five dollars. They had what they called Teachers' Institute, and they'd go and they'd train'em. Then they'd give'em their papers and have'em to work at them. And then they'd grade their papers, and they had one, two, and three—three grades, first, second, third. I never had a school teacher in my life, honey, that had a high school education. They generally went through the seventh grade, and went to this Teachers' Institute. A good scholar that had just finished the seventh grade could teach school. I'm not fooling you.

I don't want to teach school 'cause there are too many bad young'uns. I don't want that responsibility on my hands. I went to school, and I've been in school, and I know good and well that the poor old school teacher just had to sit there and take it from he or she or whoever it was. Give the child a whipping and he'd go home and tell all in his favor—in *his* favor. And here [the parents] come. Well, I said, "Shoot, I'd rather be a knot on a hickory tree than be a school teacher. I ain't a bit better yet, not a school teacher. Oh, whee, no!! I believe in correcting children myself, and I believe in whippin'em with a switch. I don't believe in hitting with a paddle. You can make black and blue spots with'em and hardly know you're using it.

The children don't have the education, the knowledge, that I had. I'm a wise guy now. They don't know anything about everyday life, about everyday living. I've questioned some of the children around here, and I know they don't know it. They don't know how to measure lumber, they don't know how to measure how much corn a room would hold with the dimensions being ten feet high, eight feet wide, and twelve feet long—they don't know how to find th'dimensions of a bushel of corn. They don't know arithmetic; they don't know English; they don't know spelling. You need those —they're the most essential subjects there are. Why these children couldn't tell me if they had two hundred to lend to someone on 8 per cent interest for two years and six months. They couldn't tell me how much whoever borrowed the money would be due them at the end of the two years and six months. Can you? I can! They don't teach that now—or they didn't teach the children around here that. That's what I call everyday living.

People had different ideals when I was growing up, different all the way around. For instance, children are not taught to work like we did—we had to work to make our bread. When we got out of school, we didn't loaf here and yonder, no sir. Now they lie in bed till ten o'clock, get up and eat their dinner—come back in twelve, one o'clock in the night. I didn't do that— there wasn't nowhere to go—none of this running up and down the road for me, or anyone else! We went to bed when dark came, and got up the next morning when the sun came up.

I don't approve of a lot of the ways that young people do, and there's no elderly people that do. You don't want to hear what I think of kids today! I think they don't care. I don't think they have any body pride. Now, I wouldn't show my knees to nobody, but you all. And I won't have my dress shorter than my knees. They don't care any more. Now, I'm gonna tell you. You asked me! They don't care no more about their nakedness. They don't care as much as Adam and Eve did, 'cause Adam and Eve was ashamed of their nakedness when they was born. Went and tried to pin fig leaves together and make aprons to hide their nakedness.

Some changes in the world are good and some are not. Some of it has degraded people. They don't observe the Sabbath as they should. They don't take care of their bodies as they should. They don't rely on nobody. They think they can rely on themselves. It gets 'em to thinking that they can do anything within themselves, when you can't do that. They used to rely more on their Maker than they do now. They have learned so much that they think, "I don't have to call on my Maker." Things won't get better, not the way the world's going. I think Judgment Day is close at hand.

I don't believe they went to the moon. I don't know. But I just don't believe they did. Why the moon is a—I never studied science in my life, I never did go to school farther than the seventh grade, and I'm glad I got that much. Children, I'm eighty-three years old. And I never did care for science. And I read the Good Book, and the Good Book said that the moon was made to rule the earth and all the heavens therein, fishes of the sea, and

the fowls of the air, and even man's body. And the moon rules the vegeta-
tion. I don't think they landed up there. You just know what they said. And
how do you know but what they carried them rocks with'em? Possibilities
that they did. And if it was made to fool with, it'd been put down in the
reach of man. I believe that, too. 'Cause we know that God created everything.

I think that the world has made great progress, but they's a few things
that I think is money spent foolish. And that is trying to go to the moon! I
don't think that's fair at all. God made everything. He made man to rule
the earth and all the inhabitants therein. And he didn't make the moon for
man to play with. If he did, he'd put it down for man to reach. He'd put it
anyhow where man could get on a stepladder and go up! I don't think that
it's—well, it's just no means! The moon is the moon. Leave it alone!
There's not a thing in the world up there but just the moon. And if they
read the first chapter of Genesis, they'll find out what the moon is—first
and second chapters, I believe it is—they'll find out how God created the
earth. And he made everything. Man was created. The earth was made.
I'm not educated, of course. But it's true. We had it in Sunday School yesterday, about the creation.

It took him six days to create all these things. He didn't do it in one day.
And so the moon and the stars—the moon was made to shine at night and
the stars was made to'luminate the sky, and the sun just warms the earth,
that's all it does. But the moon rules the earth. Now you girls that study science, don't it teach you that the moon rules the earth? And so, therefore, I
don't think that they ought to be fooling with the moon. There's nothing up
there. And what we see on the moon is the shadow of the earth. You look at
our maps and see the shadow on the moon and see if it ain't just exactly
alike. Don't you think it is? If you don't think it is, don't you agree with
me! Some night when you see a big round moon, you look at that shadow,
and see if it ain't just like the map of the earth.

I don't know nothing about ghosts, nothing about a ghost. In fact, I
never was brought up to hear ghost tales. My daddy said not to tell children
ghost tales. Said it'd make'em afraid. Well, I'm not afraid, but I tell you I
had a sister that wouldn't open a door and go out on the porch and get a
drink of water at the well. She was just afraid of the dark.

I never did know anything about haunted houses and ghosts. They's no
such thing as a haint. It's not a thing in the world but imagination. They
just imagine they hear these things, and they don't hear'em at all. Now this
is not a haunted tale—this is true—I was seven years old when I started
school, and I had to go through these wood over there. And everybody
thought they was haunts in the woods. And over yonder at that old house

where you turn in this way at that barn, Mr. Bleckley lived there, and Mr. Swafford lived down there. And they had lots of big old brood sows. And if you caught a pig or made a pig squeal, the sow'd bite you. And they'd say, "Now, Annie, don't you get out there on the side of the road (them pigs was on the side of the road) and go through there or them old sows'll eat you up." Well, they had me afraid of hogs. I'd have to go by myself through those woods over there—I'd look way out here and way out there; there wouldn't be a thing in the world. Directly I saw a thing that looked like a hog. And so I had to go by it, and I was scared. And there wasn't a thing in the world. Not a thing. They wasn't a hog within a mile of there, just some stumps a'lying there. But I guess it looked like a hog to me. 'Magination. That's so now; they scared me with hogs. And I'd look way out, and I'd see something and I'd make a hog out of it. Now that's the way ghost tales get started. [There] ain't no ghosts.

I don't read the Bible *too* much. I read it some. But I don't read it too much, 'cause I can't. My eyes won't let me. We should read the Bible, because He gives us knowledge. Your conscience tells you whether you're living right or living wrong. If you was to steal something, say my hat—which you wouldn't do—but if you was to steal my old hat, something inside, a inner man on the inside, would say you done wrong.

I know one thing. [The Bible] says, "Honor thy father and thy mother and your days will be prolonged upon the earth which the Lord, thy God, hath made." And I know another thing it says, "Whatever you sow, that's what ye also reap."

When Linda was a little girl, she came up here and she wanted me to read her a Bible story. And I said, "Well, we'll just read the first chapter of Genesis. Well, I had read it off and on all my life, and that was the first time I ever read it and got the real meaning. I'd read it, just going along through. But He didn't make but one thing a day. Had you ever thought about it? Just one thing. The earth was formed first. It was totally dark and He made light and He saw it was good—morning and evening. Then He made the fowls of the air and it was good—morning and evening. And on till the sixth day. And the sixth day, He was pleased with all He had done. And He created man, and man needed a helpmate. And He caused Adam to go into a condensed sleep. And He took a rib from Adam's side and made Eve. And on the seventh day, He rested. And who does that now? And He hallowed it and called it the Lord's day.

I'll tell you right now, God didn't intend—I know [in the] olden days, all the pictures that were made by men—and the Good Book says, "It is a shame for a man to wear long hair, and a woman's hair is her aura of glory." It's her *glory*. But it said a woman shouldn't cut her hair. But it said it was a shame for a man to wear long hair. And I *think they look shameful!*

They look sorry to me! If I was a youngster going to school, I wouldn't even look at one that had that shaggy hair as a friend. I'd just cuss him down! Do you think they look admirable? It just looks so strange—and men wearing moustaches. Now I don't like that either. It'd be like kissing a stinging worm.

Religion back then wasn't a bit more important than it is now, but they did live better than they do now. I believe they was more conscientious Christians then than they are now. In your reading and going about, don't you think they were, too? They observed God's laws more than they do now. You never heard of nobody going fishing on Sunday. You never heard of anybody going hunting on Sunday. They's breaking the Sabbath. And in my childhood days, if they took a gun and went squirrel hunting, the neighbors around were the grand jurors. They would prosecute'em for it and they'd have to pay for hunting on Sunday. Sure did. People used to observe it much more than they do now. My grandmother was reared in South Carolina, and she was Presbyterian. She said they didn't get to cook a thing on Sunday—not a thing. They cooked up food on Saturday to do till Monday morning. They made a little tea and that's ever'thing that was done. But they had to tend to the hogs and cows. But as for cooking, all their food, they ate it cold. They went to church and if somebody was sick, they went to visit'em, to see if they could do anything for'em. And if they didn't need nothing done, they'd come back home. And they stayed at home the rest of the day.

I cook my Sunday dinner of a morning. I cook my dinner when I cook my breakfast and if somebody wants to come and eat dinner with me, why they can, but they eat just like I do. Sometimes I go visiting in the afternoons, sometimes I don't. Everybody ought to have one day out of seven.

I go to the Methodist church. I walk over there and some of the neighbors bring me back home. But I walk over. I feel like that's too much trouble for anybody to come after me. I walk a mile. That'll keep my legs working. But I can still make it. I say, "Why not use what God gives you?" I am thankful that God has seen fit for me to live and be healthy and strong as I am at the age of eighty-three years. My birthday was the twenty-third day of May.

I don't know what has caused the difference. I don't know whether there's more people in the world and more conveniences. Let me tell you. You know people—they don't think about God giving them wisdom to be able to do all these things. You don't get no wisdom from the devil. He don't know nothing. But God, He gave you your life; if He gave you your knowledge, everybody ought to serve Him. He gives us everything. When we get in real deep trouble, who can we go to? Who can we call on? He's Creator and Maker of all.

HORSE TRADING

Being a horse owner myself, and seeing how people trade horses now, I was curious to find out what the old-time ways of horse trading were.

I had always sensed that horse traders had bad reputations, but I found out they're just like anyone else: Some are more honest than others. One horse trader would take a horse with a lame leg, give it a shot of morphine, and trade it; another horse trader would cure the horse of lameness, then trade it.

As I talked to many different traders, I found trading wasn't always as much of a living as it was an obsession. Once they traded for the first time, they couldn't stop. Some of the horse traders started trading when they were children and kept it going until they were fifty and sixty years old.

The old ways of horse trading are just about gone. Today traders transport their horses in big trucks instead of riding one and leading the rest in a string. Now they trade primarily saddle horses instead of work horses and mules. They tend now to go to horse auctions and deal in cash whereas they used to bring their horses to a person's farm and trade for anything they could: chickens, cows, guns, and land. However, there are still a few men here who trade the old-time way, and they really seemed to enjoy sharing their experiences with us.

MYRA QUEEN

Photographs and interviews by Myra Queen.

"Tie two or three ol' horses to one good one and take off up the road."

LAWTON BROOKS

Horse trading was kind of a complicated thing—like it is with cars now. Back in them days, it was horses they looked to instead of cars. If you was tradin', you'd keep your eye out all of the time all over the country.

M. M. Q.
'75

PLATE 240 A. Teeth are an indicator of horse's age. They may be filed down to make a horse appear younger than he is. The longer and more protruding the teeth, the older the horse is. B. Horse's relative age can be determined by the sharpness of his jawbone; the sharper it feels the older the horse. C. Depression above horse's eyes. A deep depression shows that the horse is old and/or in poor condition. Some horse traders would blow it· up with air to make the horse appear younger and better. Also, if horse has moon blindness, one or both eyes (just below C) will turn white or light blue for two weeks out of the month when the moon is dark. During this time he is blind in the affected eye(s). D. Area on face which may turn gray with age. Some horse traders would dye the hair to make the horse look younger. Also, a broad flat face means a horse will work. E. Ears are a sign of temperament. A horse with big ears is more likely to be stubborn. F. Sunken area along side of neck indicates horse is either overworked or too old to be worked other than lightly. G. Broad chest—sign of a good worker with a lot of stamina. H. Swinney—when the muscle in the shoulder deteriorates and the horse can't use the leg. One attempted cure was to slit the skin at the shoulder and slip in a piece of poke root about as large as a man's little finger. I. Straight legs—good point of conformation in any horse. The horse is more likely to remain sound and have smoother gaits. J. Ringbone—a hard gristly growth in the pastern of a horse usually results in lameness and is considered incurable. K. Twirl —where the hair on the flank of the horse forms a spiral-shaped cowlick. It is a sign of stamina. L. Area on the rump of an Appaloosa which is likely to be spotted. One horse trader we spoke to dyed fake spots on the rump of an Appaloosa who didn't have many spots of his own. M. Well-muscled hindquarters indicate that a horse has a lot of strength. N. Big foot—a desirable quality in a horse used for a lot of plowing. Large feet are less likely to sink in the dirt, and allow the horse to get a better footing.

PLATE 241 John Houck, who has traded a few horses, told us, "There ain't no use trading unless you make a little something."

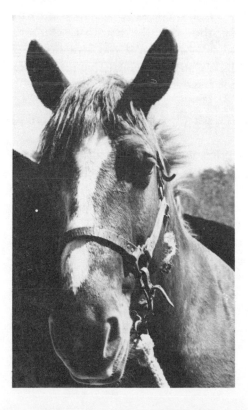

PLATE 242 Blaze, a nine-year-old work mare owned by John Houck.

I was seventeen years old when I started trading horses. I went to see my brother and I rode a mule that I had just traded for—a young mule breakin' him to ride. I married when I was twenty-three and I traded up till I was married and then traded some after I was married. Things were hard and you couldn't make over seventy-five cents a day, but you get out and trade horses and you could make two or three dollars a day. Sometimes you would make ten or fifteen dollars. Then you thought you was getting somewheres. It's just like today going out and making five hundred dollars.

I'd go to Hiawassee and Blairsville and trade. I'd get on these country roads and go to barns and go right into the field and unhitch their horses or mules from the plow and hook mine up.

When I was trading horses, I watched. Everybody farmed and logged because that was all they had. I knew everybody in the county because I was always riding.

Say you didn't have a pair that matched up—I'd go off and in a couple of days, I'd find one and get it so it would match yours. I'd put them together and talk to you about how they would look and how much you would trade, and then you'd up and trade some with me. And that was the way it went.

When I got one, I knew just where to take him and trade him because I'd already seen a man that had one just like him. I didn't aim to keep any of them myself. I had pretty'uns and some I couldn't give away. But I'd always get shed of them some way or other. I knew what to match up with the man, but all I was trading for was the boot. I'd take cash, chickens, hogs; anything I could go trade again, I'd take it. And I just kept that stuff turning around all the time. It was kind of a complicated thing, once you got into it, but once you did it, you kinda liked it.

Tie two or three ol' horses to one good one and take off up the road. Sometimes I'd have to stay and talk to a man two or three hours before he would trade with me.

You could take horses and if you tended to them right, fed 'em right and everything, you could make 'em look a whole lot better. Then there were horses that had what they called the "heaves," and they was the hardest to trade because they would show up on you. You had to know how to doctor one till you got shed of him. And [the heaves] would stay down for about a week or so, and they would come back again. You have to dampen everything he eats; even his hay, you've got to wet. Then give him a little Japanese oil and give it to him along with the hay. When you do this for a while, you can get shed of 'em for a while. When they would breathe, their sides would go in and out real big. I can stand off a hundred yards and tell if a horse has got any heaves about him. The Japanese oil worked on his bronchial tubes some way so he could get his breath, but he couldn't let it out. They would kind of whistle after a while when they got tired and they would do it bad. You could hear them a'comin'.

Then some horses had the swinney—that muscle right where his leg starts across from the bottom, he's got a muscle there. That would perish away. That muscle will go away and he'll be as slick as a board and he'll limp when he starts taking swinney. There's nothing you can do about it. It will just perish away. I never did know what caused a horse to take the swinney.

A lot of horses died with kidney colic. There is a remedy for that. The bots killed more horses than anything. That's a thing that they take and you can't do a thing about. They go crazy they hurt so bad. They'll gnaw at their sides and bite theirselves and they'll wallow and they'll do it again and again. Finally they'll go so crazy they'll walk through a fence. They don't pay attention to nothing. They would kill the horse.

Hardly ever could you do anything with a horse if he was lame. I'd always just tell the man he'd sprung his foot on something—he might get better or he might not. I've seen them change their color. They'd get some paint to make them look good but I never thought it made them look any better. I have worked on their teeth to make them look younger. That's what they go by. Looking at their teeth, a man that's ever fooled with horses can tell their ages any time—if he's ever looked in a horse's mouth any. They would take their horses and file their teeth some and make them look younger.

They could pump the holes up with air right above their eyes. There was a lot of that done to trade horses. They'd stick a needle under the skin above the eye and pump them up. It was against the law, but they'd do it.

Old man Ferd Burrell, he made a fortune tradin' horses. He owned Hiawassee at one time. I don't know how much he owned at Franklin. He died down here at Franklin, but he owned a lot. He had a lot of money in the bank, they tell me. I've heard people talk about it. I'd knowed him ever since I was a kid. That's how I got up with horse trading. I got to fooling around with him. I used to go around with ol' man Ferd. Watch him trade. Then when I got up big enough, I took his horses and traded them for him. Then I decided if one man can make money at it, another can. I got out on my own and you could buy horses cheap. I got me up two or three ol' plugs and I started. I've had some real horses, and some that wasn't worth a dime in the world. Some that you wouldn't have. Look like quilting frames goin' down the road. But they'd always trade somewhere or another; they'd always trade. Ferd Burrell used to get horses in by the carload. Mules that had never been broke. And cash them right for the money. I went up there with a man that had our place rented for his tent and built that road from Hayesville to Hiawassee—the first road that ever went through there. Costella Brothers built it. Ferd seen they was doing it with

PLATE 243   Lawton Brooks shows Myra Queen how to tell the age of a horse.

mules and things, you know. And he knew that would be a good time for him to get into mules. He used his head and watched out ahead for things and he was ready for them. He'd get two hundred dollars a pair for them mules and he got them for a hundred dollars a pair. But he was sellin' them like hot cakes. I went with my boss man up there, 'cause I worked with this man who rented our place. I carried water and when he'd go off, he'd take me with him and make some other boy carry water.

One of the funniest things that happened was Wayne. (Me and him was good buddies and he never did trade or he didn't know nothing about tradin'. So ol' Wayne made a pretty good living so he didn't have to trade no ways.) I knew him like a book, and I was raised with his wife and I stayed there most of the time. One time there was an old black man come ridin' by there and he was ridin' th'poorest old gray horse you ever seen and it tickled Wayne. It was so poor, Wayne was makin' fun of the horse. So Wayne and me had went and bought us a big ol' sheep we was going to kill. We'd kill sheep and calves and go out and peddle them around. We went over across Hiawassee River there and we'd sell out in just a little bit. You could buy all [the sheep] you wanted for two and three dollars apiece. And we'd get six or seven dollars out of that sheep by killing him. We was making money peddlin' in a one-horse wagon. And if they didn't have the money, we'd swap them mutton for a chicken and we could get turkey or anything. This ol' black guy come by there that day and Wayne, he was just laughing and going on about that poor horse. You could count every rib that horse had and his hip bones stuck a way out. It was an ol' white horse at that and that made it look ugly, you know. So Wayne hollered something back to him. Wayne said something funny about the horse and that black man looked back at him and said, "What would you give for him?"

"I'll give you that ol' sheep tied up there." That black man didn't do a thing except get off of that horse, come back, tie the horse up, and took that rope leading his sheep off. Wayne looked at me and said, "Do you reckon he means that?"

I said, "You damn right he means it. I know ol' Frank Dorsey. When you've traded with him, you've traded." He was a trader too. I knowed him. He took the sheep and left the horse there. Wayne begged for me to take it home with me. I said, "I wouldn't take that thing home with me. You can't give me that horse."

He said, "What are we going to do with it?" I said, "That's your job, son, that's your trade." That just tickled his wife to death. But I wouldn't have nothing to do with it. She said, "He traded for it? You let him trade it off?"

I said, "That's exactly what I'm going to do. I ain't going to have a thing to do with it."

I stayed busy till about dark and started to go home. Then he said, "No, I want you to stay with me awhile. I swear I've got to do something with this horse."

I said, "Well, I'll tell you where you might trade him at. You might trade him over on Crooked Creek. People over there keeps such horses as that and you might trade him over there." He says, "Well, we've got to do something."

So we got up there. We had to go over by Hiawassee and he says to me, "Lawton, I'll tell you what I'll do. Why don't you ride this thing through town?" He was ashamed to let anybody see him riding that thing through town and have people laughing at him. He said, "I'll give you a dollar if you'll ride it through town for me and let me ride your horse."

I said, "All right." I just got down off mine and got on the old poor thing and we just went rackin' on up through there. Went over on Crooked Creek and went up to a place. Now this is what tickled me. This woman and ol' man had this ol' mare and she got so old that she couldn't eat enough to make her fat. The old mare's name was Bess. They'd had her for years and years. Well, the funniest thing was he went up and knocked on the door and this lady came to the door. He asked her where Hicks Mars was. Hicks was a horse trader. Wayne said he'd just give it away if he could get anything out of it. She said, "Do you want to trade some?"

Wayne said, "Yeah, I've got a good horse out here I want to trade."

She said, "Bring it out here and let me look at it." So he got the old horse and led it around the edge of the house where she could see it. She said, "My God, that's ol' Bess. She's seven years older than God!" I just fell over. I never laughed as much in my life. He knew he was hooked there. He couldn't do nothing. He just dropped his head. He said, "What are we going to do?"

I said, "I don't know what you're going to do, Wayne, but directly I'm going home." We was about eight miles from home. It was getting late. We come to a little road up there that a family lived down. When we got to that little road, Wayne said, "Wait a minute. I'll tell you what I'm going to do. I'm going to bid ol' Bess farewell."

I said, "What are you going to do?"

He said, "I'm going to turn her loose."

I said, "Well, that's your job." So he took his saddle off. That was one of those little terrapin-hull saddles. He got it from his daddy-in-law. Those are the kind of saddles that they ride on these race tracks. That's what I called them—terrapin-hull saddles.

So he got on my horse behind and took that old horse and led it down the road and put the bridle reins up around her neck so they wouldn't fall down and sent her down the road. She went out of sight. Me and him never did hear tell of that horse anymore. Where that horse went, I don't know. Some family probably got him down there and probably glad to get him. But whoever got it had them a horse and didn't cost them a thing.

The funniest thing was I went up to Tusquitty to trade. This man had a big ol' gray horse and the prettiest mule you'd ever seen. I had this gray I'd swapped a lady out of on Crooked Creek and it wouldn't work but I didn't know it. It would kick the devil out of the cross. [When I traded for her gray horse] I asked if it was a good work horse and she said, "Oh, yeah, good work horse." I think she was a horse trader, too.

I knew this poor ol' fellow up on Tusquitty; he had this big gray horse and a good mule, and I thought to myself, "I know where to go. I'll head for Tusquitty in the morning and I'll know where to place you an order, good ol' workin' horse." So I went up there and this man was down in the field gathering corn. I asked his wife where he was and she said, "Go down that road and you'll find him down in the field."

Well, I started down that road and there was a hill right up to the barn and I was going down this hill and met him right at the foot of it. I knew that was the wrong place to talk to him, but that was the only chance I had so we got to talkin'. He said, "Boy, I like the looks of that horse."

I said, "Yeah, you ought to have this one to go with that one there. And you'd have a team just nearly alike."

He said, "That's the truth. I've never seen any two match up any better. How would you like to swap him for that mule?"

Well, I knew I would swap for that mule and if I had to, I'd give him a little boot. The mule wasn't too old and it was a pretty mule.

We kept on talkin' and he said, "Let me put the harness on him and try him up the hill." I didn't know what to say. He had me there. I knew if he hooked him to that wagon, he wouldn't pull a pound, 'cause I hooked him up to the wagon and he kicked the devil out of it. I beat the devil out of him, but it didn't do any good. I had to take him loose from the wagon. He'd walk a step or two and then go to kickin'.

Well, I knew that was what he'd do, but there wasn't a thing I could do. I studied just a minute and said, "All right." I just thought this trade was lost. Well, I'll just tell him the folks guaranteed him to be a good workin' horse to me. Of course, it didn't matter to me if he didn't take him. Someone else would. He put that ol' fool to that wagon, and he got up on his wagon and I just shut my eyes. I just knew he'd kick the front end out of his wagon.

When that other old horse started pulling, he did, too, and they pulled just as pretty as you please and pulled right up where he unloaded his corn. "Boy, that's a good horse," he says. "How would you swap?"

I said, "What will you do?"

He said, "I'll trade you that mule."

I studied a minute and says, "I can't hardly do that. I'll swap with you for five dollars."

He says, "I believe I'll do it." I just took my saddle off of the wagon and put it on the mule and come on home.

I never went back to trade with the man on Tusquitty after I sold him that gray horse. I was always ashamed of that trade. I ought not done that. I still think of that trade a lot of times.

I swapped that mule for the prettiest bay mare you ever laid your eyes on for fifteen dollars to boot off a gypsy woman. I got that off a bunch of gypsies. They'd come through here every once in a while, and they'd always park down there at what we called the Herbert Ford. You forded the river there and it was a big level place and big trees just like a parking lot now. They'd pull in there and stay for two or three weeks at a time. They had horses, mules, everything. They were just going through the country trading with anybody who would trade. I'd get in with them and trade. I traded a lot with them gypsies. If you had something they wanted, they'd trade good, but if they didn't want it, you couldn't trade because they'd gyp you. They had another one to match that mule and they wanted that one bad.

One man I knew had a big red horse, prettiest thing you ever saw and one of the saddlest things you ever put a saddle on, but that horse was the worst heaver you ever saw in your life. He would just go in and out, and if you rode him a piece, you could hear him snort. When he started snorting, he'd just rock you to sleep and just as pretty and just as fat as I had hoped. They kept him in a big meadow on grass all of the time. This fellow gave me the horse—didn't cost me a thing. He couldn't do nothing with him. He said he tried to trade him but no one would have him so he just gave him to me. I said, "Well, I'll trade him."

And I was glad to get him, so I headed up on Hog Creek out of Hiawassee. This other fellow up there had another big ol' bay horse that this'un would match and I went up there, and so this ol' man was there and I asked him about tradin'. He said, "I shore do need that horse there, but I tell you, son, I shore am short on money right now."

I said, "Well, what have you got to trade? I don't have to have money." I had me a good saddle horse I was ridin'. I was leadin' that one. I always kept me one. I always had one picked out for myself. Sometimes I'd trade for something else. So he studied a minute and said, "I've got some good hogs. Come on up here and let me show them to you."

In that pen he had some hogs. "What about the two hogs there? How would you like to have them?"

I said, "Well, they're pretty nice-looking hogs," and walked on to look at the others.

He said, "I'll let you have that one there. Ready to kill, you know."

So I said, "I don't know. I got a pretty nice horse down there in awful good shape. He's just as fat as he can be."

He had a buggy setting under a shed. I did want that buggy but I didn't have no idea of getting it. I got that buggy and the buggy harness and everything, and got that big hog and eight dollars in money off him. Now that's the truth. I never did feel right over that deal. If that man was living, if I ever laid eyes on him, I'd give him some money. I never did feel right because this was an honest old man and a good old man. He says to me, "I haven't got the eight dollars but I'll tell you what I'll do. I'll mail that eight dollars a'Tuesday and you'll get it a'Wednesday.

I says, "That's all right. I ain't worried about that." So Wednesday I went to the mail box and sure enough, there it was. That hog would have been a big price for that horse. The buggy would have been a big price for the horse, let alone the buggy harness and all of that. I just took the harness and borrowed a collar from that old man and tied that hog in that little booth on back of the buggy, tied ropes around him and his feet and went on home with it layin' on the back a'hollerin'.

I usually traded in the county. Sometimes I'd get off over to Blairsville and down around Blue Ridge and I'd stay a week at a time. Just stay here and there and trade horses with people. The biggest tradin' time was when court was on hand. Well, when court come, everybody rode their stock to town and they'd tie them up around the edges of the courthouse as close as they could get. Court then would run a week or two weeks. And that was the tradin'est place you ever went into.

Of course all of the horse traders in the country was there. Ol' Hobb Duvall and all of'em—Ferd Burrell, Will Burrell, Bud Hitchbar. All of the old horse traders were there. We'd all get in there and trade. Sometimes I would trade as high as ten times a day. That was your best tradin' was court week. If they had it at Hayesville, the same way there and Blairsville the same way. Go around to Murphy. They traded a lot there.

But I made more going out and hittin' up with the old farmers. Of course they always had some to pay boot with. It may not be money, but they had hogs or cattle or something that you could take and get the difference off of. I'd just go to the field one day and match up their team for them and they'd be pleased with it. I'd get my boot and go on. That's what I was looking for—the difference.

That horse tradin' is a good trade. I'd like to do it again. I wish horses would come back, but they ain't enough around. They don't farm with horses; they do it with tractors.

You couldn't do no tradin' now at all. All you'd find now is one somebody wanted to ride. If you could get one to suit somebody to ride, you'd be all right. If you didn't, you'd just have some horses on your hands to feed for nothing. But back then, they was working them. They had to have something to work to make anything. If you had a team, you could get out there and get a job logging or hauling for somebody and make money. That's what they were looking for. I'd always rig them up a team some way. In trading, you have to keep your eyes open and you have to know, too. You can't just start today in the business. You've got to get out over the country and you've got to know who's got what and what you think you need. Then go back and see them again. If you ever get started, there is somebody after you every day. They was a dozen at the house all the time I was gone, tellin' my daddy to tell me to see them; that they needed some kind of a horse. They wanted to know what you had. What you do, it kept you busy as a telephone operator. Once you get on the line, you really like it. I had fun.

"I don't care what you're trading, you better trust your own judgment."

KENNY RUNION

There was a fellow come by one mornin'. I was quite young. I don't guess I was over sixteen, seventeen years old. He said, "I want to trade some with you." He was a horse trader and I knowed him. He said, "I've got a horse an' buggy."

I said, "How old's your horse?" I didn't know no more about how old a horse was than a thing in the world.

"Well," he said, "he's comin' nine year old."

I said, "That ain't old." He said he was round and sound and nine year old. I had some good steers, and a wagon. He said, "I'll tell you what I'll do. I'll swap with you for twenty-five dollars."

Well, my mother couldn't get around, and I had a brother who couldn't get around, and I thought it would be an advantage to get somethin' for them to ride in. We stayed around there a while in the evenin', and I finally said, "I believe I'll just trade with you."

Now he got away with me. Well, I kept that horse around there a while, and he wouldn't work. So I decided to go to Hiawassee to see Ferd Burrell, an old horse trader; he's dead now. I rigged that horse up and took him down there. I said, "I've got a young horse I want to trade you for a mule."

PLATE 244   Kenny tells us some of his horse-trading adventures.

He said, "I'll be glad to trade with you if you've got a young horse."

I said, "The fellow I got him from said he was young."

He looked at him, shook his head and said, "No, I wouldn't have him if you give him to me. He's twice nine, then some!"

Doggone, I was beginnin' to get disheartened. He wouldn't trade with me at all. I rode him back and put him in the stable.

One day a fellow came by, an old friend of mine—I reckon he was a friend of mine. He said, "Tell you what I'll do. I'll give you a dollar if you'll take me to Blue Ridge."

I said, "I've got a horse that'll take you all right." [It was the same horse Ferd Burrell wouldn't trade for.] He had a sack with somethin' in it, and I never asked any questions. Well, I said, "I'll just gear up and take you."

I hitched that horse to the buggy, and me an' him started. We got a little out of the settlement, and he said, "I believe I'll take a drink." It was in a jug and you couldn't tell how much you was a'drinkin'. Then I took the jug, turned it up, and it was pretty heavy. After a while, he says, "Whoa. Let's have another drink!" When we got to Blue Ridge, I tell you, I was just about out of business. I was as drunk as a man ever gets. I guess we drunk half a gallon, three quarts, since the time we started. He went on this away, and I went back that away. Some folks met me there in Blue Ridge, and they said I was standin' up in that buggy whippin' that horse, and the road was straight down. I really broke that buggy down. Well I finally got home, and I seen I had to do somethin' with that horse. He wouldn't plow, barely move. So I rented a pasture; it was pretty high, too. Let him stay in there till fall, I decided I'd go down and look at him. He was just a sore all over nearly, hardly any hair. I don't remember what they called it that was wrong with him. I told my daddy, "You can have that horse if you'll go get him." He went and got him, brought him home, and the horse died.

So I lost about two hundred dollars on that swap. I got stuck on that one. All I got out of them steers and wagon was that one dollar I got to drive that man to Blue Ridge and all the liquor I could drink.

Horse traders will tell people false. I don't care what you're trading, you better trust your own judgment. They're out to *trade*. They won't give the age of a mule as over seven years, and a horse just nine. That's as far as they'll tell you. I've had some mules that wasn't no 'count. With one mule I had, it took one to lead the mule, one to hold the plow, and one to drive and whip. He wasn't worth a blame for nothin'. More money gone. Got another'un. He'uz still worse. Got another one; when you'd open the door, he'd go to kickin', and you couldn't get in that stable to save your life. He'd kick with both hind feet. I bet he didn't miss my head three inches. Boy, you better watch on horse swappin'. You shore had, or you'll lose what you have in a few minutes. You can't go back once you've made a deal. I've put out some money buyin' all them mules. I had one pretty good old mule. He was club-footed, and I swapped a stove for him. Fellow was tellin' me the truth there. He'd work.

"These horse traders here, you better look out, or you'd get home with a rope and your horse gone."

WILL ZOELLNER

There were Fred _____ and L. M. _____ and that sheriff from Cornelia. L.M. and his daddy were two of the slickest there was in this country here. L.M. had a bunch of plugs that couldn't hardly go and they had a sale down there. So, L.M. says, "We'll have a sale and I'll dope them horses up; they're all trained but they're not able to go." Most of them were old and their teeth were all filed down He'd take those horses out and file their teeth down so they'd look like a six- or eight-year-old horse. You

PLATE 245 Will Zoellner, a blacksmith, told us about some notorious horse traders who once worked this area.

know, a horse's crown runs out when he gets twelve years old. He ain't got no crown. Well, he had that all filed out just as pretty as can be. He fixed it all back and had them horses down there, but they can't eat good for a day or two. So they fixed those old plugs up and I shod them. I didn't say nothing. It wasn't nothing to me. Old Joe said, "We made a thousand dollars yesterday with [some of] those old plugs."

I said, "What are you doin' with those horses—they're all to pieces."

He said, "We're feedin' them dynamite. We give them a teaspoon of dynamite and they're just like a colt for eight or nine hours. By that time we've already got our money and we're finished."

Take them out on the road and they fall all over theirselves; get their legs tangled up. They sold I don't know how many old plugs. They cleaned up there for a while, about two years till they run out.

Old man L.M. had to leave here, he got so far along that people wouldn't put up with it. Fred got pretty smart along towards the last. He owed me sixty-five dollars for shoeing when he died. [One time] there was a lady come in here with her husband. They wanted two nice saddle horses and L.M. was at the shop where I was a'workin' and he was standin' there listenin'. I told her I would look around and see if I could find them two. I knew of several but 1 didn't know if a man could buy them. "Oh," he said, "we'll buy them if you can locate them."

Just as soon as I quit talkin' L.M. jumped in. He said, "I've got anything you need."

She said, "What have you got?"

He said, "I've got them right across the street over by the railroad. We got sixteen head down there and I guarantee any one of them."

So I knew right then that he might get that woman killed. He didn't give a durn just so he got the money. They were fixin' to go over and his wife was out there talkin' to him and her husband come on in where I was and I told him, "You're foolin' with a man who don't have no heart for nobody but himself. He's got horses over there that are okay, but the rest are no good. They'll kill you."

"Well," he said, "I'm glad you told me. We're no riders. We just wanted tame horses we could crawl on and take our time."

I said, "I'd never buy nothing from him." So they went over there and looked at them, and the old man said, "We'll take them over and let the caretaker saddle and ride them before we get on them."

Well, they took two over there and it wasn't more than an hour and they come back. I knew right then what had happened. See, the horse knew more about saddling than the man did. The horse knew who he could outwit and if it was a kid, he knew he could throw him. So they brought the horses on back.

[Another time] some fellow come in there and had a horse with a jaw tooth ground off to the side. And he said, "I want that jaw tooth pulled." Old man Joe looked up at me and said, "That tooth has got to come out."

I said, "You can't pull it."

He said, "We'll pull it. We'll get some money out of that." It was old man Rosie's horse. It was one of those French horses, a big saddle horse. He said, "We'll take him right here and put him right to sleep. We'll get your drill-bit and drill a hole down into his jaw and take a punch and knock that tooth out."

I said, "Yeah, you'd better sterilize those drills and punch before you do that."

He said, "Aw, there's nothing to that. I've did it a'many a time."

I said, "If you kill that horse, you'll go to the chain gang, because now that man has money and he doesn't want that horse bloodied up like that."

I let him have the bit and he went out and put him to sleep and laid him down on a load of hay and drilled his jaw. R.M. run the drill. They did it. An hour went by and he had never come to. I said, "You either gave him a big dose or something's wrong. That horse should have come to in thirty minutes."

He said, "He's comin', he's comin'." They gave him a shot of something else. I don't know what it was. And the horse raised on up. He was bleedin' pretty bad and he gave him another shot. The fellow come and looked over the horse and put the saddle on him and took him home. Old man Rosie lived over at Five Points and told him, "Don't ride him. Just put him in the stable."

Well, he got on home and fed him that night, but he wouldn't eat nothing. And the next morning, the horse laid down out in the orchard and died. They got the vet from Clemson College up there and he told them the horse died from blood poisoning.

There were a lot of horse traders fifty years ago, but they didn't belong here. A horse trader don't stay long in a town, because he knows it isn't wise to. They'd come and stay about thirty days and leave. Then another one would come and take his place. They swap around. We had one here from Mississippi. He bought a place up here in the valley. He had a whole string of horses that he brought with him. I was about sixteen or eighteen years old then. I come on down with my daddy. Daddy wanted to buy a horse that was broke to a one-horse wagon and we went on up there. He was a nice old fellow, stayed there by himself. He lived in a shack and had the horses loose. They were pickin' in and around the strawberries. Daddy went out and looked at them, and he had a little copper-bottomed mare there, prettiest thing you ever looked at—weighed about eight hundred pounds. He said, "I'll guarantee her to work anywhere."

Daddy said she was a little small. He said, "Well, I got a bigger one out there." I told Daddy, "That durn thing is mean [the big horse]. It snapped at me as I went by a little while ago."

He said, "This horse here is hard to bridle, but that's all. If you can get the bridle on, you have got it made." So I told Daddy to leave it alone. I said, "That little horse out there will do all the plowing we want." He wanted a small animal. He didn't want a big animal. He bought her for two hundred dollars and we took her on home and she was perfect.

Come a bunch from Highlands over there, and out of the whole bunch there wasn't but six that would work a'tall. Rest of them would kill you. When you opened the door, they would turn around and kick you with both feet. They were doped when you got them, and when you got home with them, they'd be almost normal, but when you got up in the morning, you better look out. There is all kinds of tricks.

They would trade for saddles and things like that. They get something out of it. These horse traders here, you better look out, or you'd get home with a rope and your horse gone. I know of a dozen people who went down there and swapped a durn good animal off just because he had a little age on him, and got home with one that would kill you. Wouldn't ride no-wheres, wouldn't work nowheres. That's the kind of stuff they had.

"They'd gather in and maybe come from as far as Asheville, you know, just way off that way."

HARRY BROWN

[My father ran a store on Scaly] and people would [come from] all over just to get the cider he sold; it was just a flavored-up drink. You could get peach and apple, and it sold for five cents a glass. Well, they was going to have a horse-swappin' convention at my daddy's store. They had a full thirty-gallon barrel of this cider and they drew out about three gallons, and then filled that jug back up with whiskey. Well, there wasn't none left after the convention.

My father's place was just a wide place in the road. The men-folks were the only ones there and the biggest per cent of them would get drunk. Some of them were pretty bad to drink too much. Sometimes they'd have a fight over the age of a horse and sometimes they'd have horse races. They'd gather in and maybe come from as far as Asheville, you know, just way off that way. Some of them would be on the road two or three days before they got there. And then trade horses on the way. And some of them just went

PLATE 246 Harry Brown, Sr., who with his wife now operates a thriving craft business in furniture and weaving, did some trading when he was young.

through the country just trading horses. You traded with them, you got beat. They'd get out and say, "I bet you a dollar my horse will outrun yours." They never did bet over two or three dollars. 'Course back then five dollars was money. I believe five dollars was the most I heard of them bettin'.

Sometimes when a horse was a little stiff, they got them out and got a whip and made them go around and around till they got them all livened up. Lots of times in the morning, a horse would be stiff. Those spavins was nothing but arthritis and they'd get those sores around where they wore their collar. Sometimes you'd cut a hole out in the pad in the collar to protect a knot or sore on their shoulder. All work horses had a knot on their shoulder where that bone come out.

Some of these horse traders were very slick—they could make money. And of course there was a lot of poor fellows that got beat, that didn't know.

The gypsies used to go through here trading horses. Nobody ever did trade with them that didn't get beat. I haven't seen any gypsies go through here in twenty or more years. First they went through drivin' horses and then came the secondhand cars. They used to camp over here at Rabun Gap where the post office is. They used to have that place covered up there.

It doesn't matter where you go, you'll always find someone who'll cheat on horse tradin'. At that time, they judged a horse by his teeth. They had a float [file] they called it, which they put in the horse's mouth and they come right along there and filed the horse's teeth off It'd make the horse look younger. And some of them would have a spavin [knot on their leg] and get crippled. They'd shoot novacaine in the spavin and it would last for several hours. And then they'd feed them gun powder and different things like that to pep them up. They'd give them the gun powder in with their feed. But I think that was mostly superstition, because I don't think gun powder had any effect on them.

Now there are what they call wind-broken horses [also called heavers], and weavers. They run a horse till it would almost bust their lungs, you know. Well, when they got to going a little ways, they'd go to heavin' and just fall down. That's what they called heavin'. And the weavers; when you took them out to plow, they'd have fits and they just go 'round and 'round. They called that a weaver. After you worked them awhile, they looked all right.

With a horse that wears a harness, where the trace chains are, the hair gets worn off and also on the shoulder where the collar rubs. If you didn't have these signs, it wouldn't be a work horse. And with a saddle horse, look for the signs of the saddle. And the next thing, you examine their teeth. Before you buy a horse, rent it for a little while and if it is a heaver or weaver, you catch it there. Another thing, you want to pick up one's foot and see if it can be shod. Lots of horses won't let you shoe them. And you can notice where a horse has wide or narrow hips. A narrow-hipped horse is bad to kick.

Another thing—in mountain sections, people didn't want too heavy a horse. These draft horses like Clydesdales are too big. People back in the mountain sections were more likely to have mules, and here [in the bottom land] were more likely to own horses.

You didn't keep a horse or a team much after it passed nine years old. At that age, it was usually counted a nag and slipped off on somebody.

We usually kept a team of young mules. We had a couple of mares we kept in the pasture, and raised our own mules and trained them. Sometimes they were hard to work. A mule is more dangerous than a horse.

Most of the horses we had we raised. My daddy got cheated by horse traders a time or two. Horse tradin' was just a way to make a livin' like these cattle traders. We had some that were honest and some that wasn't. It was like any other business. In any business you got somebody that's going to find a way to take advantage of you.

"I didn't play any tricks; I'd let them be the judge of what they thought."

THAD "HAPPY" DOWDLE

I used to swap horses lots. I'd buy a horse, maybe have two-three more, tie'em together, hit the various settlements in the country, and swap. And I made some money—that's the way I made what little I had. If I came along and you had two-three yearlin's, or a cow or two you wanted to sell, I'd buy'em if I could see I could make a dollar or two. I made money all the time.

When I got one that was pretty old, I'd take a rasp and file his teeth down till he could eat. He'd put on more weight, and his teeth wouldn't be s'long, as long teeth is a sign of an old horse. It'd make'em look younger. Sometimes I'd blow up the hollow above the eye of an old horse. The older the horse, the deeper the hollow. I'd take a needle and stick it in there under the skin and blow air in there with a little old hand pump—puff it up. It would stay puffed up for a good while, but it'd finally go back down. I didn't play any tricks; I'd let them be the judge of what they thought.

I'd take a rag and some good oil and rub the horse down with it, and the hair'd be all layin' in place, slick as they are after they shed. And I'd take shears and trim the mane and trim the tail, and sometimes I'd shear his ears

PLATE 247   Thad Dowdle remembers the days when one of the main purposes of trading was to match up a good work team. Here, James Wilson plows with a horse/mule combination.

if he had ol' long hair in his ears. I'd also trim up the hooves and put new shoes on'em. [To make a lame horse appear sound] I used to have a little dope and I'd give'em a load of it—linseed oil'r'somethin'—just rub it on there. And if the horse had a corn, I had a blue ointment to rub on it, and it'd heal up in just a little.

[To make an old or lazy horse look spirited] you can get you a little dope and put it in it, morphine or something. He'll be lively then. Just like a man! You see an old dead man a'draggin' around, and in two days maybe he'll be climbin' the fence if he had a good dose of dope. He'd climb that fence'r'jump it maybe.

I used to use shoe polish on a horse to change his color. Take a little brush, coat him with it. Shore did look good, but you didn't want to put too much on him, just enough to turn the color of him. And I used to use some kind of blue ointment on where they were turnin' gray around the eyes and such.

There was a fellow that lived in my settlement—he tried to swap horses all the time, too, and I got from him the prettiest little horse you ever looked at nearly. And I thought I'd made a good trade—got him pretty cheap, swapped for another'un. I took him home and put him up that night. The next mornin' when I went out to water'im, he was blind as a bat. He couldn't see a thing in the world! I said, "Well, I'm fixed now." So I fixed him up as good as I could. There was gonna be a fair, so I went up there, and a fellow had a pretty good mule. I rode up into the yard at the schoolhouse, and he said, "Where'd you get that horse?"

I said, "There ain't no use askin' me that."

He says, "Why not?"

I says, "That wouldn't make no difference about where I got him; I've got him."

He says, "I've got a good mule out here I'll swap you for that pony. I'd love to have him."

I says, "Well, if you want him bad enough, you can git him."

We went on out there and looked at his mule, and he said, "How much do you want to swap?"

I said, "You git on that horse an' ride'im out the trail there an' back." I thought maybe surely he'd see that he was blind. But no, he rode him out there, loped him back, and said, "I'll give you a ten-dollar bill and that mule for him."

I said, "Just make it twenty and take him on with you."

He said, "Well, that's a little too much."

I said, "If you think it is, don't do it." That's the way I'd do, if I think it's too much, I don't trade. He got back on him and rode him back out there again. I thought, "Well, if you had any sense at all, you'll see how he is." He didn't, and we traded. Well, the next morning before I ate breakfast, somebody was peckin' at the door at home. My dad stepped to the door, and it was the man I'd traded the horse to. He said, "Where's Thad at?"

My dad said, "He's down at the barn, I guess."

So here he come down to the barn. He says, "You know you put a blind horse on me?"

I said, "Well, yeah, I knowed it."

He says, "What's your idea?"

I said, "To get shed of it!"

He says, "I'm going t'town and take a warrant for you."

I said, "I don't care if you take a dozen for that. Anytime you buy something and you look it over and don't see that there's anything wrong with it, well, the trader ain't responsible. It's you who's tradin' for it."

I was comin' home from Toccoa. I was down there on the creek and it come a snow. I had a boy helpin' me, us both on a horse and a couple more horses in between. He was riding behind'em and I was ridin' in front of'em. Well, we crossed the creek and there was another creek comin' down that way, and the creek made kind of a bend, way off the road, and plumb around. We camped there one night, and in the night this big old yellow dog trotted between our tent and the road. It was nearly dark, and I just thought it was somebody passin' by. Well, he went on and here he come trottin' back. I had a little old shotgun in the tent and I said to myself, "I'll just see who you are when you come back again."

Well, here it come back again. I said to the boy with me, "Shall I kill him?"

And he said, "No, let's just let'im go." Near where we were camped was a laurel thicket on each side of the road.

I said, "Take your pistol and step out there and see if you can find anybody." He eased out, and directly I heard his gun go off. And they was just a'tearin' them bushes down to get out of there. They'd followed us plumb out of town to get to rob us that night. And would of done it if we'd a'been in the tent asleep. I'd sold all of my produce, and all but two or three of my horses, and shucks, they'd have got three or four hundred dollars from me, plus what the other boy had, about two or three hundred dollars.

"I wouldn't take nothin' in the world for the experience I got tradin' horses."

HOB DUVALL

The first horse I ever owned was a jack. I was eight years old, and I bought him with money that I got together from tradin'. I started tradin' from—I'd say five years old or six—pencils, knives, what have you. So I saved my money till I had fifteen dollars, and I bought me a jack. But my father, a Baptist preacher, didn't want me to have this jack, so I carried him off to a barn quite a ways from where we lived. When he got out Sunday morning to start his circuit [four churches], the jack started brayin', and he wanted to know whose that was. Finally I had to say it was mine. "Well," he said, "if you'll go to church, and be a good boy and go to school, I'll let you keep him." The temptation was so great for me to get to ride that jack and drive him to a little old two-wheel cart, that Sunday I put in the whole day with him. When he come home Sunday night, naturally my mother told him what all had happened. He said, "Take that back." That's the only time I've ever went back on a real bargain. It like to have *killed* me to have to take that jack back. This old boy wouldn't give me my money back, so he kept the money and the jack, too.

The next horse I got from an old horse trader from Hiawassee. This horse had a kidney colic and had been down for a day or two. It had rained and run in mud all around him, and the mud was about knee deep, and the trader picked up an axe and was gonna kill him. I said, "Please don't kill that horse. Give him to me."

He said, "You can't do nothin' with him."

I said, "Give him to me an' I'll show you." Well, I got me a block and tackle, put a bunch of sacks under him, tied ropes to it where I could brace him, and pulled him up. In about two hours, I had him to where he could stand, and that evenin' late, I led him home. In less than a week from then, I was *workin'* him. Then I started tradin' on that one. When I was eight years old I swapped three or four times, and I got a mare who was gonna have a colt, and I was gonna raise the colt. I carried her to a pasture, and another horse kicked her and broke her leg, and that was the end of that story. I've been tradin' horses ever since.

I worked for a man from Texas for five winters, and he shipped as high as fifty mules at a time to Atlanta, and I'd meet him there, and then we'd circuit ride. One time I didn't have nobody to help me, and I had twenty-

PLATE 248   Hob Duvall with Sidewinder, a six-year-old walking horse owned by Randy "Hoss" Litterell.

seven head of horses and mules in Lula, Georgia. I led them from Lula to Carnesville. I tied them three abreast, then I'd tie this one to the tail ahead, and when one would start, why, here they'd go. Well, I was ridin' a big gray horse, twelve to fourteen hundred pounds, and I tied a hitch to the saddle horn and got'em started, and went. Then they wasn't nothin' but T-model Fords. You'd pass maybe the mailman, or somebody now and then, but you wouldn't pass a dozen cars in a whole day. You couldn't do that today.

I want to tell you one on me an' Frank Rickman. I pulled up over there with a load of horses one day, and I had a four-year-old palomino horse on the truck, and Frank said, "Take that horse off. I want to see him."

I said, "Listen, Frank, this horse is four years old and half spoiled. He's *mean*."

He said, "Rooster'll ride him."

I said, "*Listen,* Frank, I tell you this horse is *mean!* Don't put that child on him." He grabbed him up and started to put him on the horse. I said, "If you want him rode, *you* get on him."

Well, he reached back, picked up a big old parade saddle, throwed it on the little old horse; he just bowed up. A saddle has a keeper on the back cinch, keeps it from goin' back on his flanks. Anything will buck if you put a rope around their flanks—it tickles'em an' they shore will buck. When he swung into the saddle, that keeper slipped back and hit'im on the flank, an' that horse just went straight up with all four feet, like he was on springs. I seen when he hit the ground, Frank's face turned red. It knocked the breath out of him, he come down with such power. The next time he went loose, when he hit the ground, Frank's both feet flew out of the stirrups and he threw Frank high enough to where he kicked him twice before he hit the ground, kicked him on both sides of the knees and then the bottoms of the feet. Frank said, "I felt my shoe heels go through the top of my head!"

I've raised my family by tradin' horses. I tried to farm. My wife was raised at Clairmont, Georgia, and when her daddy passed away, why he give her a little farm, and we lived there for twenty years. But I never made a dollar in my life farming. I'd lose money. But my wife loves a farm. One time when we were living in Clairmont, I went to the Nacoochee valley, driving a mule and a horse. I traded two, three times, and when I swapped with one man, I got a load of corn and a shotgun in the boot. Then I got a load of hay. And I come down the road and swapped this shotgun for a sow and a bunch of pigs. I put them pigs in a sack, tied them to this ridge pole that was holding the hay down, and when I come through Cleveland, I swapped this horse I'd been a'tradin' on. But I still had a big old mule hooked to the wagon. I got a cow for the horse, and tied her to the back of the wagon. Here I come down the road drivin' that mule, put two lines on him, put two tongue chains up here in the breast chain, and that mule pulled a whole load of corn and hay, and that cow, sow, and pigs.

One time I went off and swapped my horse for a cow and a heifer. And the man said, "How in the world will you get your saddle home?"

Well, I said, "I'm gonna put it on that cow." Well, I put this saddle on my cow, and you never saw such buckin' in all your life. Well, I held on t'her, finally got her to where she'd carry the saddle, and I tied this heifer that wasn't even broke to the horn of the saddle and here I come down the road, and her a'pullin' back, once in a while takin' a notion to run away.

I was tradin' mules in Cleveland. I had a barn full of'em, and this man lived in Batesville. I loaded four mules on the truck, and drove up there in the mud. When I got there, he began to find fault with every one of'em, and they were four good young mules. This one wasn't right, or that one wasn't right. It was cold and rainy, and I couldn't trade with him, and I said, "You don't know where a man could get a little liquor, do you?"

He said, "Oh, yeah, I've got plenty of liquor."

I said, "How 'bout gettin' me a quart of it?" and I give him a dollar and a half for a quart of whiskey. Well, there was an old boy with me, and we took two or three drinks of that, and goin' back down the road, I said, "I'm gonna fix this old man. He caused us all this trouble. I'm gonna trade with him, and he'll remember he's been traded with when I get through with him."

So we go to Atlanta and buy a big old pair of mares that was as old as I was, or older; one of'em was gray-headed, but I had their manes cut off, and trimmed'em up, and they looked pretty after I got'em cleaned up, and I give only sixty dollars for the pair. Well, I went back to that man's the next time and told him, "You said you wanted a pair of mares—here's a pair of mares."

He said, "Pull your wagon out here and let's look." He commenced talkin', "You needn't commence tryin' to hook'em. I'm gonna trade fer'em just like they are."

I said, "Okay." Then I said, "I'll tell you what I'm gonna do, I'll swap with you for seventy-five dollars. If you don't want to do that, I haven't got time to fool with you."

He said, "I'm gonna trade," and jerked out his pocketbook and counted out the money. I said, "I want a gallon of whiskey this time." I knew he was gonna come back. He didn't have any principles. I've always been this way; a poor man I was sorry for him 'cause I was always poor m'self. But when a man had plenty—that's where I always tried t'make my money— off somebody who had it t'spend. I knew he was comin' back, and I paid him for that gallon of liquor. I told him I was gonna law him, and I said,

"If you want to go to court, I'm gonna bring that gallon of whiskey in and let you pay for sellin' liquor."

That just slapped him just like that, and he went home and ain't said nothin' to me yet. Well, he crooked me, he let me make two trips up there, and I seen he didn't have no principles; he was a big liquor man, had plenty of money, so I decided I'd even up with him.

Why, I've had people to come back and want to fight and everything else. Right here at Clayton, I sold a horse to a man for four hundred'n fifty dollars at the horse show, to a man in Marietta. And this horse had taken a blue in the show. He paid me two hundred down and owed me two hundred and fifty. He was to come Tuesday to get the horse. He pulled up Tuesday like he said, and then said, "I've decided I wouldn't take that horse."

"No," I said, "you can't make that kind of a decision."

He said, "Yeah, oh yeah, I want my money back."

I said, "I don't have your money, I've got my money. You bought this horse fair and square."

He said, "Well, I'm gonna law you about it. We'll just take it to court."

I said, "Okay, we'll have to go to Rabun County to try it because that's where the crime was committed if they's been any crime."

Well, he had a man with him and his boy. We fussed around and you'd think we was gonna fight, but we didn't. Anyway, he said, "Come on, get up in the truck with us and let's talk it out."

I told my wife, "Bring my gun out here. I may have to kill these two _____'s, but I'll do that before I take this horse back. You're gonna pay me now."

He said he didn't have the money, and I said, "I'll tell you what I'm gonna do. I'm gonna take your check, and if you don't pay me, I'll kill you for two hundred and fifty dollars."

You know what he done? He wrote me a check and took that horse. My wife was really a lady, but I was *mad*. Mad enough to cry almost. Oh, I've had some awful times in my day.

I was travelin' once, and I had a blue-eyed mule. At a certain time of the month, that mule'd go blind, maybe two weeks out of every month, when the moon got on the dark side. This mule's eyes would turn white. She was just five years old, and the prettiest mule you ever looked at. This man, I'd tried to trade with him two, three times, old fellow Allison, and I couldn't never trade with him. I come by there around three or four P.M. on the truck, and I said, "Listen, I'm a'goin' over to Hiawassee and Blairsville, and here's a mule that I don't want to trade. If you've got a good mule like this, that's the one they want. I'm gonna pay you to leave her here with you. I may be gone two, three days." I just took her off and put her in the barn. I knew when I left her that he'd hook that mule when I got gone, for I knew she'd work anywhere—she'd ride, do anything you'd want her to do. But I knew then at a certain time, she'd go blind again. So I went on, then come back by, said, "Well, I come t'pick up m'mule."

Well he said, "Wait a minute, I want to swap for this mule."

I said, "What have you got to trade?" He showed me a mare and colt. I said, "I'm gonna swap with you for a hundred dollars."

"Oh," he said, "I ain't gonna give that much for her. I'll give you fifty dollars and the mare and colt."

"Well," I said, "I ain't got time to fool with you. I'm gonna swap with you." So he just paid me the fifty dollars, and I traded the mare and colt, and I just walked straight across the road, and sold the mare to a logger. Kept the colt. Anyway, I knew that he'd be back when that mule's eyes went bad, and here he come. So I swapped him a mare. He was a great big old tall man. This mare would work anywhere, but when you hooked her to a plow, she'd lay into the harness as hard as she could go. That time he give me fifteen dollars for the boot. So it wasn't no time, and here he was back again, and he said, "That mare is just s'fast that I can't keep up with her."

I said. "Well now, if you can't keep up with her, you know good and well there ain't no use for me or nobody else to try her, 'cause you're long-legged, and if you can't keep up with her, it'd be impossible for me. I'm gonna have to have ten dollars to boot and swap you for somethin' else." Seems like I traded him a mule this time. I said, "I've got t'have something for the gas for this truck. You'll have to give me ten dollars for the boot here to buy the gas."

He said, "That's what's gotten me into all this trouble is this gas you've been handin' me!"

I've traveled with every gypsy on the road. A gypsy will fight you if you've done him wrong. When you done the right thing, you stand up to a man. I don't care, let him be a murderer or what, he ain't gonna hurt you. You can take the meanest man in the world and if he tells you a lie, you can face him and say, "You're telling a lie." And he'll swallow it. Now that's somethin' I learned from the gypsies. When somebody does you wrong, if you stand up to their face, they've done you wrong, they'll take it. If they haven't, they won't take it. That's just a higher power that makes that happen, I reckon. Those gypsies was the smartest horse traders in the world. Most of'em carried their wives and families with'em. Well, they'd sell lace they'd bought in the five and dime store. It's hard t'feed a bunch of horses and travel. Well, them women would get out and swap that lace for somethin' t'eat. They swapped with ever'body that would trade with them. They always come to the mountains in the summer, and when the cotton begin t'open up, they'd go south in the winter, and spend the winters in south Georgia. They were money-makers; none of'em got any education, but they were smart people. *Smart!* They were Irish! They could sell anything. They'd never get discouraged. They'd talk to you for two hours, get your confidence the first thing, just play along with you, that they were your friend, that they'd do anything in the world for you; then when they got your confidence, then they'd cheat you. Then they'd ask you an unreasonable boot. Well, you'd offer maybe half, then they'd trade with you. But they're really smart people.

Then I began to follow these [summer] camps. I'd get horses for these kids at these girls' camps. I've had two or three boys' camps, but that would break the federal government, because them old boys'll run your horses to death. After they quit row-cropping, I went t'using horses around these camps. I've [supplied horses for] as high as five camps at a time. But it got to where you couldn't make no money at that. You had to buy these horses in the winter, and you'd buy three horses and get one, maybe two, that you could use. These kids can't ride, and they's very few of the instructors knows much. I've had'em turn down horses an' [I'd] just pick'em up here and move'em over to the next camp and them just be tickled t'death with'em. If the kid falls off, you just blame the horse, don't you see? You'd have them horses t'winter, start buyin' around the first of the year. They wouldn't use'em until June, and you had to feed'em all that time. I'd go to Atlanta, buy a load of horses; there'd be two or three of'em have a cold, and it'd go through the bunch of horses. I bet I've spent two or three hundred dollars a year on penicillin to knock the cold out of'em. It was expensive, but I'd get a hundred and twenty-five dollars a horse. I bought one little horse for a twenty-dollar bill, but he was poor. He reeled as he walked. I put him in a stall and covered him with an old quilt, and kept him in for two months, and when I took him out, he'd got in pretty good shape. I carried him up to the camp, and got a hundred twenty-five dollars for him. I used him for two summers at a hundred twenty-five, and I sold him to a little girl there at the camp for two hundred fifty. But it's a rough-and-tumble game, kind of like a gambler, you make it today and lose it tomorrow.

Had a little horse that was an awful good work horse—snow white, a pretty little horse. Well, this old man come and wanted to buy him, and wanted to know would he work. I said, "Sure." And I put the harness on, hooked him to the plow, just reached up, pulled the bridle off of him, hung it on the hames, said, "Gee," and "Haw," and he'd mind me just like my little dog.

He said, "What do you ask for him?"

I forget what, seems like a hundred and a quarter. Anyway, I priced him, and he bought him. But when he went to pay me for him, he said,

"What's the matter with this horse?" I said, "Well, he's got a nickel's worth of heaves."

He said, "What's that?"

And I said, "It's just like anybody with asthma, but if you'll keep his feed wet, water his hay and the grain you give him, he'll go on and do a good day's work."

It was two or three weeks after that before I seen him. He said, "Just how many heaves can you get for a nickel?"

I said, "You can buy a oat sack full of heaves. Why?"

He'd tell that on me. He'd get me in a crowd and he'd tell, "Swear and be damned, you can't catch him in a lie. He sold me a horse and told me it was a nickel's worth heavey, and he was *bad* heavey. The next time I seen him, I asked him how many heaves you could get for a nickel, and he told me you could buy a oat sack full!"

You could tranquilize a horse. If you've got a mean horse that you can't do anything with, you can give'em a tranquilizer. They're about the same as a man two-thirds drunk. If you've got a horse that wants to buck, give him a tranquilizer and he'll go along with you, and you can get shed of him. Put him to somebody that thinks they're smart, and let them have the trouble with him.

If you've got a horse with ringbone around the front feet, they'll go lame —a gristle starts growin' around the joints right above his hoof, and you can't cure it. But you can take novacaine and give it to the horse [to deaden the pain] and lead him around or show him, and he won't be lame. But as soon as that novacaine dies, it goes to hurtin' again.

Now you know a person who knows can tell a horse's age by his teeth up till he's eight or ten years old. You could take a regular little drill and drill the cavities back in their teeth, and paint those cavities with permanganate potash, and you could trade a mule fifteen years old for a seven- or eight-year-old. Just raise that lip and look, see those cups in the teeth, you don't have to tell him nothing. Just let him be his own judge.

To change their color, people used permanganate potash. This farmer was a leather salesman, and owned a five-to-six-hundred-acre farm, and he had an awful pretty spotted horse, and I wanted this horse. Well, I had a mule that was fat and pretty, but she was gray-headed, her whole head up here was white. Well, I took permanganated potash, a little salt, and a little hot coffee poured over that. Then take you a corncob and go over that hair. The more you put, the better it looks. I traded this mule for the man's spotted horse. It must have been two or three weeks or a month later, and he said, "You know, I like that mule fine, but I'll tell you what, you kept her in the pen with another bunch of mules, and that mule just stood and pawed she's so homesick, and you know, she's turned gray-headed?!" Now that just tickled me to death, 'cause I dyed her hair.

I had an Appaloosa horse, and he just had a few spots about on him. I said to a friend who was a barber, "Tony, get me some hair dye."

He said, "I'm gonna app this horse. He ain't got enough dots on him where the Lord blessed him when He put His hands on him. I want more spots to come on there."

Well, now, I'm not braggin', but I made the prettiest dots on him. I took me a Irish potato, stuck it down in that dye, now I had the prettiest round dot there, there's never been a artist that could beat me at dots. He traded that horse to an old boy over at Hayesville, North Carolina and after the dots faded out, he said, "I'll tell you what I'll do, I'll give a hundred and fifty dollars to find that man that dotted this horse. I want to get him to dot him again."

You get a lot of spoiled horses. I don't care how good a horse judge you are, how long you've been tradin'. Why I bought a horse at Toccoa for my grandson. He was a nice quarterhorse, pretty, fat, but he was a rig, what you call a rig. When they altered him, they didn't get but one seed, and the other one was up in his belly, but to look at him, you couldn't tell it. Then we turned him in the pasture and he killed a Shetland pony, and broke two or three calves' legs and he went to buckin'. Bucked off one of my grandsons, and got the other one afraid to ride him. All that happens. You'll get a horse that'll just go loco overnight, but that goes with it. When you're a'tradin' you get all that. A horse trader gets more than anybody, because when somethin' happens to one, they hunt a trader to put it on, but he can't eat it. He's got to get shed of it.

I've bought horses for two dollars and a half, and I've sold horses for as high as fifteen hundred dollars apiece. It's been a long experience. I've traded horses from Atlanta to Asheville. I used to follow the courts just like a judge in the circuit. I'd meet more people. Before I bought a truck and started truckin' 'em, I'd ride and lead a bunch. Oh, listen, I've been robbed. I have come in a'carryin' my saddle—I've swapped out. I've been tellin' you the good trades. I have come to the bridle—your judgment will fool you; you never learn it all. I don't care how long you trade, you're gonna get cheated. And if anyone's got somethin' that's wrong with whatever animal they've got, they'll hunt a horse trader to put it on. A poor old horse trader has the hardest time of anybody in this world. There's nobody believes him. Ever'body says, "Oh, he's the biggest liar in the world." You just watch a man when he comes a'wantin' t'trade. Whatever was wrong with his, if he had a mooneyed horse, or a windy horse, or a lame horse, he'd go look at that place first on a horse he was tradin' for. But my wife and I have raised four children, we own our own home. We ain't rich, but we got a very comfortable livin' for our age. But it's been rough for both of us.

Now I believe in feedin' whatever you have. A dog, a horse, whatever. I've made more money by buying poor. I never made no money in my life buying a fat horse; buy poor, feed him fat, then you can ask something for him and get it. And ever'body wants a pretty fat horse, but nobody wants a poor horse. Trading horses is a sight in this world. Now there's lots of expense to go along with it. You hear the pretty part of these traders and you say, "Well, that man's made a barrel of money." Well, it costs you somethin' to tend to a horse, and feed him and take care of him like he should be. It takes *money*. I've never fed a horse *yet* that I begrudged one bite that he eat. I love to see'em eat. I *enjoy* feedin' him.

It's a long old life—a horse trader—if he stays with it a lifetime he'll learn a whole lot of things that he may never even have thought about. Little things that you wouldn't dream of. You can't ever give up. You've got to fight a losin' battle. If you know you're gonna lose, you have to just keep pushin'. That's why a horse trader can get by. Determination. You've got to have the determination of an elephant to go through with it. I wouldn't take nothin' in the world for the experience I got tradin' horses.

"I'd trade for anything I could get ahold of."

ADAM FOSTER

I guess I was just born to like to trade. I commenced tradin' when I was a lad. First trade I ever made I swapped a sheep for a brood sow. I'd trade for anything I could get ahold of. I've swapped for chickens, banjos, pistols, anything.

I never did too much about changin' the looks of a horse, except dye their hair. If they were gray, I'd dye their hair around their face with permanganate potash. Mix it up in warm coffee; that made it color better. And used to, back yonder when I was a young man, I'd raise the depressions above their eyes. I'd pump that up and make'em look younger. I wouldn't do that now. Cut a little hole in there, fill it with air, and then fill that hole up. It'd stay maybe a week, long enough t'trade it.

They's a lot of people back in the olden days who'd work on their teeth, but I never did do that. They'd file'em off. It didn't help the horses any. A man older than me back yonder used to do it—he'd have a big old thing put in his mouth to hold it open, so the horse couldn't shut his mouth, and he'd take a file and cut them teeth smooth and flat. Sometimes they'd cut'em too short and the horse couldn't eat nothin'.

Sometimes I'd have'em t'have a swinney in the shoulder. They'd be hop-

PLATE 249 Adam Foster, who says, "Sometimes you make a pretty good little trade."

pin'. I'd take a piece of poke root, trim it down about like my little finger, and cut a hole in that shoulder just in the skin, not cut it in the muscle, push that poke root in there and that'd cure that swinney. The poison in that poke root did it. Swinney is a strain, and then they'll go to hoppin', and unless you do something for it, you've got a ruined horse.

I'd trim their feet and put turpentine in the frog of their hoof. The turpentine would take care of their foot, take the soreness out if they got a nail in it or got the thrush. Clean out that foot and fill it full of turpentine. I'd also burn that turpentine, set it afire and let it burn; bake that foot hard in there. That took the soreness out and hardened the frog of the foot. It didn't hurt the horse. I set one afire one day and I had let the turpentine run up his leg and the hair on his leg got afire, but I smothered it out with a sack before it burned his skin.

I used to do my own doctorin'. I never did do anything to'em to make'em look sound when they were lame. I'as tryin' t'cure'em.

Some traders would give'em shots, feed'em dynamite, make these old dead horses spiriten up. Take a piece of a stick of dynamite and mash it up in their feed. They say it'll spiriten'em up. I've tried it, but I didn't think it done much good. That's been years ago.

I was about seventeen years old when I done my first bit of horse trading. The first one I ever owned myself was a mule colt. I rode an older mule to North Carolina and got that colt. I paid seventy-five dollars for it. It was rainy, the creek was way up, and I had to cross a big creek to get home. I was afraid I couldn't get that colt through the creek. There was an old foot bridge two logs wide and floored, and I got a couple boys to help me push that colt across that footlog. I turned the other mule loose and he swam across the creek. I got him across all right and got him home safely. My father hadn't wanted me to get that colt, but I said, "I'll never learn no younger; I'm gonna go myself." When I got home, my daddy looked the mule over, and said, "Well, son, you've got a good mule."

I thought it was. So in a few days, he said, "Well, now that you've got one, just go buy you another one to match it. Have you a team." He said, "Just go borrow the money; I'll sign your note." I had my own money to pay for the first one. So I went to my uncle and asked to borrow some money to buy another mule colt.

He said, "Well, how much do you want?"

I said, "I don't know. I don't know what the mule's gonna cost exactly."

He said, "Well, here's a check. I'll sign it and you just fill it out when you buy the mule. Then come on back and give me a note for it."

Well, I had me a pair of mules then, and I thought I was rich. I kept one of those two or three years, and swapped one of'em for thirty-five acres of land, with one hundred and fifty dollars to boot. The other I kept till he was seventeen years old; then sold it to my brother.

The first *real* swappin' I done was over a T-model roadster. Me an' my brother had a good big truck to haul peaches on. I told him I was gonna buy a little old roadster, put a bed on it, and I could haul twenty-five or thirty bushels of peaches. I bought it and went down in Georgia and got me a load of peaches, started back up through the country at night, and I'd just have one blow-out after another. Well, I finally got back about daylight, and sold those peaches that day. An old man met me down the road here and said, "Would you swap that car for this pair of mules?"

He had a pair of mules to the buggy. I said, "Well, I'll swap with you for fifty dollars. I don't much want to trade this little car." 'Course I wanted to trade but I just told him that. I was sick of it.

He said, "Well, I'm just gonna trade with you. I'm gonna give you the boot. You can bring the car out in the mornin' and get the mules."

So I took the car over toward his house . . . had to cross the mountain, steep narrow roads, and I was climbin' up them hills and that old T-model got hot and went dead on me. You couldn't crank one when it got hot. They'd go dead and quit on you. I got up nearly to the top of that mountain, didn't lack two hundred yards and it was pretty flat from then on. It went dead on me. I was there a'crankin' and crankin', and it wouldn't start. I jacked up a hind wheel. When they got hard to crank, that'd help, and I was just a'turnin' and a'crankin'. And this old man come in behind me driving his mules. I was just afraid he wouldn't want to trade with me with it not cranking. He said, "What's the matter—you havin' trouble?"

And I said, "Yeah, it's got a little hot. If you hook those mules to it and pull it off, it'd crank in a few steps."

"Why," he said, "my buggy outfit wouldn't pull that car. That singletree on them's too little, don't you see that?"

I didn't know what he meant then, but as it turned out, the mules wouldn't pull nothin' but the buggy. Put a little weight to'em, they wouldn't pull, and he didn't want me to know that! I kept on till eventually I got it cranked. I got over the top of the hill and made it fine from there on in. He wanted me to stay till the next day and teach his son how to drive the car, but I told him, "No, I had to get on home." So I got my mules and started back, and got in way after dark. Next day I swapped'em for a little saddle mare and got a hundred and fifty dollars to boot. I was makin' money I thought. I just give ninety dollars for the old car.

I just kept on goin' from there on—not regular. I worked jobs lots of my life. But back through the thirties when it was so hard, I made enough tradin' to support my family when everyone else was gettin' on the WPA. I'd trade a horse, and if I got five dollars to boot, that'd do me a month. The money from horse trading helps, but I always made my crops—'taters, corn, beans—and had my hogs and killed five, six, eight hogs every year. I've done ever'thing but steal to make a living. You don't get rich when you're a trader. Sometimes you make some money and sometimes you lose some money.

I used to go from place to place—Franklin, North Carolina, Murphy, North Carolina, Clayton, Georgia, and I'd go to court to swap. And there'd be these horse-swappin' conventions over in Union County and around, and have a week's horse tradin'. It wasn't a fair, just a horse tradin', people gettin' drunk. They'd be in a different place every year. There'd be a few farmers go, but mostly it was us horse traders, swappin' with one another. Maybe you'd make a little money.

A fellow come by one day, and he wanted me to take a mule to Blairsville for him for ten dollars. I said, "All right, I'll take him." He had it traded off, but we stopped down here at Hiawassee, and I saw a man lookin' at the mule in my truck. He said, "I've got a four-year-old mule I'll swap you for that mule." The man who owned the horse told me to go ahead and trade. He said, "You just go ahead and trade the way you want to. You know more about tradin' than I do. If you can make me a good trade, go ahead." We went on down the road and the man give me a big fat hog, fifteen to twenty bushels of soybeans to boot and the old man with me just set still. He never let on it was his mule. Well, we got the little four-year-old mule we traded for, and it was wild, but we got it loaded on the truck. The man with me said, "Well, now that you've traded, what do you want to do?"

I said, "Well, if you want to, we'll go down there and swap with the man you planned to trade with." We went over to that fellow's house, and he said, "Yeah, I'll swap with you." I asked him twenty dollars to boot. He said, "All right, if it'll work. I'll just put it to the wagon." We hooked it to the wagon, and it was hitched up with his old gentle mule, and it worked all right. He swapped with us. I got us back home, and I got that old man about a hundred and fifty dollars and the same mule he had wanted to trade for. Now that's horse trading.

I started out one day with my brother over here to Young Harris to change horses for him. He wasn't no horse trader. Now he traded cattle, but he couldn't trade no horses. I told him after we finished the trade and got the horse loaded up, "You've got beat."

He said, "How do you know?"

I said, "I've owned that old mare. I know what she'll do. Let's go on over here to Blairsville and swap horses again."

We swapped over there for a good little old mule, got some boot, went on down to Murphy, swapped again, got boot again, and we come on back home, and my brother give me twenty-five, thirty dollars for that day's work. It was worth it to him. He made more that day than he expected to. In the wind-up, I give him what boot I got, and he give me the last mule I traded for. And I took it to Franklin, and swapped it for a big old mule, the prettiest mule ever I seen, from old man Doc Angel's father. He was a big fine-lookin' mule, but he was wind-broken. Couldn't get its breath when it started t'work. He said, "Oh, that's a good mule as ever you've seen."

I said, "Ain't that mule's wind a little short?"

"Oh, no," he said, "there ain't nothin' wrong with that mule."

I knew his wind was broke and that's why I wanted t'get it. Trade on it. So I swapped with him for fifteen dollars. He paid me, and just as quick as he paid me—he wouldn't wait till I loaded the wind-broke mule—he knowed it wouldn't *load* on a truck; it wouldn't *ride* on a truck. But I finally did get it on the truck, and I seen it was gonna tear the side out of the truck. It was about dark, and I went to town and got some big ropes to tie him in there with; then I just got through Franklin, coming out toward Hayesville, and that old big mule tore out of the side of the truck, and right into the road he went. I had a fellow with me, and I asked him to lead the mule to a friend's house, Ferd Burrell, and figured we'd leave him there. So I drove on slowly out to where the old man lived, and we put the mule in the stable, and I patched up the truck a little and come on home. Next mornin' I saw the sheriff—he was a horse trader, too, and I said, "Let's go over to Franklin. I've got a mule over there I have to go and get." We went over there in his truck; he swapped a time or two with this fellow, Burrell, and we finally brought the mule on back. He said, "Let's go to Blairsville and trade some this evening." So we went on over there, and an old fellow looked at that big fine sorrel mule up there on the truck, and he said, "I've got a good mare mule down at the house I'll swap you for that mule."

I said, "I don't guess you'd want to pay me the boot I'd ask you."

He said, "Just go down and look." So we went on down to his house, and he said, "I'll tell you what, I'll give you fifteen dollars, every dollar I've got." My mule wouldn't compare to his, and I knew it. I said, "Just let me have it, and here's your mule." Put his'n on the truck and I was gone. Went on back home, swapped it the next day for another'n, got fifty dollars to boot. Sometimes you make a pretty good little trade. But I've gone three months at a time with only three dollars.

MAKING TAR

When wagon axles and wheel hubs were made completely of wood, resin (or "tar") melted out of fat pine was smeared on the axle ends to minimize the friction of the turning wheel hub. In addition, the tar found other farm uses: when cattle were dehorned, it was smeared on the stubs of the horns to keep flies away; when livestock got scraped or cut, it was smeared on the wound, and when they got sore feet, their hooves were poured full of it and bound up with rags; and when sheep got "head rot," a little tar was forced down into their tear ducts to open their heads up. Even humans used it. For coughs, a syrup made of one part tar, five parts molasses, and two parts sulfur, taken one teaspoonful at a time, supposedly helped. Tar was also put on blisters, sores, and sometimes even poison ivy.

One day a neighbor walked into our office and asked us if we had ever seen tar made. He had just heard of a rock on Wolffork where the community used to gather to do it, but it had gotten turned over on its side over the years. We tracked it down, turned it back upright, and with the help of Mack and Terry Dickerson, put it back into action.

When I first walked out to the tar rock with the rest of the crew that had helped turn it upright, Mack and Terry were getting ready to make it. I felt excited. I was getting an opportunity to witness and learn about something few teen-agers my age ever get a chance to see. I felt proud that I was a part of it, and I was determined to make something out of this rare experience. I knew it was something special when some of the neighbors came out to watch it. I wondered how many other kids my age had had this chance to see how tar was made long ago. Perhaps they had read about it in books, but really getting to see it? There was something inside of me that told me to never forget so that someday I could tell my kids how it was done, and then they could tell their kids and so on. At least somebody would still know how to do it.

When I was out there watching and helping them make it, it just made me more interested in how people did do things like this long ago when there weren't any machines or devices to do it for them.

CRAIG CARLTON

PLATE 250   As a child, Terry Dickerson used to watch his father melt resin ("tar") out of fat pine on this rock. With Terry and Mack Dickerson's help, we re-created that experience, and many of the neighbors came to watch.

When I set out with the rest of the crew, I had a feeling of determination. We were going to turn that rock over. No question about it. We also had the feeling that this was just some big hunk of rock that was in someone's way all the time. We had no idea that it was a special rock for making something useful. We hadn't been told in advance what the rock had once been used for. When we got to the rock, I wondered about that depression in it. Finally I realized that the rock was once used for making tar. Then I became interested in it.

A couple of days later, Terry and Mack started to make it. All of us came to watch. There was interviewing, and a lot of pictures were taken. The making of the tar was very interesting. Even some of the community folks came to watch. It was kind of like a friendly reunion. Some of the people said that it reminded them of the past when old-timers used to make tar.

Well, though some of the people thought that the old way of making tar had died out, through the aid of *Foxfire,* Mack and Terry, and us, once again the old-timers' way of making tar was relived.

DALE FERGUSON

PLATE 251 To turn the rock over we dug the earth out from behind it and rolled it back using poles as levers.

PLATE 252 Mack and Terry first packed the iron pot full with slivers of fat pine (pine that is almost solid resin).

PLATE 253 Terry hammered the last pieces into the pot with a stake to make sure it was packed as full as it could be.

PLATE 254 When the pot was packed, it was inverted over the depression in the rock's surface, and over the tiny groove cut in the rock to allow the basin to drain. Then a piece of tin was placed between the pot's rim and the groove in the rock.

PLATE 255 Next, Mack and a neighbor brought water from a nearby stream to make up a batch of red-clay mud.

PLATE 256 The water was poured onto the clay, then stirred to make a good stiff mixture.

PLATE 257 The clay was then packed around the rim of the pot to keep the flames from the fire that will be built over the pot from lapping in under the rim and setting the wood inside on fire. The piece of tin keeps the mud from filling the groove in the rock and blocking the flow of resin.

PLATE 258 Next Mack and Terry piled wood over the pot and started a bonfire. They kept adding wood to make the fire as hot as possible.

PLATE 259   Then they waited for the tar to begin to flow.

PLATE 260   Finally the resin began to melt and run down the insides of the black pot where it collected in the rock basin and drained out the groove and down the side of the rock into a pan Terry had waiting.

PLATE 261   When the pan was filled, the resin was poured into a container for future use. It keeps indefinitely, remaining in a syrupy form. The flow finally stopped after we had filled three pans. We took one pan with us and Mack and Terry kept the rest.

LOGGING

We first became interested in logging when Bill Lamb, one of our earliest and finest contacts, told us the haunting memory that follows. We saved it specifically to work into this chapter:

"They'd take them old log carts—I don't know to this day why they wouldn't trail up logs—but they'd hook the oxen to them carts and then they'd just have to scatter around to stay out of the way of that log pushing that cart down the mountain. In the place of stringing up four or five logs like people got to doing finally in this country, why, they'd just have to out-run one log.

"I've seen poor old steers—and them with big yokes on—I've seen them have to run just as hard as they could run to stay out of the way of a log, and the log just running them over. If it run out [of the logging road] and hit something, it was just about one's neck broke, or his leg, or something 'r'nother that way. Sometimes they'd try to jay loose from one where it was on too bad a run. And if you hit a rock solid sometimes, just stall them just as dead as they could be until you pulled and twisted off.

"I'll tell you what I've seen. I've seen as high as five or six yoke of cattle to one log when they was in here logging out the old virgin timber. I've seen five or six yoke go through all the punishment that ever you see'd on any-thing. 'Course the ground wasn't level, you know. Just to get out it was over a hump or in a holler. And I've seen steers picked plumb off of the ground by the head going through a low place in here, and then I've seen them going over the top with the old wheel cattle in back next to the log—maybe them pulling over there—and them just having to slide their head right sideways in the ground to keep from catching their nose *in* the ground.

"And every once in a while an old steer'd get a foot cut off—catch it be-tween a log and a rock or something, you know—and maybe just cut their foot just about off. Have them to kill.

"Why, it was a sight the punishment that was put on the old cattle. They was always short-legged nearly, you know, and couldn't get around good. People always used a whip as long as from here to that seat over yonder, and a man could make the hair fly off a steer with that. Them old whips a'popping—they'd go like rifles sometimes.

"And sometimes five or six yoke, and them all strung out. Well, if the road wasn't straight, they'd go around a tree here and below a tree yonder —like people would do building a road through the woods. They'd dig all the roads and put in a fender log, and they'd come down through there and get at a tree, and them old cattle that was back next to the log—it was a sight to see how they'd goose them old cattle there with them whip stocks, you know, to make them wheel over to keep that log from binding against the tree here; and them other ones out yonder had lots of that load out yonder past that, you see. Well, they had to hold them cattle and their load, too. Well, that'd make the awfullest strain on them cattle ever you see'd. If it'd jerk them over and throw them over the fender log, then it was back up everything till you got them back up.

"Lord, the punishment they had. If there was ever a blessing that come on anything, it was when they got the trucks and bulldozers to log with to take all of that burden off of the old horses and oxen. Why, they'd have a great big barn full of cattle; maybe have ten or twelve head of cattle. They was some people that didn't have no mercy on themselves nor the cattle neither. That's what made it so bad. A poor old steer doing everything it could, and then a man just reach over and lift him off of the ground. Why, I've heered them whips pop as big as a thirty-eight pistol. Just, 'Ka-bow! Ka-bow!' and if you was where you could see, lots of times the blood was trickling out of them steers where they was hit. They'd take a plait on a cracker as long as my arm out of thread, and they'd beeswax that thread and they'd plait it on the end of that whip, you see. And then they'd have a big long whip stock on them.

"Why, they could just stand here and whip one yonder at the edge of the porch and just make him bounce."

Millard Buchanan, who spent much of his life logging, became our primary contact for this article largely because he has been involved with logging from the time it was done with animals up through the advent of trucks and modern machinery.

Millard's ancestors settled in the Smokies through a land grant from the Queen of England. They've been in the mountains ever since. Millard himself was raised right above Waynesville, North Carolina, on Browning Branch. He lived there for thirty-five years right up through the Depression: "That was back in the days when everything was down so low. Jim

Crawford started building a house, and back then, you know, everything was done with a hand saw, and when the hand saw would get a little rusty or something, people would carry a meat skin with them and rub that blade every time it started to bind. They'd have to rub it two or three times sawing one piece. Old man Jim, he worked and he got the subfloor and everything down on the house and started to put up the walls, and then quit.

"And some of them two or three days after that told that old man Jim was down there about drunk, and what a time for him to pitch a drunk and quit. Said to him, says, 'Jim, how come you quit carpentering?' Says, 'We thought that house was going to be put up and maybe be a little construction work around here.'

"And he said, 'Well, I was doing all right,' he said, 'if it wadn't for one of them damn old poor dogs that eased up and stole my meat skins,' he said, 'That shut the job down!' "

Millard's contact with horses and steers has been constant throughout his life. His grandfather, for example, was a cattle buyer. When he got ready to make a drive, he'd send letters ahead to the men who raised them to let them know what day he'd be coming through so they could have them gathered up and ready for him. Then he'd head out picking up several head at each farm, driving them along the road with him as he went, and camping at night. By the time he got near the end of his route, he might have as many as a hundred and fifty head. These he'd drive to Clyde, North Carolina, where they'd be sold, loaded on railroad cars, and shipped to Chicago.

Of course there were animals around their farm, too:

"I never did try to lay off and plant with a steer. They were too slow for that. But steers and a wagon might go to town just the same as horses and a wagon back then.

"We did our plowing with horses. And then we'd break up new ground —pull the roots out with horses or cattle, or work around them till they rotted loose. I've plowed many a new ground, and if you didn't watch it and the horse get going a little too fast and that plow hit a root or a stump and the plow handles catch you right under the ribs there—I've had my sides blue all over plumb up under my arms and back under my shoulders where them confounded plows have kicked me. Shey'd shore get you, and I'll guarantee you couldn't dodge one neither! It'd shore fly up and get you. Raise you plumb up off the ground sometimes it'd kick so hard.

"We used to have an old mare we called Dinah. And old Dinah, I'd put her in new ground and go to plowing her and every time that plow would hit a root or a rock or something and hang a little bit, she'd look back at you and snap her teeth. She'd pop her teeth just as fast as she could pop'em, and go to switching her tail. She'd get mad whenever that there harness jerked her two or three times. That was the aggravatingest thing's ever been in the world. I throwed rocks at her many an hour for running sideways and snapping her teeth at me! And she'd bite you too if you was in reach of her. She wouldn't just pop them teeth. She'd bite, too!

"And then, of course, I did a lot of logging with horses and steers. People have stopped raising them. Young people don't take an interest in nothing like that no more. Young people now, why they've got something else to do. If they work any at all, they get out here and work on a car or motorcycle or something like that.

"See, back then they wasn't nothing for us to do—only things like that. Wasn't no picture show. Nothing to do without you just went over and sat and talked to your neighbor a while. Wasn't no radios. Wasn't no TVs. Wasn't such a thing as lights. If you wanted a light, you carried an old lantern. [By the] time you'd carried it an hour, the globe would be smoked on it till you just as well catch a lightning bug for you couldn't see a damn thing with it. Go in the house and think you could read, and in thirty or forty minutes' time have to get up and clean the globe where it was smoked. And that was it, see? So they wasn't nothing to do much back then only just fiddle around with something like steers, you know, when you wasn't working.

"And then cattle was cheap. Beef cattle and milk cattle was cheap. The best would sell for fifteen or twenty dollars apiece. That's all they'd bring. Well, if you had a yoke of steers that was broke and matched up, well you could sell them for a hundred and fifty or two hundred dollars. You see the difference in price. Good yoke of steers would bring as much as a pretty good herd of cattle would otherwise."

The following section begins with Millard's method of breaking and training steers, and progresses through his logging days. We hope you enjoy it.

Interviews by Wendell Culpepper, Doug James, Jim Renfro, Steve Smith, Peter Reddick, and Matt Young. Photos by Doug and Matt.

BREAKING AND TRAINING OXEN

I like to work with steers [better than horses or mules]. They're slow-natured, the most of them is. I just like to fool with'em. After they've got used to you and you get'em broke, they've got a whole lot more sense than a horse or a mule. And they won't come half as near hurting you. You can work a horse or a blame mule and you think they's not a bit of harm in him in the world—maybe keep him ten years and go in to get him one morning and the son-of-a-gun'll kill you. Wheel and kick you or something. I always liked to

work a steer more than anything I ever fooled with. They're just easier natured.

And they're not near as expensive on feed. And then another advantage:
back when we was working cattle, we always fed'em high, you know—cottonseed meal and hull—and kept'em good and fat. And if one got a leg
broke or something like that, we could skin him out and eat him and we
wasn't losing a thing. If he got hurt and had to be killed, why he went
across the table!

Getting started, it takes a pretty good judge of cattle. You've got to know
pretty well what kind of cattle you've got. A red Devon is actually the best
stock of work steer they is. That's an old stock of cattle—about as old a
stock as they was. They're a deep red, and they was all horned cattle. You
dehorned all of'em. Them son-of-a-guns, they just know what work means.
Seems like whenever you first put'em in a yoke, if you start off with'em
right, they know what you're doing with'em.

But that Devon was a deep red color, and that's another thing made people like them more than anything else. The color made that much
difference on account of showing up so good. And then they was a type
stock that they wasn't too much difference in'em. What I mean, you know,
you wouldn't find a big bone and a little bone. Their bones was all about
the same size, and their heads was all made alike. In other words, they're
just matched, you know.

Now we worked Jerseys; we worked Holsteins; we worked other types,
but actually the best type was the Devon. We worked good Jerseys and
Guernseys, but for a good tough work animal, the Devon had him beat. As
a usual thing, a Jersey is easier broke than a Devon is, but they're mean.
You might work one all day, or maybe work it a week and think they
wasn't nothing wrong with it at all, and whenever you drop the bow [on
the yoke] and turn him loose, the son-of-a-gun wheel and hook you or kick
you. They're just natured that way. They're mean. You've got to handle
them a whole lot rougher than you do a Devon. They's mischief in a Jersey.
Jersey bulls is something that's bad to fight. Jersey's worse than a Guernsey.

And hybrid stock just don't make a good work steer. They've bred'em up
to where they ain't got no *sense*. You take anything that's hybrid and somehow or another it affects their brain. You can take these black cattle—these
black Angus—and you can handle them any way you want to; and then
you stay away from'em a week and go back into the barn to get'em and
they'll climb the walls. Put you out!

Now if they don't have horns, that's muley cattle. Muley don't have
horns. They're born without any. Back years ago, they all had horns, and
see, they kept improving them and got'em to where they bred'em without
horns. You wouldn't see one in a hundred that didn't have horns back forty

years ago. And if you had one didn't have horns, he was a muley. That was the name for him. He was a muley cow or a muley steer. It was just a rare thing. People was really glad to get ahold of one. That's the way they started breeding them and getting the horns off of them. They'd get them natural muleys—and they was long and far between—but they'd keep them natural muley heifers and then whenever they had a muley bull, they'd mate'em up. See, they wanted'em with no horns. That's what they was trying to do— get'em bred with no horns. And they've got it now. You don't see many *with* horns. The horns is about done away with. But they wasn't making much success on that breeding the horns off till along about '40.

[If you had young, horned cattle and you were going to leave the horns on rather than dehorning them] you could make them grow in any shape you wanted to. If you put rubber bands on them and a stick to separate them, and let it stay for a day or so and then take it off for two or three days and then put it back, you can shape them. You can make them grow any shape if you'll fix it to where there's the least little steady pull [on the horns]. Makes them look better. We used to take'em and when their horns got to be about a foot long, we'd put a small piece of brass on the ends, like a forty-five pistol hull. Put brass nubs on the ends, and they'd just shine in the sun.

And if their horns is right—if you've got'em turned like the regular old work steer—you can hear'em a'going along the road, and them old horns will just be cracking together as they walk—just making a tune nearly.

If you want to pick out a yoke, you make sure the cow's legs are the same length, and the backs are the same height. You have to have two cows about the same build—legs and all—'cause if you don't, you'll have one long lanky steer and one short one. Also you have to pick them out by the shape of their heads.

The best age to start getting them halter wise where you can tie'em and handle'em is when they're just sucking calves just being weaned—when they're about three months old. Just take'em when they're calves and start handling'em—play with them two or three times a week, or maybe once a week on Saturday evenings or Sundays. Have to fool with'em a month or more to gentle'em down and get them used to you.

And then you want to pen'em together. If you're going to work'em to- gether, you ought to pen'em together and feed'em together, and make sure one can't crowd the other out when they're eating. Keep'em together all the time, and then whenever you turn'em loose out here, they never will sepa- rate. They'll stay together, and wherever you find one, you'll find the other. That way you wouldn't have no trouble going and getting your steers when you got ready to work'em 'cause they'd be together.

These steers I've got up here, I can go up there and tie one of them and start off from there with it, and that other one would tear out and follow me if I was to lead him plumb over into North Carolina. They've been done that way all the time, see?

But get them used to a halter first. Get them to where you can lead them around anywhere you want to go. Get them to where you can hande them in any direction you pull on them with that halter and them not pull back. If you have trouble, get two men—get one in front and one in back. Then if the one in front pulls and the steer fails to come, let that'n behind have him a good long withe and *move'im!*

And then when you want him to stop, say, "Whoa," and then hold him after you say, "Whoa," and *make* him stop, see? You need to be pretty stout yourself or they'll overpower you and do whatever they want to do. I've took steers when they was nearly too big to train right and put bits in their mouth just like working a horse 'cause I couldn't handle'em no other way.

PLATE 262   Millard shows the oxen who's in charge.

And I have run a rope around through under their jaw. Just any way to hold'em to start with.

After I get my steers broke, I won't have no rope on'em. I might leave a halter on'em on account of them looking better, but I won't have no ropes on'em. If I tell one to come here and he don't come, or I tell him to back and he don't back, I'll reach up and grab that whip. I use that whip to drive with. And you don't have to use it hard.

Ropes are just in the way. After you fool with'em a little bit—get'em to where they know what's going on—you can just take that whip and throw it up and let it fall easy and that cracker'll wind around that horn and it'll stay there. You can pull it. If you jerk it right hard, it'll be just like it's tied. You can pull your steer anywhere then.

See, in other words, you've got to show them that you're a better man than they are. And until you do, you can't do nothing with'em. You want to get'em gentle to where you can handle'em, you know, but then if they won't do what you want'em to do, you've got to foul them in a shape to show them that they *have* to. And if you one time get'em showed that you're boss, that's the end of the trouble you'll have with'em. Unless one of'em was to kick you or something. Now every once in a while, any of'em will take a spell maybe. They'll kick just like a mule. And they're a something that you never know when they're going to kick nor nothing else. You'll never be expecting nothing, and one of them things'll kick you quick as lightning can strike. And when he kicks, he kicks *hard* too. I'll guarantee you he'll bring the hide! Lot of times they'll come up forwards. You'll be a'walking down by the side of one, walking up towards his head, and he'll kick forwards same as he will backwards. Mule or horse'll just kick back, but a steer'll kick sideways, forwards, *or* back! If they take a notion to hit you, they'll just about hit you. They's no way you can get away from'em. That's exactly the situation!

Now after you've got them gentled, you can put both oxen together in a yoke. Start'em off as a team and, see, they'll more or less gait together. See, that's one thing on the length of their legs and stuff that you want to watch. If you have a short-legged one and a long-legged one, then as long as they work together that there long-legged one'll be just a little bit faster than the other one because he'll take longer steps. That's the reason you've got to size 'em up that way.

And if you let them turn in the yoke a few times, they won't never do nothing only turn the yoke every time you go to work them. If you'll pick you up a club, and get one person on one side and one on the other and go to laying it on their sides from their hind ends plumb to their heads, about four or five licks is all you'll hit'em till they'll turn that yoke back and be a'standing like they're supposed to be. You've got to knock that into'em.

They're kind of natured like a horse. You don't find as many balky steers as horses, though. They work kind of like a horse. They's some of'em that are higher nerved—kind of nervy—sort of scary. You can take some of'em that is high-nerved like that and they're scary as long as they live. Just like a horse is. I mean it's in them just like it is humans. You know you can get people—they get excited awful easy and it takes'em a while to get over it. Well, you hit that in cattle or horses or anything you work with. You get ahold of one of them high-nerved ones and you've got to work him awful easy. You've got to just about pet him into [working]. You might have to knock him down every once in a while, but when you do that, then, and get him stopped, then you've got to pet him. You've got to work him easy.

And then you get some that's just plumb old down stubborn, and when you get them there stubborn ones, you've got to pick you up something till you show'em who's boss, and knock'em where you want them.

When my steers goes to cutting up, I take that whip right over there and give'em a cut or two and that straightens'em out. They know what that is! They know what it means.

They'll get used to that yoke pretty fast. If they don't, I'd take'em out there and tie'em to a tree out there in a field somewhere where all they could do would be go around and around it. I'd put that yoke on them of a morning, and I'd take it off'em when I fed'em that night. Do that about a week. Let'em wear that yoke all day long and not take it off. Let them get theirselves tangled up any way they want to. They'll come untangled. They'll not break their necks nor nothing. They'll get tangled up and they'll get untangled, and they'll find that it's a whole lot easier for'em to stand and not tangle'emselves up and they'll do it. And that's the way I'd do that now. Tie them to where they can go around and around but not get the lines or nothing under their feet. Just tie one of'em to the tree and let him control the other one. And then you might not have no more trouble. They might go to work.

So let'em wear the yoke till they get used to it, and then start pulling a little something. First thing to do is to get'em used to the rattle of that chain 'cause, see, they have to pull with a chain. Put that yoke on and let'em get used to the rattle of that ring in the yoke, you know. And then the yoke itself'll rattle. It makes a funny racket. Get them used to that, and then put a heavy log chain in that ring then, and let it pull between'em—let them drag it around till they get used to that racket. And then after four or five times dragging, put'em to a sled—something light. Let'em have that thing light four or five times, or half a dozen times for an hour or an hour and a half maybe every other day, and then go to putting weight on it. Let'em pull that [empty] sled around about a half a dozen times, and then the next time you hook it up, get on it.

Mine wanted to wring and twist a little bit when I put them to the sled, and I just got that whip and give'em two or three cuts and that was it.

Then start laying the loads to'em—not too heavy—till they see they can move what you've got hooked to'em, and then just in a short time you can just load any amount you want to. They won't *quit* pulling. They won't back up from it if they find out they can't pull it. They'll still try to pull it anyhow. But if you ever do overload one and let him quit, then you've got to straighten him out again. It's better to just give'em what they can go on with until they get used to the work altogether, and then you've got it, then. Then you can do whatever you want to with'em.

If they try that turning in the yoke again, tie their tails together with a rope—and tie it tight, too. And only give'em a little space in between where you've got'em tied. See, then they can't twist their hind ends. If they can't twist their hind ends around, they can't turn that yoke. See, they've got to step out kindly away from it before they can turn it; and if you've got their tails tied together, they can't get out there far enough *to* turn it. I've done a little bit of everything to'em!

You need to work'em in a pretty good-sized lot; and when one goes to getting ahead of the other one, hold that rope a little tighter on the faster one and give that other one a cut and make him stay up. And if they want to run, they'll not run far because they give out easy. And if they do want to run and they run a little ways, why don't let'em stop whenever they want to. Just keep'em a'going. And if one was to go ahead of the other'n, give the one that's behind another cut. That's the way you've got to do'em.

And if you want one to go to the left, tell him, "Haw," and if you want him to go the right, tell him, "Gee." Now the old way if you want one to come to the left, you hollered, "Whoa, come here." And if you wanted him to go to the right, you hollered, "Whoa, back," or, "Gee."

Your lead steer is the one on the left, but you can work'em from either side after you get'em broke. They claim the one on the left always has a little harder job than the other one. I never could figure that out. I never could see no difference in it myself. Maybe I wasn't that much educated on'em, but I've worked'em all my life—horses and mules and steers—and I never could figure out where one had it any rougher than the other.

Now if we was working and something happened to one [of the steers], if you've got one broke to where he knows what's going on and'll mind you, you can take another one that's wild—don't make no difference how wild he is—and put him in [in place of the one that got hurt] and the one you've already got broke will help control that other one. He won't let him get loose from you. He'll more or less help hold him in place.

And the way we used to work that: When we worked four or six steers together and something happened to one of them and we had to put a new one in that didn't know nothing about the work, we'd put him back here at the back with what we call the wheel cattle. You always had your [pair of] leaders up front, and the chain that was hooked on that lead yoke was hooked onto the back cattles' yoke too. Well, see, he *couldn't* do nothing only stay in line because the front ones would be pulling him till all he could do was just twist sideways or lay down! He either *had* to go or lay down. That was all. And if he laid down, why, it was so hot under his belly he had to get up! He didn't stay there long.

That new steer might have just come in from pasture. Back then when so many cattle was used, you caught them up out of the woods because it was free cattle range. People didn't have too much pasture under fence for nothing only just their milk stock. Whenever a steer got up about a year or a year and a half old, why he was took to the mountains and he stayed there till you was ready to sell [or use] him. Never did come in no more only just heifers and cows, you know, that was ready to calf. Some of them steers in the mountains would be four years old. Then time something happened to one you were working—get him crippled up or get a horn knocked off, or sometimes they'd bruise their horns and take the "swell-head" we called it and get pus in their horns and the side of their head would swell up and you'd have to bore that and let the pus out and not make him work for a month or two till he got straightened back out—we'd just go in the woods and catch one up and cram him back at the wheel and he *had* to go. In three or four days' time he was doing his part just like he'd been at it all the time. But he was still wild. He'd be hard to handle, you know, till you'd handled him two or three months.

Or you could put that new one in the middle yoke with one that had been working a long time. He couldn't get loose nor nothing because he was fouled behind and in front too. Them lead cattle in front would pull his head off if he didn't pull.

I've fooled with steers a lot. I've dehorned a lot of them. Saw'em off with a hand saw—dullest hand saw you could find. That made their horns heal a whole lot quicker to use a dull saw that didn't booger up their horn none. You go to sawing in that horn and the blood start to flying and them son-of-a-bitches go to bellering and bawling and get down on their knees—you could hear'em from here to Clayton. Had a gauge we could pull their head through to hold'em. It was bound to hurt. I've sawed horns off of'em to where blood would be running as far as from here to the barn out there— great big long branch of it. Cut off maybe fifty or seventy-five at a time, you know, and you had a lot of blood. Get so God-dang sick have to quit and leave a while and then come back and start again. We dehorned all of'em with a hand saw. Only way we knowed. Only way we'd ever been taught to dehorn'em.

And we had to put shoes on'em. I don't guess any of you boys have ever seen an ox shoe. We'd have two shoes for each foot—or two pieces for each foot. It took two pieces, you know, to make a shoe. See, their hooves are split in the middle; between their toes there wasn't nothing, and there's nothing back there between their heels either. So the shoe was two separate pieces of steel. You had to put [the steers] in a special stock when shoeing them and tie their feet down to a big heavy post where they couldn't move them—put big leather straps around their feet and tie them to that post and shoe'em while they was tied 'cause they's never been one that wouldn't kick. Aw, them things would lay down and bawl and beller and everything else whenever you started putting shoes on'em. It didn't hurt'em. You just can't hammer on their feet. Horse is a whole lot different. I guess they more or less know you're supposed to hammer on'em. Some of them, when you first go to put shoes on'em they're pretty rough, but not nothing like a steer. You just can't shoe a steer without having you a pole where you can pull his leg out from under him and put it to that pole and put a leather strap around it where it wouldn't hurt his leg; put the shoe on and then turn him loose and pull another foot up.

LOGGING WITH STEERS AND HORSES

Logging with oxen—that's nasty. It's nasty when you're fooling logging with them. The general field of logging is just hard work. Work from before daylight till after dark. That's the general field. Having to wade in mud hip deep half the time, and snow and ice the other half. That's like the kind of winters we used to have at that time. We've not had no rough winters in a long time. We ain't had no really rough winters since the early '40s.

We used oxen to drag the logs out of the woods with, and then we used horses to carry them to the mill and from the mill to the railroad siding. We used horses to wagons, and we used oxen to wagons. From the time the log started out of the woods till it got to the railroad siding, it would take about three weeks.

But you want to back up and start at the beginning? Okay.

First, your logs have to be cut to length. You allow two to four inches. If you're cutting sixteen-foot stuff, you allow a little and that way it will all square to sixteen feet. We used a crosscut saw to cut the tree down, and we cut the limbs off with an axe. Mostly you just worked up to where the limbs or knots set in and quit there. You didn't use no knotty lumber without you was going to use it yourself, or somebody wanted to build a barn or something. You either kept that yourself or left it laying in the woods. We used firewood, but we wouldn't go that far back in the woods after it. There was too much of it close by. See, where a lot of these big cleared fields is now,

PLATE 263   Six pairs of oxen hooked to a long wagon.

back then that was standing in heavy woodland—big trees. You wouldn't cut down more than four or five of them big trees [out of a field close to home] till you'd have enough wood to last all winter. You take trees that's four and five foot through—one of them six-foot saws just barely reach through it—and you don't have to cut too many of them to have winter wood. Very few. So what we left back in the woods where we was logging just laid there and rotted.

We done all the cutting with a crosscut saw. They wasn't such a thing as a power saw back then. You could set your axe head in the lead when it was sawed out, and the handle will point the way the tree will fall. I can drive pegs out through there, and cut a tree and drive them pegs on into the ground with that tree. They had contests like that back when they used to use crosscut saws.

And whenever we cut them, we had to cut'em different to what they do with these power saws, because if one [tree] was leant, you never could get a crosscut saw under it far enough to keep it from busting. Oak in particular. If you didn't cut past the heart of it, if it was leant any at all it'd split wide open when you laid the saw into the back of it. You couldn't saw it fast enough to keep it from splintering. It'd go to pulling splinters out of the middle there at the heart, and if it was fifty feet to the first limb, that's how far it would split! It'd ruin the whole tree. Ash was another thing that was awful bad to split. On sugar maple and oak too, I've chopped six hours chopping a lead the way the son-of-a-gun had to fall to keep it from splintering. Couldn't saw it, you know. Just had to set in with an axe and chop it. And once in a while you'd hit one that you'd just have to chop *down*. You take one so big that you could almost set that sofa there on the stump, and you set in chopping that down and you've got a day's work ahead of you. A hard one, too, I mean. It'd just take all day for one to fall and hit the ground. That's all.

Now with these power saws, you don't have to saw past the heart since it's so fast. It cuts faster than the tree will split.

Right after the war in '46, I cut some poplar and white pine and yellow pine that was awful big. And we had awful big chestnuts and awful big mountain oaks, and what they called hard maple—that was sugar maple—we had a sight of that that was awful big. I've worked as high as two days getting one log to a sawmill with six head of cattle.

Now cattle: if he'll work good, one steer ought to pull his weight. To load one and not load him out of reason to where he ought to go on, judge what he'll weigh standing on foot and then load just about what his standing weight will be. Say the two of them weigh about two thousand pounds. Well, about a ton gives them a load on the ground. If the load is up on a wagon, why they can pull three times that much. But if it's on the ground where it sticks, they ought to pull a ton if they weigh a thousand pounds apiece as long as it's level or downhill a little bit. They ought to carry their weight.

We had pulling contests up until World War II—mules in their class, year-old fillies up to six-year-old—like that. They'd pull weights. You keep adding on till they couldn't pull anymore. No money prize unless maybe you got two dollars and a half for having the best in the county. But everybody knowed you had the best! Or you'd get a ribbon—great big thing to hang up on the wall. Blue was first, yellow second, and pink was third. If you got that *pink* ribbon, that was something, you know. That was the starting of breeding up stock—cattle and horses—because from '30 until up about '33 was when they started bringing this registered stock in here and breeding up the size of them. See, that old-type Devon, they'd have to be seven or eight years old to get up around fourteen to sixteen hundred pounds. It was something unusual for one to get up to eighteen or two thousand pounds. He'd have to be ten or twelve year old. Well, you take the same cattle the way they got it bred up with that registered stuff, and by the time he's three years old, now, he'd weigh as much as he would whenever he was eight back then. Same way with horses and mules.

All the big stock had to be shipped in from Missouri until we got our own breeding going here. Now, then, they're breeding them back down to where they'll be small again because people have no use for the big ones. No work for them to do. And it doesn't cost so much to feed the smaller ones. We're coming back now to what it was fifty years ago.

Back fifty years ago, if you *did* see a big horse, some of these companies had him on a logging job.

I had a pair of bay horses. I reckon I kept them about three years and logged with them. And them confounded son-of-a-guns would stand and listen at me drive them grabs, and they could tell just as well when I got done driving the grabs as *I* could. And they was restless. They'd just stand and paw the ground and look back at me. And they never would move as long as them lines was laying on the ground. They'd stand there. When I went to hook the spreads—I'd just reach and get the spreads and hook onto the logs before I'd reach for the lines—and whenever I stooped over to get them lines, they'd hit that thing with everything they had in'em; and if I happened to miss the lines, I wouldn't get'em stopped for a hundred yards a'hollering at'em. But if I got ahold of the lines, we *went to the yard,* my shirttail in the air!

Boy, I pulled big logs with them. I've had eighteen sixteen-foot long ones behind them at one time. Load three trucks with one load coming off the mountain. That was over yonder above Cherokee [North Carolina] on Black Rock in that steep country in there. And that was virgin timber. We *cut* timber in there. We cut a lot in there that the four-foot scale stick wouldn't even reach across the end where you scaled it. We just cut all kinds of hemlock and chestnut in there that was bigger than the scale stick would scale. I pulled it with them little horses, too. I called them little horses, but they was big.

I'd pull that header log out and chain it to a stump or another tree standing there when I was bumping others up against it to keep it from running off. And then whenever I got them logs all trailed up together, I wouldn't have to do nothing only just get the slack all pulled out of them. They'd go to running, and I'd hook on that J-grab and unchain that header from that stump—maybe not pull the [train of logs] no further than the road there, and those logs would run [by themselves] as far as from here to Kate Cathey's down yonder [about three-quarters of a mile]. By the time that back log would pass me, it'd be making seventy-five miles an hour just a'whistling through the air!

Regular teams most of the time was six cattle—three pairs for heavy work and heavy logging. As a usual thing, it was a six-head team. If you was on level ground, you wouldn't move too much in a day, but if you was on steep ground, you could take six head of cattle and in places trail as many as fifteen logs behind them. Just looked like a freight train. And lot of times, just one trip a day is all you'd make. Bring in anywhere from fifteen to twenty logs at a time. Take a half a day to go get'em. Maybe be two o'clock before you ever got'em all trailed together and ready to go out with'em. And that one trip a day's all you'd make 'cause you might be pulling two mile, two mile and a half. Pull so far and stop and rest, you see.

I've worked all day many a day and not even get one log to the mill. Maybe take two days to get one log out pulling him all the way. Flat ground. Big logs was hard to move. Sometimes you'd walk up to one lying on the ground and it was all you could do to see over the top of it. They don't have nothing like that no more. When you go to moving one like that, you've got to *have* something. Now they've got equipment to move it with, but we didn't have nothing but cattle and horses. We had double and single and triple tackle blocks—blocks with rollers in them. Put two of them together, and sometimes put three of them together. Thread three into two and then on down into one. Sometimes we'd have to do that to move it. And then a few times I've had as high as twelve head of cattle to one log. Me and my buddy had three yokes apiece, and we'd put all twelve to some of the big stuff to move it. It'd be so big they'd have to bore it and put powder guns in it to split it before it'd ever go on the saw carriage—quarter it up. You don't see nothing like that no more. Not in this country. It's all gone.

Back then they wasn't no roads. Roads was just what you made wherever you went through. If we was going to move a whole lot of logs, and a good distance, we used corduroy roads. You'd use that three, maybe six months. Fix the road just for that. Them logs going over it would keep the dirt off the top of the pole for a while, and the logs would just slide across the poles. That would make them slip across easy. But you wouldn't hardly be able to snake on it for much more than three months because the poles would keep getting pressed down into the dirt from heavy logs going over them until the dirt would be level with the tops of the poles, and then you'd just have the road.

Where the road had a dip in it, put long poles in it we called bull poles to hold those logs up and get them over the dip.

Them corduroys had to run just about the way they grade a highway now. What you chopped out with an axe was the road you had then—or what you dug with a mattock and shovel or one of those old scrapes or slip pans. Only way you ever used that wheel scrape would be building a road to where a sawmill was going to be sitting for three or four years.

Now if it was to come a dry spell like this, you'd turn branches into the road to make it muddy and to make it slicker to pull on. The rainier the weather was, and the harder the ground was froze, the more you could

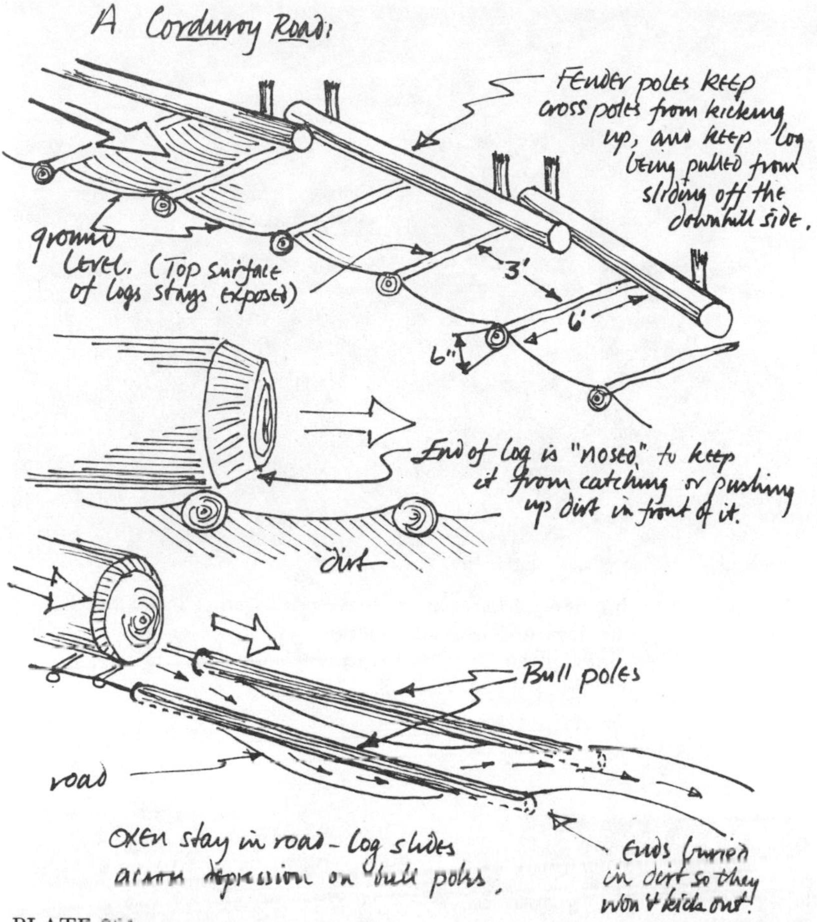

A Corduroy Road:

FENDER poles keep
cross poles from kicking
up, and keep log
being pulled from
sliding off the
downhill side.

ground
level. (Top surface
of logs stays exposed)

3'

6"

6"

End of log is "nosed" to keep
it from catching or pushing
up dirt in front of it.

dirt

Bull poles

road

OXEN stay in road - log slides
along depression on bull poles.

Ends buried
in dirt so they
won't kick out!

PLATE 264

move and the better you got along with it. Logging was better in the winter than it was in the summertime 'cause the ground froze. You really didn't have better weather; just better logging weather, 'cause it was cold and the ground froze. You'd pull a few loads on the road, and it freezing ice, and that's when you could move a whole lot. When it would go to freezing and getting icy, that would be the time to get the logs. When it was too rough for most people to get out of the house, well that's when loggers worked and got a whole lot done. I never did quit on account of rough weather. That was the best time to move stuff.

Now, when you go to pulling a log, you've got to find the heavy side. A log will run a certain way. It has a bottom and a top. There's a heavy side on all of them, and he'll pull on that heavy side. Then knock off that leading edge with an axe. Slope the leading edge. That makes it run easier—

PLATE 265   In order to drag several logs out of the woods together instead of having to drag each separately, the logs are hooked together with "trailer grabs"—metal hooks connected by swivel links so the logs can turn independently—and two links of chain.

PLATE 266   When the logs are hooked together, Millard's horse, Charley, is backed up to the lead log and chained to it via the singletree at the end of his harness, and a "J-grab" or "header grab" that connects the singletree to the lead log. At a signal from Jack, Millard's son, Charley lunges forward to get the train of logs moving.

PLATE 267 The logs are dragged down a skid trail to the truck. Dogwood posts are driven into the ground at intervals to back up small fender poles along the downhill edge of curves in the trail which keep the logs from rolling out. Such skid trails are still visible, more than thirty years later, throughout the mountains.

keeps it from kicking up dirt in front of it and slowing it down. That's what we call nosing a log. And in the summer, you nose it and bark it too. You can pull a heavy log that way 'cause it will be slick.

And you want to put your biggest log in front, your next biggest one behind, and so on down to the last. Leave about eight inches in between them to get slack. You just keep trailing on back. You have a swivel in the middle of your grab chain that will let the log turn the length of the chain. I've pulled eighteen and twenty logs in a line that way. That was on steep ground. We used a J-grab on that header [biggest] log. Put your J-grab on that. See, if you fix your road right, they'll be a lot of places where you can let [the line of logs] run by theirselves [without being pulled by the steers]. Sometimes they'll run as far as a mile and a half. In them places you jay your steers off and let the logs go on by theirselves.

And whenever you go to jay, you just turn your spread hook over and put it in that grab and your spread hook turns loose and it just goes right on by. I've jayed off eighteen and twenty of them, and the cracker [the last log in the string] would go past and he'd be a foot off the ground when he passed. He'd be going as fast as any of these cars that go down through here [on the highway past our house] a'racing. That gets your team out of the way so they don't get run over 'cause it's exactly like a freight train behind'em, and I mean by the time they passed, they would really be *flying*. Over there in the Smokies, you turn some of them loose on some of them mountains and it'd sound like a thunder storm. You could hear them a'roaring for miles.

It was a long time before they ever done that jaying with steers. Instead they had old big log chains that weighed about a hundred an' fifty pounds. I guess the inside of the links was about six inches. They was made out of three-quarter- or seven-eighths-inch stuff. Well, they was so heavy it'd take two men to handle one of them. And they called that a dull chain. If the ground was steep enough for a log to run, you'd put that dull chain around it along about four feet from the front end of the header and that made the son-of-a-gun plow in the ground till it wouldn't run and hurt your steers. Then, whenever you got down to leveler ground where it wouldn't run, you'd unhook the chain and the log would slip over it and you'd go on with it.

Then they got to learning steers to where they'd jay. After they learn it, whenever they start to one of them jay places after three or four trails of logs passed them for four or five days in a row, they wouldn't even stop in the hole. They'd run plumb on through it getting out of the way. Now they moved!

But if the ground's not level enough for a team to get out of the way when you jay off, you've got to dig that J-hole into the road bank for them to get into 'cause when those logs run, they've got to get in that so the logs can pass them up and leave them standing there. They can't stay in front of the logs 'cause the logs run so fast they'll kill'em—break their legs and kill'em. We broke a few steers' legs, and two or three's necks.

Actually, I didn't never kill none myself, but I've skint'em all over. And I never was hurt myself. Just skinned. Get jerked down or knocked down. Shins skint all over. Elbows. Knees. Maybe a limb fly up and hit you across the back or shoulder or something. You'd be sore for three-four days. But as long as I worked'em, I never did get no broken bones.

Now those teams, we never did switch jobs much. We had our job skidding every day. When we worked at that, that was every day business. Nobody didn't fool with your teams of cattle. Nobody didn't fool with what you drove. I drove and fed and took care of mine, and the other feller done the same way with his. Nobody didn't fool with your stuff.

Sometimes we'd switch our driving horses and wagons when one driver would be out planting crops or something and we'd be hauling acid wood in the summer and not using the cattle. Take somebody's else's team like that, you know. But every man had his team and he fed and took care of'em, and he worked'em and he worked'em every day. Nobody didn't swap back like they do trucks now, you know: one drive one day and one the next. That didn't go. Whenever you got your team, you kept it.

Well, the cattle knowed who their boss was so a stranger couldn't do nothing with them nohow. Somebody else fooling with them, it'd take'em two or three weeks to get used to him before he could get any work out of

PLATE 268 At the truck, the logs are loaded by rolling them over skid poles onto the bed. They were often loaded onto wagons, years before, in the same manner.

PLATE 269 Large logs that would be very difficult, if not impossible, to roll by hand roll very easily using a peavee —one of the most important tools in logging.

PLATE 270 When the truck is loaded, the logs are chained down with chains tightened by log binders for the trip to the mill. Before leaving, the men put Charley in the shed they have built for him on the site and feed him. Charley spends each night there waiting for them to return early the next morning with an empty truck.

them. A steer's sort of a quare thing, the majority of'em is. Some of'em's different, but the majority has more or less got one master, and that's all that gets anything out of them. They won't work for half a dozen people at one time. They're strange characters on that. They're called a dumb brute, but they're a long way from being dumb. They're well-educated when it comes to that kind of business 'cause they know who's who.

Back whenever we worked steers, we raised them all the time. Back then we *had* cattle. They was took to the mountains and turned loose. Lots of times they was left in the mountains all winter—all except heifers and cows that was going to bring calves. You bring them in. And we marked them— ear marks. Every outfit and every family had his mark and it was registered at Raleigh. Once or twice you might hear of one being stole, but that was something people didn't do back then. They didn't take the other feller's stuff. They was different to what they are now. They wouldn't bother nothing that didn't belong to them. You didn't run into none of that—hardly ever. Our older generation wouldn't be bothered, nor they wouldn't bother nobody.

And we wouldn't log'em much until they was three years old. Then some of them we might work as much as three years—never over four years.

Now if the logs was going to be hauled a long ways, you'd haul them with teams and wagons. Wheels six-foot high—great big old wide tire on'em. Took six head of cattle—three yokes of oxen to a wagon. You had the big pair behind next to the wheels, and you called them your wheelers. The smaller ones went up front to lead with, and they were your lead cattle. In other words, the front ones did the controlling of the work. And the number of teams you used depended on the size of the logs and the distance you were going.

It took two men to operate one of those wagons. They were heavy concerns. Mud knee-deep. Them old wagons would cut down deep.

Now the team that was on the wheel—the ones that carried the wagon tongue—now they caught it rough. That front wheel would hit a rock, you know, and that tongue would hit that steer hard if they was making any speed—especially downhill. It'd just about knock'em off their feet. I've seen'em knocked plumb down to their knees. See, you've got that tongue right in that yoke, and if a front wheel hits rock or something solid, the tongue slams over and it hits that steer and jerks this other one's weight on him too. Now that was rough on'em. Really hard on'em. Wagoning is hard work on'em. Reason it took two men was one to drive, and one to run the brake. You've got a brake on that wagon. The brakeman walked behind— had a steel guide with notches on it. You started going downhill, and he'd just mash down on that brake handle and hook it in one of them notches. If it got to going too fast, you just rare down on it and hook it in another one.

Then when the wagon got down the hill and went to getting too hard to pull, why he'd raise it a notch, you see? And he walked behind and the driver walked up front. Didn't have reins. He'd just talk to'em and they'd mind.

They'd pull wagons more with mules back then than they did with horses 'cause a mule would go further and didn't take hardly as much to feed him, and he was much faster with a wagon than a horse was. You can feed a mule—just feed him of a night—put him in plenty to eat tonight and just get him used to that and you won't have to feed him no more till tomorrow night. You've got to feed a horse three times a day to hold him up if you're working him hard, but a mule, you don't. So they'd use a mule—haul long distances with'em and just feed'em once a day.

Now steers were the same way. You don't have to feed them but once a day if you feed'em good. You can take and feed'em—like we fed'em cottonseed meal and hulls—and feed'em plenty of a night. They've got four stomachs, you know. What one eats tonight, he'll belch that up and chew his cud, and what he eats tonight don't do him no good until tomorrow. He's got to belch that up and chew it and let it go back into that other stomach tomorrow before it does him any good. And then they'd eat buds along the road, you know, and leaves and so forth and so on while you was working'em. They'd be a'grazing along while you was loading and resting them. See, they'd fill that one stomach up there where they'd chewed that other out, and then you'd lay the cottonseed meal and hulls to them that night and that'd finish it. So that one big meal a night was all they needed, and they'd stay fat all the time. That was another advantage of having them.

To conclude this section, we asked Millard to explain to us something of the economics of one of the old operations—how the orders came in, what sort of money was involved, etc.

We just cut the best back then—the biggest and smoothest. If you want to saw out good lumber, you've got to have good trees. Back whenever we was logging with oxen, we didn't cut nothing but the best because there wasn't no sale for nothing else, hardly, and even what we got out didn't bring much. We hauled many of a load of number one timber—oak boards that was eighteen to twenty inches wide and sixteen foot long. Wide enough to almost make a table top. And it was clear all the way through. And we hauled it from the mill to a railroad siding and loaded it inside a railroad car and shipped it to Chicago for twelve dollars a thousand [feet]. The same lumber now would run at least eight hundred dollars for the same amount. We got twelve out of it. And it *had* to be good to sell at all. If it wasn't the best, you just didn't sell any of it. Cherry and walnut and oak sold better than any of it did. And we sold curly walnut, curly birch, curly cherry and curly maple. And it wouldn't bring but twelve or fifteen dollars a thousand!

And there was big chestnut. I've cut chestnut trees that had twenty-one cord of wood in them. Load a full railroad car load of wood out of one tree. I've cut a lot of it six and seven foot across the stump. And chestnut wasn't worth nothing till Champion Fibre Company went to making a lot of paper. And even then it was a dollar twenty-five a cord—that was a hundred sixty foot. A cord and a quarter is actually what you sold. And that was to cut it and take it to the mill! And a lot of chestnut sold for light poles and phone poles for a long time. Back years ago, young chestnut was about the straightest thing growed in the woods. We used to get them out and load'em on a car fifty foot long and them be ten inches at the little end. Put them on flat cars. We loaded them with a block and tackle and a team of horses.

And back in them old dark coves in the Smokies they used to be a lot of sugar maple that would go up six foot across the stump. And it was just as curly as it could be—what they called bird's eye back then. Lord have mercy, if a man had it now, what *would* it be worth? And they made *flooring* out of it, now. And then a lot of it went to Chicago where they made furniture out of it. And some got gunstocks made out of it. And a lot of it was exported to Finland and Sweden. It was precut here to where it could be handled and put on the boat—four-by-twelves, six-by-sixes, six-by-eights. And then they recut it down to smaller sizes over there. What they done with it, I don't know. And then black walnut went to Sweden too.

But we'd start logging wherever the kind of trees we wanted were. We'd cut one kind one time and another the next. Maybe be maple one time, maybe poplar one time, and maybe walnut or oak. We cut more oak than anything 'cause there was more of it than anything else.

So we'd just go where the most of it was, and the best.

A lot of times, we'd get orders, and whatever they'd order, you'd cut. A car would hold about twelve or fifteen thousand feet, so we'd get orders for a car load at a time, you see. Mostly oak, and then we got a whole lot for hickory, see, to make wagons out of.

But we would go to the depot and tell the depot agent, and they would have the cars sent for when we'd be ready to load. They were set on the side and the brake was left on, and if we needed to move them, we just took the brake off and moved them down to where we wanted them and then tighten the brake back. Then you'd load.

Back then, the Government didn't own nothing. It was all private or company land. The Government never went to buying land until right after the Depression. When things started picking back up, the Government went to buying land. Sometimes they did it, they claimed, to preserve the forest.

They might buy up a big company, or shut'em down. Did it in 1925 with the Suncrest Lumber Company. There's timber there that never has been cut yet. But mostly they didn't buy land until along about '33.

Then, after World War II, they had everything took over, and if you logged any at all, you had to have an OPA card to do it. You had to take it to the rationing board and get them to approve it to get your card. I know, because there was one time during all that that I had over two hundred and fifty thousand feet laying on the ground ahead of me and me logging with three pair of horses.

It was all stamps then. You had to have that stamp before you could buy anything. The stamp wouldn't buy you *nothing*. And your money wouldn't buy nothing if you didn't have the stamp. On lumber, if you didn't have that stamp, you couldn't buy it. They was trying to allot it out to where everybody'd get a equal share. Lumber was still going that way till plumb up after '46. And see, there was a ceiling price on it. They couldn't sell it but for only so much. Seems to me like it was selling for forty-five and fifty dollars a thousand then. See, there was a ceiling price on the lumber, a ceiling price on cattle, a ceiling price on hogs—there was a ceiling on everything regardless of what someone would give you for it. That set price was all you was allowed to sell it for. The millionaire couldn't buy no more than the poor man could. You were allowed so much at such a price, and that's all you could get. If you wanted to build a new house, they would allot you so much lumber for it. You couldn't get but so much. You couldn't get out here and build any kind of house you wanted. You built according to the size of your family, and then you got so much lumber to do that with, you see?

And now that about takes us up to the more modern logging with trucks and all that.

SAWMILLING

Back then you took your sawmill to the woods with you. You'd put it back in the mountains middleways of what territory you was going to log. Then you'd pull logs into it from all around, saw them up, and then move your lumber out. It would have cost too much to move the logs out if you had very many of them to move. You wagoned some, but you wouldn't wagon too many.

You just took the mill to the woods, maybe saw a half-million feet or something like that at the place, and then move the mill to the next place. Just kept on moving it back into the woods as you went so you could pull your logs to it on the ground. And the lumber, then, it was all hauled out on wagons and took to a railroad.

The sawmill had to be in kind of a flat place—a place where there was plenty of water on account of your boiler. You had to have plenty of steam. Had to have it on a good-sized branch. And then, too, they was a lot of wood moved by branches. See, they had flumes. I don't guess none of you's ever seen a flume. It's just a water trough made out of twelve-inch-wide oak boards, and two of them nailed together here in a trough—"V"-shaped. Or some of them be twenty-four inches wide and wouldn't be "V"-shaped. Then you turn water into them. Maybe go four or five miles back in on the head of that branch where it come out of the mountain and run good, and build what you called a splash dam—just a dam that would fill up overnight, you know. Hold several hundred gallons of water. Next morning, then, turn the water into that flume trough and go to putting wood in it—just one stick of wood right against the other one. The water'd take it down. It'd maybe go three or four miles like that.

Then somebody would be down there at the lower end where it levelled out picking it up and loading it on a wagon and taking it to a railroad car. That was acid wood, mostly. And lumber too. They'd pick up lumber the same way after it was sawed.

See, that was a cheaper way of moving it, and it saved a lot of time. Take a pretty good while to build one of them flumes, but they'd keep on lasting. Wasn't too much repair to do on them either. If the water went to freezing, they'd take the water out of it so there wouldn't be nothing to break it down. And then if it got a whole lot of frost on it, it'd run without water. It would run on that ice. But lots of times that was *too* fast. It'd run so fast it'd jump the trough 'cause there's places that'd have to be curved on it.

PLATE 271 Acid wood (chestnut) was essential for the production of paper. Companies like Champion International would build miles of flumes up into the mountains in order to get this acid wood out. A flume would begin high in a watershed nearly at the head of the creek. A splash dam at the head of the flume would hold water to be turned into the flume. The chestnut would be cut into five-foot lengths and split up and stacked beside the flume at intervals along its length during dry weather. Then, in wet weather when the stream was running full, water would be turned into the flume at the splash dam and the split wood would be loaded into it and carried to its end. The flume pictured here was on Big East Fork. (Photo courtesy of Champion Paper, a division of Champion International Corp., furnished by C. W. Hardin.)

PLATE 272   The flumes usually ended at a road. Here the wood piled up and was loaded into wagons or narrow-gauge railroad cars for the trip to the plant. (Photo courtesy of Champion Paper.)

PLATE 273   This photograph shows acid wood being moved into the plant's yard by narrow-gauge railroad. The engine, called a "little Shay," pushes twenty-five to thirty "dinky cars" at a time, each loaded with six to eight cords of wood. (Photo courtesy of Champion Paper.)

And it wasn't easy to carry that wood back uphill to put back in. It *shore* wasn't!

But a two-inch branch would carry that. You'd cut the acid wood and pile it up all along the flume, and then when you'd turn the water into it from that splash dam, why just put the wood in. Then that flume would be full all the time. You'd flume enough wood there to haul a dozen teams, then, all day long on down to the railroad siding. Load it on a car.

But now that sawmill: it took a big inch pipe running free about all the time running water for the mill. And then the branch run through under the saw and carried the sawdust off. They used to put the sawdust in the creeks there if they was one close enough to where they could have that saw box right over the creek. Then you wouldn't have to have nobody to move no dust. The branch would wash it off—take it away.

The mills was steam engines—steam boiler and steam engines. Fired him up and got a good head of steam up—enough to pull the engine—and you throwed the steam on the engine and that's what done your sawing. Had your saw just like they've got it now, but it was pulled with steam in place of gasoline engines.

PLATE 274   Narrow-gauge railroads were also used for hauling large logs, such as balsam, to the mill. Often trestles were required, and a man like Rube Mull and his crew would be called in to build them. This trestle probably went up into Little East Fork, an area that is now the Pisgah National Forest. (Photo courtesy of Champion Paper.)

PLATE 275   A finished trestle. (Photo courtesy of Champion Paper.)

PLATE 276   More often than not, this was the only method of getting a log to the point where it could be reached by the cable from the overhead skidder, or loaded onto a wagon or railroad car. Logs such as this would be dragged down a skid trail from the places where they were cut to the loading area. (Photo courtesy of Champion Paper.)

PLATE 277 At the head of the railroad line, an overhead skidder (far right) powered by a steam boiler would be used to drag the logs out of the woods, where they had been cut, to the loading area. There a log loader (or "stiff-necked loader"), visible in this photograph on the tracks beyond the steam engine, would load the logs onto the railroad cars for the trip to the mill. When one car was filled, the loader would pull off the main track onto a short siding so that the engineer of the train could move another empty car into position to be loaded. (Photo courtesy of Champion Paper.)

PLATE 278 A "stiff-necked" loader at work. The loaders were steam powered, and their boilers were often called "coffeepot boilers." (Photo courtesy of Champion Paper.)

One of them steam boilers—one to pull a big mill—was a pretty good-sized thing, and the engines were just about twenty horsepower. Wasn't none of them over twenty horsepower.

They was a little drive wheel—about an eight-inch wheel—on that engine and it was cast iron. *Heavy* son-of-a-gun. And when that thing got started and picked up his speed, why it took a lot to slow that old big cast iron wheel down. Long as you kept a boiler with plenty of fire and water in it, you could have steam to saw on. Had a pop-off valve on it. They only got so hot and then the steam pressure would open it up to keep it from blowing up. When that pop-off valve opened, it was ready to go to sawing then! If a man knowed how to fire one, he could just about keep that pop-off valve going all day long, 'cause while they was changing logs, his steam would build back up and it would pop again. Back when timber was so heavy and so big, it took'em a good while to saw a log up.

The way they operated was something similar to what they operate now.

PLATE 279 Bud Allen or Suel Medford moving a steam sawmill. Eight pairs of oxen (one pair is not visible beyond the lower left corner) are hitched to the boiler (far right), and four more pairs behind them are hitched to the long stack and saw box. This scene was probably photographed in the Pigeon Valley. (Photo courtesy of Champion Paper.)

One outfit would saw—he'd do customer sawing but the most of the time he logged his own mill and just sold the lumber. Buy timber, you know, and sell the lumber. Once in a while there'd be somebody haul some logs in on wagons wanting it sawed to build a barn or a house. They'd come in and swap work instead of paying. Most of the time if they wanted lumber, they'd just come and work around the mill or work in the woods a few days, you see, and take their pay in lumber. And that was one of the ways they got their building material back then. Sometimes it was a problem getting men to work in the woods and the mill both 'cause the population was thin then. They wasn't too many people. So that was the way they'd do. They'd swap work for something they needed.

If they were going to be sawing there for a long time, they'd build a bunkhouse for the men working the mill. Shirley [Millard's wife] ran the bunkhouse sometimes and cooked for the men. We had our own little place to stay in, and the men stayed in the camp. Then, when the sawmill moved out, they left the camp behind. People coming in gathering herbs could stay there, or hunters. Sometimes moonshiners. They got used a lot, so they were kept up. Someone would come along and stay over a night or two, and do a repair here and there to keep it up, and the next man the same way. Some of them camps stayed there for years and years that way.

MODERN LOGGING

Back then when we was working steers, they wasn't such a thing as a truck. You either skidded your logs to a sawmill, or brought them to a wagon. They wasn't no trucks used in the woods up till '35, and they was very few then. See, you didn't even have a dual-wheel truck. The first one of them was made in '32. And the trucks that was first used back then was pulled with a one-wheel sprocket drive. They didn't even have a drive shaft on'em. They was just one wheel that pulled.

And they wasn't no roads to run'em on because everything that was hauled was hauled with teams and wagons and steers and wagons and it was just out of one mudhole into another one. They wasn't nowhere for'em to go so they wasn't no good, see?

But the truck took the place of the wagon to start with. He only delivered the lumber after it was ready to load on the railroad car. After he took the place of the wagon, why then he gradually went to going back in the woods and taking the place of the horses and steers. They got to building roads and putting them back in the woods. But they wasn't too much of that done, now, until up in '37 and '38 when they started taking them back in the woods.

The first trucks was a very small rig. Well, they hauled an awful load for their time, but they didn't move too much because they was too small, and their motors was so small they didn't have much power. I know you know what an A-model Ford is. Well, you know about what you can move with a A-model motor. Well, now, that's the size motor they had in them. Four-cylinder Chevrolet. It was they same size motor the A-model was. A-model was about as strong an order as they was, so you can tell by that how much you could move with it. That's the way it started out. If you had one you could haul three-quarters of a cord of wood on, you really had a *good* truck; but you could take a team and wagon and haul a *full* cord! And you couldn't go much faster in a truck than you could with a team and wagon because they wasn't no roads. So if you wasn't hauling something but six or eight or ten miles, you could get along just as good with a good team and wagon as you could with a truck.

But then, you see, the state took the roads over and they got to building roads. Back then they wasn't no road tax, and the way you built a road back in them days was with what they called a poll tax. You paid two dollars a year to vote. That was poll tax. Well, in place of *paying* any taxes [in cash], you worked on the road one day out of the year for that poll tax. You either had to work a day yourself, or hire a man to work in your place. And that's all the road work they was. They wasn't no state taxes or county taxes or nothing on the roads, so the individuals kept them up with that one day of work. And then maybe going by somebody's house here along the edge of their field it'd get real bad, and the field would be covered over in rock, and they'd want to get them rock out of the way where he was tending his field, so he'd haul them rock and pile them in the road and work it down so far [in distance]. Well now, that's the kind of work there was.

And then the state went to charging taxes and took the roads over and just went to building strips here, yonder and about, and trucks then got to operating and cars got to operating and they got to raising the tax on gasoline and stuff, and that there's what made the whole thing go to building.

But see, all during that time they wasn't no way for it *to* build because they wasn't taking no taxes in.

It was just like—if you started to go somewhere, they was half the time it'd just be like hitting that field out there; getting out there and picking out a hard place in the field to drive on and hoping it would hold up a few days for you to haul over. Keep somebody busy filling up the potholes where you'd mire down. Somebody was hauling rock all the time filling up the ruts. That's the only way you went.

When it rained, you done work whenever you had teams and wagons, but you didn't do nothing when you first started off with trucks. When it set in to raining, they stayed parked 'cause you couldn't get nowhere with 'em. If you was hauling downhill where it was fairly steep, you could take a good team and hook it in front of one of the trucks and pull him up the mountain and load him. He'd *come down* all right! But he sure wouldn't go up. Every time he went up there, you had to pull him up! Pull him up there and get him pulled around, and then you could load him and come on out. But that was the way you done it, and the only way you *could* do it then.

[Even when the first dual-wheel trucks came it, it was hard. You could haul the logs to the truck with a dozer and load it, or drive on in and if you got stuck, get the dozer to pull you out, or put a twenty-foot pole in between the dual wheels and run the truck on that pole until you got out of the mud.] I've poled out of many a mudhole like that. That, or pull out with a pair of horses or a skidder if you were close to one. Or if you was hauling downhill, put on a set of chains and go in, and then take'em off when you brought him out.

You know, you could outrun one of them old trucks anywhere 'cause that [drive] sprocket wouldn't let it go but so fast—it wouldn't turn but so fast. You could turn one down a 45 per cent grade and outrun it if you wanted to 'cause it wouldn't go no faster. It just had one speed, and when it got up that far, that's as fast as it would go!

Now coming on up to more recent times, I worked for the Dayton Rubber Company in Waynesville, North Carolina, for three years. That was '50, '51, and '52. I quit logging and went over there and went to work. Thought I wouldn't log no more. Got kinda aggravated at it. I just decided I'd quit a while. Daddy kept on talking to me trying to get me to quit logging altogether and go to work on the public works.

So I went to Dayton, and I built pickers there for cotton mills. It was an assembly line. And then about the last sixteen months that I was there, I was on the experimental end of it. We made some tires over there and put them on trucks, and we run some on them semitrailers a hundred and ten thousand miles and half the tread wasn't even wore off them. They wouldn't never let nothing like that get on the market. That was when they come out with that Double Eagle for a car that was guaranteed for sixty thousand miles. But they was so high that poor people couldn't afford'em so they just quit making them. But they could make a tire there that would wear a car out.

And then during the war they made them pontoon bridges; and they made them throwaway tanks out of rubber that they dropped off planes whenever they was emptied. And they made some tanks that held as much as five hundred gallons, and they could take one of them tanks and take a fifty-caliber machine gun and shoot all the way through that thing and they wouldn't be three quarts of gas spill out of it. There was something in that

PLATE 280 A loaded truck approaches a saw that cuts the logs in half while they are still on the truck.

PLATE 281 Truck being unloaded after passing under the saw.

rubber that when the gasoline hit it, it made the rubber dissolve and seal that hole.

Then when the war was over, they just kept adding on to the plant, went to making radiator hose and, well, just anything that was rubber. And synthetic sponge. I guess they hire something like five thousand over there now 'cause they're spread out all over that bottom. I've cut tobacco right out through that bottom right where that thing's setting. It belonged to old man Jule Welch.

But when I first started working there, me and Shirley got a prize there for being the youngest married couple. It was ten pounds of sugar for the prize. That was in July before they started putting all the machinery in. They started putting the machinery in the Monday after that. I made a dollar to a dollar and a half a day there.

And I'd been there about three months when I went to logging for Genett's [Lumber Company]. I worked graveyard shift at the Dayton Rubber Company—went in at eleven o'clock and come out at seven—and then crawled in my truck and went to the woods. I'd get in home sometimes six-thirty or seven—lots of times eight o'clock in the night; and then go

PLATE 282   In the woodyard—trailers that haul wood to the paper mill.

back to Dayton at eleven that same night and do it again. I'd work that way
till Saturday. Quit about four o'clock Saturday evening and I'd sleep from
then till about eleven o'clock Sunday night.

Yeah, I worked there on graveyard and logged every day. Shore did.
They was weeks—Shirley'll tell you herself [she did]—they was weeks that
I never slept six hours a *week*. And by God I was working too. I wasn't lay-
ing around. I was *working*.

Whenever I'd come in on Saturday evening—the kids was all small—I'd
take them to a drive-in show, and it'd take her thirty minutes to get me
woke up to get them back home. And I'd fall into bed, and about dinnertime on Sunday, I'd get back up. I'd make up for [lost sleep] on those
weekends.

But I'm a son-of-a-bitch if I didn't go week on top of week and never
sleep more than six or eight hours a full week. Took a whole lot of pills—
them there no-sleep pills. I took a whole lot of them, and a whole lot of that
dope to keep from going to sleep. And drank a whole lot. Drunk a whole lot
and worked all the time too.

But while I was logging, I was either operating a skidder or driving truck
about all the time. I was hauling off a place over there called Wolf Pen,
and couldn't get nobody that could drive a truck and get out of there with
no load. It was steep and they'd mire up too much. Had to drive myself to
get anything done. Had two trucks. I'd drive one of them and an old Moss
boy drove the other. Contracting for Genett. You got paid for what the log
was worth in board feet—all contract work.

Genett would buy a boundary. You know what that is? It's not any cer
tain size territory. The Forest Service just marks an area off—blazes it with
paint. They either mark the trees they want cut, or they tell you to clear-cut
and you take what you want. Used to be that way. Now [when you clear-
cut] you have to take it all. Firewood and all.

But Genett would bid on that boundary, and if they got it, I'd go cut it
and bring the timber to the mill. And then sometimes I'd buy a boundary
myself and go cut it and sell it to Genett. I made more money that way.

I've went many a time in the winter—go in in the daytime and load up
and the ground would thaw till I couldn't get out. I'd mire down and just
back out of the hole. Know I couldn't get through it. And I'd stay there till
three or four in the morning till the ground would freeze down again
enough for me to get out. Take my load on in and come on back and go
back to work then. Get out one for the next morning. But now that's hard
work. I rolled a load of logs off on myself over yonder at Genett's one time.
I was about half asleep. They'd filled up a hole—I guess it was five-foot
deep where we'd wallered it out with the trucks. They'd filled it up with
sawdust, and it was soft, and I pulled up to the edge of it and went to

unload a load and chopped my standards out to roll'em off, and they was five of them logs rolled over me. Mashed me till my eyes swelled shut. I didn't even know when my kidneys acted or my bowels moved for over a week. And you know it never broke a bone? But now it shore messed my muscles up! But I was in the sawdust, see? They'd just filled the hole up with the dozer and smoothed it over, and them logs just rolled over me and buried me in that sawdust. 'Course the sawdust was hard. Hard enough that, God, I'll tell you, it give me a mashing. I was in the millyard, and they shut the saw down and all run to me, and one of'em run in and called the ambulance. They thought it'd killed me. I told'em to cancel the ambulance call 'cause they wasn't nothing wrong with me. Rolled around on the ground there a few minutes and finally made it up and got up and got in the truck and thought I'd go back to the woods and get another load. But time I got to the foot of the mountain, I seen I couldn't load when I got there. So I drove on to the house; and when I got to the house, I couldn't get on *to* the house, and they took me to the doctor. I was out about two weeks, I think, before I went back. Went right back at it again. Didn't have enough sense to quit.

After I quit Dayton, I went back to logging full time. I was using a truck and skidder and horse all. Two trucks. Two of my own trucks. Had somebody else driving one.

Mostly we hauled overloaded. Eighteen thousand pounds to the axle is what you're supposed to carry. That's back axle. Front axle you're not supposed to carry but twelve. That was the limit. But I was carrying way over that. And it was a cent-and-a-half a pound plus a fifty-dollar fine plus three-cent-and-a-half a pound for what you had over plus court costs—if they caught you. That'd wipe out [the profits of] several trips when they got done with you. You'd already worked about two weeks for nothing when they caught you. And then that'd make the son-of-a-bitches go to watching you closer then.

Here we asked if he really ran overloaded that much, and Shirley answered, "Well he done it!" Millard laughed, "I done it and I mean I done it plenty too."

I lived over in North Carolina. I outsmarted Fergy [nickname for a state patrolman who is legendary in this part of the country] a few times, and you were sharp when you done that.

They come up down here—I was parked right above that State Line beer joint on the old 441—but they come up there that evening just a little before dark, and I was overloaded to hell and back, and Fergy'd been trying to catch me. And him and the Macon County Sheriff come up there and looked the truck over. Ralph _____ down there—he happened to be going home and seen them there and come on down to my house and told me. Says, "Buck," he says, "they're going to get you tonight."

I says, "Well, maybe not."

He says, "I wish they was some way or 'nother you could go around and dodge'em."

I says, "I'll figure out something before I leave out."

Earl [one of Millard's sons] was out a'courting that night, and he come in about eleven and he says, "Daddy," he says, "they're sure going to get you whenever you start through in the morning."

I says, "Ah, maybe not, son." And I told Shirley, I says, "Heat the coffee up. I'm gonna drink me some coffee and I believe I'll pull out."

She says, "Why, you're crazy."

I says, "You heat that coffeepot. Make me some coffee." I says, "I'll figure out something."

Earl says, "What are you going to do, Daddy?" Says, "You know you've got more sense than to pull out now." They was at Otto [North Carolina] then.

I says, "Well," I says, "when I drink this coffee," I said, "you can take me up there to the truck." I says, "I'm a'going through."

He says, "They're waiting on you." Says, "They'll get you too."

I says, "No, I don't think they will." Says, "I'm going up through Highlands [North Carolina] and down through Cashiers into Sylva and leave them son-of-a-bitches sitting there all night."

I come up there and crawled into the truck and went up across Highlands and down through Cashiers. Come back through the next morning about seven-thirty. They was still sitting a'waiting on me, and I just give'em the highball as I come through.

Boy, old Fergy, you talk about a feller blowing his top, he shore raised hell!

[Shirley: It's a wonder he hadn't shot the tires out from under the truck!]

But I'd load the truck of a day and then get up anywhere from two to three o'clock in the morning and go through at them time of hours. I was going through to dodge'em, you see? Without they had a special report like that, they very seldom ever got on the road before daylight. They was asleep then, see, and before they got on the road, I went through. I didn't care for them to stop me when I was empty. They couldn't do nothing then without that load.

Old Fergy pulled me over down there one Sunday night, and I had on three high racks of wood. I was going to Canton that time. Had on a Georgia tag and had a North Carolina tag too. He wrote up a bunch of stuff on me. I knowed he couldn't do nothing with me 'cause he didn't have the authority to. Old J. P. Long was the head man. He lived over there at Bryson City [North Carolina], and he was the pay man. Fergy says, "I'll have Long to get you before you get to Sylva."

I says, "Well, he might and he might not."

So Fergy, he radioed Long to get me, and I knowed that Long would come, too. So I just pulled out from the service station, and Fergy, he come back to Franklin. I just pulled out from down there and went over out the other side of Franklin and pulled up on the old road where they couldn't see the truck nor nothing, and got out and walked back down there on the side of the main road. And I hadn't been there more than about thirty minutes till old Long come through. And he come on to Franklin and missed me. Come back and went back the other way, and I just waited about an hour after he went back the other way. I knowed he'd seen I dodged him or done something—or maybe thought I'd went back home. I waited till he'd been gone about an hour and just crawled in the truck and went on through to Canton.

PLATE 283   The present-day Canton Hardwood Company in Canton, North Carolina. Most logs are brought to this mill by truck. The hardwood lumber produced here goes into furniture, flooring, and building materials. The loader at middle right is putting the logs into the electric-powered sawmill itself. (Photo courtesy of Champion Paper.)

PLATE 284 The Canton Hardwood sawmill. At far right the loaded carriage is ready to move the log through the band saw. Operations like this one are almost completely automated and controlled by men stationed behind panels for safety. (Photo courtesy of Champion Paper.)

PLATE 285 The Canton Hardwood lumber yard. Some of the lumber here will be kiln dried and then resawn and planed for furniture and floorings. Other lumber will be simply air dried and used for building materials. (Photo courtesy of Champion Paper.)

But back then, I'd come in of a morning, go to the woods, load up, take and park the truck, go home, and then go out early the next morning. I used to cut and load that truck myself. If the boys come and helped me load, all right. They helped me. But I'd cut and load three high racks on that a day by myself. Sometimes Shirley'd go with me and cook dinner. And she drove a mule and pulled in whole lot of stuff. And she'd scotch when we'd roll big stuff up. Me and her'd put just as high a load of logs on a truck as they put with these loaders—her scotching and me rolling with a peavee.

And then I done it myself a lot. Put on three high racks—I mean three *high* ones. High as any of'em. I was pulling anywhere from thirty up as high as thirty-four thousand pounds at a trip. And I'd cut that much wood and load it in a day by myself after I come back from delivering the last load to Sylva. And I was loading, by God, with my damn hands. I shore was. [Pull the truck up to a high bank and roll the logs down poles that went from the bank down onto the truck.] I'd cut and load that son-of-a-gun as long as I could get a stick on. That was back, too, when things, you know, was pretty cheap. I only got a dollar and ninety cents a thousand for a long time, and pulling it to Sylva, too. Seems to me like the last I got was two-twenty a thousand when I was doing all that heavy hauling. I'd pull anywhere from ninety-six to a hundred and ten dollars a trip. Loading heavy was the only way to make any money. Pull everything you could go with. The trucks just stood it. Yeah. They just had to stand it. You had to drive so far that you wanted to take all you could 'cause it took a whole lot of gas to pull that load over there. And tires too.

But I'd just cut and load till I give out and sit and rest a while and go at it again. Lots of times it'd be eleven o'clock when I got in of a night, and then get up and pull out at two again. And then I'd rest on Sunday—get drunk on Sunday and sleep all day.

I finally had to quit. Old Fergy got wise and I finally had to quit before he *did* get me. I quit pulling and let Junior Bryson go to pulling for me 'cause I knowed Fergy'd get me if I kept on. Junior, he always hauled about standard. He wouldn't overload. But he told me he'd pull it for me. Well, he did pull it for me for sixty cents a thousand pounds. That was cheaper than I could pull it by the time it took me to pull it and the wear and tear and upkeep on the truck, so I just quit pulling it. Let him pull it.

It was hard work, but I'll tell you the reason I followed it. That's a thing they's fast money in. It's hard work, but it's fast money. Pays good money. I'd go out here by myself when the wages was seventy-five cents an hour and make seventy-five *dollars* for me and that truck in a day? They was people making four and five dollars a day and me making that kind of money? I *couldn't* quit.

Every load of wood that goes through here—them big high loads of wood that goes through here every day—is bringing at least a hundred and fifty dollars a trip, and they's some of them making three trips a day. And they're working at it like I worked at it [for myself and my family]. They're *well* getting paid for it. Pine bringing seven twenty-five a thousand at the mill, and them big trucks going through here with thirty and thirty-five thousand pound every time they go through. You figure yourself whether they're making any money or not.

They're making a pile of money. That's the reason I fooled with it all the time and wouldn't fool with nothing else.

LOGGING CAMPS

Shirley Buchanan

During one point in his career as a logger, Millard Buchanan operated a logging camp and worked fourteen men who lived on the job in bunkhouses except for the weekends when they went home. Millard paid all expenses such as stumpage on the timber, upkeep on the equipment, and food and salaries for the men, and kept the balance of what he made selling the logs to the Blue Ridge Lumber Company as his share.

The work went on all year, and so Shirley, his wife, and their children lived at the camp with him. Her job, aside from taking care of the children, was to cook for all the men. Curious about what that life was like for a woman, Cam Bond and Lynnette Williams went to talk to her about that life as well as her husband's work. About the latter, she said, "That's all he ever done—log and cut pulpwood. That's what he loved to do. See the trees fall."

What she said about the former follows.

We lived down here on Warwoman [in Rabun County]. That's where we was logging at. The men would go out and log all day long. We had some horses. One of them was named Scott and the other was named Harry —a pretty brown team of horses that they logged with. The men would eat breakfast, then go out and harness them up and go off and come in at lunch and eat; then they'd go off again and come back at night and eat again.

That was in 1947. We was there three or four years. We had fourteen men besides me and Millard and the children. We had two to be born while we was there.

We all lived in these big long camps. They built them out of wood. They was little bunk houses in rows all the way out through here. Just enough for a bed or two was all they had in them. Then ours was bigger because that's where the men came to eat. We had our beds in [the back room], and our big wood cook stove and big wood table and a cupboard to keep dishes in [in the other part of the house]. We didn't have a whole lot of stuff.

We'd get up in the morning about five [to have the men fed] by the time they went to work. At seven they'd done be fed and gone. I had this big old dishpan that I made my biscuits up in. I knowed just how much milk to put in. I had a big container that held about a half a gallon, and I put the milk in that. Then I put my flour in the middle of this big pan and put a whole lot of shortening in that and mixed up biscuits. We'd make about six or eight pans full. That's a lot of biscuits for that many men. And we'd have maybe oatmeal or applesauce or grits or gravy and eggs and jellies and butter and all kinds of things like that to go with it. But it was really something to get up of a morning and know you had to cook all that many biscuits. They'd be good and brown cooked on that wood stove. You'd just put them in there and in a few minutes you'd have a meal ready.

Then we had two great big old pots for coffee. We'd make one and they'd drink it while the other was being made. The old cook stoves weren't that big, and the one I went to housekeeping with was the one I had down there. There wouldn't be too much room on top, but we cooked them three meals on that stove and kept it going.

We usually kept pine knots to build a fire with [in the stove]. Keep the fire quick with pine knots. And the kids enjoyed getting out and picking up the pine knots and helping with the fires and stuff and cooking. Sometimes that hot fire would burn some of the biscuits, but anyway they was all eat. Every one of them.

Then I'd start right back after that [meal was finished]. By the time I got the washing done on the rub board, I'd cook that meal at lunch, and then cook again that evening. All I got done was washing, ironing, cooking, and trying to keep house a little bit, though there wasn't much house to keep. But we enjoyed it.

Now we didn't have refrigerators down there. We had just a stream that went down the side of the back of the house out in the back yard. We kept our butter and milk and stuff in that stream, and we'd go out there and get it and it would be good and cold. For dinner, we'd buy other kinds of meat that we could keep for several days, and we'd put it out there in that branch and go get it. Sometimes we'd cook bologna, and we'd have a big old platter and gravy and stuff to put on the table. And then at night we'd have fried potatoes and green beans; and then the men liked onions so we'd buy onions by the bushel, and we'd fry these onions. And we cooked mashed potatoes—just anything you'd mention. Blackberries. We'd have blackberry pies and all that stuff. But it was something to cook for that

PLATE 286   A logging camp high in a watershed. The buildings would be family homes, stables, a dining hall, outdoor toilets, and so on. The flume through the middle of the camp indicates that this was one of Champion's acid wood operations. (Photo courtesy of Champion Paper.)

many men, you know, and get all that ready and get it on the table. They'd come in starved to death and eat a lot.

I didn't do all the cooking by myself because there was this old man that stayed with us that [was from] Waynesville, North Carolina. His name was Deacon Ledford, and he couldn't do no work. He was just a little feller. And he couldn't do no work, but he could help me in the kitchen. They told me when I went down there that I'd be cooking for these men, but that I'd have a woman to come in there to help me. She didn't never show up. I didn't ever see her. But Deacon come and helped me. He'd get up of the morning and help make biscuits and help me wash and put on the coffee and stuff. And Millard helped a lot with the cooking and getting things ready to eat.

Then we'd go to town every Saturday for groceries. It was fourteen miles to town is how far it was. And it rained the most down there that I've ever seen. We lived out on this dirt road, and sometimes we'd have to go out in the sled to get to the highway, and then sled our groceries back in there. That was the muddiest place, I know, that I've ever seen in my life. And then during the week, as Millard took the logs out [to the sawmill], if we needed anything else he'd bring it back in that day. But we went out once a week and bought groceries. We'd be there by ourselves on the weekends, so that's when we got all that done. We'd go out and bring in hay on the weekends for the horses. Buy big slabs of fatback to season with, and big buckets of lard. Everything had to be bought in quantity because they was a lot of us to feed. We traded out here at the stores in Clayton. Goldmine Branch is the name of the place down on Warwoman [where we had to drive from]. Fourteen miles out of town. You can see the little road where it turns up to go in there now. I'd like to go back in there sometime—see if it's still as muddy as it used to be. Get the young'uns on that sled and go out to the road and catch the truck from there on out. There was a lot of times they had to pull the trucks out of there with the team because it'd be so muddy they couldn't get out. Put on chains and everything.

Then the men would come back in Sunday night ready to work the next day. During the week, we'd get through every night about seven-thirty or eight o'clock. There wasn't nothing much to do after supper. They just eat and went and rested. They had these instruments, and sometimes they'd pick and sing and play outside the bunkhouse. Everybody seemed to enjoy theirselves. They worked hard, but they enjoyed it.

And we'd have lots of company. They'd come from Waynesville and everywhere else. Our people all come to see us. And there'd be a lot of people from Warwoman come to see us. Had a right smart of company. You know "Preach" Parsons? He'd come out there and eat with us sometimes. He remembered us way down in there.

Earl "Preach" Parsons

"Preach" Parsons was an employee of the Forest Service for most of his adult life before he retired two years ago. His job took him to camp after camp—large and small—checking on the operation and marking timber for selective cutting. His career spans the development of the industry from steers and up and down sash mills through band.mills (he remembers when there were seven in Graham County, North Carolina alone) to modern pulpwood operations and clear-cutting.

Now in retirement, we asked him to tell us about some of the camps he saw and some of the experiences he had during his years in the field.

Now Millard and Shirley Buchanan—I visited in there. Their camp was typical of the smaller ones. They didn't have many men in their camp compared to the big commercial operations. Too many people get the conception that all camps were small—just little shacks out in the woods, you know. Some logging camps took care of a hundred and two hundred men. That meant they had to staff it, you know.

The people who cleaned up in the camp, they didn't call them maids. There weren't women anyhow. They were old loggers that they called "swampers." They swamped up. That's what they called it. And they were meticulously clean. Boy oh boy, they were clean as a pin. Now there would be bedbugs because, you know, out in the forest and everything, and men traveling here and there with their belongings on their backs—they'd bring them in. But they had their different treatments for bedbugs—kerosene and all that sort of stuff. They were really clean. And you didn't make your bunk. They made it for you. Clean sheets. It's surprising. It was really surprising now.

And one of the things about a logging camp that was always interesting to me was when they sat down to one of those long tables—and two hundred men, now—you wouldn't hear a word spoken other than to pass something. There was no idle gossip, no talk about the day or anything. That

PLATE 287 Another logging camp, this one at the head end of a narrow-gauge rail-road line. The dwellings are log sides with canvas roofs. The long, narrow wooden building behind the dwellings is probably the cook shack. An operation like this one might have seventy-five to a hundred men living there at one time. (Photo courtesy of Champion Paper.)

was just a place to eat, and that was just sort of an unwritten rule. Somebody sat down and went to talking, boy, they'd give him a look. Not supposed to do that in there. You sat in there, you ate your food, you got out.

Now they had good food. Particularly the better camps. And they were proud of their food. Way back there it was hard to get good loggers. They were scarce. So [the companies] would entice them with a good camp. The pay probably wasn't too hot, but nevertheless, they had good hard staple food, and clean surroundings. That was the pride of the logging superintendent—his camp. If a logger went off and talked about his camp [and criticized it], boy, he was through.

At the same time, they had what they called logging tramps. Now they were not tramps the way we think about a guy going down the road without anything to eat, and unshaven and all that sort of stuff. Down on the world. He just went from one logging camp to another. Probably no folks or anything. And he'd stay in camp "X" a while—maybe two or three months, maybe two or three weeks—and then he'd cross the mountain walking and go to the next camp. He just made the rounds, you know. He never drew his pay, and so he never was out of money. Whenever he hit that camp again the next time, there was a paycheck there for him from the last time. If it was a year later, or if it was five years later, there was a paycheck waiting. So he had that little store-up all the way around.

And, as a rule, they were characters. They were quite colorful. The men loved for them to be in camp because they were entertaining. And then they

PLATE 288   Another camp. More substantial buildings like these were generally located at the lumber mills themselves for the mills were permanent operations while the camps were moved periodically from area to area as the supply of wood was exhausted. (Photo courtesy of Champion Paper.)

brought news from the other camps, you know, and from the outside world. They liked to see them come.

The most colorful one was "Tramping Jimmy" Helton. I guess it was forty or fifty years he just tramped the logging camps. And, buddy, he loved it. He could tell some of the doggonest tales. Now I met Jimmy one time in his later years. Some of the tales he'd tell, you couldn't print them. You couldn't tell them before mixed company. His tales were something.

He might take a notion to leave, and he might take some driving grabs— that's these short chains with hooks in the ends they use to hook logs to-gether in trains [so they could pull six or eight logs at once down the mountain]. Give the sign and the teamster way down there would take off. Well, old Jimmy, he was liable to drive one hook into the end of a log and the other into a stump, you know, and a freight train couldn't pull it. Give the sign and then he'd take on off and they'd never see him for six months. These tramps were very colorful, and they were sort of a necessity to keep the morale up, too.

But loggers were proud of their camps. And the camps had to be good because that was the main attraction for securing good labor. They'd take them once or twice a month on the logging train to town to celebrate, you know; and then back to the woods they'd go again. But those people just got it in their blood just like anybody with anything else. That's all they wanted. They worked hard. They worked under hard bosses. They were fair, but they were hard. They had to be. They worked six days a week. That old logger was quite a feller, I'll tell you that right now. He'd go out and rough it. They had boots with [spikes in the soles], and they were deadly weapons too. They were fighting men. But most of the time they'd peel the bark off the logs, and they'd be as slick as grease; so they used these boots to walk the slick logs. They'd run those logs just like a coon. They were experts in their line. Generally you think of a logger as just common humdrum—anybody can do that. But it took an expert in every line of it. They had these splash dams, for example. That was about 1905, I believe. And they brought these river rats in from Pennsylvania and Ohio. That was people trained to run logs on a river. Boy, they had to be just like a squirrel, too. They lost a lot of people in this Chatooga River here.

The way that worked—they built these splash dams on the tributaries going into the main Chatooga, like up Holcolm Creek. And what they'd do is cut logs for three or four months and pile huge piles of them on the banks. Then when the wet spell came and the rivers began to come up, they'd roll these logs into the river bed and then open the splash dam above them up, and that water would take them on down to the main Chatooga River. They'd aim to drive a couple of million feet that one day. That's a lot of logs, too. And then they rode those logs, floated them down in below

Toccoa, Georgia, someplace, and sawmill them. The [sawmills] had booms across the river that would stop the logs, and they'd take them out. But once those logs started, they had to keep them going. There wasn't anything such as quitting. They had relief crews, but those crews were going all the time. And men had to follow those loggers with food and everything else till those logs went through. But those river rats had those boots so they could run the logs—had about fifty spikes to each shoe.

There were experts in every area. Cutting and felling and notching. They took pride when they'd fell a tree. They could take a tree a hundred and fifty feet tall, and mark a spot out there on the ground around the hill, and they'd drive a little stake in the ground. And those experts could almost fell that tree to where it would finish driving that stake in the ground. It just took people like that [with that kind of skill] because they couldn't split their timber. If it split [while they were felling it], and that crack shot way up the trunk, they'd ruin the log. And then it had to fall in position, particularly if they were logging with horses, so that the horse could pull it. They'd throw that log in position, pointed the way they were supposed to be carried out, so that the horse could get to them.

[Then if they weren't going to float the logs] they'd haul them to a narrow-gauge railroad. The best ones they had in the logging woods were the railroads with Shay engines. They ran off cogs—like gears in a car—and they were much more powerful [than conventional, piston driven engines]. Either that or they had tram roads. A tram didn't have an engine on it. It had switchbacks. They'd load this car and let it go down the hill under its own power. It came down to a point, and by the time it got to going a little too fast, it turned upgrade. [That's the way the tracks were constructed.] Then, just before it got to the apex of that upgrade, then here went another track back this way [to take it farther down the hill]. Just before it went up the upgrade, it would go through an automatic switch—a "frog" they called it—and that switch automatically just fell back over [after the car went through heading uphill so that it would be in position to direct the car onto the next downhill portion of track when it reached the apex of the upgrade and headed back downhill]. Over here on Tray Mountain, they'd switchback seven times getting down the mountain.

All those big logging camps are gone from this area now. There just isn't the same type of stuff to cut. The small timber we have now doesn't necessitate that kind of camp. And the mills now can't take care of the big logs anyhow. They have to keep turning it and turning it on that carriage until they lose at least one-third of that big log by just pruning it down to where they can get it through the saw. They had those big bandsaws then that could take a log that was six feet through—back then they cut for the widest width they could get—but now they very seldom ever cut anything

PLATE 289 The Champion Fibre Company operation at Sunburst (now Lake Logan). The log trains would come into this area and dump their logs into the log pond so the dirt would be washed off them before they were sawed. Soaking the grit and dirt off would protect the saw blades. The logs would be drawn into the band mill on a chute (visible leading from the second floor of the building at the head of the lake) where they would be squared by a band saw. Then they would be moved into the resaw area where twelve circle saws operating in tandem would saw them into twelve boards at a time. This mill was shotgun fed and steam operated. Stacked lumber is visible in the far background behind the stacks. A large operation like this one might cut 100,000 feet of lumber a day, and have as many as five trains operating simultaneously hauling logs from the camps to the mill. (Photo courtesy of Champion Paper.)

over ten inches. That's the marketable timber today. They take that lumber and laminate it and put it together and come up with all the wide stuff they need. So logging's entirely different now. Used to, they wouldn't fool with that smaller stuff. They couldn't. Took too much work. What they wanted was the big logs.

Will Zoellner

Will Zoellner worked as a blacksmith at several of the logging camps in our area. When we asked him what a blacksmith's responsibilities were in those camps, he said, "Everything in the world! The blacksmith had to do it all! Even a damn table leg breaks in the kitchen, they send for the blacksmith."

"Everything in the world" included such jobs as repairing the band mills, putting in new tracks and levelling them up for the carriage that carried logs through the saw, repairing or rebuilding the log turners that rolled the logs into the carriage, as well as making singletrees, tools, tool handles, and wagon wheels. Sometimes the jobs required far more in terms of time than most loggers were asked to give. Will might put in a ten-hour day, for example, and then at the end of that day, when the steers were brought in from the woods, put in an additional several hours shoeing them. He'd have to put them in a set of stocks to hold them still, and then raise their legs one at a time with a block and tackle to attach the two-part shoes. And sometimes the jobs were tedious and time consuming. Harnesses and traces, for example, had to be made to fit the animals exactly so that they wouldn't rub their hide raw. And the yokes he made for the steers had to fit exactly so that the steers couldn't turn in them and get fouled or hurt themselves. In addition, he had to know what type of wood was best for each job: he had to know, for example, that a poplar yoke might be fine for use in plowing in a field, but for heavy work, like logging, sweetgum was better as it would give but wouldn't break under the tremendous strain put on it. His job was vital because, in many ways, he kept the whole camp going.

Since he had so much experience with steers, we asked him first to tell us a little about his work with them. Then we asked him to talk about the importance of having the kind of well-run camps that "Preach" Parsons had told us about.

When I first started logging, we used steers. I like to work with them. Horses is hateful. They get to fretting. They get nervous. I don't like to work with horses. Especially in muddy ground like in a creekbed or something. A horse, he don't want to stop there. He wants to run through that and get out of it, but he can't run through with fifty tons. You have to take your time to go through it. I'd rather fool with cattle with the exception of getting in an old field or on a big mountain range with no water and no ditches and no [obstacles] much. There a horse can be mighty handy. But in the roughs I'll take a steer.

I started working with steers early. I used to break them when I was a boy. I had five or six yoke of little ones. I'd play with them. I was working with them, by gosh, when they were still sucking the cow—three or four weeks old. I'd put a little bitty yoke on them and just drive them up and down the road and let them drag a bush or a chain or something between them, and I never would have no trouble. They got used to it. And when you'd take them out, after maybe two days you holler "whoa" to them and they'll stop just like anything else. They get onto it quick, young. Especially if you handle them every day. Later I'd break them to make a living with.

PLATE 290   Will Zoellner (center) with five yokes of steers.

I've logged with them; I've put harness on them and plowed them single like a mule. They'd do anything.

But they've got to be over three years old [to do heavy work]. They're not stout enough to do anything heavy [before that]. They're bones are soft yet. And you don't want to strain them. Some of them takes it awful hard. They pull too hard. And some of them lays down on you. He wants to go faster than the rest and he gets mad and he lays down. Then you have to just whop him up. But you have to be easy with them, of course. The easier you are, the better you'll come out with them later. You can very soon break one.

Then sometimes they turn in the yoke. The bow is not exactly right and one will run around this way and leave the other one standing there with his back end the other way. One's got his head upside down, so one's got the yoke underneath and the other one's got it on top and then it's an awful shape. They'll get one killed. You have to go ahead and knock the bow out and push them around in there and put the bow back. You've got to make a yoke to fit so they can't do that and so his neck won't turn in the bow. I've had them to walk on their hind feet—get up in the air ten feet and jump and rip and tear; but you get them working with other teams in a procession and they'll soon stop that. That chain goes from one yoke to the other, and he can't do that.

Once you start logging with them, you can teach a pair pretty quick if you're logging with more than one pair. You put a trained yoke ahead and then they'll show that [new pair, also called a "yoke"] what to do. The new ones can't get away 'cause the front [pair] just won't let them run, and when you hook them [together], the front ones make them go where they tell them to go.

Now what they call a team is three yokes. Now in the middle you've got to have a pretty good yoke on account of pulling around a ditch. If they don't, the front cattle put them down in overboard. They have to be pretty stout cattle, heavy cattle, to push each other and hold that load up there. A youngster, he'll go straight through and get in the ditch and get killed. He don't look out for himself. He don't know how. So the lead ones have to be perfectly trained, and the middle ones has got to be heavy enough to hold them in there.

But the butts—the last ones—it don't make no difference whether they're broke or whether they're not. If they want to pull, they can pull; and if they don't want to pull, the others'll drag them. They'll go. They'll have to go. They'll soon learn it; and if they don't look out, the other cattle'll drag them along. [They'll see that if] the other cattle can do it, they can too.

But the butts should be heavy cattle too because they've got a lot of pushing and pulling to do against each other going in through the ditches and limbs and holes and stuff like that. They have to be stout enough to hold their own. But the leads have got to be absolutely trained. When you holler, "Whoa," you want him to stop. It don't make no difference where it is. And they soon learn it, and they get so they look back and watch to see if the other cattle is not hung up or anything like that. They buddy up in less than a week.

Sometimes one of the butts will try to lie down on you. They get mad and lay down. When they lay down, why, just shoot them one with the ox whip and let the others pull him up. Then he'll go get mad, and he'll go on. And don't overload them. Make sure that they can pull it if they want to. Then after you log them a week or two, why, all the trouble is over. But don't take two yokes or three yokes of cattle in the rough land like cliffs and rocks. If you do, you're going to get one killed.

In loading logs—we didn't have no way of loading logs then. We'd just load them with the cattle. Take the leads off and wrap a chain around the log and back the wagon up there. Run two chains under the log and on over and hook the cattle to the ends and let them cattle pull that log up there. You stand up there with a peavee and watch and see if anything slips. Then just holler, "Whoa," and they'll hold that log. They won't let it go back. Then you spike him where you want him and tell them to get up a little. They'll ease on up there and as quick as the log hits the standards,

PLATE 291 A large operation like Champion would also have a commissary where its men could obtain food, dry goods, tools, feed, and other supplies they might need. This one, on the head of Sunburst, like other commissaries, had its busiest day on Saturdays when families would be free for the weekend. Since they were only paid every thirty days, employees would make their purchases with what they called "doogaloo" —credit vouchers against their forthcoming paychecks. At the end of the month, they would draw the balance of what was left in their accounts in cash. Such a commissary might serve as many as twenty camps, the band mill, the general public, and the independent loggers, like Millard Buchanan, who cut boundaries of timber themselves, were paid by the thousand feet of timber they brought in, and could make purchases here on credit against what the company would owe them at the end of each month.

Though most of the people in this photograph undoubtedly work for the company, only a few of them would be loggers. The list of employees required by a large operation was staggering, and would include: cooks, "cookies" (cook's assistants), "lobby hogs" (men who served the food and cleaned the dining hall after meals), "swampers" (the men who made the skid trails the horses and oxen used to drag the logs to a loading area), "road monkeys" (men who maintained the skid trails), "grab jacks" (men who drove grabs into the logs so they could be pulled), teamsters (men who drove the stock), blacksmiths, stable boys, foremen, timber cutters (the men who felled the trees and trimmed and cut them to length with crosscut saws and axes), sawyers, block setters (men who positioned the logs so they could be sawed at the mill), firemen to fire the boilers, "off-bearers" (men who took the lumber away from the saws), "cutoff men" (men who cut the bad ends off lumber and squared it up), "trimmers" (men who edged off the bark that the main saws didn't get), "pickup men" (men who hauled the lumber to the woodyard), "stackers" (men who stacked the wood in the woodyard), "skidder men" (men who operated the overhead skidders), flagmen to signal the skidder operators, "tong hookers" (men who hooked the choker to logs so they could be dragged to the loading area by the skidder), train engineers, and so on. (Photo courtesy of Champion Paper.)

they'll automatically stop. They know it's loaded. Then you just turn them around and get another. You load plumb on up to the top.

Now when I worked in camps, there was some good camps and some bad camps. One I stayed in had seventy-two men. They come from Hayesville [North Carolina] and up on Shooting Creek [North Carolina] and several from Franklin [North Carolina]. There was one horse man that took care of the horses. Seen that they was, well, fat. He was from West Virginia. He was a big old feller. Nice, quiet, easy to get along with. He looked after the horses, and if the harness didn't fit, he'd get out his whittling knife and fix it. We never lost but one horse. And then the Government had sixteen men in the woods day and night [marking trees to be cut in the National Forest lands]. Get out in these mountains and they wouldn't go home. They'd just get in the barracks and go to sleep and pay the board. Then we didn't do a thing but hunt the marked trees and cut them.

Now that camp had anything you wanted. Makes no difference what it was. They had the nicest beds you ever looked at, and they kept clean. And those beds, they'd go where we'd go. They were in barracks that could be moved. You could pull them wherever you wanted to. They could move a whole camp in two hours. And the boys that would go out on a shift hunting the timber to cut way off, if that company didn't bring the dinner to them, they'd go and get them and bring them in. But most of the time the mess sergeant would send the dinner out and meet them at the campground wherever they were logging.

They had tools and equipment and everything. And the cooks, they had their barracks connected with the kitchen. Had a dining room, living room, and kitchen. The living room was a separate building so they didn't interfere with the men and women who cooked. We had both men and women cooking. It's really a man's job to cook in the woods, but if a woman wants to do it, why, she's cleanest. I'd rather have a woman cook than a man. They were handiest.

But all the camps weren't like that. I had to quit one. I left there. They didn't have brain one. Never thought a man had to sleep at night and had to have something to eat dinner and supper. They'd just put him on out and let him go on with it. Tell you what to do and not make no arrangements for you out in the woods. I got full of it.

There was one old head man about seven or eight feet high with a great big old black moustache—old bony feller. He didn't have brain one. I told him, "I always work for people that's got a little sense, but now I overguessed it so I'm through. Give me my pay and I'll leave."

"Why, you can't do that."

I says, "I'm going to. If you ain't got the money, I'm going to anyhow."

"But what's the matter?"

I says, "Nobody's got any brains here to know how to log! That's what's the matter. Don't you know that a man has to eat a little something once or twice a day? I come in for supper and you put me on a truck—have to go to Virginia to get some cables and a compressor and stuff. You never thought about the bath, and you never thought about the eats. You ain't got brain one!"

He hung his head a little bit and said, "Well, I thought you had arrangements made."

I says, "Where could I make arrangments in the woods?"

But I never seen such a mess in my life. Man would have to fix him a place to eat on the table when it did get there. Wasn't no place fixed to set. You had to get your own stool or a piece of board or something to sit on the table to eat.

I told him, "When Saturday comes, I'm going home and I'm going to stay there."

"Oh," he says, "we've got a place for you [to stay]."

"Yes, I see you have. Sleep in the sawdust pile, by gosh, and lay down in the shade of a tree [to sleep] when it's hot," I says. "Eat when we find it. If it ain't fair [weather], why, do without."

"Well," he says, "how did you all do it [in the other camp]?"

I says, "We had a mess hall. We had a cook. We had KP's. We had a housecleaner. We had a bed fixer to strip the beds." And I said, "If you want to log, that's the way you got to go at it. You can't work seventy-five men and have them sleeping on the trees and the bushes and rock cliffs and get them on the job the next morning."

He looked around a little bit, says, "We can't do without a blacksmith."

I says, "You'll do without me. I'm gone. I'm just the same as home now."

Looked around there, "I'll have to call headquarters."

I says, "You can call them up and tell them I'm gone."

So I stepped on out.

The kind of camp you ran made a big difference when you expected men to work hard all day long and into the night.

Jake Waldroop

On July 21, 1976, Jake Waldroop took four of us from Foxfire to see the "big poplar" in the Nantahala National Forest, not too far from his home in Cartoogechaye, North Carolina. He has a special interest in this tree, which is reputed to be the "largest yellow poplar in the United States." His grandfather, also named Jake Waldroop, once owned all the land in Sugar Cove where the poplar is located and had sold that land to the U. S. Gov-

ernment prior to its being logged. Jake remembers as a child coming to the big poplar, much larger than any others in the area, with his mother looking for ginseng. It was a landmark even then.

Zeb Waldroop, Jake's father, ran a logging operation in this area about sixty years ago when Jake was a young man. When the Sugar Cove area was being cut, Jake had to make a decision about cutting the big poplar tree. He apparently had no esthetic reasons for saving the tree. Even then it was at least thirteen feet in diameter and the crosscut saws were only ten feet long. The logging company said they would get a longer saw. Then Jake realized that even if the tree were cut, they would have a very difficult time getting it out of the woods, and then it could not be cut at the sawmill because of its great width. Therefore the big poplar was spared.

Several years ago a trail was cut through the woods to the tree by the Forest Service and dedicated to John Wasilik, a former forest ranger well-liked by the North Carolina residents of this area.

Because his father was a logger and his mother ran a logging camp for the men he had hired, we asked Jake to tell us about that life.

PLATE 292   Jake Waldroop before the giant yellow poplar.

Oh, Lord, I've logged ever since I was just a boy. I used to help my daddy log. He had a big operation over in Nantahala with a splash dam and everything. We've worked back in those coves ten hours a day. In the wintertime you'd have to take you a lantern to see your way out. Sometimes he'd have forty or fifty thousand feet of logs loaded on them skids ready to roll into that slide when they turned that splash dam on. It would take sometimes a half a day or more before they'd get them all dumped in [the river]. And then them men, they'd drive them all the way to the mill—ride the logs down through there. When they'd jam, they'd have to get in there and break that jam and get them to moving on.

Now when he was doing that splashing and we was down at Tate Cove, I was a small boy. He always boarded his hands, and my mother run the boarding house there. All I was big enough to do was carry out the lunch or dinner. She'd get the dinner ready and we'd carry it up to the Tate Branch where they was logging. Then they'd come in for supper.

A few of the men boarded at home, but we always had ten or twelve stay with us. Then they'd go out on Saturday and come back on Sunday evening and they'd be ready to go to work on Monday morning. On Saturday, if they was bootleggers around, they'd get a quart or a half-gallon and that would do them over till they come back in. Never would have much drinking in the camp. They had to do their drinking outside. They'd have their "drown" on the weekend.

But this camp, my daddy built it and moved us into it. Them that wanted to go home walked the three or four miles home after work in the evening after quitting time. Others stayed. We had a big garden. Make our own potatoes and raise our own corn, and had two or three acres of wheat. The thrasher would come around at the fall of the year and thrash that wheat. We'd take it down here at the roller mill and that's all the flour we'd get. And we'd raise beans. We'd raise the awfullest sight of beans you've ever seen in your life. I've seen ten, fifteen bushels piled up in a room and everyone around stringing them. They'd have leather britches beans and shell beans too, but most of them would be for pickling. They'd pickle a big barrel full of them. They'd hold sixty to eighty gallons. Fill one of them with pickled beans, and have big sackfulls of leather britches beans. And wasn't no trouble about meat. We just grazed hogs back in the mountains. I remember one time my daddy had twenty-seven killed one day. He got a bunch of men to come in and killed and dressed and cut up and packed up twenty-seven. We had a big smokehouse, and we'd salt that meat down in that smokehouse. So we had the food.

Mother would feed them potatoes, meat, bread. Every morning she would make them a big pan of sawmill gravy. She'd have a great big skillet and she'd put some meal or flour in it. You could make it out of corn meal or flour, but you generally thickened your gravy with flour. She'd put that flour in that pan and she'd let it brown a little bit. Then she'd dump milk in there—or water if she didn't have milk. So they'd have gravy, and they'd have eggs and bacon. A lot of times it would just be the whole big middling. She'd just slice it up. And ham, and shoulder meat. And she'd have fruit. We dried sacks after sacks of fruit. And she'd bake these dried fruit pies, or sometimes just have big platters of that dried fruit on the table. And it was good, and they'd eat it. And she'd have applesauce and jelly. They'd just make worlds of jelly up in the fall of the year. Why, you could pick just bushels of blackberries and apples. She was busy. Worked all the time.

Then either they'd come in for lunch, or they'd send somebody to come into the boarding house and they'd have the dinner ready all packed in big buckets and carry it out to the men. And depending on how many men was going to be at the lunch ground, we'd have a big coffeepot and make it out there. It was too hard to pack coffee. It generally took two good husky men to carry out the lunch for them men to eat anyway. They could eat, them loggers did. Lord goodness, they could take care of some of it. It was a sight! On a great big platter one would just rake it full of beans and meat and fruit and vegetables and whatever they had.

It was a good life. I enjoyed it. You didn't have all that much to worry about. You didn't have all this confusion—killing and everything. Once in a while one of them would fall out, but hardly ever in them logging camps. You'd never hear of any trouble much there. Some of these bigger camps, sometimes some would break over and have a little shooting streak. A man would get killed over a card game. But not often.

In the evenings, sometimes the men would get out and gang up and play them a game of setback. I've played setback with them for hours at a time. It would get so dark we'd have to go in. And 'the gnats would eat us up in the summertime. We'd have to build up a smoke and we'd set around that smoke and play setback. And sometimes some of them would bring in a banjo and make a little music.

And one time we had a fellow—he was the blacksmith. And every Wednesday night we'd have services—preaching—for the loggers. He'd wait till after supper and the cookies had gotten everything cleaned up so they could listen too. Then George, he would preach in the lobby. Pretty much every one of them loggers would come in and be just as quiet and listen to him, you know.

We called them "the good old days." And they was.

Interviews and photographs by Cam Bond, Lynnette Williams, and Brenda Carpenter.

AUNT LOLA CANNON

I hope everyone is fortunate enough to have a special place to go to—a place they'll always remember. A place that involves a trek down a tree-covered hill, across the creek, and up the opposite hill, just for a short visit. A place where you can always smell something cooking even before you get to the house. And in that place is the person one will never forget.

I remember Aunt Lola as far back as my memory goes. To me, she hasn't changed a bit and never will. She has always offered me some cake, pie, anything sweet, and I have always eagerly accepted. A long time ago, she gave me a little red Bible on my birthday, and because she gave it to me, it is a treasured possession.

Aunt Lola is the sort of person you can turn to when things aren't quite right, when you need advice. She's the person who can tell you right from wrong without making it sound like a lecture; instead it sounds like good common sense. There's a kindness about her which is impossible to articulate. A very generous and gentle-natured person, I have never heard her say a harsh word to or about any other person. She's very close to God, and tries very hard in her own delicate way to help other people know God the way that she does.

Aunt Lola was born on March 26, 1894 in the Warwoman community. She's actually my great-aunt, but to me she's been more like a grandmother. I guess I could sum up all my feelings for Aunt Lola in the three words, "I love her."

ANITA JENKINS

Photography and interviews done by Bit Carver, Anita Jenkins, and Myra Queen.

PLATE 293   Aunt Lola with Anita Jenkins outside her little home.

My grandmother said that she could cover my face with an ordinary coffee cup when I was born. The house that I lived in on Warwoman was a huge log house. It was wide. I don't know the number of feet, but anyway the beds sat like that [headboards against the wall] in the back and there was still plenty of room in between them to go in and out. I can still see it. It was sealed with wide poplar boards.

[We later moved to Chechero because] we didn't own a good-sized piece of land. Mother had been raised here on Chechero, and she had never liked living over there. She was always a little homesick for this place. Daddy got a chance to buy this property here—all of it. We bought this place which was Mother's grandfather's property. And we moved into the house where my sister, Bessie, lives now.

The Godfrey place, as it was called, had the first white settlers in this end of the community. There was a family, the Coffees, that settled about where Kingwood [Country Club] is now, and then the Godfrey family was settled here and it was about three miles across Big Creek to another family. The cemetery over here has always been called the Godfrey Cemetery.

The house that my great-great-grandfather Godfrey built was somewhere near the cemetery. Their little girl played under a big oak tree [near the cemetery]. She had built a playhouse and once, while he was gone back to buy supplies, she got sick and died. Grandmother bathed and dressed her, and put her up on a board between chairs and she kept for three days till he got back. They buried her under that big oak tree. That was the beginning of that cemetery.

Most of the country was in little settlements. The first man who got up in the morning would go outside his door and holler just as loud as he could two or three times to wake the other people. In a little bit, you would hear from another house over on the ridge somebody had come out and hollered off his front porch. And it was like that until every family had gotten up and had their morning hello. I think now if we heard it over the community, we would be alarmed. We'd think something was happening. That was one thing that was always done when I was a child. We didn't have an

PLATE 294   The Godfrey Cemetery, with Malinda Godfrey's headstone in the foreground.

alarm clock at our house until long after I was married. Mama had one of those great old big ones. I thought that alarm clock was the most treasured thing—that you could be waked up any time you wanted to be.

People who keep a mixed flock of chickens [can use roosters as alarm clocks]. So many people don't keep chickens now. I don't know what it is about it, but to hear the roosters crow just before dawn brings something back from my childhood. If you had a rooster in your flock that crowed before time to get up, you got rid of him. A great many people claimed that they could tell the time of day by their rooster's crow. Most of the time, they crowed about half an hour before dawn. You could judge pretty well.

At our house, we used to sing a lot after supper sitting around the fire. Mother would probably be knitting. Daddy would make axe handles and hammer handles and different things like that at night. We didn't buy them. Boys grew up feeling like they had accomplished something when they learned to make a good axe handle or a good hoe handle. They were tasks that we could do at night around the fire and there was a lot of good fellowship in families. There was a habit among people in our area; we'd get an early supper and go over and visit the neighbors and stay until bedtime. That was quite an event. If there were children, they got together to play and the old folks talked and sang. Sometimes two families would get

PLATE 295   The view from Aunt Lola's house. "I wish I could put it on canvas or paper to show all of the people how beautiful it really is here."

together and sing. Smaller children would get sleepy quicker and probably go to bed. And some among the group would stay up as long as the parents stayed up.

It was a right good time to live then. Now you don't find a lot of fire-places for families to gather around after supper. And so many people work at different jobs that take them away from home, that families hardly ever are all at home at one time. I think we had a closer family relationship in those days than people do today.

One thing that we enjoyed as youngsters—we always had a Christmas tree at the church during the Christmas season. Most times it would be a day or two before Christmas. We'd meet several days before to decorate the [church] house. We'd cut holly, white pine, and anything that was green, and decorate each window and each corner of the [church] house. To keep it from looking bare, we stood greenery up all the way to the ceiling. That took a day in our lives. But we stretched out a day. Oh, we thought we were really living it up when we could spend a whole day decorating the church for Christmas. And then we felt we must go back and clean it up afterward, and that took another whole day. Oh, we were just as busy as youngsters are now who work.

My parents didn't talk religion as much as they just worked it in our ev-eryday living. I wish I could tell you exactly, but somehow you just got up in the morning and they made you feel like this was another good day if you used it well, and that's what God wants us to do. They stressed more, I think, to me about the things that God wants us to do than they did what you'd call religion. But that is religion, isn't it—what God wants us to do. And of course, we went to Sunday school and to preaching service at the country churches. Back then we had preaching service twice a month. There would be a Saturday service and a service the following Sunday, and the other Sundays we had Sunday school. Mother always saw to it, and so did Daddy, that we had our Sunday school lesson read.

They taught us a lot about God, religion, and our future life in planting the garden and the fields. Whatever they planted, they expected to get a harvest from, because they planted it in faith and cultivated it. That was one of the things that seemed [to leave] more of an impression on my life than anything else. Now you plant this little, pitiful-looking seed, a grain of corn, or a bean, or a pumpkin seed, and then think of what a harvest it would make. And I remember Mama telling me one time that that was the way your life was. You were just one person and if you did a good deed for somebody, that made them want to do a good deed for someone else, and it spreads. That was a valuable lesson to me. Even though you're just one per-son, you can start a good thing going.

When I was little girl, I was the only child for about ten years and I had to figure out my own amusement. There weren't any radios or television. I don't think I'd seen a phonograph till I was about ten years old, so my play was games my daddy would play with me after supper every night, like Fox and Geese, and guessing rhymes, and a game we'd play with some object in the house. One person would say, "I see something that looks like something else," so then the rest of them would try to guess what it was. Or, I could say, "I'm looking at something in this room that's green," and everybody would start guessing. Or I would say, "I see something in this room that's round," and the person who guessed the most questions won. That was a great game.

Another pastime at home before I learned to read was dolls. I wanted more clothes for my dolls and my mother would be busy, so she cut me some little patterns and I learned to sew. And when I knitted that doll a sweater, I really thought I had made something.

Once in a while, we had company with a child my age and we made up a group of little rag dolls and took them down to the creek. We baptized them and we sang songs that they sing at church, and then later we had a hospital. We knew nothing about a hospital except what we'd read. There wasn't one in the county then. So we had the hospital and some of our patients would die and we had a burying ground for them, and the next time these girls were there, we'd go dig up the dolls and see if they were still dead.

There were no bought toys in my home. Of course, people near town had more of those things, but we made our toys. I made lots of corncob dolls and dressed them up like people. We made corn-silk hair for them. We learned to improvise. I guess it stood us in good stead. It was really good for us, and especially when the Depression hit. We had to improvise so many of our things, so early training of making toys was good for us.

We girls would build elaborate playhouses, and work so hard our mothers would wonder, "How did you get so dirty?" Usually we looked for a thicket, a laurel thicket was the nicest place to build because the little trees made the partitions for the walls. We roamed the country looking for pretty rocks and mosses to furnish our houses. And our bathtub was a whole heap of pine needles piled up and shaped out for a bathtub. We'd take pieces of lace or something from home to make the pillow shams and table covers.

At school, sometimes the boys and girls played together in a game they called "Tap me." [The children made] a ring and one was left to tap one of the others. He'd run around the ring a time or two to draw the others' attention; then tap someone and run. The one he tapped, to catch him, had to go around the circle again. That's about the only games boys and girls played together. Now some of the larger girls liked to play ball and were good ball players. The boys liked to have them join because they were good. The smaller girls and boys wouldn't play ball too much. They were apt to get in the way and get hurt.

I went to school at Warwoman my first years in school, in one of those little weatherboard, one-room schoolhouses. All the children were in that one room. I think the most pupils that were usually in school were thirty, and you know it kept the teacher pretty busy. We went to school from eight until four, but we had an hour recess at dinner time and a short break in the morning and afternoon, about fifteen minutes. It gave us time to go to the spring and get water. There were no buses. We all walked to school.

In those days, there would be one time along in the autumn when a traveling photographer would come through the county and make the students' group picture. I had a couple, one made at Warwoman and one made here [at Chechero]. I don't know what became of those pictures. I would have treasured them a lot now. I didn't think so much about them then.

Our school days were really fun. We had only five months of school. It was out early in the fall. Later on, we got to having a seven-month school. And I went to school a couple of years after they started having nine months of school. Schools weren't graded when I went. I finished what I guess was the seventh grade. They started the grading process about the time I was in the last year of school. If you had applied yourself, you had a pretty good basic education when you finished the seventh grade.

I had a very eventful school life. I enjoyed it. I don't think my mother ever had to drive me off with a switch. Some children didn't like school; but I liked it even though I wasn't such a good student. I just liked the companionship.

My education was pretty limited, and as my children went a little way in school I helped them with their homework and pretty soon had to do a little studying in the daytime to keep up. I thought at that time, when my children are all on their own and I have no responsibility, I'll go back to school. I didn't think at that time that I wouldn't have a retentive mind and wouldn't be able to go back to school. I tried to keep reading when I could. I tried to use the best language for [my children] and I studied a little harder to express myself better.

We had lots of fun in those days. The farmers would gather up their corn in the fall. There was always a [corn] crib, most times it was a log crib, a log building that would have a big shed alongside it to protect the corn. They'd pile the corn up there. One farmer would invite everybody to a corn shucking on a certain day. That was quite a treat—to go see a lot of young people and a lot of older people. We shucked the corn. I don't think I was ever at a corn shucking where they had the jug of moonshine hid in it. They did at some places. The person who shucked to that jug first was the top of the evening. We had such dinners, such big dinners, cooked—all cooked on a wood stove or in the fireplace. A lot was done by the fireplace. The stove wouldn't hold all the pots and pans. We had a fabulous dinner. We'd have big kettles of pork, turnips and turnip greens, cabbage, potatoes, and beans. There wasn't much canned stuff then. In fact, I can just remember the fruit jars that Mama bought and they were such a novelty. All of the good things that you can think of to eat—big platters of baked sweet potatoes, butter, buttermilk. I don't believe we had much cake served at dinners like that, but there would be countless stacks of dried apple pies, "half moons" they called them. Roll out a real flat surface of dough and cut it out by a plate. Spread the fruit on half of it and turn the other half over it. Seal it together by mashing the edges with a fork. Oh, my, they were good.

Families did lots of things together like that. There was a lot of land that had virgin timber which had to be cleared if you wanted to make some more farm land. Some farmers would have their trees marked and how they wanted them to fall, and what they wanted done with them. They cut the big logs into something to build with and burned the brush and got the land all ready for planting. [We'd have a log rolling then.]

The girls had quiltings. They'd put up a quilt on the frames that hung from the ceiling. The girls and women would quilt, and then at night they'd have a party. Some fellow in the community that played the banjo, and maybe a French harp, would gather in and we'd all have a party. Sometimes it lasted until after midnight. I wonder how many of the young people today could work all day and then dance until that time. But we had wonderful times and when I tell my grandchildren about it, they look at me wide-eyed like they thought, "Well, Granny, isn't that tale a little too thin?"

Washing was done usually at a creek near the house. The people searched out a spot that would be near a good spring or a good creek, and built their house there. We usually washed at the creek with a big iron pot to boil the clothes in. The men searched the woods for hollow logs and would saw them off in six-foot lengths or more, then hollow them on out into a smooth hard surface and put a bottom on and that was your tub for scrubbing.

There are a lot of the old habits when I grew up that I still like to sit and think about. So many of them were really good habits. Young people learned to work, of course. I expect the young people learn to work as quickly now as they did then, but it was a different type of work. It was all rural and there was no going to town except on Friday or Saturday to buy the necessary things. We grew most of them at home. The children were all taught little tasks. We had chickens, and they were to be fed and looked after. Then there were always cows and calves. Cows had to be taken to one

PLATE 296   Aunt Lola with Bit
Carver.

pasture and the calves to another. Many little tasks to be done. The wood
stoves were all that we had up until some years ago. They required a lot of
petting with wood. You'd have to get wood for them so you'd have a good
fire.

It was right amusing. There were lots of little things that brought a laugh
in those days. Nobody got their feelings hurt. If somebody made some mistake or did something not just right, why everybody just laughed it off.
Today, you all know how it is when the boys reach a dating age, or before.
They've just got to have a car. They just must have it. Well, back in those
days when a boy reached that age, they just had to have a horse or a mule.
It was the same way it is with cars now to what kind you could afford. But

they worked terribly hard then to get them a buggy. And if they were pretty well-to-do, they'd have a top on it. That was still a little higher up. Every fellow had his buggy and kept it just as clean and cared for as the boys do their cars today. And the harness for the mules or horses was all shined up and nice for Sunday. I guess the poor old horses had a harder day on Sunday than they did the rest of the week. We really had a time then.

Mothers at that time thought you must know how to card and spin, how to cook, how to quilt, and you must know how to keep your house neat and clean. You must behave in mixed company very quietly, and you were never to be isolated with any man. There must be a group of you. I expect a great many girls grew up [with] a kind of fear that they didn't know how to go out to meet the world. Each girl was taught how to save the field seeds and the garden seeds, and when the best time for planting was. One thing went in one time and another at another time. The older people used the signs of the zodiac much more than they do now. My mother wouldn't have planted a bean at any other time than the arms [see *The Foxfire Book*, page 212]. My father had a time when he planted potatoes. He would have missed a crop rather than plant at a different time.

The boys were taught early how to chop properly and carefully, they were taught methods of planting, and when to plant such and such, and if the father had a carpenter trade or other trade, they taught their sons that. Most communities had at least one or two basketmakers. A lot of the boys liked to go to this basketmaker's place and take lessons from him. That way they learned to do the work, not only baskets, but chair seating and making stools. Very few boys learned how to cook. They didn't teach boys as much back then about housework. They were taught about cattle and how to notice for signs of the mating season for the cows and the horses. When a young man grew to where he could plow a straight furrow across a good-sized field, he was very proud. He considered himself a man. The boys were taught what types of firewood was best in the days when we all made soap from the wood ashes. Most mothers liked hickory or oak for their ashes to make soap. The boys were taught how to fell the trees, and how to make them into whatever type of wood they needed. No two fireplaces were exactly the same length. They had to know how to gauge their wood. And you most always saw a little boy with a roll of hickory bark in his pocket. That was a string then. You wet that little hickory bark. You take it from a little tree and peel it off in tiny little sections, some you could take down to just a fraction. Little boys traded their hickory bark rolls sometimes. Sometimes one fellow didn't have any, but maybe he had some marbles that another fellow wanted. They traded like that. That was their wampum, really.

As each girl grew up and began to get to the dating age, she liked to piece quilts. Girls pieced their quilts and had them all ready [for their own homes]. They had their sheets and pillowcases ready. We knew nothing then in our part of the world about seamless sheets. You bought sheeting. It was in several grades, thirty-eight or maybe forty inches wide, and you sewed two lengths together to make your sheets. That's the way we made our sheets and pillowcases. Most of us learned to crochet or embroider to trim those pillowcases. We took pride in having all the bedding ready that we would need. And usually the groom's mother gave him a set of bedding, too, I think.

I married Raleigh in 1917, and we went to housekeeping in that little twenty-four by sixteen-foot schoolhouse. We didn't have a great deal, but we got it all in that house and we lived in it, like that, until a year later. When I went to housekeeping, I had made four quilts, and I had some more started. I had six sheets and that was many more than lots of the girls had. A lot of them just had two. I thought that I had really set myself up when I had six sheets. When I went to housekeeping, a lady that my husband worked for (she spent her summers up here) gave him two big old porchlike rockers. I had a bedstead and he bought a bedstead. Two was all we had room for in that little house, along with those two rockers. He had made a round dining table from walnut, which was my treasure. I had a clothes press that my daddy had made me, a big trunk, and a tiny little number-eight cook stove. How we got all those things in that little house, I don't know, but we did.

We didn't have all the cookware and things that people have today. I had bought a set of blue enamel ware. There was a water bucket, a preserving kettle, a big spoon, and two little boilers. Then I had a few dishes that my grandmother gave me. But I didn't want to use those—they were for best. It was very plain ware that we had those days. Now the more wealthy people did have china and nicer things.

Raleigh built a porch across one end and along one side of the little house. I was so happy over that porch. One end of it was sunny in the morning and the other end was sunny in the afternoon which was very nice when the children began to come along. He put up a sort of banister around and we let them play out there.

The first year we kept house, my husband bought a pig. We raised it as a pet. We didn't keep the door shut so she came into the house. Anywhere we found her outside, we'd call her and she'd lie down for you to scratch her. We spent hours teasing that pig. And when she got big enough to have baby pigs, my husband gave me one of my own. I raised it and sold it. With the money from that, I bought some Alaska silverware (I think that's what they called it), a set of knives and forks.

I don't remember when we first got electricity. The line came out to the Methodist church. Then it was some little time till it came on out as far as

Mrs. Pollard's. And we all got impatient about it down here in Chechero. They kept promising, "As soon as we can, it'll be out there." One day my sister and I stopped in and talked to the power company people and told them that if we didn't hurry up and get electricity down in our section of the country, there were going to be a lot of divorces.

One man in there said, "Well, how's electricity going to help?"

I said, "The men are getting tired of wearing shirts that have been ironed with a flat iron by a wood stove, and they're going to divorce us if we can't find something better."

I think that must have been my happiest time of life. I didn't actually realize the responsibility of raising a family, so I didn't have that to worry about. I could just enjoy my children. Raleigh always made plenty for them to eat so I didn't have the food to worry about—just to make their clothes. I knitted their bootees, socks, sweaters, and caps. I said if they ever got large enough that I didn't have to knit for them, I would never touch another knitting needle, but I have taken it up again. It required a lot of forethought and planning to be able to have what they needed for school.

I did housework before I was married. When Luther Rickman was sheriff, I worked with his wife for three or four years. Then I worked in a little cafe for an old German lady. When the WPA came in, I worked in a school lunchroom and that's the only out-of-home work I've done. I enjoyed it, but we didn't have many conveniences. The patrons brought in firewood for the wood stoves in the lunchroom. I had to do it a lot of times. Sometimes in the winter, the pump would be frozen and we'd have to carry water from a spring a far piece off. It was hard but I liked it. However, I would rather work at home. Yes, there are so many little intimate things you can do in the home. For years my husband wasn't able to do much but just sit around. He liked someone around, and I didn't get to do as much housework as I would have liked to. There was one thing I had always hoped to do and prayed to do—to take care of my husband as long as he was living. I had that privilege until he had a stroke and I couldn't manage him and he had to go to the hospital. I got a lot of satisfaction knowing I did everything I could for him and I could supply all his material needs and read to him and pray with him. Since he's been gone, I just can't pin myself down to anything. I start something and don't get it done, but however many tasks the Lord wants me to do, He'll give me the ability and time to do them in.

I have done a lot of things, but the most satisfying was a good productive garden. I got such a thrill out of putting up fruits during the fall before the freezer was introduced. I found a lot of pleasure in making a quilt just like I wanted to. Maybe I would put it in the frame you see hanging from the ceiling. And when I finished, I had so much pride in it. I don't quilt now because I can't see well enough.

If I learned how to bake a different cake and it turned out well, I loved that. Just about everything I did, if I had done it well, I thought I really had accomplished something.

And I liked working outdoors. A great many women helped to do the outdoor work. Most of them in my environment helped saw wood or chop wood and do any of the outdoor tasks with the men. A great many mothers were wise enough to teach their sons to help in the house, too. Women in those days did a lot of work in fields alongside their men if there weren't a lot of small children. If there were small children, they'd take a quilt, a bottle of milk, and maybe a piece of bread to the field and find a shade to put the pallet down in, and then sit the baby on it while they worked. Women did more outdoor work then. People worked in those days from early to late; it wasn't from eight to four. People considered themselves quite industrious if they got to the fields before sun-up and worked till sundown. I don't see how they did it. And we couldn't now because it seems like we've gotten out of that way of doing.

I have six children, five girls and one boy. They learned to do all sorts of work. All of them but one can milk a cow better than I can now. Of course, they don't have to do it now. They finished grammar school here on Chechero, and then they went to work. Ruth and Estelle worked during the summer for some of the boarding houses. There was nothing for girls to do

PLATE 297   Aunt Lola's barn.

then as they can now. [After finishing grammar school], they went away to Tallulah Falls [for high school], all five of the girls, to board there.

I wouldn't know how to cope with youngsters today. I certainly wouldn't. I think that I would rather have raised my family back in those days than today. I think it was easier to impress them with worthwhile things of life, because there weren't so many distracting things. I'm sure that I couldn't cope with training youngsters today. They are given so much more permission when they're little fellows, and then when they get larger, I'm at a loss on how to handle them. My children weren't the best brought up children in the world by any means, but they did learn that "no" was "no" and that it didn't do any good to whine and pout and cry like I see some do today. I think that saved me a lot of worry later and was better for them.

I used to go to bed and cry when I made the children do things that were too hard for them. But today they tell me that it influenced their later lives. Today, it seems like people are a little too permissive with their children. While they are small, that's the time to get in your best training, before they start to school. What they learned from their parents then really influences their lives. It's just as easy to teach them good manners and good language as it is to teach them bad language and bad manners. It's the early training in the early years that really counts.

One of my neighbors taught school. She said that when she had class every morning, she could tell which child had had discipline at home. When they were given their books, she could tell a child that had been read to and that had grown up with the influence of pictures and books. She said it was very easy to pick out that child. It goes to prove that the early part of their life is [the best time to train a child].

We tried to give our children good training at home and a good religious background. We had an event in churches then that I don't see so much now, Children's Day. The churches almost every year had a Children's Day, sometime in May or June. The children would practice for weeks, and they'd go to church and their teacher or instructor would meet them there once or twice a week. They would practice their recitation, the songs and the plays that they'd use. We'd go a day maybe beforehand, and clean up the church and decorate it with whatever was available. That was a great event for us. People came from miles and miles to the church for our Children's Day. The smaller child who could memorize some little thing would get up and speak his piece. Why, it helped their ego a lot.

When we went to church, we went in when we got there and sat down. Our children didn't run around the churchyard laughing and playing and making noise. They went into the church very reverently and then when the singing would begin, the little fellows tried to sing. All they did was kind of crow around but at least they made their noise. And between the Sunday school service and the church service, we had what was called an intermission, a little time to get out and walk about and maybe go get a drink of water. They always looked for a place to build a church near a cool spring so they could get water. Then they gathered back in the church and had song service and then a preaching service.

My children had a better advantage than I did, church-wise. I was able to go with them every Sunday, and for the most part, we had two preaching services a month. They had more chances to learn, and back in those days religion was taught in the school a lot. Most of the teachers either had the group of children stand up, and they grouped around and sang one or two hymns each morning and had the "Lord's Prayer." I think that's mostly been abandoned lately. But that was quite good and more than once, we've had teachers, since my children were going to school, who didn't rely on the "Lord's Prayer," but prayed a little personal prayer. I understand that a lot of children don't hear the Lord's name mentioned except profanely at school now. I'm sorry that [the prayer and hymns] were done away with. There wouldn't have to be any denomination talk. It could be just basic religion, belief in the Lord Jesus Christ.

Being a Christian is important to me. I have a friend up the road who owns a little apple stand. I taught him when he was in Sunday school; he was thirteen or fourteen, at the age when boys are apt to be noisy. This group of boys and girls were unusually good children, I thought. I just loved them everyone. And when they grew up, some of them went to service and some didn't come back. But this boy came back and he had some nerve-racking experiences and it left him in a nervous state. He went into business and after awhile, it didn't succeed. He married and his marriage broke up; then his mind seemed to go haywire all together and he was in a mental hospital for quite a bit. I got his address from one of his brothers and wrote to him. I sent him a copy of the Clayton *Tribune* and he wrote back and told me how much he enjoyed it. We sent him the *Tribune* as long as he stayed. Now when I meet him, he almost always mentions that. If anybody from this community stops by to buy anything from him, he gives them a bag of apples to send to me. And I feel that it is bread on the water.

I'll tell you another one. Women didn't have a lot to say about politics then. They may have influenced their family some, but they never got out and took any part in it. After they had the vote, you could begin to see a pickup in their attitude. I was old enough to vote when women got the vote, but I didn't vote for a few years after it was permissible. I didn't realize that, even though I was not too well posted on things, my vote might do as well as anybody else's. The first few times I went to the voting place

PLATE 298

(then most every little county had a voting spot, or a law ground and a law house), I felt a little bit out of place. I'd never been used to voting. But now I think nothing about it because everybody does.

I remember the first time I went to the election. One of the managers said, "Well now, Aunt Lola, I want you to vote the right way today."

I said, "Will you tell me how I must vote to vote the right way?"

And he began to tell me who to vote for. And I said, "I'd already made up my mind before I came out here. I had talked to a person that gave me an idea how to vote."

He said, "Who was that?"

And I said, "The Lord."

That man wilted like you had poured hot water over him. He didn't say anymore to me about it!

That faith is one thing that really stands out about Aunt Lola. As she said at one point in the interview, "If God should call me tomorrow, I've had so many good things happen in my life, I'd be ready."

After the article about her appeared in our magazine, Anita received a letter from Aunt Lola which she shared with us. It said in part, "The magazines came today. They had followed me back to my mountains. I was so happy when I read your note at the beginning, for I had never dreamed when I used to wonder 'if I would see little heads bobbing across the field this day,' that it meant anything more to you than just a little trip outside your own playground. If it meant something to you, I am very glad; it was a bright spot in my day.

"It is still a lovely thing to remember all of you growing up into such industrious, helpful women; people who can help the world to be a better place for those who follow after us. My love and prayers will always be yours."

The selection of a site for a new farm was always based, in part, on the availability of a good supply of clean, cold water. "I've got a good, bold spring," is a sentence we have heard hundreds of times, and it is always said with pride and satisfaction.

The methods used for tapping that water are bewilderingly varied. At one end of the spectrum is the system that is so simple that all that is required to make it work is a bucket and a pair of hands to carry it. This is the system that nearly all the earliest families used, and it is still used by people like Hillard Green. A spring is located. Often the basin is enlarged, deepened, and lined with rock—not cemented, of course, so that water can come into the basin not only from the bottom but also through the sides— and this causes a small pool to form from which water can be dipped, or into which containers can be set to keep their contents cold. The top of the basin on the side out of which the overflow runs is kept level with the original stream bed so as not to interfere with the water's natural flow.

One thing that has always confused us somewhat is why, at the vast majority of abandoned, original log home places we have explored, the house was set some distance *above* the spring on a hillside or on top of a knoll when it could just as easily have been set closer to the spring. Most of the people we've asked don't know, but the ones that venture a guess say that since the spring is often in low ground, building a house there would prevent the occupants from being able to look out over their land and fields and keep their eye on things. Being up higher let them watch to see if deer had gotten into their corn crop, or if visitors were coming up the road, and so on.

Whatever the reason, there were some disadvantages to this system. Water had to be lugged uphill (there were no pumps), and there was always the danger that the spring could become contaminated by sewage from the barn and/or outhouse above unless a good distance separated them.

PLATE 299   Hillard Green still gets his water in buckets from a spring and carries it to his house several hundred yards away.

Gradually, some families moved away from this system toward others. Aunt Arie, for example, finally got so irritated at the fact that the water from her spring was always full of tiny, flashing specks of isinglass (mica) that she made her husband dig a well beside the house. Then they set their springhouse over the old water system (see section on springhouses). Other families must have tired of finding leaves and dead animals in their uncovered springs. Some built up the walls of the rock basin so they were flush around the top, with an exit hole in the lower side for the overflow, and fashioned a removable wooden lid. Others began to look for other, better ways.

We guess that the one event that changed the means of getting water most dramatically was the eventual availability of pipe. Making wooden water pipes (see section on same) had always been possible, but when stores began to stock cheap metal pipe, suddenly everyone was talking about "gravity water." What this involved was finding a new spring—this one *above* the house—and piping some of its water down the hillside to the house, letting gravity do all the work.

One of the earliest systems of this sort that we have seen was built as follows: a covered collection basin of the type we've already mentioned was built around the spring to keep out animals, leaves, and surface water. The exit hole was plugged except for a pipe. A second exit hole slightly above the first allowed any overflow to escape easily and take its natural course down the original stream bed. The pipe led from the spring directly down to a sink in the house itself. There was no faucet. The pipe simply ran twenty-four hours a day into the sink. The biggest problem this kind of system created is one that Charlie Ross Hartley talks about in another section in this chapter: what to do with the overflow. In this case, a pipe carried the overflow out the bottom of the sink, into an open fifty-gallon wooden trough near the barn so the stock could be watered, and from there to a nearby stream where it was set loose again. In the case of Oma Ledford's combination springhouse/water supply (see section on springhouses), the overflow went directly from the end of her indoor trough into a stream behind her house.

Later, as more and more demands were put on the system by the addition of such things as flush indoor toilets, bathtubs, and hot water heaters, another major alteration was made. Faucets and valves were installed so that the water only ran when a valve was opened. The rest of the time it sat, unmoving, in the pipe. This necessitated two things: first, the pipe had to be buried to keep the water inside it from freezing in the winter; and second, a reservoir had to be installed somewhere along the line above the house, for any major demands put on the old system drained the line almost immediately and reduced the flow of water to a trickle. Early reservoirs were

PLATE 300 A primitive reservoir. Water from the spring is piped into a metal drum, and from the bottom of the drum to the house. When the drum is full, it overflows into the original stream bed.

PLATE 301 Noel Moore's cement-block reservoir after a winter of freezing and thawing.

PLATE 302 Noel Moore with the round cement sections he uses as a reservoir now.

simply fifty-gallon wooden barrels. The water ran in at the top, filled the barrel, and overflowed from the top either into the original stream or into a channel that led to that stream. The pipe leading to the house exited from the barrel at a point some six or eight inches above its bottom so that any sediment that collected in the barrel over time would not get sucked into the line. Later reservoirs were more elaborate. Two or three barrels might be hooked together, for example.

Today, many people use large, precast concrete tanks made for use as septic tanks but acquired for this purpose instead. Round sections of cement culverts, or tiles for lining wells do equally well when set on end and sealed at the bottom with six inches of cement.

Some experiments failed, of course. Noel Moore's first attempt at a reservoir was doomed. Noel built it with cement blocks, but neglected to fill the holes in the blocks with cement. Water seeped in and, during the first winter, froze, expanded, and broke the sides open. Some people still use cement blocks, but they fill the center holes, plaster the inside walls with three

PLATE 303   Walling up a spring. The water flows out from under a rock cliff at a point to the far left, not visible in the photograph. Leroy Tice is preparing the exit area for the water, which will flow out of a hole in the middle of the wall. When finished, the rock wall will close the opening to the spring completely except for a screened door above the exit hole that will permit access into the spring for cleaning.

inches of plaster, and often coat that lining with a waterproofing compound that will prevent water from being absorbed into the walls and freezing during cold spells.

Today, gravity systems are still popular in the mountains, but those who want to build one are urged to go to the office of the local health department official and pick up a free set of guidelines. These guidelines recommend a system that is completely sealed from spring to house so that at no point along the line can the water become contaminated by such things as animal feces, chemical fallout from the air, or surface water from a neighbor's hog lot.

At one point, that may not have been such an important consideration, but now, with more and more houses being built closer and closer together, and the risk of contamination more serious than ever before, the guidelines serve an important purpose—insuring that water that is not treated chemically remains as pure as possible until it's used.

WOODEN WATER PIPES

When the first settlers came into the mountains, there were no stores where they could buy metal pipes for their plumbing: They had to carry their water in buckets from the spring to their cabin or barn.

I Water System Using Spring Below House

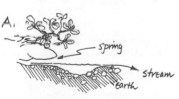

A.

spring

stream

earth

spring is located, and house is built nearby. Water flows in direction of arrow from under rock

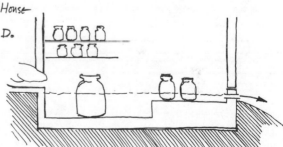

D.

In final stage (above) a spring house is built over the spring. The original basin is carved out and lined with cement creating an eighteen to twenty-four inch wide trough for cold storage of milk, butter, etc. The walls are lined with shelves for storage of canned goods. A small basin with dipper for drinking water may be added.

B.

water

Natural pool is dug out and lined with rock creating basin so that pail can be filled easily without picking up mud and pebbles.

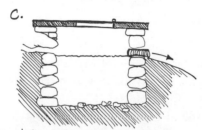

C.

Later, rocks are built up over basin and wooden roof with hinged door is added to keep out leaves, animals, etc. Sides and bottom may be cemented.

PLATE 304

II. Water System Using Spring Above House
note - water pressure builds in lines at rate of ½ psi for every foot
of vertical drop between source and end of line. If using plastic pipe, check pressure,

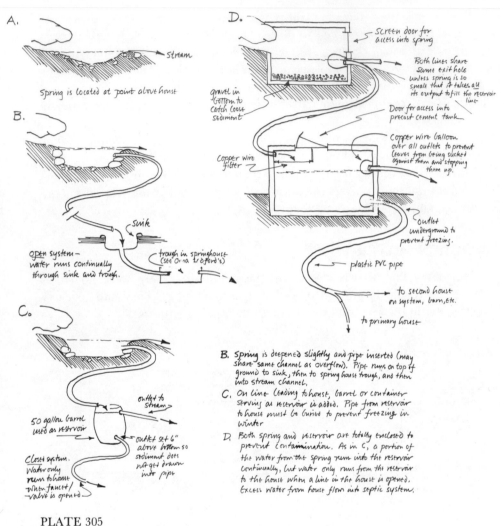

A.
Stream

Spring is located at point above house

B.

OPEN system —
water runs continually
through sink and trough.

sink

trough in springhouse
(see Orna Loford's)

C.

50 gallon barrel
used as reservoir

outlet to
stream

outlet set 6"
above bottom so
sediment does
not get drawn
into pipe

Closed system.
Water only
runs to house
when faucet/
valve is opened.

D.
Screen door for
access into spring

Both lines share
same exit hole
unless spring is so
small that it takes all
its output to fill the reservoir
line

gravel in
bottom to
catch loose
sediment

Copper wire
filter

Door for access into
precast cement tank

Copper wire balloon
over all outlets to prevent
leaves from being sucked
against them and stopping
them up.

Outlet
underground to
prevent freezing.

plastic PVC pipe

to second house
on system, barn, etc.

to primary house

B. Spring is deepened slightly and pipe inserted (may
share same channel as overflow). Pipe runs on top of
ground to sink, then to spring house trough, and then
into stream channel.

C. On line leading to house, barrel or container
serving as reservoir is added. Pipe from reservoir
to house must be buried to prevent freezing in
winter

D. Both spring and reservoir are totally enclosed to
prevent contamination. As in C, a portion of
the water from the spring runs into the reservoir
continually, but water only runs from the reservoir
to the house when a line in the house is opened.
Excess water from house flows into septic system.

PLATE 305

As time went on, they found that they could split logs in half lengthwise
and hollow them out to make water troughs above ground so the water
could flow to the springhouse.

Later they found a way to make a tool to make wooden pipes out of
green poplar or yellow pine. This tool is an auger. Some are larger than
others, but they all have the same purpose: to bore out the center of the
logs. After fitting the logs together (see Plate 313), they buried them under-

ground in a pipeline that would bring the water straight to the spigot that was made out of poplar, and then to the springhouse (see Plate 316). They found that these underground lines would last fifty or sixty years.

For a long time we looked for someone who could show us how to make these pipes. Finally we found Garnett Lovell who came from a family of blacksmiths. His father, George Lovell, sharpened the steel for the tools used to make Rabun County's Lake Burton Dam. Both his father and grandfather, Elijah Lovell, had made these water pipes. In fact, Elijah had made the auger that Garnett still has. Garnett agreed to show us exactly the way it was done if we would bring a six-inch diameter, ten-foot long pine log. We brought him the log and he showed us how the pipes were made.

BOB O'DWYER

Interviews and photographs by Bob O'Dwyer, Jeff Fears, and John Matthies. Diagrams by John.

PLATE 306   Garnett Lovell.

PLATE 307 Garnett holds the auger he will use upright to show us how long it is. The auger was made by his grandfather, who was a blacksmith.

PLATE 308   The handle of the auger.

PLATE 309   The drilling end of the auger. Garnett's grandfather flattened the end of a round steel bar, bent the sides up to form a scoop, put the twist in the end, and then sharpened the edges of the scoop.

PLATE 310   Garnett begins to bore out the log as his grandson looks on.

PLATE 311   To make a twenty-foot section of wooden pipe with a ten-foot auger, Garnett bores into one end as far as the auger will go, and then switches ends. He has to be careful not to let the auger bore out the side of the log as it gets in deeper and deeper. He constantly sights along the shaft to make sure it's going straight.

PLATE 312 When the pipe is drilled, he uses a drawknife to taper one end.

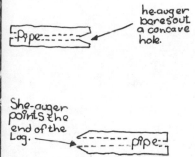

he-auger bores out a concave hole.

Pipe

She-auger points the end of the Log.

pipe

PLATE 313 He then takes another auger and bores a concave hole in the other end of the pipe.

PLATE 314 The tapered end of one pipe fits into the concave end of the next. Just before the pipes are locked together underground, a rag is wrapped around the joint to minimize leaking.

PLATE 315 The finished spigot. The plank on top is nailed firmly in place to prevent the water from shooting out the top through the bored hole instead of the poplar spout in the side.

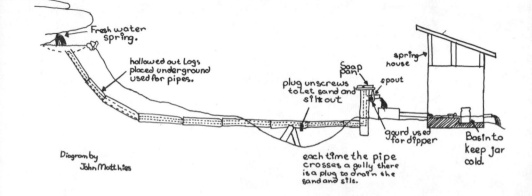

Fresh water spring.

hollowed out logs placed underground used for pipes.

Soap pan

spring house

plug unscrews to let sand and silt out

spout

gourd used for dipper

Basin to keep jar cold.

each time the pipe crosses a gully there is a plug to drain the sand and silt.

Diagram by John Matthies

PLATE 316

SPRINGHOUSES

Long ago before electricity was brought to the mountains, people were faced with the age-old problem of preserving their food. They came up with many methods for doing this. Meats were dried or salted and smoked. Vegetables and fruits were either dried or pickled in brine or canned. There was still the problem, however, of keeping things cool during the warm-weather months. Milk, cheese, and butter had to be kept cool, and many people preferred to keep their pickled and canned foods cool also. They solved the problem by building springhouses.

Springhouses are buildings that are constructed over or near springs. Cold water runs through them to serve the same function as a present-day refrigerator. This section is about springhouses, their design, their uses, and their advantages and disadvantages.

There is an abundance of fresh springs, rocks, and lumber in the mountains, so these were the primary materials used, but we discovered that all springhouses are not alike. We researched four springhouses. Two were constructed entirely of rock, one was made from wood, and the fourth was built of both wood and rock.

Wooden springhouses were constructed faster and with less effort than rock springhouses, but wood buildings were more vulnerable to the weather and did not last as long as rock ones. We found that the deciding factors which determined the materials to be used were the availability of either rock or wood and the amount of time available to build one. Rock buildings require more skill and time to construct. We know of one man who used pieces of old T-model Fords to serve as a framework for the rocks to speed up the construction process.

In the next few pages we'll present the floor plans of each springhouse, the people who remember its construction, and any small details that make each one unique. The springhouses that we documented were Aunt Arie Carpenter's in Coweeta, North Carolina, Harry Brown's, Mrs. Oma Ledford's, and Mrs. Jay Hambidge's, all located near Dillard, Georgia. The information given in this article was taken from interviews with Aunt Arie and Harry Brown.

We hope the following diagrams and photographs are easy to understand, and through reading this you might further understand and appreciate the ingenuity that mountain people displayed while overcoming one more obstacle that they were faced with in their daily lives.

Article and photographs by Gary Warfield and Claude Rickman.

Harry Brown's

In Harry Brown's yard is a rock structure half-buried in the ground. The entire building is made of rocks and cement and is covered with ground ivy. At first glance one might think it is just a mound of dirt, or even a bomb shelter, but closer inspection reveals a cleverly built springhouse.

In the summer of 1932 Harry Brown started work on the springhouse. "First I built the form out of culled lumber. Then I'd throw down a shovel of cement, and throw me a rock in it. Throw me another shovelful or two and throw more rocks down in it. I didn't try to keep the outside smooth."

When Harry built the walls up to the desired height, he took "the frames and axles from two T-model Fords and laid them on top. Then I started dumping cement by th'wheelbarrow load and then threw rocks on it. I did most of it by myself. I worked on it about three months. I'd set rock a few days, then rest a few days, then set more rock. It's like when you build a chimney, you haul what rocks you need, then you get that many more, then you get a few more t'finish up and you might have enough rock. It was that way here."

We asked Harry if he likes a refrigerator more than his springhouse. He favored the springhouse. "You can keep things in here [the springhouse] for about five days. We've put our milk in here, and gone off and visited three or four days and come back, and the milk would still be sweet."

Harry mentioned another advantage: "If you keep your stuff sealed up in a frigidaire and you put fish or something like that in there, everything you've got will taste like fish. But in a springhouse, you see, the air's not compact and that don't happen. And the temperature wouldn't vary ten degrees."

In the top of the springhouse is an air vent that measures about ten by twelve inches. "That gives it air. See, if I had it closed up in here, it would be like a refrigerator. It would condense and begin to get thick. You'd have dead air in here like in the refrigerator. You ain't got much space in a refrigerator and the same old air stagnates, while in here in the springhouse, it circulates. And if it weren't for that vent, there'd be water dripping in here all day."

In addition to the vent, the springhouse also has a window for light, an entrance door, and an inner door. The inner door is used to keep the dogs out. "If they's anything t'eat, a dog'll get ahold of it."

Before the Browns had electricity, Harry kept his springhouse full. "We kept our milk and our butter, and anything you put in your refrigerator, like your beans and your meat, and even if you got more fish than you can eat. You can even put them in there. You use it for nearly anything that you use a refrigerator for."

Harry said his springhouse was good all year round. The water never froze in the winter because it was from a deep spring, and it was always cool in the summer for the same reason.

The springhouse is practically the same today as it was when it was built in 1932. The shelves for storing canned goods have rotted out, but it is still used when the power fails or if the refrigerator in the house is full.

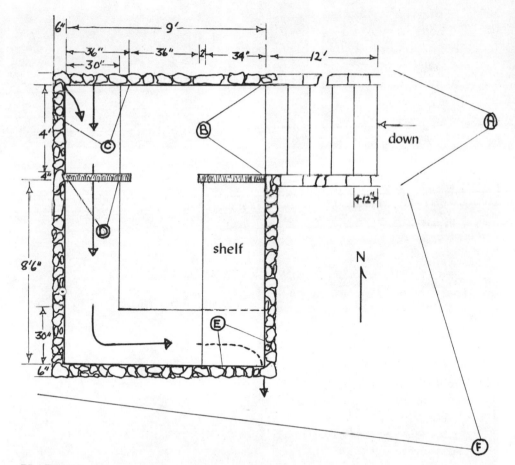

PLATE 317   Diagram of Harry Brown's springhouse.

PLATE 318　Point A on diagram, view of the steps leading down to the springhouse.

PLATE 319　Point B, looking from inside the springhouse.

PLATE 320　Point C, view of water inlets.

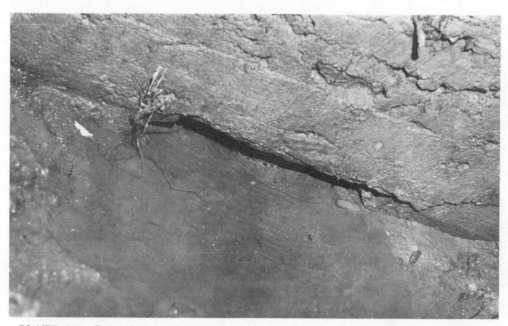

PLATE 321   Point D, view of water coming under a small partition as it goes through the trough.

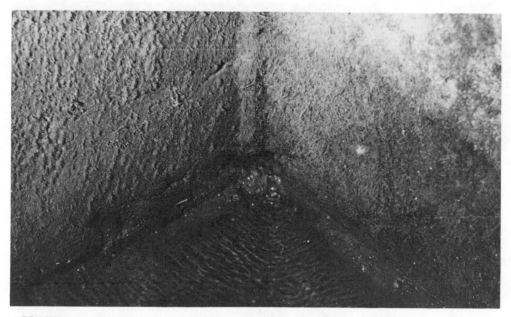

PLATE 322   Point E, view of outlet for water going through the springhouse.

PLATE 323   A 10″×12″ vent for condensation, from the inside looking out.

PLATE 324   Point F, overall view of the springhouse.

Oma Ledford's

With the help of Mr. L. D. Hopper, R. H. Ledford built the Ledford springhouse around 1937–38. It was built onto the house out of lumber Mr. Ledford sawed at his own sawmill.

The trough in the springhouse was fourteen inches wide and seven feet, two inches long. The water fell about three feet from the pipe into the trough and drained out through a small hole in the end of the trough which was outside the springhouse.

There were also some shelves in the springhouse on which canned fruits and vegetables were stored.

PLATE 325   Diagram of Oma Ledford's springhouse.

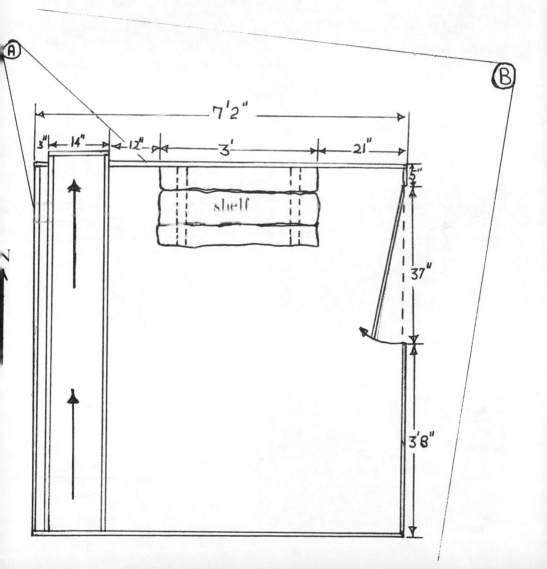

PLATE 326 Point A, view of the springhouse.

PLATE 327 Water running out of the trough from inside the springhouse.

PLATE 328   Point B, another view of Ledford's springhouse.

Aunt Arie Carpenter's

On Aunt Arie's little farm, a springhouse that was built by her husband, Ulysses, sits just below her house. The springhouse has a rock floor. The lower half of the back wall is built below ground level and is also made of rock. The four walls and door are made from rough-cut lumber, and the roof is covered with wooden shingles.

When we asked Aunt Arie whether she preferred a refrigerator or a springhouse, she quickly replied, "I wouldn't trade one frigidaire for a thousand springhouses." She stated that you can get your milk and butter and not have to worry whether it was raining or not. Aunt Arie also said that it saved many unnecessary steps. "I wish I had a dollar for every trip I made to that there springhouse. If they was silver dollars, I wouldn't be able to lift'em."

Aunt Arie's springhouse features a simple rectangular design with a single channel of water flowing on one side which is "just wide enough t'put a churn in."

Even though the springhouse hasn't been used for several years, it is still standing and in good shape. The roof needs a little repair and weeds have grown up around it, but with a little work this springhouse could be converted to function as it once did.

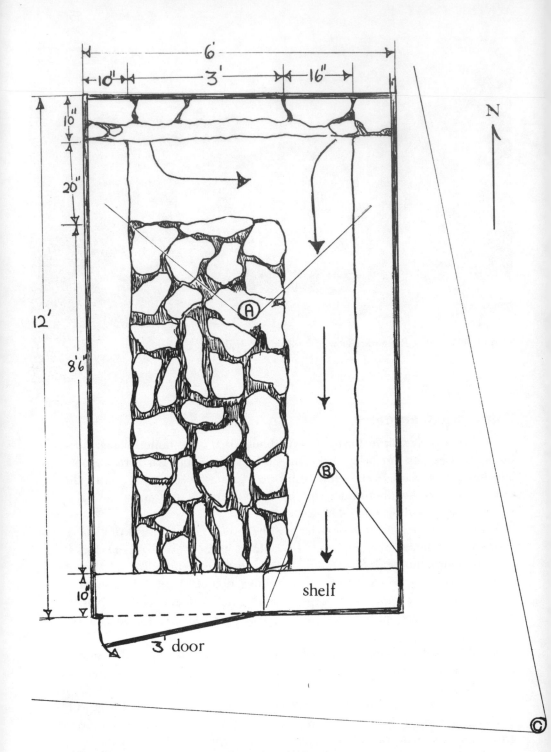

PLATE 329   Diagram of Aunt Arie's springhouse.

PLATE 330 Point A, view of water coming into the springhouse.

PLATE 331 Point B, view of shelf and the water leaving springhouse.

PLATE 332   Point C, overall view of the springhouse.

The Jay Hambidge Art Foundation's

The Hambidge springhouse was built around 1918–19. It was used to keep the milk and butter cold for the Hambidge Center. Canned fruits and vegetables were also kept cool on shelves in the innermost part of the springhouse. In 1939 the springhouse was replaced by electric means for cooling.

The springhouse was built completely of stone and has two main rooms. The outermost is not completely enclosed and contains a holding trough for the water to run in before entering the springhouse. Also there is a springhead next to the holding trough. This is where people used to get water for household needs.

The other room is the largest and was completely enclosed so no animals could get in. It has one door and a vent in the top for air circulation. The water entered the springhouse from the holding trough through a four-inch pipe and emptied into the troughs in which the milk and butter were put. The troughs were eighteen inches wide and had steps which kept the water moving and provided different levels of water. The water followed the "L"-shaped trough and drained out through a four-inch outlet at the back of the springhouse.

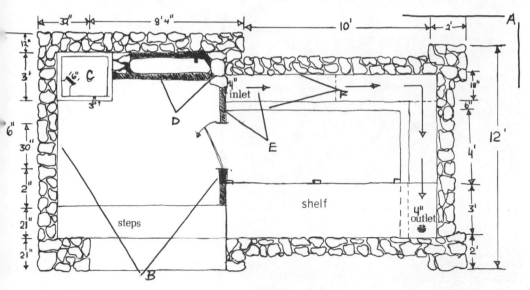

PLATE 333   Diagram of the Hambidge springhouse.

PLATE 334   Point A, view of Hambidge springhouse.

PLATE 335   Point B, view of the steps and water inlets.

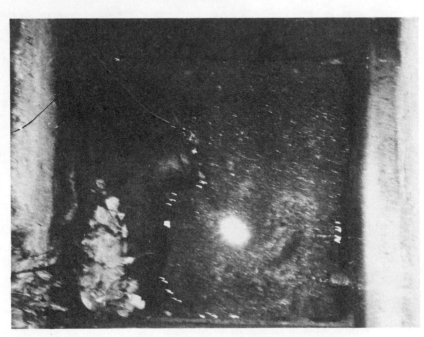

PLATE 336   Point C, the springhead within the springhouse.

PLATE 337   Point D, close-up view of another water inlet.

PLATE 338   Point E, view of pipe that carries water from the water inlet areas to the trough in the springhouse.

PLATE 339   Point F, view of the long trough.

DOWSING FOR WATER

After several months of searching for a well dowser who would talk to us, we finally found one. There are not too many traditional dowsers around our section anymore, so we were fortunate to meet C. M. Arrowood who had a reputation for finding water with a probing rod and a "V"-shaped stick. He talked quite freely with us, and even came to the school to demonstrate his skill to our class by finding all the school's main water lines.

As everyone expressed amazement at the "V" stick which bent forcefully to the left or right each time Mr. Arrowood crossed a water source, he said, "I don't know how it's done, but I can do it. Back before you kids was born, I had a good job, but I lost it. So I built me a log house myself, and since I wasn't able [financially] to have a well dug, I went to see a man who knowed how to dowse and he found where the water was so I could dig the well myself. Well, I forgot where he marked the ground. So I got me a stick and retraced where he'd been and found it myself. I dug seventeen feet on Christmas day and hit water. Well, when I got down to the water, my father-in-law come and said his well was muddy, so I had dug right into his stream. I been doing this since—about fifty-five years."

When asked how he could be sure the stick was working, Mr. Arrowood replied, "When I have it in my teeth and on my thumb, I can't control it. It has to be free. The pressure would break this stick [when water is present] if I held it tight. About the only way to tell how much water is down there is by the stronger the pressure or pull."

We wondered if it mattered what kind of stick to use. Mr. Arrowood didn't think it did, as long as it was green and pliable. "I never go hunt one stick in particular. The stick is easier handled, though, if it is forked—in a "V" shape."

He also puts a knife, open, in the straight part of the stick. When asked why, he said, "I was just taught to use the knife. It'll work without it, but it works better with it. It moves easier."

Then he added, "I don't ever charge anything for this. Oh, if the people are satisfied with the well [after it's finished], they might give me ten or fifteen dollars, and I turn around and give it to the church. I don't do this as a way to make money for myself.

"They is water all under the earth, but you can't afford to dig here when the water is over yonder. You've got to pinpoint it [to save time and money]. I just find the water and tell them to dig. I've found hundreds of them. Missed one. They drilled for it. Might have missed it six inches. I've also hit in other counties where it is not as damp as here in Rabun County. I got my first well over near Dawsonville, Georgia."

PLATE 340   First, Mr. Arrowood cuts a "V"-shaped stick and trims off the loose branches.

PLATE 341   He sticks the blade of his open pocketknife into the part of the stick just below the fork to give weight to the end and make it more sensitive to movement. Then he places one end of the fork between his teeth and the other end presses against his thumb. This is done to prevent his hand from having any control over the stick's movement.

PLATE 342   Mr. Arrowood follows a stream of water near his home. He crosses back and forth over the stream, the stick moving from side to side as he crosses back and forth over it, to pinpoint its direction of flow.

PLATE 343   Ken Kistner, one of *Foxfire*'s editors, tries his hand at dowsing.

After the water is found, the well is dug [see following section]. He can't tell you how deep you might have to dig. It could vary greatly.

We had a chance to see a well found by Mr. Arrowood, and we talked with the diggers, Tom Ramey and Harold Embrey [see following section].

"Money is why we dug the well. He found the well with a probing rod. That's a copper wire. He can also use a peach-tree limb or a clothes hanger. I don't know anybody who is as accurate as Mr. Arrowood in finding water. There [pointing] is a stream, and here is a stream, and they cross right here where he told us to dig. We hit it, too. We are going to dig four or five more feet to make a reservoir for the water to store in."

After watching the process of dowsing for water, we all agreed that we could not explain it. We just had to believe it works. As Mr. Arrowood said, "It's just a gift from God is all I know. It don't matter what kind of stick you use. I think the main thing is to believe in it yourself."

Interviews by Barbara Taylor, Phyllis Carver, and Mary Thomas, with help from Sheila Vinson.

PLATE 344   Mr. Arrowood found our school's main water line using a piece of wire which swung from side to side as he crisscrossed over the line. He used this coathanger to locate the spot where Tom Ramey and Harold Embrey should dig their well.

PLATE 345 Buford Garner showing Bit Carver how to find water. The stick is a
green peach-tree fork which Mr. Garner is holding straight, but the water below it is
causing it to bend toward earth. His method of holding the stick is different from
C. M. Arrowood's, but it works. As he moves away from the water, the end of the stick
comes back up of its own accord until it sticks straight out in front of him.

DIGGING A WELL

Whenever a house was built where there was no spring close by, the people dug a well.

Digging a well was a dangerous task. The men we interviewed told us that there were a lot of problems in digging one. They could be digging and have something fall in on them. When you're down sixty to seventy-five feet and a rock falls in and hits you, you're as good as dead. Or others could be hauling you out in the bucket, and just as you get to the top, the rope could break and back you'd go. Or you could hit a gas pocket and pass out.

One thing that scared Kenny Runion was looking up when he was way down in the hole digging. He said the hole at the top of the well looked just like an auger hole. He felt like he was trapped in there. Mr. Ledbetter agreed: "When you're down in there and the sun is shining on top, the hole don't look much bigger than a nickel. Some people say that when you're deep enough to hit water, you can look up and see stars, but I never have."

Starting a well usually required three people: one to do the digging and two to wind the windlass that cranks the bucket up, and also to keep the rim of the well cleaned off so that nothing would fall in on the person digging it. The bucket is used to bring the dirt up and to bring the man up when he is finished. Sometimes men used horses to pull the bucket up. Mr. Ledbetter said, "I pulled the dirt out of my well at home with a mule. Somebody used a horse once and ran around with a big knot on his head

PLATE 346 Aunt Arie Carpenter about to take a drink of cold water from her well.

PLATE 347   An abandoned well in the mountains. Note the wooden curb built up over the hole to keep things from the surface from falling into it.

because the horse pulled him up so fast. I wouldn't trust a horse; not unless two people were holding it."

Some of the men, when starting a well, used the rim of a wagon wheel and traced around it. Then they started to tunnel their way down. The tools used in digging a well were a short-handled mattock and shovel. They dug straight down until they hit water. Kenny knew a guy that had to go forty-five feet deep through rock, blasting with dynamite, until he finally hit water.

Once they hit water, they would continue on down about another eight feet to make sure they had a good strong vein and lot of storage space to hold the water in. Then they'd rock the walls up to four feet above water level, or all the way to the top if the walls were weak. The well was then ready to use.

In doing this article about well digging, I gained a lot of respect for the men who dug for a living—it's a dangerous job and would be scary.

DALE FERGUSON and MIKE DRAKE

Interviews by Dale Ferguson, Randall Hardy, Mike Drake, Donald Wright, Ford Oliver, Ridg MacArthur, Keith Head, and Tommy Lamb.

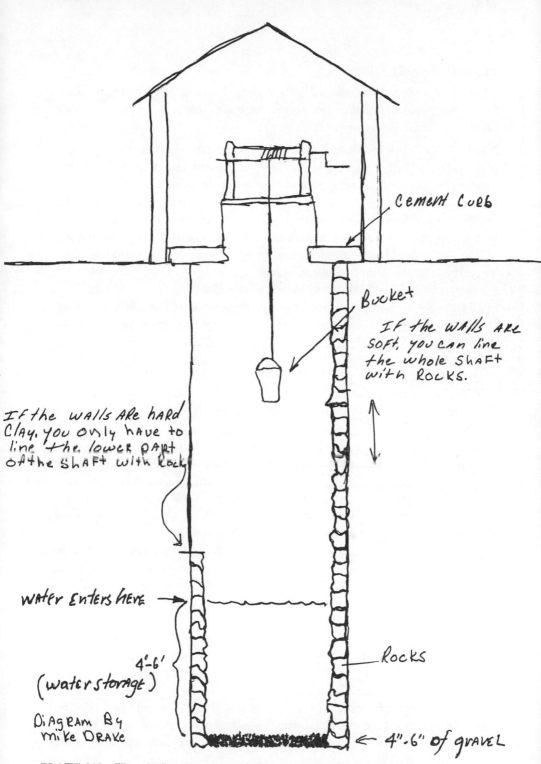

Cement Curb

Bucket

IF the walls are soft, you can line the whole shaft with rocks.

If the walls are hard clay, you only have to line the lower part of the shaft with rock.

Water Enters here →

4'-6'
(water storage)

Diagram By mike Drake

Rocks

← 4"-6" of gravel

PLATE 348 The windlass is gone; probably the victim of souvenir hunters.

How to Dig It

The four men we interviewed were Kenny Runion, Harley Rogers, Law-
ton Brooks, and Mr. Ledbetter. In the following pages, each of them talks
about his individual experiences.

KENNY RUNION: When I was a teen-ager, I used to go from place to
place with my father digging wells. We'd dig them about three feet across
through the center. The way me and my daddy done, we used a wagon tire.
We'd just lay that down and mark it plumb around and cut into the
ground about three or four inches. Then I'd follow that to get started. If I
ever got down a foot deep, I had it made. A man could dig his length a day
in dirt. And when I got done with that thing, it would be as round as a dollar at the bottom. Round as a gun barrel.

About the only tool I'd use would be a shovel with a foot-long handle. If
the whole handle was broke out, you'd be better off. It's so narrow in there
you just can't use one. And you can dig three ways: on your side up against
the bank, or on your knees, or stand on your head and shoulders. And if you
hear that bucket a'coming, you hit on your head and shoulders or it's
gonna knock a place on your head.

When we started, Dad would help me as deep as where it got to his head.
Then he wouldn't work no more down in there. It was all up to me then.
I'd stay with it. The first day or two you could go pretty fast because you
could shovel the dirt up and throw it right out. But now the next day you
were stuck. You would have to have the dirt pulled out with a winch. Dad
would do that part and I would shovel. There was a rope tied to a
bucket, and when it came back into the well, I'd fill it with dirt and rocks
and he was on top and would roll it out. All I'd have to do was dig, shovel,
and load up when he sent the bucket back. Dollar a foot.

And now the walls had to be straight to where the bucket wouldn't hit
them and chunk out rocks as it went up. It had to be done right like a gun
barrel. And it can't angle. If it does, it'll slide out on you or the water'll hit
that high place and get muddy every time. It's got to be just as square as
square itself if you're to get good water.

If you come to rock, you have to blast. You used to get dynamite. It
looked like sawdust, but, boys, it was more than sawdust! And black
powder—you could buy it in twenty-five- or fifty-pound cans, and it was as
good, if not better, than dynamite.

Now digging the holes for the dynamite was slow, I reckon! It'd take you
a day or two to get them holes down. They had to go down about two feet
to get that dynamite in there. I guess you could just drill one hole in the

PLATE 349 Lake Stiles took us to visit Mr. Ledbetter who was digging a well in North Carolina. Here Dale Ferguson, Mike Drake, Lake Stiles, and Mr. Ledbetter look down into the half-finished well.

middle, but it would tear up the bottom and leave it in a bad shape. You want to blast it to where the walls are smooth, so you should drill clean around the edge and put in about six holes. Put about a half-stick to each hole; and then the dynamite would just blow back to the wall if you drilled right.

To drill those holes, a fellow turned and I drove with a hammer. He was a small fellow, and he sat flat down and he'd put that drill right between his legs. He'd double up some way or another, and I'd put the eight-pound hammer to it. If I'd missed, I'd of hurt him, I guess, but I never did. And it'd take a half a day to put down one hole in that blue granite rock. 'Course if it was soft, it'd go quicker. After you got the holes drilled, you'd take dynamite down, fill them holes full, put in your cap, light it, and get out if you could! You'd better get out. That stuff burns about a foot a minute, so you'd put about three or four feet of fuse. It'll give you time to get out if something don't happen. Now if the rope breaks, you're a gone man! You wouldn't have time to tie it back, and you couldn't put the fuse out. A man might jerk it out, but the blamed cap would blow. You just can't put that fuse out. And that cap is might' nigh as bad as the dynamite. Tear your head off! I've see'd a fellow here at town—him and another boy got out some dynamite caps and was hitting them, and every one of his fingers is off and his thumb too. That's one thing, boys, you've got to be careful with. You can't light them with a match, either. You got to get a stick of fire and just take the coal and stick that coal to the fuse and she's gone!

Or if you were using powder, you'd pour some powder in a bucket and take it down in the well. You'd pack it in the holes. That's a dangerous thing, ain't it? If the powder don't go off, it's dangerous to go in there. You can't get it out 'cause it's packed.

And after you blasted, you'd have to stay out a couple of hours. That dynamite smoke will hurt you. Can't get your breath. Then when you go back in, you have to get the rocks out. If there's a rock down in there too big to lift out in the bucket, you have to bust it with a hammer.

Now how deep you go depends on when you hit water. You could go down anywhere from thirty feet on. I've been in them so deep that if you look up toward the top, it looks like an auger hole—about the size of a silver dollar. The best thing, boys, is to never look up. Look down. If you look up, it looks smothersome. You be down seventy-five or a hundred feet down in the ground in that small of a hole and it'll smother you if you ain't careful. You'll get scared. The best way to do is don't never look up no difference what comes in.

When you first hit water, go right on down. Some people want you to have at least six feet of water in there, but you could get out with four. If the water is boiling right straight up, you've got it. If it's running out of rock, it's pretty doubtful that it might go dry during a dry spell. Then when it's dug, you want to wall it. You start at the bottom and go around and around. It's best not to put a flooring on the bottom because you need to let the water come in. You stick the rocks in the mud all the way up and the wall will hold up itself. At the last round, you want to lean the rock back towards the dirt and that'll hold it. If you wall a well right, it won't ever give you trouble. You don't have to wall it all the way to the top, but I have done it that way. There's a well up here in town where me and my daddy walled it to the top and put a rock curbing on it. We took a big rock and put it there on the side where she could set her bucket.

And then you have to keep it clean. I've cleaned out a lot of wells before. You get a lot of cans and bottles in them. When you go to clean a well out, you draw the water out of it to where you can see what's in the bottom. You'll find dippers and bottles and no telling what in there.

It's dangerous work, but you only made forty cents a day on top, and you could make fifty cents a foot through dirt and a dollar through rock digging wells. But you were always taking chances. Rope break while you were being lowered into the well, and you'd go to the bottom and I don't mean maybe. I used to just go down the rope—just swing down it, slide down it to the bottom. That's pretty dangerous. Or that bad air down at the bottom. It's dangerous work.

LAWTON BROOKS: I've dug four wells myself. I've cleaned out several of them, but I've dug four from the start to the finish. Usually it don't take but three men—two to rope and one to do the digging. Can't but one work down in there anyway. Ain't got room for two down in there.

To start, I always just lay out about a four-and-a-half-foot round circle. Then I commence in the middle and dig out to the edge plumb around there. Then I get it started and keep it down straight all the way. After you get down head deep or a little better, then you can tell by looking at your walls if it's off and if everything is going straight. You dig down about two or three foot with the maddock; then take your spade and get all that out and straighten your walls. Send up four or five bucketfuls of dirt and then set down again and dig. The fellow up on top is a'resting while you're a'digging. The man who's digging is the man with all the work because he has to dig and he has to load, and all they have to do is roll up the dirt. While you're a'digging, they're talking or smoking or even eating.

The reason I start with a four or four-and-a-half-foot circle is because you've got to have room so you can use your short-handled tools in there to dig with. You're down on your knees doing the digging and the shoveling. The only time you stand up is when you're smoothing your banks [walls] down. It's pretty hard swinging that maddock because you have to dig sitting on your knees. You can't come back like you would if you had a long-handle. You could dig as fast again then, but you can't do it. It's a lot like driving a nail with a hammer you do just a little at a time.

Then when I get ready to come out for lunch, or to quit, why they just send the bucket down and I just put one foot in the bucket and the other on the side of it and reach up there and get ahold of the rope and ride right up to the top.

Then when you're getting to the water, your dirt will go to getting damp; and if you keep on, it will go to getting a little bit wetter. After a while, you'll see the water heaving in over on one side and maybe on the other side, and you just keep on going down until after a while you will hit a good vein of water. Dig down about three feet below it. Then you will never have no trouble about water coming in.

One trouble is that most of the time when you dig a well, you hit rock. Now me and a Hopper boy dug one in solid rock. Me and him dug one for a fellow, and we just barely got under the top of the ground and hit solid rock. He told me to go right on and dig. He wanted that well right there, so I did what he said. We just put in a little piece of dynamite and blowed out two or three little chunks. Then we drilled another hole and blowed out another chunk or two. Kept on going around and around. Blow out a chunk or two and throw them out; then drill another little hole and take a piece of a stick of dynamite and blow out another chunk or two. We done that till we got on down there and hit water. Now it had a rough bank. It didn't have no smooth bank. 'Course when it would stick out too far, we'd take a hammer and beat some of that off the best we could. But it was a job getting that one done. But we didn't have to wall it since it was all rock to start with.

Sometimes when you're getting pretty close to water you might hit a streak of sand, and it might just cave out. When you dig down and it goes to doing that, you might have to wall it with rock. Just take you some rock and come in right down here at the bottom and lay your rock around and just go on around with it—wall it up just as high as it's caving and a little above that. That rock will keep it from caving anymore. And the water won't let your rocks fall out of place if you place them right. Make them fit just as best as you can, but don't put anything like cement between them. Your water has to come through there.

And you dig it to where you have anywhere from six to eight foot of water in your well. You ought to have that much water in your well for a good well. Then your water don't get muddy when you go to drawing, you know. These ladies used to have to draw the water to wash with, and it took a lot of bucketfuls to do a good washing, you know. If your well wasn't pretty deep, then you going up and down with that old bucket so many times would get it muddy. But if you got plenty of water, you ain't bothered with that mud or nothing.

When you finish the well, it just takes a day or so for the mud to settle to the bottom. The next day you can go out and draw the water out. Then let it fill back up. Then it will settle down again and the water will be just as clean as it could be because after that your bucket never goes down to the bottom. You'll have anywhere from six to eight feet of water, and you never

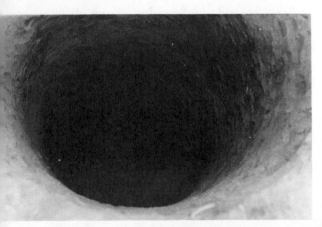

PLATE 350 The Ledbetter well. The short-handled shovel and maddock used for digging are on the bottom of the well.

let your bucket go down and hit the bottom until it has to be cleaned out. Stuff will fall off the banks and get in there and that's what causes you to have to go back and take out all that old mud and stuff out back to the bottom. Then you'll have your clean water again right off.

HARLEY ROGERS: Whenever I dug a well, I always charged by the foot. If I was to take a contract to dig it, I might make a little on it, or lose a little on it, see? So I always dug it so much a foot.

And the only tools I use is a shovel and a maddock. I cut the handles off them. And I dig them three, maybe three-and-a-half foot in diameter—just as little as I can and still work in them. How long it takes depends on how deep you have to go. You might dig one here and go down maybe twenty-five or thirty feet; and then another one might go fifty-five or sixty. Then it starts getting a little bit slower. You can't work near as fast.

But I very seldom had to go over thirty feet till I struck water. The last well I dug, I believe it was twenty-nine feet, and it was high up on the mountain. I reckon we just hit a vein or something down in there.

You can go pretty fast in dirt. The first day, two hands can go down twelve or fifteen foot, and then from there on you gradually go off a foot or two a day. Some days you don't get maybe three foot because the dirt gets harder down in there, you know, and you got all that that has to be loaded

PLATE 351 Harley Rogers describes how to keep the hole round while digging a well.

and hauled out, and that takes a little time. You have to do that with a windlass and a big rope and a bucket. You ride down in the bucket, and stay down until you change shifts or get tired, and another one goes down and you come up and roll the dirt out for him. I generally stayed down there most of the time myself. It's easier down in there than it is to load and unload on top. And you really need two men on top—like you need two surgeons when they're operating on you. One man could pull me up himself, but something could hit him on the arm, or it cramp or something, and it would just jerk right out of his hand. So you got the other man on this side who carries you on out where it could have dropped back down and killed you. That's the only reason why you got two men to help you.

And then after you go down, say, twenty foot or so, I've always found that you've got to take it steady. You can't hit that lick or two real fast. If you do, well, your breath is all gone. And don't never smoke a cigarette down in a well because that seems like it takes the oxygen out or something. It just fogs it up.

Then if you hit rock, you have to drill. I always just used a hammer and a piece of steel. I always had somebody to chuck my steel for me. I never could get nobody to drive for me. I always had to drive myself. Afraid they would hit me. I didn't care if I hit them!

Then when it goes to getting damp, you've got it. If the dirt is soft, they tile the walls nowadays; but used to you just dig it plumb on down and then rock it up—wall it up. That ought to be six feet below where you first hit water. Ought to have six foot of storage on account of you use more water now than you used to. You used to just draw it out in a bucket, and if you could make it with one bucket, you made it. But now you don't care how much you use. And if the walls are good, hard clay, you're okay. Just rock it up, say, two or three feet above the water level. Then it'll never cave. You don't use cement. You just lay the rocks in there. Go right to the bottom, and then lay some rock in there—down into the bottom, you know— for the sand trap.

Then once in a while you have to clean it out. You draw all the water out just as fast as you can, and then you go down in there and clean it out. Get the dippers and everything. It used to be we might get ten or twelve dippers out of the well when I was a boy. You'd keep dropping one and leaving it—just go get another one. You'd have those to get out.

Problems

Well digging was just about as hazardous a job as could be found in the mountains. One man we talked to told us about a friend of his who almost got killed one day: "He was cleaning out his daddy's well. They were bringing him up and he got to the top, and just as he got to the top the rope broke and he went back down—him, the bucket, and all. It broke his leg twice, but he finally got all right. He limped all the rest of his days though. I don't know how many feet it was he fell, but just as he started to climb out he put one hand on the bank and the rope broke and back he went bucket and all. That's what got me studying about that, too. I was kind of scared after that. But it was a job, and jobs was kind of hard to get and I had to do something to live, so I worked at it."

Perhaps the most terrifying possibility was that of a cave-in. In fact, a near miss of that sort is what ended Kenny's career as a well digger. As Kenny tells it: "I dug a well over in town that was fifty foot deep, and it was pipe clay—white looking dirt. You could slap the bank with a shovel and it would shake up ten feet. I got it done and I told the woman, 'You'd better have it walled now. I'm a'feared it'll cave with you.' But I got it done, built her a curbing and everything; plenty of water. And a few days later I went back to see how it was doing, and you could reach the bottom with your hand! It filled slap-dab up! I was crazy for working in there. When I see'd that bank shake, I ought to have got out of there. Of course I was digging on a contract and I wouldn't have got no pay.

"You couldn't dig it out again because it would just keep caving. I wouldn't have took a job putting that well back for a thousand dollars. I could have dug a new one easier than I done that. Now boys, you can't run in a well! They ain't a thing you can do only just take it. Anything comes in from the top, you just set right there with it. And if it caves, if they've got time they'll pull you up. If they don't, they just kill you up. Now it comes in quick, boys. Ain't no fooling. When it starts, it starts pushing out the bottom and just comes in like that [clapping his hands together once]. They might as well leave you. You're done dead anyhow, and you're sure enough down in the ground—done buried. I don't know whether you could get a man out of a well or not.

"That well digging and topping trees is two things that I've quit. I'd eat bread and water before I'd do her again. I never aim to dig another well. When that one done what it done in town, I said, 'Farewell, I'll never dig another one.' And I ain't."

Harley Rogers agreed about the danger: "If you hit sort of a slick place that's easy cut, you better be watching that. Maybe you get down in there about twenty-five feet and the whole side of that just drop off. If it's any bit slick, you better tile it from there. And I'd take caution if the wall had a crack in it while you were digging it 'cause that crack could lead to a slide-off, you know. A load of dirt falling in on you—it'll kill you. Smother you to death."

Another common problem associated with the job was that of gas and bad air. Lawton ran into that sort of thing several times: "We had an old home place, and we had a well there that my daddy and I dug right on top of a mountain. I dug eighty-two feet and I hit bad air in there and that liked to killed me. I didn't finish it up. It wasn't but about three more feet to dig till the water was there, but he went and got this old colored man that dug wells to come on over there and help. But I liked to passed out. I hollered and they sent the bucket down. I got to the top and couldn't get out of the bucket. They had to drag me out—laid me on the porch till I finally come to. It's a funny feeling. It felt like me and the well and everything was just a rising up. My head felt as big as the top of that table. It's some kind of dead air, and it just makes you feel plumb old funny. My head felt as big as that bucket that I was riding up and down in. It felt like everything was just moving—wheels—like you were rolling on earth.

"My daddy wouldn't let me go back down in it no more after that, but this old colored guy came and he said, 'Well, you're getting pretty close to water.' Then he asked if we had any newspaper or anything, and they said, 'Yeah.' So he went and got himself a big old bunch of newspaper and lit it and threw it down in the well and let it burn. Then he got in the bucket and said, 'I'm ready to go down.' And he went on down there and dug on down, and sure enough, he hit water. It was still a good old well when I left home. Never had no more trouble with it.

"But all the old well diggers I have talked to said that if you're going to hit that air, you will hit it within two to three feet of the water. It could kill you if you don't get out and get you some air. They have been people killed with it. I had a lot of well jobs offered me after that, but my daddy said, 'You ain't going to dig any more wells.'

"And I listened to him."

Kenny also ran into gas sometimes. "One thing I dreaded was that gas. If you had a moustache, a heap of times you'd come out of there and it would be black as a crow. You'd have gas on your beard. Yeah, that gas'll kill you, man.

"And don't talk none when you're digging a well—only when you have to. Don't talk. You're sucking that gas in your lungs. You can hear that gas spew out of the banks every once in a while. When you get to where you throw a newspaper around and it won't burn, you better get out. You've hit her then. Wait till that gas gets out and then you can go back. And if the gas gets to where you can't stand up, don't come up. Just stand there till that gas gets weaker because when you come to the top and hit this pure air, back you'll go, by the way. You're dead. You got to watch that stuff, man.

"That there gas generally comes out between two crevices of rocks. You

PLATE 352 We visited Harold Embrey and Tom Ramey who were digging a well in our county. They had hit water at forty feet by the time we got there and were finishing up. It took them six days to hit water with seven men digging off and on. Here, the bucket is being lowered into the hole to be loaded with dirt and rock.

PLATE 353 Harold Embrey being lowered into the well to continue working. The Embrey/Ramey well is 52″ at the top and tapers to 42″ at the bottom. The first five feet were through dirt. Then they hit white flint rock and had to use a hammer and chisel. After four or five hours, they cut through that and had dirt again until they hit solid rock above the water level. They had to blast with dynamite twenty-five times to get through it. Below that level was water, running at a rate of five gallons a minute.

can hear her a'spewing. If you burn newspapers in there, that'll help you some if you can get a match to strike. A blamed match just won't hardly strike down there.

"That's one place you won't smoke. If you're a smoker, you'll not smoke in there. You'll choke.

"See, no air can't hit you. Just what you suck in from the top. I believe a man digging a well needs air pumped into him."

In addition, there was also the danger that a prankster—or someone who simply wasn't being careful enough—could knock something into the well while a man was down below. As Lawton said, "No, that's one thing I told them to do is that every time I go down to keep everybody away from there. Better be nobody fooling around on top of that well while I was down there. I got people I could depend on standing right there on top so nobody could come in and look in—sightseers, you know. They could kick off something in on you. You take a real small rock and drop it and it could kill you dead as a hammer down there at eighty feet. The people working with me would always draw out a few buckets and as they did it, always keep that stuff clean back away from the well. I've had dirt to fall back on me, and I've had my head cracked a time or two with little bitty rocks. They weren't big, but it doesn't take much to crack your head when you're way down in there. Feels like someone's hit you with a baseball.

"I cleaned one well that was ninety-two feet deep, and that's when I was scared because there was a big old rock there that went out in the well about a foot out from the side. It was so big, you couldn't get it out. You had to bypass it. After I got down below it in under this rock here and looked up and just seen the bottom of that thing there with nothing underneath to hold it up, I just thought, 'There ain't a thing to keep you from coming on down here with me.' I tell you, you feel funny looking up at a big old rock like that. But I told him I would clean it out, and I did."

Harley remembered getting hit a few times: "Even a little rock as big as a marble down there about twenty feet—it'll flatten you. You have to wear a hard hat down in there, and then it goes like dynamite when it hits you in the head!"

Kenny had some even wilder things happen to him while he was digging: "I've had halves of buckets of rock and mud poured back on me. No protection at all. Just the hair on your head is all you've got.

"I was working down in a well one morning and some old boys were standing around on top. Had an old pistol—they was up there trying to sell it—and the cylinder fell out. Just as it happened, I was standing up against the bank and it mired up in that dirt, believe it or not! If I'd been over thataway at work, it would have killed me as sure as you're setting there.

PLATE 354   A finished well. Note the handmade wooden windlass, and the sliding wooden door that covers the well itself.

"And one time a boy caught an old cat and put that thing in a sack and shook it down on me. That thing tore me up! The first time, he didn't lack over ten feet getting out, but after a while, he was just down there with me. And catch that thing—you couldn't. I said, 'It's going out or me.' I hated to kill it. My sister—I guess she was on top crying about it—but I finally sent him out in the bucket. If I hadn't had on a new coat, it'd'a'tore me to pieces! I had on a jacket, and it hit me on the back with its four feet. A cat's eyes sparkle in the dark. I was down in the dark, and you couldn't see a man digging down in there. That thing tried its best to tear me all to pieces. I was scared, and I couldn't run. I had to kill it with a shovel.

"I don't reckon I got out till about dinnertime that day. I'd a'whipped that boy or he would me. I was wild. I'd'a'tore him up, and he knowed it, too. He left. They wouldn't let me out of there till he left. I hated they didn't throw a dog in on me. I could have caught a dog and held him. Them blame cats are tough. If I'd been outside, they'd a'been somebody hurt.

"Then I went one time to finish up a well. Had two old boys there, and it was deep. They said, 'Get in and we'll let you down.' Have you ever seen a well windlass? Well, when I got in the bucket, they turned me loose. You talk about hitting the bank and bottom, I hit it! The bottom was rock, by the way.

"That's a bad way for a man to get water. There's too much water on top for a man to risk his life in a well."

BERRY BUCKETS

Berry buckets are traditional containers made of bark. Jason Townsend's parents used them for picking berries on Grandfather Mountain. Jason has continued to make them, as there is a big tourist demand for them. While they can be made from the bark of tulip poplar, chestnut, white walnut, hickory, or box elder, the most popular, and the bark Jason uses exclusively, is that of the tulip poplar. Jason gathers the bark when the sap is up (about the first of June

PLATE 355

through the new moon in August), and at the same time gets hickory strips for lashing the buckets together at the top and sides.

To peel the bark off the tree, Jason uses either a "spud," a chisel-like tool, or a sharp stick. After he has peeled the bark as high as he can reach, he will cut the tree down, take the remainder of the bark off the tree, and use the wood for stovewood. He has to make the buckets within a week. If he doesn't, the bark dries out too much. To prevent the bark from drying out while waiting to work it up, he puts it in a creek or damp place, which keeps it pliable longer.

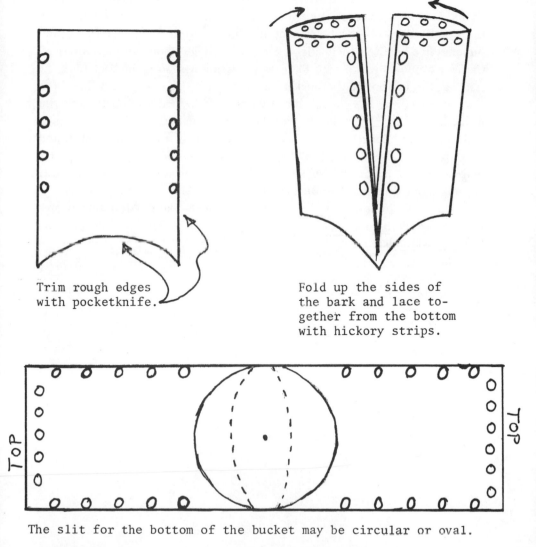

Trim rough edges with pocketknife.

Fold up the sides of the bark and lace together from the bottom with hickory strips.

The slit for the bottom of the bucket may be circular or oval.

PLATE 356

In order for him to make the buckets, Jason also needs hickory bark for the laces. When he gathers it, he makes a slit around the tree and yanks upward. If the bark becomes too hard to peel, he waits till the new moon when the bark again loosens. He "rosses" or takes off the top layer of bark, and uses the second or sap layer for the lacing, the hoop, and the bail (handle) of the buckets. He stores the extra hickory strips in rolls and wets them as he needs them.

Here is how he does it:

He cuts the bark to twice the length and the same width as he wants the bucket to be. He shapes the bucket bottom by carving a deep oval or circular slit around the outside center (see Plate 356), into but not through the bark. Jason then folds up the sides, creasing the bark at the slit. They should be even if the oval or circle was cut in the correct place. He trims off the rough edges on the bottom of the bucket with his pocketknife, and punches five holes on each side and a row of holes about an inch apart all the way around the top (see Plate 356). Using a strip of hickory bark, he starts at the bottom of the bucket and laces it up like a shoe. When both sides are laced, he has enough hickory bark left to lace around the top rim inside the bucket. To make the rim, he takes a hickory split about an inch wide and a little longer than the circumference of the top of the bucket, and overlaps the ends into a hoop that will just fit inside the bucket top. He places the rim inside the bucket and laces the hickory bark all the way around in one direction and then comes back the other so the laces cross.

For the bail, he uses hickory because the tourists like it. Mountain people used to use cloth so it wouldn't cut into their shoulders: overall galousies (straps) were ideal.

SCOTT BRADLEY

Photographs by Ken Cronic.

CHEESE MAKING

On our most recent trip into the area around Vilas, North Carolina, we were visiting Charlie Ross Hartley and his wife (see chapter in this book) when his neighbor, Milton Hodges, came over to see us. She's been enthusiastic about *Foxfire* for some time, and, knowing that we were interested in meeting people who could show us how to make cheese, offered to help us meet them. It was through her that we met Mrs. Monroe Reese and Mrs. Thelma Earp —she actually set up the interviews for us and showed us the way to their homes. She's that kind of person.

We were also able to pick up some additional information from Tedra Harmon (see sled-making chapter in this book); and, from our own area, Harriet Echols and Aunt Nora Garland (see *Foxfire 3*, page 465) told us how they make cottage cheese.

The first person we talked with was Mrs. Reese (Plate 357). Her hus-

PLATE 357

PLATE 358   PLATE 359

band was out working around their farm when we arrived, so we went straight up to their house where she showed us into her spotless, sunlit kitchen. As we took pictures, she showed us the process she follows for making the blocks of cheese that she and her husband like best. She has occasionally sold some to bring in a little extra money.

Mrs. Reese begins with two and a half gallons of refrigerated, whole milk from their cow. She pours this all into a large pan and heats it on her wood stove (Plate 358) until it is a little past lukewarm. She prefers a wood stove as it gives a slower, steadier heat.

When the milk is warm, she takes the pan off the stove and adds one-fourth of a Hansen's Cheese Rennet Tablet dissolved in one teacup of water, and one-eighth of a Hansen's Cheese Color Tablet dissolved in one teacup of water. Both these tablets are available in drug stores, and directions for their use are listed on the containers.

She lets the milk sit for from fifteen to thirty minutes until it stiffens and gets jellylike. Then she cuts it with a knife or spatula into tiny squares, also running the spatula under the surface as if cutting it into layers.

Letting it sit briefly, she then works the mixture until it is all broken up into pieces that are about the size of grains of corn. She works it gently

PLATE 360   PLATE 361

(Plate 359), squeezing the custardlike substance until it is completely broken apart. Then she puts the pan back on the stove and heats the mixture slowly until it is almost as hot as the touch can stand—but not boiling. While it is reheating, she stirs it constantly so that the curds will stay separated and not melt back together. She then removes the pan from the stove and lets it sit for from fifteen to thirty minutes to cool, and then strains the contents through cheesecloth in the colander she has ready on her sink (Plate 360). She does not squeeze the mixture dry—she lets it drip naturally and then returns the mixture to the pan, adds a heaping teaspoonful of salt, and massages it in well (Plate 361).

Finally she puts the contents of the pan into a homemade press which she has lined with cheesecloth (Plate 362). Adding weight in stages (Plate 363), she leaves it in the press overnight, or twelve hours, to press the cheese down into a firm block. She then removes it from the press (Plate 364), and dries it for a week in the open air with a cloth underneath the cheese to absorb any additional moisture. She turns it two times a day during this drying process, during which the cake of cheese forms a dry crust on the outside. It should keep fine without spoiling for a month or more.

Before rennet tablets were available, cheese of this sort was still possible

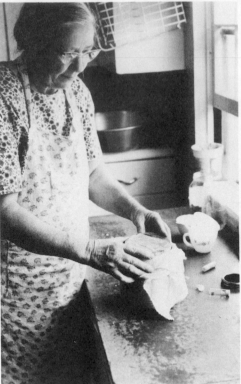

PLATE 362   PLATE 363

to make. Tedra Harmon remembers that when they killed a cow for butchering, they would get the stomach out, cut it open, and clean it well. Then they would stretch it out in one piece to dry like a banjo hide. After it was thoroughly dry, they rolled it up and hung it in a bag from a convenient rafter. Whenever his mother made cheese of the sort just described, she would use a tiny piece of the stomach lining (about the size of a thumbnail) to curdle the milk, just as the rennet tablets are used now. He also remembers his mother using a small piece of the stomach lining when making light bread. He remembers it giving the bread a sour taste.

The cheese his mother made was pressed into wooden hoops that were from twelve to fourteen inches in diameter. The cheese would be set up in the attic to dry for six to eight weeks before being cut, and he remembers that the older the cheese got, the better it tasted.

Mrs. Thelma Earp, also introduced to us by Milton Hodges, makes a different kind of cheese. It can be eaten right away. In fact, it was so good that we wound up taking half a cake along with us in the car and nibbling on it all the way home.

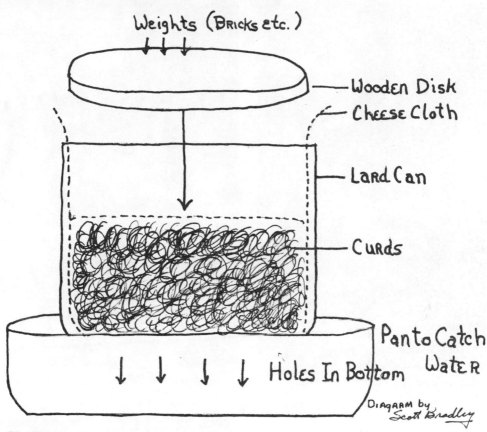

Weights (Bricks etc.)

Wooden Disk
Cheese Cloth

Lard Can

Curds

Pan to Catch Water

Holes In Bottom

Diagram by
Scott Bradley

PLATE 364

Before we got to her house, she had clabbered the milk and had it waiting in the refrigerator. To do this, she took whole milk, allowed the cream
to rise, skimmed it off and made butter (Plates 365 and 366). Then she
added two–three tablespoons of buttermilk per gallon of skimmed milk and
let it sit out for two days and sour. She put this in the refrigerator to await
use.

When we arrived, she went right to work, pouring two gallons of the
clabbered milk into a pan and heating it on the stove until it was a little
hotter than lukewarm. She said it should be pretty hot, but not boiling, and
not so hot that it would burn your hands.

Once the clabbered milk is thoroughly heated, she pours it into a strainer
made with a cotton cloth pinned over a bucket with clothespins (Plate
367). She then gathers up the corners of the cloth and squeezes the whey
through the cloth, leaving the curds. "The best thing to do with the whey,

PLATE 365

PLATE 366

PLATE 367   PLATE 368

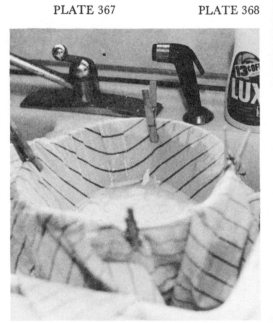

PLATE 369

now, is feed it to the hogs," she laughed. Going outside, she poured the whey into the slop bucket.

She then puts the curds in a bowl and adds one and one-half teaspoons of salt and a raw egg. She prefers barnyard eggs to store-bought ones as they make the cheese yellower. She mixes it all in with her hands (Plate 368), readying it for cooking.

Now she puts a lump of butter about the size of a large hen egg into a big iron frying pan and melts it. She prefers a wood cookstove because it heats more evenly and slowly. The electric stove used here belongs to her daughter, and it heated the cheese too fast and got some burned flakes of butter mixed in with it.

When the butter is melted, she adds the curds and keeps turning them in the pan over medium heat (Plate 369). When all the curds are melted enough to run together into a cake, she puts them out into a dish to cool (Plate 370). As they cool, they automatically form a cake.

She recommends that you, "Go to eating on it" (Plate 371), but you can wait several days. It should not be refrigerated as it should dry out somewhat. After a short while, it gets hard enough to cut into slices. It should keep about a week.

Article by Scott Bradley, Lynn Butler, and Debbie Thomas. Photographs by Ken Cronic.

PLATE 370

PLATE 371

COTTAGE CHEESE

We asked Mrs. Harriet Echols to tell us how she makes cottage cheese for her family and below are her directions with some additional comments from Mrs. Nora Garland. Mrs. Echols was unable to get raw milk to actually show us the steps at the time of the interview, so we do not have pictures of her method, but felt that her instructions would be quite clear to you.

To begin the process of making cottage cheese, pour about a gallon of raw (unpasteurized) whole milk into an enamel or other metal pan. Any amount of milk may be used. The amount used here is what is preferred by Harriet Echols for her family. Mrs. Echols lets her pan of milk sit on the back of the wood stove in the winter or just out on a kitchen table during warm weather, so that it can sour slowly. This process may only take one day, or perhaps two, according to the temperature. Mrs. Echols does not heat the milk at all before it clabbers. When on the stove, it is not over direct heat— only in a warm place.

After the milk clabbers, the cream is lifted off and refrigerated. The cream may be used later as sour cream in any recipe, or it may be mixed in with the cottage cheese after it is made to make the cheese creamier.

The skimmed, clabbered milk is then heated over a low fire until it curdles. It is removed from the heat and poured into a colander or cheesecloth to drain all the water. This usually takes a couple of hours. It may also be hung in a cloth overnight. Mrs. Nora Garland remembers that she put the curdled milk into a clean flour sack and let it drain overnight outside.

Both Mrs. Garland and Mrs. Echols told us that they would then work the cheese by putting it back into a pan or bowl and squeezing it with their hands or a spoon or spatula, getting out any remaining water. Mrs. Echols warned us not to work the cheese too vigorously or get the curds too fine. Then a little salt may be sprinkled in to taste, and to make the cheese creamier some of the sour cream may be mixed in with it. The cottage cheese is then packaged in small containers and refrigerated. It will keep several weeks in the refrigerator.

Mrs. Monroe Reese also makes cottage cheese, but her method is slightly different. She removes the cream first, lets the milk clabber, warms it on the stove, strains it through cheesecloth, adds salt and pepper to taste, and then adds some of the cream back to keep it from getting dry and hard. She eats it either warm or chilled, and tries to finish it within two days.

Article by Debbie James, Karen Moore, and Debbie Crowell.

REV. A. RUFUS MORGAN

ufus Morgan, semiretired Epis-
copal minister and native of
Macon County, North Caro-
lina, is now eighty-nine years old, somewhat hard of hearing, and with such
poor eyesight that he subscribes to the Library of Congress's talking books
for the blind. He recognizes his friends and acquaintances only when they
step close to him. In spite of these apparent handicaps, he still hikes the
Nantahala Mountains within sight of his home, and the Smoky Mountains,
with his hiking friends. He still ministers to the small St. John's Episcopal
Church of Cartoogechaye.

He has such a wonderful memory and such a way of telling about events
in his life that we asked him to start at the beginning of his life, October 15,
1885, and tell us all about himself. Since his great-grandparents were
some of the first settlers of this area, we were able to tie in Indian history
and other early stories that he had been told by his parents and grand-
parents. He told us so much in such an interesting way that we want to
share it all with you so that you might feel what we do about him.

Dr. Morgan is a tall, fine-looking man who speaks in a deliberate, kind
manner. He has a son and a daughter and several grandchildren and great-
grandchildren. He has many cousins, nieces, nephews, and young friends
whom he mentions often in conversation.

Lucy Morgan, one of Dr. Morgan's sisters, helped to establish the
Penland School of Handicrafts in Penland, North Carolina, and has led a
most interesting and productive life, also. She has now retired and lives in
Webster, North Carolina. Their brother, Ralph, was educated as a pharma-
cist, and two of their other sisters went on to college, too.

We asked Dr. Morgan what he felt had influenced so many of the chil-
dren in his family to leave home and work as hard as they had to, to get a
higher education than they could get in their local area, when this was
definitely not a tradition here in the early 1900s:

PLATE 372   Reverend Morgan.

Our family was always very conscious of education. My mother had attended the St. Mary's School in Raleigh, probably under the influence of
her father, who had studied law at the University of North Carolina at
Chapel Hill. My great-grandmother Siler was a sister of the then Governor
of North Carolina, who had also served as President of the University of
North Carolina during the War Between the States.

My oldest two sisters went to a school that our aunt conducted, a girls'
school down in Hickory, North Carolina. It wasn't college, but it covered
some of the territory that now is college work. My sister Lucy went to a
church school in New York when I was in the seminary up there, and then
she went to the University of Chicago. It's an interesting thing—she never
received an A.B., but she has two honorary doctors' degrees, one from
Chapel Hill and one from a school out in the Middle West. My brother,
Ralph, finished high school and then went on to pharmacy school and became a registered pharmacist. That leaves my youngest sister. I don't think
she graduated, but she went to a teachers' college up in Virginia, where my

oldest sister was living at the time. She lived with her and went to this school. So most of us had some college work.

My mother was always interested in my going into the ministry. She died young and when I decided that I wanted to go on and get training, I talked with my father about getting more education [than I could get at the local school].

I knew that I'd have to go somewhere else to get even a high school education, so my father said, "Why, son, you know that I don't have any money to send you to school."

I said, "I'm not asking you that. I'm just asking permission to go."

And he said, "Why, of course, I'd be glad for you to."

I went one winter to school at Andrews, North Carolina, and then to a mission school, Micadale. Then I went to Waynesville to public high school and graduated there in 1906. In each case, I had worked my way doing chores. In Waynesville, I stayed in the rectory and did the chores around the church, Grace Church, mowing the lawn, building the fires, ringing the bell, sweeping out, all that, and then although I was just a high school student, I was made a lay reader. I conducted the simple services, both there in Grace Church and in a little Negro mission on the edge of town. I went from there to Chapel Hill and worked my way there.

We first met Dr. Morgan when writing the chapter on "Old-time Burials" for Foxfire 2. *He gave us a beautiful account of his thoughts on burials, years ago and now, and how he'd like his own final service. Much of the personality of this remarkable man comes through in the comments he made on those two or three pages.*

Then, during the summer of 1973 we were invited to attend the Siler reunion in Macon County and behold, there was Dr. Morgan—wearing a name tag with "William" and his own name on it. We talked to him awhile at that time. He explained that his great-grandfather William Siler had migrated into the Macon County area with his three brothers, John, Jacob, and Jesse, in the early 1880s, and all had settled there and reared their families. So for many years, the descendants of the four Siler brothers have come from many areas in the United States, and occasionally from England, Australia, and other countries, to the annual family reunion in Macon County, North Carolina:

The four Siler brothers had originally come from Germany or from Switzerland, I'm not sure which. They sailed from Holland with their father and came first to Pennsylvania. An interesting fact was that they discovered sweet potatoes and liked them. They were told that sweet potatoes came from South Carolina, so they came down to what was then the Pendleton District of South Carolina. Then they came on to the mountains. They

PLATE 373   Dr. Morgan's grandparents, Albert and Joanna Siler.

came up to Buncombe County in the region where Asheville is. Then they
drifted over here—all four of them settled in here. William Siler was the
oldest and he had this valley in here—the Cartoogechaye valley. Jackob settled just beyond in the next part of the valley. Then on farther down, John
settled. And Jesse settled in what is now Franklin. He was the most prosper-
ous of the four. He started with an Indian cabin in Franklin and built on to
it. Now it's a three-story house, quite large, and I guess it's the oldest house
in Franklin. Descendants of the Siler family still own and live in the house.
Then Jesse Siler and his family built the old Dixie Hall which stood where
the new courthouse now stands. He also built some other buildings on Main
Street there. And he owned nearly a thousand acres over in what is now the
Smoky Mountain National Park.

*In early October of 1973 some of Dr. Morgan's family called and asked
if we had any* Foxfire *students interested in attending an unusual birthday
celebration—and he came into our lives again. None of us here could go at
the time and we've always regretted missing a most unique experience—that of climbing Mount LeConte, elevation 6,593 feet, with a man
celebrating his eighty-eighth birthday to stay overnight at LeConte Lodge
overlooking Gatlinburg, Tennessee. The Lodge is accessible only on foot by
climbing any of several trails a minimum of five to six miles.*

Since then, he's celebrated another birthday on Mount LeConte, his

eighty-ninth. He's been up LeConte nine times this year and 152 times alto-
gether. And he performed a wedding ceremony there a few weeks before his
birthday this year:

I had this telephone call from up in Pennsylvania, and the man wanted
me to perform his wedding ceremony for them up on Mount LeConte.
These two medical students at the University of Pennsylvania had fallen in
love, and had been up to LeConte and had fallen in love with it.

So I told them that we would arrange it, after asking various questions to
see if they were people that I could marry—not divorced and so forth. We
arranged the date, and they got their reservations and we got ours. Meantime, of course, there'd been a lot of correspondence—they had to know
about the marriage laws of Tennessee, and I had to know whether I would
be allowed to perform a ceremony in Tennessee.

A couple from Highlands went with me and a great-niece of mine, and
we picked up an Episcopal minister in Gatlinburg to go with us also. There
were five of us and five in the bridal party—the couple and her mother,
sister, and brother.

Our group went up the Trillium Gap trail; they went up the Alum Cave
trail, and we arrived at the lodge about the same time. I had wondered how
they had known there was such a person as I. It turned out that when they
had been up at LeConte sometime before, they saw a picture that a cousin
of mine had taken up there on one of my birthday trips and asked about it.
Then they decided that I'd be a good person to ask to marry them. That
was the reason they got in touch with me. The bride belonged to the
Roman Catholic Church, and the groom belonged to another church—I
can't remember which one.

I had time to talk with them, to counsel with them. Then we had quite a
wedding dinner in the LeConte Lodge—salisbury steaks, string beans, applesauce, baked potatoes—the usual LeConte fare. Afterwards, we walked
out to Cliff Top where we go to see the sunset. They had brought a shawl
or something to spread down in front of the couple. I had brought only my
surplice and stole. I got the minister from Gatlinburg, Bruce Green, to hold
the book in case I should stumble, but I didn't; so I performed the ceremony right there—a beautiful sunset evening. The bride had picked along
the way some of the simple wild flowers—mountain aster and some of the
others. Then we went back to the lodge and in the new building which
they've almost finished, we had cake and refreshments. The proprietor of
LeConte Lodge, Mr. Brown, and his staff had prepared the wedding cake.

When Dr. Morgan goes on hikes these days, he doesn't go alone due to
his eyesight, and rarely sleeps out overnight now because he can't see to
cook. He usually goes with friends living nearby, or with others who contact

him that want to go—as long as it's not Saturday or Sunday and might interfere with his conducting church services. Sometimes they have hair-raising experiences:

There are a good many people whom I suspect of using pain as an excuse for not hiking. I never know how seriously to take injuries of people. Occasionally I have a few pains here and there, but I don't let them bother me very much and I don't let my blindness bother me too much, although I ought to. But I must tell you of one of my most recent experiences.

There's quite an interest now for establishing a William Bartram system of trails. William Bartram was a naturalist who came down through this section and went on through Georgia and Florida.

Well, there are some trails taking off from the Appalachian Trail up here in the Nantahalas, and we have been trying to find out, as near as we could, where he went because he went through Franklin [read the *Travels of William Bartram,* published by Dover Publications, New York, 1955, a republication of the work published by Macy-Masius in 1928 and edited by Mark Van Doren] back in the Revolutionary days—two hundred years ago. We've been scouting out some of those trails. I've been over some of them in years past, and recently [in October] one member of our hiking club, Sally Kesler, who is the most knowledgeable of our hikers, was assigned the task of scouting out this trail over Wine Spring Bald down to the Nantahala Lake. Well, one day she wanted to scout out one section of it over which I hadn't been for years and years, and she asked me if I'd go with the group and I said, "Yes."

I like to start out early in the morning, but it is hard to get these folks with city backgrounds started early. It was almost noon when Sally asked me about going. So she said, "I'll have to round up a few others to go with us."

She rounded them up; there were five of us, two men and three women. By the time we got started, it was about two o'clock that afternoon. There's a new road that we call locally the Dirty John Road. It turns off at what used to be called the Dirty John Johnson place. We left Sally's car on that road, and drove down to the lake and parked the other car where Wine Spring Creek [so-called because the water from it is so invigorating] runs into the lake.

So we started. Well, we ought to have had sense enough not to start that time of day. The old trail was obliterated, grown up in rhododendrons and laurels and all sorts of things. We had to walk almost in the creek and had to walk over rocks or logs to get across. I couldn't see very much, of course. I had one fall and fell backwards. My head sounded like an empty gourd hitting the rocks—I was so glad it didn't burst. Then after a while I fell into a pool in the creek and got wet all over—just sat down. I still have a wound that I have to favor somewhat.

As we started up a steep ridge which was slippery, the sun got low and we made it very slowly. I couldn't see the trail because there wasn't any trail there, but I knew where we were headed. It got later and later, and finally it got so dark, nobody could see the way to go. So they said, "Well, we'll just have to stop."

I said, "We can't spend the night here."

They said, "The rescue squad will find us."

I asked, "How will they find us here?"

After a while, they suggested that we start a fire. It was pretty cool. It went down below freezing that night. I said that we couldn't—the woods were too dry, it was too dangerous.

Well, they insisted that we had to have a fire, so they built one. By that time I was just shivering, I was so cold and wet almost all over. So the fire was welcome. We didn't have any food; we hadn't brought even a sandwich. I had three or four apples, but they refused to eat them. I had a little jar of water. They refused to drink that. We stood around the fire, turning one side and then the other, trying to keep from freezing. Occasionally, one or another of us would lie down beside the fire and try to get a little cat nap. Fortunately it was a beautiful night, stars all over the heavens, clear as could be. At two o'clock in the morning, the moon rose and then after four o'clock, we began to see an outline of the mountains. Finally, it got light enough so that the others could see the way, so we poured my water on the fire and dug up some dirt and put on it and got it out. We went on, and about nine o'clock in the morning, we reached the road where Sally's car was parked. It just happened that the husband of one of the women of the party got anxious and started out at midnight, waked up one of his neighbors and they'd been driving around ever since, trying to get some inkling of where we were. They had discovered the car down by the lake, and when we got to the road, there they were with a pickup truck. So they took us on out a little way to Sally's car and they went on down to get the other car while Sally and I came on home. We hadn't had anything to eat since lunch the day before. When we got down this side of the mountain, we met my daughter and son-in law in their pickup. They had started off to hunt us. So they turned around, followed us in, and came here and cooked breakfast for us at ten o'clock. It was a foolish sort of thing, but I loved it very much. Everyone was in good spirits.

This gift he has of welcoming experiences that would make others shudder—and of welcoming people—is immediately felt by those who have never met him before. Marie Auten, for example, picked up on the inter-

views with Dr. Morgan where Linda Warfield had left off with her gradua-
tion in 1974. She felt that warmth immediately upon meeting him, just as
Linda had the first time she went into his home. It was Linda, when inter-
viewing Dr. Morgan on wild plant foods, who had said that she'd love to do
an extended article on him. The obvious answer, "Why not?"

Here is Marie's impression of her first visit to Cartoogechaye and Dr.
Morgan's home:

As we all know, first impressions stand out in our minds—the meeting of
a new person or visiting a new place. The feelings we collect on our first go-
round of a new experience are what dominate our mind and also what we
tell others.

My first experience with meeting Reverend Morgan left a very warm,
loving feeling in me. It wasn't as though he thought of me as a "stranger"
or an "intruder." The love he has for people surrounded me and filled me
as we shook hands. That greeting was more than an introduction to him; it
was a real welcome to *his home,* the invitation to stay awhile and to come
back whenever I wanted to. This really made me feel good inside, because I
knew he was meeting me as a person, not a school child or because it was
the proper way to greet someone.

Dr. Morgan's two-story frame house is a large house for one person. His

PLATE 374   Dr. Morgan lived alone in this house until it burned to the ground
recently. It was built by his grandparents, the Silers, and named "Nonah"—the name
the area had when his grandparents lived there. Friends of Dr. Morgan have since
built him a new log home on the same site.

porch stretches all the way across the front of the house with rocking chairs spaced out so one can relax facing the mountains in any direction he wishes, and ponder his thoughts.

The front door is always unlocked and open for anyone to come on in. This really impressed me as I am very accustomed to "being sure the door is locked when you leave." And yet this man always leaves his door open.

The house is spacious on the inside with a long staircase right in the front hall going to the upstairs rooms. There is a room to the right of the entrance which reminds me of a "guest room." On the left of the entrance hall is the door to his living room, the real heart of the house, where we enjoyed our visits in front of a large stone fireplace with a crackling fire, with shelves of books on subjects ranging from birds and trees, plants and mountains, to fiction, to religion and philosophy on two walls. The fireplace mantel has a number of statuettes of St. Francis of Assisi with hands outstretched, welcoming us into that warm, hospitable room. I later learned why Reverend Morgan would choose St. Francis as a favorite of his.

At the back of the entrance hall, under the staircase, is an area for his backpacking equipment. His pack looks all ready as though if he at any time wanted to go out hiking, he'd pick up and go. He has several sturdy hiking sticks near the front door, which I suppose he uses for different hikes.

Reverend Morgan has shared with us some of his life's experiences, his

PLATE 375   The fireplace Marie describes.

accomplishments, and his disappointments. He has helped me to realize that everything in life has something to offer—experiences good and bad, people, nature, everything!

He has lived his life as he felt he should. People have not always agreed with him, but he has few regrets for the way he had chosen to do things.

Through his words, we have visited many places and witnessed the beauty of mountaintops through his eyes, things and places we may never see otherwise. He is a very special person to many people, and we hope you will enjoy knowing him as we do.

Interviews by Marie Auten, Linda Warfield, and Craig Carlton. Photographs by Al Oakes and Marie.

Well, I don't know where to start except where I started. My great-grandfather William Siler settled over across the valley about 1818. The story goes that his house was the first house in Macon County that had windows. I remember the house quite well—a long two-story log house with a porch both upstairs and down the whole length of that house. I've used some of the logs that I bought from the man that tore the house down. The owner wanted to build a neat little compact cottage in place of the lovely old log house. The mantel over the fireplace here is made from one of those logs and the legs from that rustic table are from the same log.

The top of the table itself is connected with the Cherokee Indian Reservation over at Cherokee, North Carolina. It's a part of the boundary tree which was the beginning corner of the land that was bought for the Cherokees for their Reservation. I like that connection between the boundary tree of the Cherokees and this log because, if you remember your history, 1818 was just twenty years before the removal of the Cherokees from their mountains here to what was then Indian territory, when the government armed forces rounded them up at the point of a bayonet. They put as many Indians as they could capture on the "Trail of Tears." The local chief here in the valley, Chief Chuttahsotee, and his wife, Cunstagih, were taken along with the rest. But when they got over into Tennessee, they escaped and came back to their mountains and, as the story goes—which I love very much—they came directly to my great-grandfather's house for protection. He took them in and then, in order that the government might not remove them again, he deeded them a tract of land on which they lived out the remainder of their lives. The government couldn't move them if they owned real estate. So naturally, I connect my great-grandfather Siler's home with the Cherokee Indians.

I was born up there between where my great-grandfather lived and the property that he deeded to Chief Chuttahsotee—born there in a log house in 1885. I can't remember the log house, but I do remember moving from it

PLATE 376 The historic boundary tree table. It, and everything else in the home, was destroyed in the fire.

to another little log cabin that I own at the present time. I remember the moving. Of course, we got around by walking in those days, and I've kept it up ever since. I was three years old then and the log cabin we moved into had been built about five years before I was born. I walked across the dam of the fish pond that my grandfather Albert Siler had built. He loved fishing and he had two ponds with fish and bullfrogs—one down near the cabin where we were going and one up on the mountain above here. He raised carp and liked to have them to eat.

I remember quite vividly coming into that log house over there and the other people were busy carrying things in and out. I went in the cabin and got into a seat that was behind a table. It was a little bit hard for me to get out and I had a desperate feeling wondering whether I would ever get out, but the others came along soon.

Two or three things I especially remember about life when we lived over there. We carried water from a spring down the hill a few hundred yards and my sister was with me. My father had given me a little axe just the right size for a five-year-old boy. My sister Anna and I stopped at an old log that was lying beside the trail and began playing there. We picked some bark off of it, and all of a sudden we came upon a big, long beetle. Her instinct was to reach out and catch the beetle; my instinct was to use my axe and chop it in two; and unfortunately, we met about the same time and I almost cut off her little finger. She recovered, however.

Another thing that I remember is crossing what we called a buck fence. Some people call them galloping fences. I was crossing that fence and I discovered, much to my delight, a twenty-five-cent piece. Well, of course I picked it up and came home rejoicing and showed my mother what I had found. She inquired around and couldn't find whose it was, so she decided, since we seldom had any money to amount to anything, to let me buy material to make kilts because boys at that age wore kilts until they were five or six years old. We bought the material and my mother made me the dress.

Another thing that I remember about life there at the cabin—we had been playing there in the yard and a man came to the yard with a load of tobacco leaves, and of course I wanted one. I wanted to know what to do with it since my father didn't use tobacco and he said, "You chew it." So he tore off a piece and suggested that I try it. So I tried it. It made me sick, and I haven't used tobacco since, so I guess it was a pretty good thing.

I was about five years old when we older children were sent up to the home of a man we called Uncle Elam Slagle—no kin of ours although the families have intermarried since. We stayed up there for two or three days. When we got back home, we found that twins had been born while we were gone, a boy and a girl.

Most of the farm of my great-grandfather has gone out of the family because we made a mistake back in those days. My great-grandparents had nine children, and of course the property which was all of this part of the valley had to be divided among them. Then my grandparents had nine children and it had to be further divided. My parents had nine children, but we moved over to the next county of Cherokee when I was six years old.

The people traveling then went across Wayah Gap. That was the road people used in hauling potatoes and apples, and driving turkeys, sheep, hogs, cattle from way back in the mountains down to Charleston, South Carolina. They'd camp along the way with a covered wagon and sometimes stop at stopping places like the Slagles' up on Wayah Creek.

We moved across to Cherokee County in a four-horse covered wagon, and of course it was slow going. It's only about sixty miles, but it took us three days. On the way, climbing up the Nantahala mountains by what we called then the "W's" (because the road went back and forth and formed a "W" on the side of the mountain), on one of the turns of a "W" I fell out of the back of the wagon, and of course I let it be known. I had been sitting on top of what we called a chest—a big wooden box nearly as long as a sofa. I still have it in my bedroom. Of course, they stopped the wagon and picked me up. My uncle put me up on the front seat by him and let me hold the lines and pretend that I was driving.

The first night we stopped at the Monday House and spent the night. I remember still a swing attached to the limb of a white pine, and the other children and I amused ourselves by swinging there. The next morning we started out and crossed the Nantahala River on a covered bridge. They used to cover them to protect the fabric of the bridge from the weather to keep them from rotting out. That bridge stayed there until the local power company built a dam across the river below that and formed a lake and covered up the Aquone area where we had gone across before.

So Aquone had to move, and the present post office is right down below the dam. We stop in there occasionally coming from our hikes.

Then the next day we went as far as Andrews and spent the night there. A tragedy in my young life occurred there—a friendly neighbor over here had given me a white bantam chicken, so we took it along with us, and to rest it there at Andrews we put it in the chickenyard. When we went on the next day to Murphy, we forgot the chicken and I've never seen it since.

Of course there was plenty of work to do. When we boys got a little bit older, I naturally drifted to the work on the farm, looking after the sheep, milking cows, chopping wood; and my brother worked in my father's printing office. He was quicker than I. He could set type faster than I, so he got into that and I did the farming.

During the summer, a lot of times the sheep and the cattle went back in the mountains to eke out a living feeding on the grass and shrubbery. I remember one trip especially that my father and I took to look up some of the wandering sheep. We lived on the point of what was locally called Fort Butler. It was near where a fort had been during the War Between the States. It continued around until it became Wildcat Mountain. We went on around on the side of Wildcat, and this old ex-slave lived back there. Well, we had gone out before breakfast and stayed out longer than we'd expected to, and old Aunt Clairsy, as we called her, discovered that we hadn't had breakfast. She was troubled and certainly we had to have some breakfast, but she was also racially conscious. So she thought and decided, "Now I'll put your table out here in the yard and you folks can eat out there."

Well, we were very happy to take advantage of it, so she went in the house and made some biscuits, fried some eggs and fatback, and I've never tasted a better breakfast than that. That was the first time that I can remember that I was impressed by the dew on the grass. At certain angles, there was just the small sparkle of the dew with the sun coming up, and it was as beautiful a thing as a diamond bracelet or any other gem. That impressed me then, and I still love it—that and the spider webs covered with the dew.

After I was up, oh, thirteen or fourteen years old, I would sometimes work for a relative who lived between our house and town, plowing and chopping wood and gathering apples and various farm labors. I received a dollar a day at that sort of work.

In going back and forth to town, we would usually walk, and in those days there were paths because so many people walked. Quite often, especially in the wintertime, you couldn't walk in the road because it was too muddy and there'd be the paths either down the Hiwassee River or along the road bank.

Our groceries and whatever else would be carried, and I quite often carried twenty-four-pound sacks of flour out home—a couple of miles. When we had anything more than that, we had an old mare and we'd hitch her to the buckboard and drive into town when the roads were passable and get what we needed and bring it back out.

When we moved over there to Murphy, we lived about two miles out from town, Cherokee County, and about two miles on farther out was a country log schoolhouse that we, being country people, instinctively went to rather than going in the other direction into Murphy. I don't remember how long we went to that school, but I remember it quite distinctly. It was built of logs completely; the floor was what we called a puncheon floor— that is, it was made out of split logs flat-side up. The seats were not like modern desks, but were made out of split logs without any backs. There was one shutter to let the light in when it wasn't too cold, but as well as I remember it, there was no glass and the fireplace chimney was at the end of the room. The teacher—it was a one-teacher school—was a Mrs. Sherrill and we enjoyed her very much. Certain smells carry me back to that school-house, because we took our lunches with us. I remember especially the smell of sweet corn—roastin' ears.

The school in Murphy was made of bricks and part of the fabric of that is still standing. It is a part of the hospital that the Roman Catholics built over there years later.

I got along fairly well with school, I guess, in view of the interruptions. Of course, like any boy, I would get into fights with the other boys. I remember one event where some of the boys had disobeyed the rules and they were in for a thrashing. So the principal of the school [this was in Murphy], Mr. Monty, sent me out to get some switches for his use. I don't know whether it was because I was sorry for the boy or afraid of him or what, but when I brought those switches in, Mr. Monty looked at them and said, "Those won't do." So he got one of the older boys to go out and get his switches.

In those days, they had all sorts of traditions, at that school, at least; and when vacation was approaching, they had a habit of what they called "barring the teacher out"—getting there before any of the faculty, closing the doors, fastening them, putting desks and tables up against them so the teachers couldn't get in. Sometimes they would keep the teachers out and the teachers would go home, if it was near enough vacation, but sometimes the teachers would work various tricks. They might send somebody up on the roof and force some inflammable substance down the chimney and smoke the boys out. It didn't always come out so well. We had fights among the older boys. I can remember a couple of the boys of rather prominent families of the location getting into a fight, and one of them had a knife and he went for the other boy intending to cut him down the front. The other boy bent over, and he ripped him up the back. He lived to tell the tale, though.

Of course the schools weren't up to the present standards, and then I had to stay out to work on the farm when I was needed, so I was just a little bit slow. I attended to the cattle, did various things, and a bit later I was a butcher on the farm. In raising sheep, we had some to be killed and dressed and I was the man to do it. If we had a lamb roast, I would go into town and peddle what we didn't need from house to house.

Back then, we received from ten to twelve cents a pound for lamb, quite a contrast to present prices. I got so I enjoyed doing that sort of work—there was an art to it and good, clean work. I didn't like the goats so well. We had some angora goats in those days. The billy goats among the angoras can be quite militant. My brother was younger than I and the old billy seemed to take a dislike to him, and when Ralph would come into the lot, the old goat would knock him down and I'd be afraid he was going to kill him and I'd get a stick and knock the old billy off. Somehow he didn't seem to hold anything against me, but I had to protect my brother.

I did work in the printing office sometimes, because part of the time when I was at home, my father was editor of the *Cherokee Scout*, the weekly paper, and I would have the job of running the old press—the old Washington press, I think they called it. A variation of it was the old Franklin press, and printers then and now were not always on time. So I would have to work late at night and run the paper off. You've probably never seen one of them, but the type is set and put on a platform and then a roller is rolled over the type that has been run in printer's ink to make the surface for printing the paper and you put a sheet of paper on that and you run it under a press. Then there's a lever that you have to pull which you put all your weight against to pull it to press the paper down onto the type. Then you roll it back out and take the paper off and repeat the process. Of course, a man would never get a modern paper printed that way. And then my father did various other printing—books and programs of various kinds.

During my childhood in Cherokee County on the farm, my father, being a printer, was in Murphy two miles away a good part of the time. His health wasn't too good; besides, he was not a good business man, so he tried all sorts of things like canning, raising fruits and vegetables. We had grapes, gooseberries, raspberries, and asparagus beds. He got equipment for canning vegetables in tin cans. We all helped with that. He had a motto, both in his printing and his canning, because we sold some of the canned goods like beans and corn. His motto was "Morgan's Best." Some people thought he was bragging, but he said, "No, I don't claim it's better than anybody else's. It's just the best I can do."

He always had dreams. I remember that our place there, on what is now called Morgan Hill, was named Montevista Farm. He loved the out-of-doors. He hated to see forest fires. I've known him to fight the forest fires on his property and on adjoining property practically all night at a time. He also called our place "The Great Appalachian Park and Forest Reserve," before we had thought about our national parks. He liked to keep things beautiful.

My mother was always busy helping with the canning, drying fruit, and cooking of course. And in those days we had the privilege of churning, making butter in the old-fashioned churn with a dasher. She would sit there churning, and she wouldn't waste her time—she would read to us while she was churning. My first acquaintance with Dickens and Shakespeare and Scott were her readings to us.

Then she would make us stockings—knit them. She would knit away and read at the same time. In our living room, up overhead, there were four hooks in the ceiling for quilting frames. She'd cut the pieces for the quilts and do the quilting, and all sorts of things to help make things go.

They would have preaching at the school on Sundays. The Baptist preacher would come and preach. My brother, Ralph, was quite a mimic and after we would get home, he would gather the rest of us children up at the edge of the woods and preach us a sermon going through the motions that the old man with his bandana handkerchief would go through at the service.

My parents both belonged to the Episcopal Church. They wouldn't stay away from the church of their inheritance, and it wasn't long before we started services there in Murphy. My father was what they call a lay reader. He started the services in a room above a furniture store with a piano box serving as an altar. My mother was the organist and Sunday school teacher. My father conducted the services except one Sunday a month when a man would come out from Asheville and hold services for us. So we shifted from the country log school to the school in town and from services in the log schoolhouse to the room above the furniture store in town.

We had some neighbors in our community—colored people—who had no religious instruction at all. Sometimes they'd be working for my mother and begin asking questions and she would teach them. Very often she would gather them on Sundays onto our back porch and she'd have a Sunday school for them. Later, somebody enabled her to buy a little log cabin near our house which she used for a Sunday school for the colored people.

My grandmother Siler had been a Chipman before her marriage, and she was born in New York State of Canadian stock. She was brought up as a member of the Church of England in Canada—that's the same as the Episcopal Church in the United States. She had a half sister who had married and had come down to Murphy, North Carolina. My grandmother came down to visit her, and she met my grandfather. He lived over here in'this valley. He was born just across the valley over here. She stuck to her Episcopal Church, although there wasn't one here. The nearest one was over in Waynesville, forty miles away. When there were children to be baptized, she would take them over there. Then she let the Bishop know that she was here and a member of the Church, and that she wanted to keep her contact with the Church. So the Bishop would call that to the attention of any ministers passing through, and they would come by to see her and give her the service.

In 1877, a minister finally came, Reverend John Archibald Deal. There wasn't any parsonage, so Reverend and Mrs. Deal lived with my grandparents, and I'm pretty sure that it was in this house in which we sit. My grandparents had gone to housekeeping in a log house just a few hundred yards from here—one of the old-fashioned log houses with two rooms under one roof with what was called then a dog-trot, an open space in between the rooms. But I'm pretty sure it was in this house that the minister and his wife lived with my grandparents.

So after Reverend Deal came, he began immediately to make plans for building a church, and it was the first St. John's Church here that he built. The land was given by my grandparents, and with the help of money that he was able to get, as he said, from the North (I think he came originally from Connecticut) and from what gifts he could get here, contributions of materials and labor, they built the church. According to his record, my mother was one of the chief contributors to the building of the church. She was just out of prep school but at that age and at that time, she gave one hundred dollars toward the building of the church, which was quite a sum for a school girl, and she fed the carpenters while they were building the church.

While the church was being built, there was an incident that is brought to my attention every time I think of St. John's Church. There is a marker up there at a double grave for Chief Chuttahsotee and his wife Cunstagih—I told you earlier about their escaping from the Trail of Tears and coming back to my great-grandparents' home. My grandfather visited them, read the Scriptures to them, offered prayers and sang hymns to the old man. While the new church was being built, the old chief died. He had requested to my grandfather that he be buried with the white man's burial. So, since my grandfather was giving the land to the church, he had him buried there. And the chief's wife, Cunstagih, died the next day. She wasn't sick, just passed. So she was buried there with her husband. I am always proud of my family's participation in that episode. Their graves are the most prominent in the St. John's Cemetery. They have a large stone for a grave marker. We were friends of the Indians. Occasionally, not as often as I'd like, I come in contact with their great-granddaughter and great-great-grandchildren over there at Cherokee.

After St. John's was built, the Episcopal church just nine miles over in Franklin was started, then one in Highlands, one in Cullowhee, all over the place, because Reverend Deal was a very missionary-minded man. Another thing that he did during the expansion of his work was to establish a small church between here and Franklin for the colored people. There weren't very many of them here, but he was a very practical man, and he built the church for worship, but also developed work for crafts, cabinetmaking and so forth. I used to minister to that congregation, and last Sunday I had some visitors. After our service at St. John's, we were out there on the porch and a pickup truck turned into the drive. This man came up with a bundle in his hand. He was a member of that colored congregation. While I had

PLATE 377   The grave of Chief Chuttahsotee and his wife, Cunstagih, buried in 1879—the first people to be buried in the churchyard of St. John's.

charge of the church down there, he loved rabbit hunting, and would very often give me a rabbit he had killed, so that was what he had. He had a rabbit that he wanted me to have that he had had in the deep-freeze, and then his mother-in-law had made some jelly and pickles, and she had sent that to me. I keep that contact. When their minister happens to be away, I go down still and hold service for them. The man who came up from Columbia, South Carolina, to teach cabinetmaking built various things for the church, including a baptismal font for St. John's. He got inspired to go into the ministry and he told me—he was a very young man when he came here —that he studied under Reverend Deal for twenty-three years before he could get far enough along to be ordained for the ministry in the church, and he worked in and for the church until his death just a few years ago.

The time came when I wanted to go off to school, because at a very early age I determined I wanted to be a minister, I guess largely under the influence of my mother. She probably influenced me more than anyone else. We shared appreciation of flowers, beauties of nature, that sort of thing, a very great deal. I admired her for her devotion to the church in so many ways. She played the organ; she taught Sunday school. She let me know very early in my life that she would like very much for me to go into the ministry. She told me about a prayer when I was sick with typhoid fever and the doctors didn't expect me to live. She gave herself to prayer in addition to her ministry to me physically, and she said that if God would spare me, she would do what she could to give me to God's service, and that had a real influence on me.

We didn't have any high school over there then, so I tried to find some high school that I could attend by working my way. There was probably a year in between. For a few months I went up to Andrews, the next town in the county. I did the chores—building fires, chopping wood, whatever came handy, milking cows—for my board. I still remember the whistle of the local tannery before daylight. That was a sign to get up and do the chores before school. And then I also went to a school at Micadale, a church school outside of Waynesville, and lived in the home of the local minister who had several scattered churches, and I did the chores there for my board. My oldest sister was teaching in this school. She wasn't so much older than I but she had gone to a preparatory school operated by our Aunt Lucy down at Hickory, so she was ahead of me more than her years would indicate. And then those schools didn't prepare me to go very far. I went to the Waynesville High School, a public school. One year I boarded with the local Episcopal minister and looked after the church, sweeping it, building the fires, mowing the lawn, whatever came up. And another year, I boarded with the same sort of arrangement, with a Mr. Thomas, and did the milking, and the fire building and other chores around the place. During the summer I would get whatever job I could—driving a team sometimes to haul material for paving the main street in Waynesville.

Some things follow you in life. James Thomas, the man with whose family I was staying that winter, was a descendant of Bill Thomas, who was a white man but adopted by a Cherokee Indian chief, so he was always interested in the Indians' plight. When the government hunted out all the Cherokees they could catch from these mountains, they finally gave up and just had to let the rest of them go. Later, Bill Thomas asked permission to get from the Indians the little bit of money the government had allowed them for taking over their property, to buy a tract of land to settle these Indians on. The government gave him permission and so we have what is called the Indian Reservation of the Eastern Band of the Cherokees, which authorities say isn't technically a reservation because it is owned outright by the tribe of the eastern band.

Anyway, I stayed with this family and a baby was born to the Thomas family. The mother was a staunch Episcopalian, and she asked me to stand as sponsor, godfather, of this baby, Sarah. I still keep in touch with Sarah who lives in Waynesville. She is Sarah Thomas Campbell, Mrs. Roy Campbell. She has a niece who lives with her, Sarah Jo Thomas. They're both very dear people, both very devoted to the church and active, and Sarah Jo is interested in our summer conference ground at Kanuga Lake. She's especially interested in an open-air chapel there that I had a hand in building down by a stream with a stone altar. Some of my hiking friends gave the money to construct that chapel. We call it the Chapel of St. Francis of Assisi. My daughter was married there. I performed the ceremony in that little woodland chapel. That friendship with the Thomases has continued to be very dear to me.

I enjoyed those years and did better than I expected to in school. When it came to the year of graduation, which I think was through the tenth year, rather to my surprise I had an average for the two years I was there of ninety-nine. It was the only creditable grade I ever made. And, of course, being the highest grade in the class, I was valedictorian. I remember one event that rather embarrassed me at the time. I prepared my valedictory speech and then I had to practice it. I wanted to hear what it sounded like, and I couldn't very well practice in the home where I was staying, so over across the creek that runs through the town there's a ridge, and I went over there to practice saying my speech. One evening I was over there on the side of the ridge and I heard voices down below. I wondered who was there and what they were coming up there for, so I waited. They called and I answered, and they came on up. I found it was some folks who had a feeble-minded son who would get out and yell and call, and they thought I was he. I think they were somewhat dismayed that I was out there in the twilight saying my speech.

While I was there, I had a little practice in church work and Sunday school teaching, and then I became what we call in our church a lay reader. The folks in the church there at Waynesville thought that I could help out, so although I was just a high-school boy, I got a license as a lay reader. Most of my work, besides Sunday school, was holding service in the Negro church over on the other side of town. I enjoyed that very much. I always had a liking for people of other races, whether Negroes or Indians or whomever.

I remember once the minister got me to go over from there to Cullowhee to hold service in the St. David's Church. The principal member in the church was old Colonel Davies, who was a Welshman. I went over and held service and the old colonel was also a lay reader, and he wrote to the minister in Waynesville telling him that he didn't think it was necessary for the minister to send that high-school boy to hold services—that he could hold services just as well and save the trouble.

Well, I graduated there in 1906, and that summer I got a job with a lumber mill, Soco Flume Company over on Soco Creek on the Indian reservation.

Then I went, contrary to the expectation of some of my friends, to Chapel Hill. They thought I would go to Sewanee, University of the South, which is a church college. But I thought since I was planning to be a minister, I ought to have experience with people who are not church-connected and who are not planning to go into the ministry, so I went into the University of North Carolina.

I found it very difficult there for two reasons: The sort of high school that Waynesville had didn't prepare a man for college and so I had to make up almost a year during my freshman year, and then I had to earn my way. I found that more difficult than it had been in high school, but with what work I could get, sweeping up buildings and tending fires and acting as sexton to the church, I managed to get through with the help of summer work.

One summer while I was there, 1909, the Bishop asked me to go to Canton, a paper-mill town, and start a Sunday school there. Because we had no church there and no church building, we rented a tent and called it the St. Andrews Tent Sunday School. Later on the church was built there and they took that same name.

In that and various other ways, I got jobs that just barely made me enough to eat, but I enjoyed that. Lately I've been interested in all these talks about the comet [Kahoutek]. It was during my senior year, spring of that year, that Halley's Comet appeared. It was very much more easily visible than the one that was supposed to have come across this past winter. I can remember watching it.

Part of my work there at Chapel Hill was looking after the church. I would build the fires and sweep out and ring the bell. One morning I was feeling down in spirits and I needed the communion service—at least I felt I did and I still think I did—which was to be at 7:30 in the morning. I rang the first bell thirty minutes before the service was supposed to start; then I rang the second bell just five minutes before and the minister wasn't there yet. In a few minutes he came rushing in, saying he had slept late. Nobody else came to the service. He said, "Well, since there's nobody else here, we just won't have a service this time."

That was a terrible disappointment to me, and I've thought of that a great many times when there were just perhaps one or two or three for an early communion. I've been very much pleased to go ahead with the service if there was just one.

Well, I graduated from there in spite of the hardships. That was the hardest period of my education. Then I considered the matter of seminary and university work, and again I wanted to go somewhere beside my own local habitat. I decided to go the seminary in New York City, General Theological Seminary. I don't approve of what the arrangement was there entirely, but it helped me very much. In the churches there in New York City, they get so hard up for qualified Sunday school teachers, they'll pay seminary students for teaching or acting as secretary or doing social work in the church, and so besides the scholarship I got at the seminary, I got paid for that sort of thing—at Trinity Chapel up on 25th Street, the Chapel of the Incarnation down on 14th Street, sometimes over in New Jersey across the river, and various places.

I got along very well, not making any outstanding marks but I enjoyed it. I played handball at the gym we had there. I played basketball, but I didn't get along very well there because I didn't know much about it and I was too rough, I guess, for the authorities. I got penalized quite often at it, but I did enjoy it.

While I was there, there was a mutual arrangement (and still is) between Columbia University and the seminary. Seminary is way downtown, 20th Street and Ninth Avenue; Columbia is up on Morningside Heights. I had to go by elevated train back and forth. I studied there as much as I did at the seminary. The course at the seminary is three years, but at the end of that time, I managed to get a fellowship at the seminary and I was ordained deacon that spring, 1913, and I got a job during that fellowship year at a small church right near the seminary as assistant rector at St. Peter's Church. I had a very pleasant year there. I enjoyed the contacts. I lived at the seminary—one of my classmates also got a fellowship and we roomed together. The building was four stories high and no elevators. The rooms were in groups—two bedrooms and a living room. The heat was from a grate and the coal was in the basement and we had to carry it up four flights of stairs. But we did have maids who looked after our rooms. I had some complaints by the maid to the seminary authorities that she just couldn't look after my room, because I just froze her out. I'd leave my windows open. She didn't like that especially. The shower baths were in the basement, too. I'd go down there and take a shower the first thing in the morning and by the time I got out and back up to my room, there were icicles on my hair.

The minister with whom I lived one year when I was at Waynesville had gone back to his native state of Vermont. He had a church up there in Swanton, Vermont. He invited me to come up and help him for the summer, 1912, while I was still at seminary. I went up and helped with the Sunday school, painted the church roof, various other things. Then I discovered that it was just out of the kindness of his heart that he had invited me to come up. He didn't have enough work for me. So I got a job in the marble mill down by the Missisquoi River, and I worked there in the drafting room practically all summer. I enjoyed getting down to the river, and then sometimes out on to Lake Champlain in a canoe after work was over. I'd take a sandwich along and share it with the mosquitoes, of which there were plenty.

So I worked there until nearly time to go back to the seminary. When I told the mill authorities, they offered me a permanent job in the mill at a salary of more than I received for the first several years in the ministry.

The winter before, I had met a young lady in New York. Her family had a summer home up above Gloversville, New York, and we thought we were pretty much in love. Her family invited me to come by on my way back to New York City and make them a visit in their summer home. I went, going down through Lake Champlain, Lake George—a beautiful trip. We got to talking things over and her mother didn't like the idea of her daughter marrying a minister. Her mother was something of a climber, and so she talked with me and with her daughter. She said, "I won't allow it, unless Rufus will promise to do all that he can to get the best position that he can in the ministry." Well, that's not my idea of the ministry. She would like to have had me a bishop or something of the sort, and I wasn't about to do it. So the young lady said, "Well, whatever Mother says, I have to do."

I said, "Well, if that's the way you feel about it, it's all over as far as I'm concerned."

So I went next morning down to Gloversville which is above Albany, bought a frying pan and a blanket, almost nothing else, and started out walking it off. I walked from there to Boston, two hundred and seventeen miles, sleeping out at night, averaging more than forty miles a day. I got to the outskirts of Boston and found a restaurant and got supper. I had walked forty-three miles that day. Then, when I had satisfied my hunger, I went out and looked for a policeman to inquire the way to the nearest "Y." He gave me directions and then as I started off, he noticed that I was a little bit stiff, and he said, "Look here, fella." I stopped. He said, "Have you got money enough to get out of here on?"

I told him I thought I had. I still tease some of my Boston friends about their trying to run me out of town the only time I was ever there. So I toured Boston that day on a sightseeing bus and that night I took the boat, the Fall River Line down to New York, back to the seminary.

I was studying at Columbia University aiming for a Ph.D. in Political Science. I met most of the requirements, but I had never studied German. I had taken a lot of French and Latin and Greek and Hebrew—never good at any of them—but I had never had any German. My sister Lucy had been at the Deaconess School on the Cathedral grounds there near Columbia University and I was in and out there, and she or somebody told me there was one of the students there who had studied German, lived in Germany for several years, and she heard that I needed German and she volunteered to help me. That broke up my doctorate, and I married her instead of learning any German to amount to anything. I never did get my Ph.D. Later, the seminary there awarded me an honorary STD [Doctor of Sacred Theology], which is the only one that I ever received.

The school at Penland was my interest when I started out in the ministry. While I was still in the seminary studying for the ministry, the man who was bishop over this section of North Carolina talked over what I wanted to do, and I told him I wanted to come back to the mountains to do what I could here. He gave me a choice. The Episcopal Church had a school founded in 1842, Valle Crucis, in what is now Watauga County. It was first started as a training school for ministers who wanted to go to work in the rural sections, especially in the mountains. Later, it was changed into a boarding school for mountain girls that would train them as they would like to be trained, but who didn't have money enough to go off to school. The church owned quite a large tract of land there, several hundred acres, and the school was started and the Bishop was interested in it. He got people to come in to teach them, not only the academic subjects, but various industries. He established at one time, a dairy, including a cheese factory. He used part of it for some time as a poultry farm. He planted apple trees and raised apples commercially. Before industries came in and before electricity was brought in, he had erected a power plant for the immediate community.

His sister there was in charge of the school locally, but he wanted a minister there.

He offered me the choice of that position in this old established school or a farm at Penland where a man had tried to establish a school for mountain youth and had failed to make a go of it. He had just planted some apple trees on it because the one at Valle Crucis had done so well.

I chose Penland because it was virgin territory so far as the Episcopal Church was concerned, and I could determine the policy of it. I had been at Valle Crucis one summer studying, intending to write my Ph.D. thesis on that community, and one phase of the work there really distressed me. That was the "old clothes room" where people from the cities would send their old garments to be given or sold to the people—the so-called poor mountain whites. I didn't like that approach. I preferred the idea of training the mountain people in things that they could make a living at themselves and give them a sense of dignity.

There have always been those who have laughed at the idea of helping mountain people become economically self-sufficient. You probably know that President Theodore Roosevelt appointed a commission to study the Southern Appalachians, and they made a report on the conditions and some of the things that ought to be done, like preserving the forests. Most of those things were good, I thought. There was one man on the commission that disagreed with the findings of the majority and resigned. He wrote a book entitled *Child That Toileth Not*. I'm quite sure that that book is out of existence at the present time. I don't remember the man's name. I was in the seminary at the time and a friend of mine who was studying art was commissioned to paint a picture for the cover of the book. The author's point was that he thought this was no place for people to live, and he urged that the population of the southern mountains be moved down to the cotton mills where they could find labor and enough to eat. Well, I thought of course that it ought to be gone about in a different way.

People said, "Well, they have the mills down south. The mills can make the cloth and other products much faster than people can make them by hand, so it would never pay to develop the old crafts and teach the people." Even some of our church authorities were perfectly willing to ask the people in the cities to send old clothes and that sort of thing to help these "poor mountain whites." Help them out in *that* way and give them charity, so-called, but not help them become less dependent. They took that stand when my sister Lucy and I conceived the idea of developing the crafts at Penland.

I was always more in favor of the approval of men like John C. Campbell, who was a Presbyterian minister. The leaders in education, public health, crafts, recreation got together beginning back in 1913 under the leadership then of Dr. Campbell and explored through this mountain section to see what the needs really were. And Dr. Campbell envisioned the John C. Campbell Folk School at Brasstown. Unfortunately he died before it was actually put on the map, but his wife, Olive Dame Campbell, went ahead and with others who worked with her, established the school [still in existence today]. Meanwhile, Dr. Campbell organized what was called then the Mountain Workers' Conference. It met in 1913 in Atlanta. I was still in seminary. But the next year it met in Knoxville, and I met with them then and was a member and often a member of the board—one time chairman of the board—until after the Second World War, and that organization put out several reports on health, education, and religion.

Another significant thing that came out of that council was and is the Southern Highlands Handicraft Guild. They laid stress on quality work of handicrafts throughout the mountains. And they've established shops for handling the crafts. They have certain requirements for members. Sally Kesler is a member and John Bulgin down in Franklin is one in wrought iron. There are quite a number. The Guild has prospered. You'll find shops throughout the mountains that handle the products of these members of the Southern Highlands Handicraft Guild. [Their annual fairs in the summer in Asheville and the fall in Knoxville are the most popular, well-attended crafts fairs in the mountains.]

From that angle, the mountains are coming into their own, that is reviving the things that are their heritage here in the mountains.

So, as I said, I chose Penland and called it the Appalachian Industrial School. I spent the summer of 1913 there, although I was going back for further study at the seminary and Columbia University, then I came back spring of 1914. I fixed up an old log house there quite comfortably—it was just a plain cabin. Then there was an old farmhouse on the place, and I made it over into a school building with space for a couple of teachers to live and the classrooms. During that first year or two, we did what we could to put in plumbing. There wasn't any electricity then. We bought a site down on the Toe River, intending to put in a power plant for ourselves and the community.

We started in giving the first students, who were boys, a chance to work there on the farm—working in the orchard, helping with the plumbing, putting in a pumping station for the water, pumping it up to the buildings. We put up a building we called Ridgeway Hall, and then put up a simple, but more suitable, building for a family than the log cabin. Later on, it was used as a dormitory, and the people who followed me named it Morgan Hall. Instead of continuing, as I had planned it, a school for boarding pupils, learning farming, orchardry, so forth, they discovered there was a greater need for smaller children from broken homes, and so it was run by

Mr. Peter Lambert for a number of years. Then the church felt that the public schools and orphanages were adequate to take care of that type of work, so this was discontinued.

All the time I was planning with my sister Lucy to put in crafts, reviving the old hand weaving, spinning, basketmaking—teaching the women of the community these arts so they could earn money for things they needed in their homes—to give them a greater feeling of worth. But after I had been there for four years, I felt that I would have to leave Penland. The Bishop wanted me to travel, raising funds and begging money, going to Philadelphia and New York and other cities in the North. There were others doing the same kind of thing, and I was having to follow them. I didn't appreciate the methods some people used, and I felt that I couldn't do this.

Penland continued with Lucy heading it up. She had already taken some training in Chicago in weaving from a Mr. Worst. Later he came down to Penland to help her set up additional weaving classes. Then she got a lady,

PLATE 378   Reverend Morgan and his sister, Lucy, at the 1973 Siler reunion.

one of the few original people who is still there, to do the spinning and weaving, and she trained the local women in some of the crafts. They were then able to do things that they couldn't do otherwise—improve their houses, make curtains for their homes, give their children dental work, and do all sorts of things that made life somewhat better. One of the first things that she did was to have a log raising where the men came in and brought logs to make this log house for the weaving and spinning, and basketmaking and other crafts. Then she worked valiantly replacing one building that was on the property that had burned down, and erected a stone building that they called "The Pines." Then the men helped build a larger log building that is still used, and the women helped by feeding them.

They have a number of buildings now. Instead of remaining as a community project which she intended it to be, people began coming to take training from outside. They'd learned about the school because Lucy had to market things that were made there in order to purchase the materials and run the school. She attended the general church convention, which meets once every three years, in New Orleans in 1925, and took some of the materials, articles that had been woven. I was a delegate to that convention so I went down and helped her all I could in the marketing. After that, she went to various other conventions and people got acquainted with what Penland was doing until, before she retired, people were coming from forty-eight different countries besides all over the United States, some to learn the crafts and some to teach. From the Scandinavian countries, she got several teachers. [The Penland School is still operating today in Penland, North Carolina.]

I went down to South Carolina and ministered to three small churches in neighboring towns for a couple of years. During that time, there was the flu epidemic of the First World War.

That was 1918 and I was thirty-three years old. I lived in the little town of Barnwell, a characteristic lower South Carolina town. Sherman had come through during the War Between the States. He used the Episcopal church to stable his horses. I also had churches in a little town south of that, much newer, Allendale, and another town about the same distance, fifteen miles maybe. Each one had its points of interest. They were the old South Carolina type of communities. There in Barnwell, soon after I came, I was to have an evening service. I went down to the church and rang the first bell half an hour before service, turned on the lights, got ready, and five minutes before the service rang another bell, and nobody came. Well, I am rather a crank, I guess, about promptness, so I waited about fifteen minutes after the time for the service—no congregation. So I just turned off the lights, closed the door, and went on up the street. I met a group of the congregation. "Why, Mr. Morgan, what's the matter? Not going to have any service?"

I said, "I intended to, but there wasn't anybody there at service time."

"Well, we were going to church, and thought we had plenty of time."

So I went back and held the service. After that, they were prompt.

One thing that interested me there, because that's low country with sandy soil. They don't have clay the way we do here. Instead of just digging a grave for a funeral, they dig it and then a brick mason builds up the walls of the grave for fear it will cave in. Then after the casket is in place and the service over, he builds an arch above it, so that it is encased in brick. That was quite new to me, of course.

The school authorities where I was living in Barnwell were without a principal for the high school. They asked me to pinch hit for them. I said, "Well, provided you get a man just as soon as possible." For the whole year, they didn't find anybody else. Workers were scarce. So I did church work and the school work together, and during the flu epidemic I ministered through the Red Cross and saw more people die, I think, that year than I have in all the rest of my life. I ministered to the people out in the country and in the town, and then to the chain-gang Negroes, who lived in metal vans. I couldn't see why they didn't freeze to death.

I went from there to Chester, South Carolina, a mill town, and was there for six years. Then I went to Columbia [South Carolina], and there I was executive secretary and general missionary for the diocese of upper South Carolina. I visited churches that had been closed or without a minister and did various things—reorganizing congregations, etc. After five years of that, I became rector of St. John's Church there in Columbia. I enjoyed ten years there. They had a comparatively new stone church and were still in debt, and the vestry wanted me to jump right in to raising money to pay the debt on the church and on the pipe organ. I said, "Are they pressing us for the debt?"

"Well, not exactly. There it is and we're paying interest on it."

I said, "As I understood it, you called me here as your spiritual leader, and that's what I propose to try to be. If we take care of the spiritual life, the money part will take care of itself."

So we went ahead and built up the work in the Sunday school and the congregation. I spent ten very pleasant years there.

One thing that I remember with a great deal of pleasure was that I did some planting around the churchyard. There were some great stones that had been left over from building the church and I managed, with some help, to get them arranged in a circle serving as seats, and very often we'd have our young people's meetings there in that circle. I planted some roses back of the seats and later, after I had left, they put up a parish house right where that circle was. Some of my friends who were interested in flowers and gardening rescued one of the roses, took it home, and when they had an opportunity, they gave it to me, and it's growing out here in front of my porch. I planted another rose there next to the church, and I have started cuttings from it and have them growing here. Another thing that I did—those of us who were interested in flowers and trees formed a dogwood garden club and we planted dogwood trees along many of the streets and there at the church.

During the time that I was there, I served also as business manager for our summer conference grounds, Kanuga Lake outside of Hendersonville. I had had no experience in that sort of thing, but somehow we worked it out. I had had young people's camps for the Church in various other places before we took over Kanuga Lake on an option. We tried it in 1928, and liked it well enough and were able to raise enough money to purchase the buildings and a twenty-five-acre lake and four hundred acres of land. Fortunately we had a good dietician and other help. That first summer there were heavy rains and they washed out the dam to the lake. We had to have that rebuilt.

I've kept in contact with many of the boys and girls. Some of the men have gone into the ministry; one or two have become bishops. It renovated the life of the youth of the Church in the Carolinas, especially. Some came from other states.

We would spend summers there at Kanuga, except I would go back down to hold services at St. John's Church. All that time I was homesick for the mountains, and the work in this section here had gone down terribly. I heard the minister at St. Agnes Church in Franklin was leaving, so I got in touch with the Bishop and I came up to take charge of the work.

The first day of November 1940, a very significant day in our church calendar, All-Saints Day, was the day I returned to Franklin and Macon County, North Carolina.

The work in this section had gone down, mostly through neglect in our church and in some of the others. We treat the country work as a stepchild, do not support it, do not send good men, so some of the churches that our first ministry here in this area had established had been abandoned, some of them torn down. I wanted to begin to get them on their feet so I could reestablish them or establish new ones. Bishop Gribbin told me, when he asked me to come, to take charge of the church in Franklin, St. Agnes, and the Church of the Transfiguration in Highlands, and temporarily hold services over at Murphy. Well, that's a stretch—from Highlands to Murphy—of about eighty miles. So I started in with that and then I saw other needs.

The man who was conducting service at the colored church, St. Cyprians, lived in Asheville and came over to Franklin once a month. I asked them if they wouldn't like to have service every Sunday, and I gave them services. The church in Sylva was being neglected, so I called it to the attention of the Bishop. The next year, 1941, the minister who had been serving it from Waynesville resigned and went to Florida. So the Bishop said, "You see what you can do with it."

So I took charge of it. They had no minister and the church had been closed at Cullowhee, so I went over there and for the time being, as the church wasn't suitable to have service, I held services when I could at the Student Union. Then I had some funds that people had given me when I left Columbia, and I spent about four hundred dollars just patching things up so that the building wouldn't deteriorate. Later I got the women of the national church to give me ten thousand dollars to renovate the church and add a wing for students' activities and meetings.

Then I discovered that the Episcopal Church never had a service over at Cherokee, and since my people had always been friendly with the Indians, I started going over there and finally built the church from other gifts from the women of the church amounting to twenty thousand dollars.

I built another church over at Murphy, a colored church, and started a little congregation which has been abandoned since over at Andrews. I knew that I couldn't do an adequate job, but I wanted to start things going, and there are six of us working now in that same territory—eleven churches that I had charge of when I had to retire.

I think I started to tell you about my present love which has been my love ever since I was born—St. John's at Cartoogechaye.

The first Episcopal minister came to Cartoogechaye in 1877. At the urging of my grandmother, the Bishop sent him. He came without anything tangible to work with or to work on. He and his wife lived with my grandparents until he could get a log house built about a mile from here. That's right across from where St. John's Church stands. The stipend, or salary, in those days was very, very small. He would teach in the subscription schools —that is, people would send small sums to send their children. He would teach during the week, then minister on Sundays. The first church that he undertook to build was right across from where he lived in his log house. My grandparents gave the land, two acres, and according to his records, my mother was a contributor. That was the beginning of Reverend Deal's work. He says in the preface of the book, *Parish Register,* that he went North to get money to help build the original St. John's. He came in 1877 and he built the church about 1879. The first wedding that was performed in the church was that of my father, Alfred Morgan and my mother, Fanny Siler, according to the records. My parents were married in 1881 and my oldest sister was born in my grandparents' house in 1882, and then I was born there in 1885. I was baptized in the church.

It was only about six years later that my family moved over the mountain to Cherokee County. I remember that quite well. As far as St. John's was concerned, it went along fairly smoothly until that first minister, Deal, retired about 1909. There is no further record of services there, but the congregation went down through neglect, mostly. I can't find out just how long the church stood. After the building was torn down, the place was neglected, and the people who had loved ones buried there—most of them—moved the graves. There were a few left, those of Chuttahsotee and his wife, Cunstagih, and my mother's grave and two infants', and Mr. and Mrs. Gillespie, Mr. and Mrs. Oliver, and just one or two others. People supposed that the church grounds would go back into wilderness and that would be that.

While I was living in South Carolina, I heard that the church authorities were planning to sell the land where the church had been. I wrote to them and asked them to please not sell it, but if they did, to give me the chance of buying it because, when the graves were moved, some of our relatives wanted to move my mother's grave and the two infants, and I protested, so they didn't. I started whenever I could on vacations, before I moved up here, clearing out the underbrush and dreaming of building a church back. Just by raking and scraping, getting up what materials I could, I started the building and we held our first services there in 1945. I had moved back in 1940. We have continued since with just a handful. Last Sunday, for instance, we had seven in the congregation. Sometime in the summertime, there will be twenty-five or thirty. The church, with crowding in, will hold about forty-five people.

I had to retire from the other churches officially when I was seventy-two, because that's our age limit in the Episcopal Church. So that's been my only charge since that time—from seventy-two to eighty-nine. I say my only charge because there is another little chapel that we've finally built, nine miles beyond St. John's, in Rainbow Springs. I'd been holding services in the remnant of an old schoolhouse, one room, and then the people over there, the few of them, wanted a church. We had no money for it until 1962. We got together enough stone and started building just a very small chapel, which is an open air chapel—no walls to it—just a stone floor and stone altar, with locust posts to hold up the roof. The wall around the floor is high enough to sit on. During the summertime, we hold services up there, from May to October. That cost only a little over a thousand dollars to build, but I took that out of the offerings that St. John's had given.

In regard to money, St. John's is unique in the way of a church. We do not take up collections as they do in most churches, except when the Bishop is here. We always give to the Bishop, for his discretionary fund, the offerings when he is here; so in order to have it, we pass the plate. Otherwise, we just put a handmade pewter plate on the organ and those who know our

PLATE 379 View of St. John's Church at Cartoogechaye from the road.

PLATE 380 The cornerstone (arrow) of the church is the tombstone of Joanna Siler, Dr. Morgan's grandmother.

PLATE 381 The Siler cornerstone.

PLATE 382 The large plate-glass window behind the altar looks out into the forest behind the church.

PLATE 383 The church bell is housed in a unique belfry at the end of the walk leading to the church.

PLATE 384 Dr. Morgan's gravestone is already in place in the church cemetery. The back side, in simple lettering, reads: "Albert Rufus Morgan, 1885– . Thanks be to God who gives us the victory."

custom and want to put in something put it in after the service. So there's enough to take care of our expenses and to make a missionary donation to the Church. I do not and never have had a stipend or a salary [from St. John's].

As I grew older, I realized that I couldn't be on hand there many more years, and I began to think about what would happen to St. John's after I died, or became disabled. So I got a lawyer, relative of mine, to incorporate the St. John's Nonah Foundation, in order to start a fund and make it grow as fast as possible for a background fund to help look after somebody who would volunteer to do the same thing I've done—just to serve in a voluntary capacity to hold services up there after I'm gone. Well, the principal of that fund, like the cemetery fund, is not to be spent. Only the interest. And since it is for the continuance of the work after I die, even the interest is not to be spent until I have to give up.

Not long ago, a member of the church died who had been very faithful. She and her husband had volunteered to clean the church every little while, to repair the cushions, do various jobs that they saw needed to be done, and then after a while, she brought her tape recorder to the church and recorded the services. After her death, we received several gifts from five to twenty-five dollars in her memory for this fund. I have a friend down in South Carolina who, when she has a friend who dies, instead of sending flowers, sends a small check in memory of the friend for that fund. So it's slowly growing. If we get a gift not designated for anything special, we just add it to the fund.

The present church has been used about the same length of time that the old church was used. In the record for the old church, there were eight weddings recorded. Recently, I performed the forty-first wedding in the present church.

There are various things that are of interest to me. One is that a few years ago, I realized that people in my family would wonder what kind of marker to put at my grave, so I decided to make that decision for them. I got a lovely stone back in the mountains, got the monument man to put the lettering on it and to erect the stone where I want to be buried.

There are some boxwoods on the church grounds, some of them were given by a couple for whom I performed a wedding ceremony—one of the oldest couples that I've served in that way. The man was seventy-five when he got married to his second wife. Others were given by a family for whom I performed the marriage ceremony for their daughter. They do not belong to the Episcopal Church—one is Presbyterian, the other Roman Catholic— but they were doing some work around their place and they had some English boxwoods, and they asked me if we could use them at the church and I did. Besides that, I had done various plantings—bulbs, amaryllis, pink dog-

woods that somebody gave me, hydrangeas, and then where I needed a
break by a hedge, I planted one little hedge of white pines and another of
Canadian hemlocks. Then I planted some rhododendrons and various other
plants. We left quite a number of trees around the church, because I don't
like the barren look of a bulldozed lawn. That's one thing that has attracted
people to decide that they want to be buried there.

We try to minister to people no matter what church they belong to. We
have people buried here who are Baptists, Roman Catholics, Presbyterians,
Christian Scientists, whatever, but *before* they die, we try to minister to
them, too. Sometimes we have groups who come in there who are on a re-
treat asking my permission for meditations, and sometimes they request that
I give them a holy communion service, and I do. I don't question to what
church they belong. I am just happy that I can minister to them in any
spiritual way. That has been my interest so far as the church is concerned
here in these latter years.

I am quite handicapped. I've got to the point where I can hardly read at
all unless I use a very strong lens, so I read the portions of Scripture over
and over again through the week to memorize the passage, and then I'm
ready on Sunday to conduct the service. Sometimes I get what we call a lay
reader, and he will help to read the lessons or the songs in a service. I can't
memorize all the songs, so when I lead them, I choose some of the shorter
ones that I have memorized in times past. I hold services there twice most
Sundays—Communion at 8:00 Sunday morning and Morning Prayer, or
Litany, at 11:00, and then in the summertime a third service at 4:00 in the
afternoon in the Chapel of the Ascension up on the mountain. Naturally, I
can't tell how long I can continue, but I am on the lookout for somebody
who, after he retires from the active ministry, will take over on the same
basis that I've been carrying on these last few years.

I haven't mentioned a couple of things that gratified me. One is that several years ago, maybe twenty-five years ago, I was chosen as the rural pastor
of the year for the state of North Carolina. This was not denominational
but out of the whole bunch, and that pleased me.

And after I'd been out of the seminary for thirty years, the General Theological Seminary, from which I graduated, awarded me the honorary degree of Doctor of Sacred Theology, and that's the reason that a good many
people call me "Doctor."

But many of those who knew me before I received the doctor's degree
just call me Mr. Morgan. Some of them have the habit of calling me Uncle
Rufus, or if they are approaching my age, of course they call me Rufus, so I
come to any of the calls. Some people call me other things that I do not like
so well. Some call me Preacher Morgan, and that seems to indicate that a
minister doesn't do anything but get up and preach once a week. I think a

minister's duty is much more than that. Some people call me Father Morgan and I don't like that because Christ somewhere said, "Let no man call thee Father. You have one Father, Who is in Heaven." But in certain areas of our church, the ministers encourage people to call them "Father," Father Smith, Father Jones, etc., because they like the formality of it, the distinction of it—the old idea of the Middle Ages of "father confessor," but I don't like it. Christ's reason, as I gather it from the Scripture, gave instructions to keep His followers from being proud. Most of us like the distinction of being noticed by people, and if they call you "Father," you sit up a little straighter and no matter how high you go, even the Pope of Rome—that's what "pope" means, "papa, father"—I don't think it ministers to the spiritual humility. Christ always taught humility. When James and John, the two brothers, wanted special places at Christ's side when His kingdom was established, He rebuked them. He said it was not His to give. It was for those who earn it.

We knew that Dr. Morgan had done much work with the Boy Scouts and Girl Scouts. In fact, he was awarded the Silver Beaver award, the highest honor of a volunteer working with the Boy Scouts. He didn't really tell us a lot about his work. To him, there was not too much extraordinary about it. To be with young people and help them out is just an everyday thing for him.

For most of my life since 1920, I have been connected in one way or another with the Boy Scouts—scoutmaster, district chairman, member of the council board. I'm still an honorary member of the Daniel Boone Council which is this western end of North Carolina.

My first contact was down in South Carolina, back in 1920. I didn't know much about scouting, but I knew that the boys needed some activity, and so I had the bunch of boys down there at Chester get a troop together.

I had a rather amusing experience when I got to working with them. We had a ministerial group and they called me to task for starting the scout work without consulting them. I thought it was none of their business. If I saw a need, then I tried to meet it.

While I was working with the scouts there, some of the younger boys, under twelve, wanted activity, so I got them together and then I discovered that in England and in Canada, they had what was called the "Wolf Cubs" (the Cub Scouts, now); so, I sent for literature for the younger boys, and we tried to follow that.

Then when I left Chester and went to Columbia, we had a troop under the sponsorship of the St. John's Church of Columbia. And then when I came up here, we had a troop connected with St. Agnes in Franklin, because I lived down there for a few years after I came back. I went out with them a lot camping and studying wild life and so forth.

I was elected district chairman for the Boy Scouts in this district, and then became a member of the Daniel Boone Council, and later I was also on the board of the Nantahala Council of the Girl Scouts. They later merged with the Pisgah Council, which now includes this territory.

We hiked the mountains—the Boy Scouts and I. I used to get them to help me with the Appalachian Trail maintenance that goes the length of the Nantahalas.

Dr. Morgan has also been an active member of the Appalachian Trail Conference for many years. He has hiked parts of the Appalachian Trail in New Hampshire, Vermont, Virginia, and Tennessee. He's hiked practically all of it in North Carolina and down to the end of the Trail in Georgia. He is still an avid hiker, in spite of very poor vision.

The first meeting that I attended of the Appalachian Trail Conference was at Fontana Dam, North Carolina. At that meeting, a change was decided upon which displeased me then and has ever since. I've been over the section of the Trail through the Smoky Mountains National Park and loved it very much. At that time, the Trail extended from the northeastern end of the park to the southern end, going over Gregory Bald and Parsons Bald down to the highway leading to Maryville, Tennessee. Fontana Village, a resort village, was off the Trail. Probably under the influence of the place of our meeting, a motion was made that the southern end of the Trail through the park be changed, and come down a side ridge of the Smokies which is called Shuckstack, on across the Fontana Dam, and then come into the Trail as it then was, on Yellow Creek. Well, to me, Gregory Bald and Parsons Bald are two of the most beautiful sections of the Trail. I'd been over them and remember especially one trip when a group of us camped at a spring on the side of Gregory Bald, having no tent but just sleeping out. We built up a fire near the spring, and about ten o'clock rain came. Well, we got up and chunked up the fire and tried to keep as warm as possible until morning. By the time we started out in the morning, the rain had ceased and we climbed up Gregory Bald. And there greeted us one of the loveliest scenes that I've ever witnessed. We were above the clouds which had settled down in the valleys, and we looked over the expanse of clouds, seeing only an occasional island where a mountain peak came above the clouds. Then the sun rose. There we were on the top of the world.

Well, that is what the Appalachian Trail, I thought and still think, ought to be . . . a wilderness trail, foot trail. And to change it from a scene like that to a recreational area of commercial interests seemed to me incongruous. I objected to the change, but as I remember it, I was the only one to object. I guess I was the only native mountaineer in the group. Anyway, that's the only section of Trail, that new route, in the southeast down into Georgia, that I've never been over, and I doubt if I ever will.

Going along the Appalachian Trail, you get all of the beauties that you could ask for in the way of majestic trees, wild flowers of various kinds at different times of the year. Going north from the southern end between Siler Bald and Clingmans Dome, the highest peak in the Smokies, you come across wood lilies, purple-fringed orchids, and all sorts of other wild flowers. Going on from Clingmans Dome to Newfound Gap, I remember one memorable trip under the leadership of Arthur Stupka, who was formerly the naturalist in the park. All along the way from Indian Gap to Newfound Gap, during that late April day, we came across carpets of spring beauty— trout lily, trillium, and other wild flowers. Then going on north from there, you strike other areas just as beautiful—witches hobble barely coming out at that time of year coming into full bloom later, then changing later still to the foliage that turns sometimes a yellow, sometimes bronze, like others of the viburnum family. Then, of course, at different times of the year you run across trees in bloom—sarvis trees, as we call them, or service as they are otherwise called; silverbell; and later mountain ash. Then, in their turn, the shrubs, like the red elderberry with its beautiful white blooms in the spring and then later on their brilliant red berries. Then the various members of the heath family, like the azaleas and rhododendron, sand myrtle, and such a great variety of the wild flowers.

If you go north on the Appalachian Trail for two and a half miles, there is a trail called the Boulevard Trail, that turns left and follows a spur ridge into Tennessee, which leads out to Mt. LeConte which is the third highest mountain in the Smokies. That is one of my favorite mountain climbs. It is 6,593 feet. It has many advantages—wonderful lookout to the west to watch the sunset, and then in the morning the beautiful coloring before sunrise, and then the sunrise itself at Myrtle Point, so-called because the sand myrtle grows beautifully up there. And then there is a lodge on top of LeConte and a shelter for hikers. There used to be a campground, but the campers left so much litter that finally the Park Service forbid camping, but if you get ahead of the other fellow, you can make reservations and get a permit to camp in the shelter.

Another advantage of Mt. LeConte is that it is accessible only by trails— no road up there. I like that because an automobile road destroys the spirit of the mountains. One of the trails, Rainbow Falls Trail, is the one that the pack horses come up to bring provisions for the lodge. You have comfortable accommodations up there and you can get your supper and breakfast, quite hearty meals, and you need them up there. Then the next day you can come down. Quite often you run across bear up there. They're not apt to

PLATE 385   Rufus Morgan on his way up Mt. LeConte.

harm you, although sometimes they rather resent interference, but as a rule they're just looking for something to eat. That's not a very serious thing unless they get at your supply that you're depending on for the next day or two.

As you look out toward the sunrise, you're looking toward the main ridge of the Smokies, and the sun rises sometimes to the right, sometimes to the left of a mountain which is the second highest in the Smokies, Mount Guyot. It's a pyramid sort of peak and you always look for it. The Appalachian Trail doesn't actually go up to the top of Mt. Guyot, but circles around to the left as you go north. You can break through the fallen timber and seedling firs or balsam and get up there to the top, but you don't get a very good view because of the seedling balsams, but it's nice to get up on top.

There are sections of the Trail that are very lovely. You go farther north out of the park and find Roan Mountain. Many years ago, there was a hotel right up on top, but it burned down or was torn down. I've been up there when that was the only sign of having been trodden upon that was there. There had been a furnace room under the old hotel, and I've slept in that depression where the furnace room was, and let the wind blow over me. On one trip I came across a man who lived not too far away, and he told me about his father telling him that he had been up there many times when the mountain grass was luxuriant, and he could see the deer, especially with their antlers, going through the grass, and you could just see the movement of their bodies. I was interested in the southern approach to Roan Mountain one time, and saw quite a lot of wild larkspur. I believe that's the only place in North Carolina that I have seen it. Years before, I had seen it up in the mountains of Virginia around Dante. It was in abundance up there. Likewise, up there I had seen a great many beechnuts. I find beechnuts in North Carolina, but they very seldom mature. They don't have any nut inside, but up there in Virginia, they were very abundant.

I spoke of the meeting of the Appalachian Trail Conference. We meet every three years. It is a wonderful fellowship and the group is made up of representatives of the hiking clubs that maintain the Appalachian Trail from Maine to Georgia—two thousand miles. They meet at various points from north to south. The last meeting, 1972, was up in New Hampshire. I went up to that, did a little hiking on the Trail up there. A few years before, there was one up in Vermont and I attended that and got onto the Trail. And then there was one up in Pennsylvania and before that in the Virginia mountains and then one in Cashiers in our adjoining county. The next meeting is to be in 1975 in Boone, North Carolina, in the Watauga section. I hope to get to that. [He, in fact, did make the meeting.] At several of these meetings, they allow me to conduct the sunrise service which is a privilege I appreciate very much.

Boone, where this next meeting is to be held, is near the crest of the Blue Ridge Mountains and there are some wonderful hikes along there, especially Grandfather Mountain, which contains, so geologists tell us, the oldest mountain mass in the world. The mountains through there, I have been told, were at one time higher than the Himalayas are now . . . perhaps 39,000 feet, which is quite impressive. Grandfather Mountain was my pet mountain to climb before I learned about LeConte. On the Monday after the meeting of the A. T. Conference, I have a date with one person to go up Grandfather Mountain, and since they "civilized" that one end of the mountain, I go up the other end. In a way, I like that even better. There's the beginning of an old trail, the Calloway Trail, not used much now, near Linville Falls, and this is where we'll go in. It goes up to the Calloway Peak, which is considerably higher than the one they've messed up. The balsams and the mountain ash grow up there. The balsams, by the way, grow as far south as the Smoky Mountains. If you're going south from Clingmans Dome over Siler Bald, all of a sudden they give out, and you have hardwood trees from there south. Farther south than that, you never see balsams or fir, except where they've been planted. I have some in my yard, which I cherish very much.

It's been a pleasure to work with the A. T. Conference. I was on the board for about thirty years, but six years ago they thought they needed younger blood, and so they accepted my resignation. However, I shall always be just as interested in the Conference and the Trail.

It's difficult to keep the Appalachian Trail as a wilderness foot trail because the Wildlife Commission tries to protect the game and doesn't allow shooting of deer along the way, and they plant pastureland in open spaces along the Trail. To get in with their machinery, they make jeep roads, which interfere with the Trail. And then there are always people who want to bring in horses for horseback riding or bring in motorcycles for riding along the Trail, but the organization as it was originally intended and is so designated now by the U. S. Government is for foot travel only. There have been some objections to the Trail going over private land, but the objection stems from the misuse of the Trail by motor vehicles and horses, and not from the foot travelers.

The headquarters of the A. T. Conference were in Washington for a number of years, but recently they have moved to Harpers Ferry, West Virginia, which is right on the Trail, and which is much more satisfactory than a big city like Washington. They get more visits from hikers, and it's a better atmosphere for the meetings.

The Appalachian Trail was conceived of back about 1920, but I used to hike over the mountains here nearly twenty years before that. I can remember hiking from the adjoining county to which we moved, over here to my grandparents' home when I was twelve or fifteen years old, sometimes the whole distance—sixty miles. Sometimes I'd take the train to Andrews, cutting it down to forty miles. Sometimes we'd come by covered wagon, but usually just hiking, and we always rejoiced when we got to the border of Macon County, because that was coming home.

The Siler Bald here in the Nantahalas was named for my great-grandfather, William Siler. He ranged cattle back in there and was one of the prominent citizens of the area. That was probably the reason it was named for him. I've hiked up it many times, slept on the side of it. There is a shelter on the Appalachian Trail, right on the slope of it. Then there is the other Siler Bald in the Smokies named for Uncle Jesse Siler, who used to range cattle back in there. And there's another mountain nearby named for my grandfather, Albert Siler, Albert Mountain. You can see that between

Rabun Gap and Franklin. There's a fire tower on it, on the Appalachian Trail.

The only botany that I had in school was just one course one year when I was in high school. I didn't learn very much. My mother loved the wild flowers, and my father liked everything in nature. If you look there on the bookshelves sometime, you'll see that I have several wild-flower books and some on trees. There are so many things that you can pick up if you just keep your eyes open. I've also had the good fortune to know people who were botanists, or knew quite a lot about it. I knew Mr. Arthur Stupka for years, a naturalist for the Smoky Mountain National Park, and I shared with him some programs at the Penland School. Then I used to attend what they called the Wild Flower Pilgrimage over in the Smokies at Gatlinburg the last week in April. Members of the botany faculty at the University of Tennessee in Knoxville used to lead some of those hikes, and so I knew them, got a little information from them. And if you once become bitten with the interest in wild flowers, you find leads. Like the orchids—you get accustomed to noticing the characteristics of the blooms and the kinds of places that they grow, and you follow these signs.

I have one book on our wild orchids. Then there are the ferns, which are not wild flowers, because they have no blooms, but they are plants. When you once find out that the way to identify ferns is to examine the sori or spore pods, they'll tell you just where they belong, and what the name is. You must just observe well enough. And then, of course, you have to have a fern book, and fortunately there are some very good ones. One that I used for years was by Dr. Blumquist, who is head of the botany department at Duke University. It is *Ferns of North Carolina*. You will discover that there is one native American fern which is a climbing fern, the Hartford fern. I understand that that is the only climbing fern in this country. There is a Japanese climbing fern; I got some roots of that last year from a friend in Columbia. The native climbing fern is quite interesting.

After telling us quite a lot about ferns and wild flowers, Dr. Morgan turned to recent highway development that has taken place right at his property line. A super-highway has been built in his front yard.

The building of this new four-lane highway has distressed me. And all that goes with it. I've sometime said that I wish a bulldozer had never been invented. I can say that with a good deal of conviction. There is much in our present world that distresses me, because it seems to me that the emphasis on the part of modern man is exactly contrary to the standards of Christ.

The emphasis on commercialism, including our government's emphasis on cutting the timber, clear-cutting, which is devastation in my language, and people coming in with the modern ideas of standards, not valuing our traditional values here in the mountains, not valuing what you can do with your hands, and handing out money to purchase a lot to build on, and in that way reducing the possibility of the mountain people making a living on their lands—all that bothers me. Having a government that doesn't know its financial limits and is dominated by commercial groups, it's hard to hold on to anything. For instance, you have your lobbyists in Washington for modern machinery. They are pressing our legislators all the time for roads, bigger roads, straighter roads. They're not thinking about the people along the way. They're thinking about getting work for their machines, and sales for their machines. They're backed up by commercial interests that want to come in, by the tourist trade that wants the most direct route to get in, the fastest way to get in. And the Forest Service is tainted by the same paint. They want to sell timber. And one of their principal pleas is, "If we don't cut the timber, then your schools will be without the income that comes from a certain percentage of the returns from timber from your national forests." So you have pressures on every side. We worship money.

The Forest Service is threatening to build a road up the Nantahala River and across Deep Gap down the other side into Georgia to connect up with a highway down there. This is just cutting through national forests. And then another group is threatening to establish a recreational area in the corner of the three states, Georgia, North Carolina, and South Carolina. It includes much of Macon County, and you know what that would mean, of course. Commercial interests would come in to cater to the tourists, and just spoil the whole area.

I've never been enamoured very much by the tourist idea. For instance, when I was connected with our church camp and conferences over near Hendersonville, every little while somebody would want to organize a group to go to the Vanderbilt estates (in Asheville). I'm sure they're very beautiful, but they're manmade, and I'd much prefer going back into Pisgah Forest, which Vanderbilt also owned and turned over to the government, so I've never been to the Vanderbilt estates.

I've been on the radio recently for morning devotions—the local station. I took the very simplest thing that I could think of for my subject—the Lord's Prayer. One morning I spoke on the petition for material things: "Give us this day our daily bread." Not overflowing bins, not millions of tons for our own profit, but give *us*—the people who *need* everywhere, and let us realize that it's given to us to supply our *needs*. I quoted St. Paul, "Let him that stole, steal no more, but rather let him labor, working with his hands that he may have to give to him that needeth." And then Christ, "Be not anxious for your life, what ye shall eat, or what ye shall drink, or yet for your body, what ye shall put on."

And that, to my way of thinking, is exactly contrary to what we are actually engaged in now. We are beginning to discover that that can't satisfy our needs. The fact that so many people are held for ransom is an indication that the people who are trying to get it from the millionaires, realize that the millionaires shouldn't have it. And the hijackings are in the same category, as is the scandal in our government. It's all the result of man's being completely occupied in the thing that Christ told us not to do. Of course, it leads to the downgrading in our estimation of God's creation. In building our roads, we are influenced by politicians, by big business, by people who make the modern machinery to grade the roads. They grade the roads in order that man might have higher speed. We come up against the situation that we have, for we've just been overreaching ourselves, cheating ourselves, by going too fast, too far. That sort of thing is distressing.

Sometime back I went in to see a lawyer to get a deed made, giving to my daughter and her husband their part of my property. I have very, very little. I bought some of it for around twenty-five dollars an acre. A man from Florida sometime ago wanted to know what I would take for it. I said, "It isn't for sale."

"Well, if I offered you twenty thousand dollars for this little tract, would you take it?"

I said, "No, it's not for sale, anymore than my children are for sale."

"Well, I think I could get twenty-five thousand for it for you."

I said, "No, it's not for sale."

Well, of course, it's for sharing. My daughter and her husband—he's retiring—are moving back here and I'm giving that part of it to them. I love my place, and I've planted most of the trees and the shrubs and other plants on it. I've loved each one of them, and that's what it means to me—it's God creation. We go roughshod over the whole thing. The business people and those who live on business are against the idea of saving those things or establishing wilderness areas. The Franklin *Press,* our local newspaper, *fights* against the idea of wilderness areas, which might be kept for our descendants in all their primitive beauty and grandeur, because it will take a few dollars of our tax money which comes back to the county when we cut down the trees in the national forests. It's that sort of thing, you see—we're just in it for the dollar, for the accumulation to ourselves, regardless of the destruction that we're bringing on our world.

But I hope we'll wake up in time. In the meantime, I walk along the trails in the Smoky Mountain National Park and my companion stops and he says, "Listen to the silence." We had left the bulldozers, speeding cars, other machinery, down here. We go up there where there's peace.

What brought me back to these mountains was my heart. My mother loved them intensely, as had my grandparents and great-grandparents. It was just inbred. I've loved this place all my life. When we used to come back and forth from Cherokee County, over here where the county line is marked (between Macon and Cherokee counties), coming this way we'd get down and kiss the earth, because we loved it so. When we'd go back, we would get down and kiss Macon County good-by.

When I was fifteen years old, I came across the mountains for a wedding in the family. When I went back home, I took back with me three seedlings of the Canadian hemlock; and planted them out over there. One of them is still living at the old homeplace.

The cabin that my daughter and her husband are fixing up is the first home that I can remember. My people moved into it when I was three years old, as I've told you. When I was a child, we used to play on the big rocks that are still in the backyard. We'd rake up leaves and play various games in them. A group of us would bury some of the rest of us under the leaves and then when they were ready, we would say, "Rise, Jupiter, snuff the moon." And those under the leaves would get up and scatter the leaves everywhere. Oh, there are so many memories! Climbing the chinquapin tree—there aren't any such now, but there was one back here on the knoll then. There was another one over at the cabin that we used to climb and shake the chinquapins down. It's just all in my blood. I've watched my grandfather here in this room with his post office there in the corner, attending to the mail, and I've loved those white oaks out in the yard—three lovely ones. And the hemlocks!

Well, to me it's just too beautiful for words. They have succeeded in spoiling some of it, like building the roads, but they can't take away the mountains as they stretch along here.

I can't express it, but somebody will have to prove to me that it isn't as lovely as I think it is before I will be convinced.

These last years, since 1940 to 1975, have been particularly happy, both within the church and in my relationships with other people in activities that I've been able to carry on—climbing mountains, studying God's hand in His creation, and the increasing number of friends—it's all been very lovely.

A little question in our prayer book, in the section called "Offices of Instruction" is: "What is your bounden duty as a member of the church?" The answer is: "My bounden duty is to follow Christ, to worship God every Sunday in His church, to work, to pray and to give for the spread of His kingdom." And if you want it expressed in a prayer, I can think of nothing finer than that which is called the Prayer of St. Francis of Assisi: "Oh, Lord, our Christ, may we have thy mind and thy spirit, make us instruments of thy peace. Where there is hatred, let us sow love; where there is injury, pardon; where there is discord, union; where there is doubt, faith; where there is despair, hope; where there is darkness, light; where there is sadness, joy. Oh, divine Master, grant that we may not so much seek to be consoled as to console; to be understood, as to understand; to be loved, as to love; for it is in giving, that we receive. It is in pardoning that we are pardoned, and it is in dying to self that we are born to eternal life."

I've been trying to live by that.

UPDATE

*S*ince publication of The Foxfire Book, Foxfire 2, *and* Foxfire 3, *we've come across additional material—or had new experiences—that relates to subjects covered in those volumes. In some cases, information was sent to us by readers who, by virtue of their background or research, had accurate knowledge of customs or beliefs common in our part of the mountains, and their expertise was welcomed.*

SASSAFRAS TEA

An unexpected visit paid to Pearl Martin might find her in the woods behind her house digging roots for tea—most likely sassafras roots.

Sassafras is a wild plant that grows in the Appalachians. Left alone, this plant grows into a medium-sized tree with an irregularly shaped trunk. The spicy, distinct flavor of sassafras makes the tea a popular beverage, served hot or cold. It is also used frequently in the Appalachians as a diaphoretic and diuretic medicine.

Pearl makes sassafras tea, and she also uses the tea to make jelly. Mint and spicewood teas, although not Pearl's specialties, are also made in her home from mint leaves and spicewood stems she gathers in the woods. Pearl has a field behind her house which she keeps bogged down (cleared of brush) to allow her sassafras to grow freely. When the sassafras reaches bush height, she digs it for tea.

Pearl told us that she could gather the roots any time of the year without affecting the taste of the tea. However, the roots should be gathered young, so they will be tender.

PLATE 386 Pearl digging some sassafras bushes in the woods behind her house with her hoe.

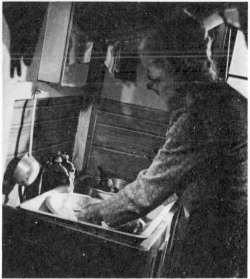

PLATES 387–388 She chops the roots from the plants, then washes the roots in cold water.

PLATE 389 Next she scrapes off the outer layer of bark and discards it. Either the roots or the bark can be used in making the tea, but Pearl prefers the roots. They can be used dried or green.

PLATE 390 She brings the roots to a boil in water. The longer they are boiled, the stronger the tea. To make a gallon of tea, she boils four average-sized roots in a gallon of water for fifteen to twenty minutes. She then strains it, and serves it either hot or iced, sweetened with either sugar or honey.

Pearl's recipe for sassafras jelly, which is made from the tea itself follows: To make the jelly, mix one package of Sure-Jell with eight cups tea in a large saucepan. Bring quickly to a hard boil, stirring occasionally. Now add eight cups sugar and bring to a full rolling boil. Boil hard one minute, stirring constantly. Skim off the foam with a metal spoon. Pour at once into jelly jars and seal with paraffin.

Bit Carver and Annette Sutherland. Photographs by Russell Arthur.

PLANTING A GINSENG PATCH

Several weeks after. Buck Carver showed us how to build a still furnace (see "Building a Still Furnace"), he came by and asked if we had noticed the ginseng plant down by the still. We said we hadn't. So Buck said, "Let's go take a look at it." We all went down to the still.

At first Buck wouldn't show the plant to us: he wanted us to spot it ourselves. When we couldn't find it, he pointed toward it and smiled as we all recognized it. He said he thought we ought to move it to another place, "To keep it from being tramped down. People will always be in here looking this still over, and ever so many of them won't know what sang is and will step

PLATE 391   Left to right: Buck, Jeff Hay, and Tom Powers dig the plant Buck found.

PLATE 392 Buck with another plant he found nearby. He said, "I *have* dug them with just over a hundred berries on them. [The ball of berries then] is bigger than a golf ball. They're a pretty thing to look at, too. It's a beautiful thing."

on it. And then a few of them *will* know what it is, and they might stick it in their pocket and take it off."

Buck told us to pick the berries off the plant, and I stuck them in one of my top shirt pockets; then he dug the plant up and took off the fat roots, which I put in my other shirt pocket. Then he gave us each a few leaves and sent us out into the woods to see if we could find any more plants. We found four or five plants that day and dug them up. Buck told us to replant them in dark ground shaded by poplars and hickories close to Wig's house. Buck said, "If we don't put it here, someone will get it. Now Wig can sit on his porch and watch his sang patch, by the way, and do his work too. You got to keep an eye on that stuff. There's people that will steal *that* stuff that wouldn't steal bread to eat. That's 'cause it's so expensive. And the big reason it's so expensive is that it's so scarce."

He showed us how to plant both the roots and the berries, setting them out just under the ground and raking leaves back over them. And while we were planting them, he told us what the roots were good for:

"Now I'll tell you something that stuff will do. One morning about thirty years ago we lived over here at Brian Kelly's, and I took a notion to go up over in Joe Cove sang hunting. I said [to my wife], 'Have you got anything left from breakfast that I could take for lunch?'

"She said, 'I got a few baked sweet potatoes and a few rashers of meat and some biscuits.'

"I said, 'That's aplenty. Throw them together.'

"So she split some of the biscuits, and put some meat between them and throwed in two or three baked sweet potatoes. And my ulcer was giving me a fit at that time, and sweet potatoes would set it afire. Well, I never thought, you know.

"Well, I went on over there in that cove and dug a pretty good bunch of sang. Come dinnertime and I sat down and eat. Well, when I ate them sweet potatoes, just in a few minutes I was a'burning. Oh brother, how sick I was. I throwed up my socks I think. Down on my hands and knees a'gagging and retching and trying to vomit and sometimes I could and sometimes I couldn't.

"Pappy Swanson was right down below me in a field cutting some tops, and tell you the truth, a time or two I thought I would die. I was so sick I come in a little of hollering for Pappy to come up there and help me get out of them woods. I was afraid to start out of there by myself. I was so sick I couldn't see nothing, and it was just as full of rattlesnakes and copperheads as it could be in that country.

"I thought, 'Well, Lordamercy, Pappy's working and I don't want to bother him.' I'd crawl out to the branch and drink water every few minutes and here it would come just as soon as it got warm. I'd just throw it up, and the burning in that stomach, oh boy, was just like a ball of fire in there.

"After a while, I got to studying, 'Well, maybe if I wash a root of this sang and chew it, it can't make it no worse and it might help me a little.' And I crawled out there to the branch and washed a root of that stuff good and clean, took my knife and cut me off some little bites and put them in my mouth and chewed it and swallowed that juice and spit the pummies out. The pummies wouldn't have hurt me a bit to have swallowed them; they probably would have helped me, but I didn't want to swallow them so I just spit them. And you know it wasn't no time till I didn't have no pain in my stomach or nothing.

"And I got up from there and I went on and sang hunted until durn near night. And that's how good that was on that. It's the only thing I took, and it's all I had to take. Boys, I was miserable, I'm telling you. I thought my time had come there.

"And then you can chop it up right fine, or let it get good and dry and put it on a food chopper or a sausage mill and grind it up and drop it into a bottle of whiskey. And you don't take a bath in it! You just pour you out a little of it if you take diarrhea or dysentery, and I mean you can have it bad. Pour you out a little of it in a teacup and strike a match to it and set it afire. It'll catch afire and burn. Burn it until that cup will be so dang hot you can't hold it to your lips. You'll have to pour it over into another cup that ain't had the fire in it. Drink it while it's good and hot. It's a bitter dose—I don't mean maybe. And you don't have to drink much of it. Two or three swallows. Turn it up and drink it, and if that don't stop that diarrhea you better get to a drugstore or to a doctor's office and don't lose no time getting there.

"And another thing—old-timers used to go a'courting, and they were nearly always ashamed to eat dinner with their girls and so forth, you know. And their intestines would get to growling because they'd get empty. They'd always carry a little piece of sang in their pocket and chew them a little piece of that sang and they'd stop that. They called it guts growling. And it'd stop them things from growling, too, I mean. It's embarrassing. _____ said he guessed he'd eat a pound of it to keep them from growling in front of his girl."

When we had them all planted, Buck told us to get some water in buckets from Wig's house. When we brought it, he poured it gently over the loose soil to help settle the dirt and give the roots a good start.

TOM POWERS

Article by Tom Powers, Jeff Hay, Wendy Guyaux, and Lynn Butler.

APPLE CIDER

In the early fall, the *Foxfire* class went to visit Mrs. Harry Brown of the Betty's Creek Community who showed us how to make tasty, old-fashioned cider. The entire class loaded into Wig's truck and headed out to the Browns'.

Upon arriving, we were greeted by Mr. and Mrs. Brown and Aunt Arie Carpenter. Aunt Arie had come over from her home in North Carolina to witness the cider making and to visit with some of her friends.

Mrs. Brown had the equipment and apples ready to start making the cider. This consisted of the cider press itself, washed apples, pans to catch the juice, or cider, in, and cheesecloth to strain the cider through. Of course there were cups and a pitcher for us to sample the cider as soon as it was poured.

Mrs. Brown explained to us that she and Mr. Brown prefer to use a proportion of half sour and half sweet apples to make their cider. One can use any type of apples available, and to make the cider sweeter or more tart, you only have to add more sweet apples or more sour apples.

The cider is preserved by either canning or freezing. Mrs. Brown felt that

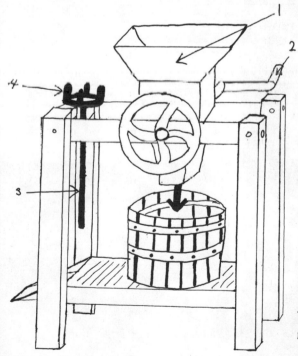

PLATE 393 Diagram of a cider mill. The apples are placed whole into the wooden hopper (1) as the mill crank (2) is turned. The apple pulp comes out the bottom of the mill (arrow) and drops into a slatted, bottomless tub. When the tub is full, it is moved to the left under the screw (3). A wooden disc is fitted into the top of the tub, and the screw (which fits into a metal socket in the top of the disc) is turned by means of the crank (4), thus pressing the disc down onto the apple pulp and squeezing all the juice out. While one person is squeezing the juice, another places a second slatted tub under the mill and begins crushing another round of apples.

the process of canning took away the "fresh apple" taste of the cider. She prefers freezing her cider in plastic containers.

Aunt Arie told us how the old people used to make their cider without a cider press. A wooden trough with holes drilled in the bottom, was filled with apples. A maul was then used to mash or crush the apples. Then a plank was pressed down on top of the apples to squeeze the juice out. The cider was then stored in wooden barrels, some in the springhouse for drinking, and some to be used for vinegar after aging.

Some of the class was curious about the difference between the taste of apple cider—which we made—and apple juice. According to some of the ladies in the community, apple juice is made by slicing the apples and boiling them in a small amount of water. Then the liquid is poured off this and either canned or frozen. Apple cider is the juice extracted from the crushed apples, as we have explained above.

Text by Phil Conner, Joey Fountain, and Keith Head.
Photographs by Rusty Leggett; diagram by Tom Carlton.

PLATE 394 Tom Carlton and Bit Carver feed whole apples into the hopper.

PLATE 395 The wooden disc is placed over the pulp in the slatted tub, and the tub is positioned under the screw.

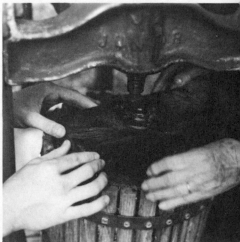

PLATE 396 Tommy Lamb, using a board for extra leverage, turns the handle of the screw to press the juice out. Matt Young and Jim Renfro begin to fill a second tub with pulp.

PLATE 397 Cider comes pouring from the tub as the pulp is squeezed.

PLATE 398 Suzy Angier holds the cheesecloth as Mrs. Brown pours one tubful of juice through it. She then gathers the ends of the cheesecloth and squeezes the bundle to force all the juice through. It is now ready to drink.

BLEACHING APPLES

We have mentioned bleaching apples as a means of preservation (*The Foxfire Book,* pages 181–82), but had never had the process demonstrated to us. Recently we heard that Mrs. Edith Parker was going to bleach some apples for the winter, and we asked her if she would show us how.

Mrs. Parker has lived in Rabun Gap all of her life. Her children attended our school. Since both Mr. and Mrs. Parker have regular jobs away from home, they share the chores at home. Together they bleach about one and a half bushels of apples a year. She prefers bleached apples over dried apples because she feels they are easier to prepare. Both her grandmother and mother have bleached apples in the past using the method they passed on to her. One of her fondest memories is of her grandmother's churn full of bleached apples. The kids would just pull out some and eat them. In the middle of winter, they were like fresh apples to them. They have the taste and consistency of apples cooked briefly without sugar or spices.

As well as bleaching apples, Mrs. Parker also cans corn, beans, and tomatoes, and makes her own jellies. She makes pickled beans, pickled corn, and sauerkraut.

Apples are usually bleached in late summer and will keep a year. A small amount of water will be drawn out of the apples upon standing. This doesn't affect them at all.

PLATE 399   Aline Richards and Edith Parker begin by peeling, coring, and quartering the apples. The Parkers prefer Ben Davis apples as they are drier, stay firmer, and thus preserve better. They are unblemished apples that are not fully ripe, and they do not wash the peeled apples before bleaching: this will make them soft, and they won't last as long.

PLATE 400 While the apples are being peeled, Mr. Parker has built a small fire in the yard. When the first batch of apples is ready to be bleached, he and his wife put some hot coals from the fire into a shallow dish.

PLATE 401 The prepared apples are put into a box and pushed up to the sides, leaving a depression into which the dish of coals is set. Then powdered sulfur is sprinkled over the coals. There is a short burst of blue flame when the sulfur hits the coals, but the apples don't scorch as it does not last long enough. The lid of the box is then shut, and the whole box is completely covered with a heavy towel to keep air from escaping.

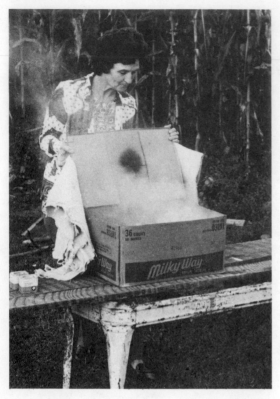

PLATE 402 The apples are smoked until they become white (about thirty–forty-five minutes). After about twenty minutes, Edith lifts the lid to see how things are going. If the smoke has thinned out, she adds more sulfur. The apples shrink somewhat during the process.

When they are completely bleached, the apples are removed from the box, put into a crock churn, covered with a clean cloth, and kept there until used. The sulfur helps keep insects away from them.

In cooking the bleached apples, use as little water as possible. Water brings back the taste of sulfur, which is not noticeable at all when the apples are eaten.

The Parkers enjoy apple pies made with bleached apples because they taste so much like fresh apples. Mrs. Parker's recipe is to place several cups of bleached apple pieces in an uncooked pie crust and add butter, sugar, and cinnamon to taste. The pie can be covered with pastry strips or a second crust if preferred. Bake in a preheated oven at 350° for 30–35 minutes or until the crust is a golden brown.

ALINE RICHARDS

Photographs by Rusty Leggett.

FRIED-APPLE PIES

Six of us went to Blanche Harkins' house the other day to watch her make fried-apple pies the way her mother did when Blanche was young.

To make the apple pies she uses either dried red or yellow apples. She really prefers yellow apples as she feels they make tastier pies.

To dry the apples, Mrs. Harkins first peels and cores them, then cuts them into thin slices, soaks them in salt water, drains them, and lays them out in a single layer on either a flat board or in a pan on a white cloth. She puts them outside for several days in the sunshine to dry, and they shrink to

PLATE 403 In order to dry the apples, Blanche first peels, cores, and slices them.

PLATE 404 The cooked apples are spread onto half the circle of dough, and the other half is turned over them to enclose them in a half-moon shaped envelope of dough. Then the pies are fried.

PLATE 405   The finished pies.

about half their original size. When completely dried, she stores them in sacks in a dry place until she's ready to cook with them.

To prepare fried pies, she adds a small amount of water to the dried apples, cooks them until they are tender, and then mashes them up with a fork. She says, "Add enough sugar and cinnamon or allspice for your own taste. For four small pies or tarts, use one quart of dried apples."

Mrs. Harkins' measurements for the pie crusts are approximately 4 cups self-rising flour, ½ cup Crisco, and 1 cup water. She makes the crust like a regular pie crust. She divides the dough into balls about the size of her fist for each pie, rolls the dough out into a very thin circle, then places the cooked apples on one half of the circle. She then folds the crust over the apples and presses the edges together wtih either her fingers or a fork. She makes tiny holes or slits in the pies—either with a fork or knife—to let the air out as the pies cook and to prevent the edges from turning up.

She puts enough Crisco into a large iron frying pan to almost cover the pies as they cook. They can be baked instead, if preferred. To make the crust crisp, she spreads melted butter on the pies before she puts them in the oven.

ARTICLE BY BETSY MOORE, CHERYL STOCKY, AND SUE VAN PETTEN.

Photographs by Dale Ferguson, Ridg MacArthur, Robbie Moore, and Randall Hardy.

HEWING

When I first started this article, I had no idea what I was documenting. When I found out, I still could think of no purpose for a square beam as opposed to a round log. I soon found out. Beams are used for everything from mantels to flooring supports, benches to stairs. Besides these, there are hundreds of other uses, most of which you wouldn't think of until the need arose. The particular beam we documented was used with its duplicate to form the sides for a staircase.

The man who showed us how to hew was Millard Buchanan. Millard has lived most of his life in the Southern Appalachians, and worked on his first cabin at the age of thirteen. He knows and can do everything for a traditional cabin from felling the first tree to fitting the last stone of the chimney.

Millard used only two tools for the entire hewing operations (*The Foxfire Book*, page 41): a double-bladed axe and an adze. It took Millard about fifty minutes to hew this log, but it would take a novice anywhere from two hours to two days, depending upon his skill. When the hewing was finished, it was very smooth, except for occasional places where the adze bit too deep.

PLATE 406   Millard first splits the poplar log in half and hews the inside smooth.

PLATE 407   Then he turns the log flat side down, and, straddling it, begins to smooth the rounded side with powerful strokes. He works forward, taking out large chunks in 4″ bites and leaving a trail of chips behind him.

The adze was extremely sharp. Millard proved this to us by shaving about an inch of hair off his arm. He said he had to sharpen it before each log or it wouldn't work properly. Even with sharp tools, it is still hard work.

The easiest wood for hewing, he said, was white pine, and the hardest, oak or hickory. This beam was made of poplar, which he said was about as easy as pine.

The photographs show Millard at work on one of the beams.

PING CRAWFORD

Photographs by Ford Oliver, Scott Bible, Ken Cronic, and Wendell Culpepper.

PLATE 408 Now, working backward, sometimes standing beside the log and sometimes straddling it, he goes over the rough-hewn side once again with smaller strokes to take off another 2″ (thus getting the beam down to the thickness he wants) and smooth the side.

PLATE 409 From the center of the log, he measures off the width he wants the beam to be, flips two chalk lines as guides, raises the log onto sawhorses, and slices off the sides with an axe. He first scores the sides, then goes back and hews to the line.

PLATE 410 The finished beam.

THE SADDLE LOCK NOTCH

There is a cabin on the Foxfire land that has the rafters hooked to the plates in a unique way. The notch used is called the "saddle lock notch" by some of our contacts, not to be confused with the "saddle notch" used for joining wall logs together at the corners of a building.

The cabin came from the Savannah Community near Webster, North Carolina. We think it is from two hundred to two hundred and twenty-five years old. This notch was not used very often for it was difficult to cut, and there were not the accurate measuring tools we have today. Most rafters were just notched to fit over the plate (see Plate 411), but the "saddle lock notch" works differently. With it, the rafter sits down in a series of notches cut into the plates. The dowel pins lock each rafter securely to the plate (see Plate 411). Each rafter overhangs the outside edge of the plate by about four inches.

JEFF FEARS

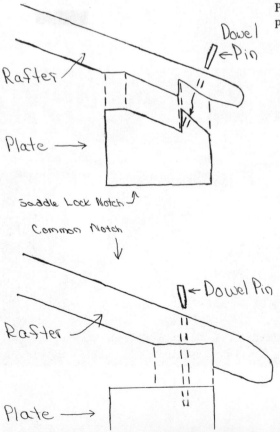

PLATE 411 Two methods of pinning rafters to plates.

PLATE 412 The top of the plate shows the notches with the pegs used to hold the rafters still in place. After this article appeared in *Foxfire* magazine, one of our readers, John Kline from Reamstown, Pennsylvania, wrote and told us, "This notch is common in old buildings in my area. It was used not only in log buildings but almost all types of structures built before 1860. . . . I believe this is a Pennsylvania German innovation, and your example could have been built by a Pennsylvanian who moved down there."

BOTTOMING CHAIRS WITH CORN SHUCKS

Chair bottoming by hand with natural materials is an art that has just about disappeared due to mass production and the development of artificial materials such as plastics, vinyls, acrylics, and various other cloth and leather fabrics. Many people today don't care how well a piece of furniture is made as long as it is pretty and will top or at least equal what someone else has. Those people who *do* care about the quality of their possessions often can do nothing about it because items of genuine quality, when they can be found, are priced out of reach.

Mr. Harry Brown, Sr., still maintains an old craft tradition of high quality at reasonable price. On a warm sunny day in September, he came to the campus for an interview with the journalism class. He was glad to share a little of what he knows about the art of chair bottoming with corn shucks. Mr. Brown said that when he was a boy, people made most of their furniture. He also stated that he was not taught by anyone how to make a chair

bottom—he just picked it up as a hobby. Mr. Brown wove his first chair
bottom in 1910 out of white oak splits at the age of twelve (*The Foxfire
Book*, page 137). He has been making and caning chairs since that time.
Originally, he made his chair frames only from oak, but he now uses either
oak or cherry.

It takes about four to five hours to complete a chair bottom using corn
shucks. The completed chair has three layers of woven corn shucks and is
really a strong seat. Mr. Brown jokingly said that it would look like a pile of
corn shucks when it was finished. It doesn't though.

The weave that Mr. Brown used is called a raffia weave and is used quite
commonly.

The materials needed to make a corn-shuck chair bottom are: a bucket
for soaking the shucks, scissors, tape, clothspins, a clamp, corn shucks, and
plenty of patience. The corn shucks should have dried naturally, turned
brown and crisp. Do not use fresh green corn shucks. Mr. Brown said the
longer the corn shucks, the better.

Mr. Brown selected the longest corn shucks, put them into a bucket, and
poured warm water over them. He let the corn shucks soak for about fifteen
to twenty minutes.

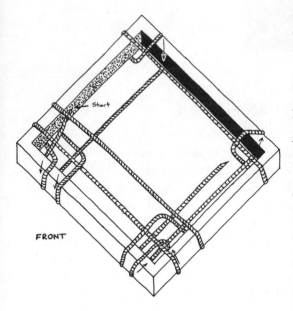

FRONT

PLATE 413 The pattern for the
weave. If the chair you are working on
is wider at the front than at the rear
(and most will be), measure and build
out on the front enough to make the
widths equal before starting on the pattern shown.

Build out by tacking as shown—
following the directions across the front
—looping the corner as shown, then
cutting the material and tacking it.
Tacks should end up on opposite sides
of the frame.

Once you have built out enough to
equalize the widths, start the pattern in
the diagram.

Since most chair bottoms aren't
square but rectangular, the pattern will
need to change when you get to the center. When you reach that point, the
original pattern no longer works. Simply loop around the frame in a figure
eight running between the longer ends
of the frame. When finished, tie the end
to one of the strands on the under side
of the chair bottom.

When they were ready, Mr. Brown took out a shuck and cut the shank (the part of the shuck that is originally attached to the corncob at the base) off so it would be even. He then tore the shuck into strips of about ¾-to-1" widths.

Next Mr. Brown took about three or four strips, placed them together and twisted them in a clockwise motion, much as you would wringing out some article of clothing, to form a "rope." He put a clothespin on the end to keep the rope from unraveling. Mr. Brown continued adding strips to the rope, staggering them every three or four inches to keep the rope as uniform as possible. He placed clothespins on the rope whenever he needed to. When Mr. Brown had twisted about two feet of rope, he taped the end of the rope to the left side crosspiece about three inches from the front. Mr. Brown then started the weaving process. He told us that in starting the weave not to pull the rope very tight because, as the rope dried, the corn shucks would constrict and pull apart. Also as you weave more and more onto the chair, the weave would tighten naturally.

Mr. Brown continued adding corn shucks to the rope, and, as often as he could, he wove the rope onto the chair. Every time that he wove the rope on the chair and pulled it around a crosspiece, he took a clamp and clamped the rope to the crosspiece so the weave would not loosen.

When the chair is finished and has had sufficient time to dry completely, he puts a varnish on it to prolong the seat's life. Mr. Brown said that we could probably find some chairs around that had been bottomed with corn shucks that were fifty years old or older.

Text by the journalism class.
Photos by Rusty Leggett and Phil Conner.

PLATE 414 The shucks are soaked well before being used.

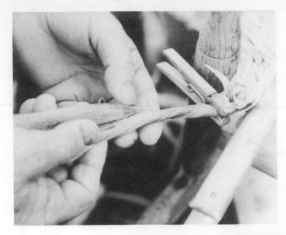

PLATE 415 As the rope gets used up, Mr. Brown twists more shucks, leaf by leaf, into it.

PLATE 416 He makes a long section of rope, clipping it at intervals with clothespins to help hold it together, and then weaves another round.

PLATE 417   He works with the chair upside down.

PLATE 418   The finished bottom. When completed, the pattern the shuck rope makes on the top of the chair is an "X".

A TRADITIONAL LOOM

In *Foxfire 2* (page 217), we ran a composite photograph of an old loom owned by Gertrude Kenner. The photograph was not a good one, however, because the conditions under which we were shooting made it almost impossible for us to get the photograph we wanted.

Recently, Harry Brown, Sr., was brought a similar loom for repairs. It was constructed 216 years ago by Levi Swain out of yellow pine, and put together with wooden pegs. Mr. Brown called us so that we could get photographs of it that would be better than what we had in stock. Then, over a period of several months, he made a copy of it for us, and helped us move it to our center where students now use it.

PLATE 419   The loom from the rear.

PLATE 420   The loom from the side.

PLATE 421   Detail of the cog wheel that fits on the end of the cloth beam (see *Foxfire 2*, page 229).

PLATE 422 Marinda, Harry's wife, threaded the loom and wove a rug on it to make sure it was in working order before it was returned to its owner.

PLATE 423 Harry reassembling the copy he made in a log building at our center.

CASKETS

As late as the early 1940s, many people of the Appalachians were buried in homemade caskets (see *Foxfire 2*, pages 304–23). Usually some of the men in the community built the casket after a person had died; the ladies would sew a lining for it while the men built it so that it was ready by evening. There were several men in the community who were regularly called on to make caskets. They kept lumber cut and cured, ready to be used when needed.

One such person in our community was Harley Thomas, a man who makes spinning wheels, repairs and builds cabinets and gun racks, and can do almost any other kind of woodwork, including making fiddles.

Some people liked to build their own casket or have it made to order long before they needed it. It was usually kept in the hayloft of the barn. Various people in our community told of having seen one stored in one of the farmer's barns near here. We inquired about its history and found that it had been made for this farmer's uncle, but he was staying with a daughter in another state when he died, and the family had him buried there. The kids remembered the casket being up in the barn for years after that, but it has since disappeared.

We asked Mr. Thomas, since we couldn't find one already made, if he would make us a child's casket, so that we could see how they were made and how he decided on the measurements. It took him quite a while to acquire some suitable white oak wood, and he never was able to procure the brass hardware he wanted for the handles. So he improvised, as he would have done fifty years ago, and made wooden handles.

Mr. Thomas told us that during the Depression, when the CCC camps were located throughout this area, he had a contract with the government to build caskets. His regular job was running a sawmill and building cabinets and furniture, but he made caskets as needed.

When we lifted up the casket he made for us, we were startled at how heavy it was for its size. He stained the white oak wood with a light brown

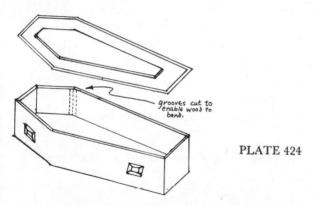

grooves cut to enable wood to bend.

PLATE 424

PLATE 425

varnish and lined the inside with cotton batting and quilted white satin tacked on over that.

Mr. Thomas shaped the bottom of the casket with the sides angled out somewhat to make room for the shoulders of the body. He used to decide how long the casket would be by adding a few inches to the length of the person to be buried in it. The widest part of the casket is one-third the way down the length of it. It then tapers back inward with the foot of the casket being the same width as the head.

The pieces for the ends of this casket are $6\frac{1}{2}''$ wide and $8\frac{3}{4}''$ high. He nailed these onto the bottom first. He cut two white oak planks $8\frac{3}{4}''\times33''$ long. To bend these pieces to fit the bottom, he cuts three grooves with a hand saw or power saw from top edge to bottom edge about $\frac{1}{2}''$ apart and about half way through the boards, as shown in Plate 424.

He then nailed on one side, starting at the head and forcing the side to meet the bottom by placing the nails rather closely. By the time he reached the foot, the board was securely attached to the bottom and bent at the desired angle. He then nailed that side to the end. He did the other side the same way, and when finished, the entire casket has the shape of the bottom.

He shaped a top to fit the casket, gluing on a smaller piece of wood shaped like the top as a decorative touch. The top is attached to the casket with three screws placed on either side. He used two wooden handles on each side of the casket, although when he could get it, he used to use brass hardware.

Text and photographs by Al Oakes, Phil Conner, and Cheryl Stocky.

BUILDING A STILL FURNACE

For years we half-joked about getting someone to build us an actual-size still so we could photograph the steps. Suddenly our wish came true, and there was Buck Carver, one of our most faithful and most generous contacts, down in a four-foot-by-four-foot hole, building a duplicate of his old furnace for us and adding a whole new dimension to the work we had already done on moonshining (*The Foxfire Book*, pages 301–45). In the process, a whole new set of tricks came to light. From Buck:

"Face the opening for the firebox downhill toward the stream as there's usually a breeze coming up the branch to feed the fire.

"The hole in the throat needs to be about the same size as the opening of the firebox to keep from choking the fire.

"Get as many rocks as you think you'll need; then lay in two or three more loads, and if you're lucky you might not have to go back for more than one or two loads more!"

And this: After we had made a trip to the site, Buck noted how people scoffed when he told them it only took a couple of trips in to make a really obvious path for law officers to follow. We smiled, then looked backwards as he gestured with a grin toward the very obvious trail stretching out behind us through the woods. . . .

DENNIS MAXWELL AND JAY HOLT

PLATE 426   The first step is to choose a suitable hillside hidden in the woods. Buck always sets his stills into a bank so that he can stand on the ground behind the still and get to it without using a ladder. The site selected, he and Joey Fountain, one of the *Foxfire* students, dug out the hole for the furnace.

PLATE 427 Here Buck and Joey smooth up the hole, the floor of which will be the floor of the still's firebox.

PLATE 428 Next, Buck cemented into place the first two courses of flat rocks thus outlining the firebox walls. Years ago, red clay would have been used instead of cement, and the site for the still would have been partly determined by the availability of clay. In the left foreground, notice that the flat rock at the back of the firebox is set on its edge and sloped backward slightly so that it will deflect the flames upward around the still (see also Plate 431).

PLATE 429 When the walls of the firebox were high enough (see Plate 431 for measurements), Buck set the large flat rock he had chosen for a bedstone into place so that it spanned the firebox. As it wasn't quite long enough, he set a second, smaller rock into place behind it and cemented the two together to make one flat platform for the still to sit on.

PLATE 430 The hole left at the back of the platform is for the flames, which will come up from the firebox below and wrap around the still, heating the contents to a boil.

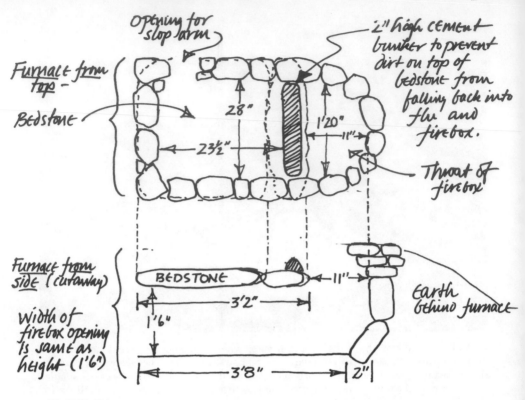

Opening for slop arm

Furnace from top —

Bedstone

28"

23½"

1'20"

11"

2" high cement bunker to prevent dirt on top of bedstone from falling back into flue and firebox.

Throat of firebox

Furnace from side (cutaway)

Width of firebox opening is same as height (1'6")

BEDSTONE

11"

Earth behind furnace

3'2"

1'6"

3'8"

2"

PLATE 431

PLATES 432–433 The next step was to set the still itself, a thirty-five-gallon copper outfit, in place on the bedstone and mark the spot where the slop arm would stick through the furnace wall. Then he started putting the next layer of rocks into place making sure to leave space for the flames between the still itself and the rock walls of the furnace.

PLATE 434 When the walls were up about a foot above the bedstone, Buck removed the copper still and placed a 3"-thick layer of red clay on top of the bedstone to insure that no flames ever hit the bottom of the still and burned a hole in it. Then he proceeded with the next round of rocks, leaving an 11½" hole in front for the scuttle hole or smoke vent.

PLATE 435

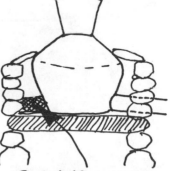

Buck builds a small bunker of rock and mud the size of the base of the slop arm and opposite the actual arm to keep the flames even around the still.

PLATE 436   When the rock sides were high enough to reach the cape of the still, Buck set it back into place.

PLATE 437   Then he sealed the hole around the slop arm with red-clay mud while one of the students helped by lining the sloped inside back wall of the furnace with cement and smoothing it up.

PLATE 438   Next Buck set flat rocks in place around the cape to form the top of the furnace.

PLATE 439   When the rocks were selected and in place, he cemented them in completely to seal up the furnace except for the firebox hole and scuttle hole in the front. This forces any fire built in the firebox to expend its heat around the sides of the still before venting out the front. The operation is now ready for the addition of the cap, cap arms, and so on.

After the still was cemented into place, another reason for the use of red clay over cement by many moonshiners became obvious: most wanted the mobility that comes from being able to dismantle their operation quickly and move the copper still to safety when in danger of being discovered. Walls cemented with red-clay mud are easily knocked down.

ASH HOPPERS

One of the best-designed ash hoppers (*The Foxfire Book*, page 156) we've seen was shown to us during a visit to Lookout Mountain, Tennessee, to talk with potter Charles Counts. We were staying at the Fairyland Motel, and in the back yard sat the ash hopper pictured here. It was built by Martin Pilgrim, now deceased—an old mountain man who helped the owners of Rock City lay out the stone paths through the rock cliffs of their tourist operation.

The hopper, roofed with shingles, has a hinged roof for easy entry, and a tin spout at the bottom from which the lye dripped whenever water was poured onto the ashes.

Articles and photographs by Ray McBride and Don MacNeil.

PLATE 440   PLATE 441

BENDING OX YOKE BOWS

Tommy Barnes showed us his method of bending bows for ox yokes (*Foxfire* 2, pages 115–16). Recently, Will Zoellner, a local blacksmith, showed us another.

Article and photographs by Jack East, Annette Sutherland, and Steve Horton.

PLATE 442 Will first boils the hickory in water in a trough he designed for this purpose. Boiling the wood makes it temporarily pliable and speeds up the curing process.

PLATE 443   He then takes the wood to a pipe he has mounted horizontally onto the side of one of his outbuildings. He places one end of the bow into this pipe and the other end into a second pipe which he uses to pull with. As he pulls the section of hickory into an arc, it splits a little as is normal. At the point where it begins to split, he attaches a "C" clamp to help keep it from splitting any further.

PLATE 444   Will inserts a piece of board in the curve to keep the bow from snapping, and bends it on around. When it is bent far enough, he holds the bow in place with his left leg while he attaches a wire to keep it bent.

PLATE 445   Then he slips the bow out of the pipes. The clamp will be left attached until the wood has dried. The bow can either be placed in a yoke and the wire removed, or it can be stored for later use, leaving the wire on to hold the curve.

THE DISHRAG GOURD

In the past, some families in our area raised *Luffa cylindrica,* using the young gourds for food, and the old, mature fruits for sponges. What happens is that as it ages, this unusual plant develops a tough, fibrous inside that is spongy, durable, and ideal for use in scrubbing dishes and pans clean. To get at the inside, one simply has to peel off the brittle outside crust (some soak the gourds overnight before peeling, but it can be done dry also). The seeds, which are loose in the hollow center of the fruit, can be saved for replanting in the spring as soon as the danger of frost is past.

Many families in our area buy the seed for this plant from the George W. Park Seed Company, Greenwood, South Carolina 29646. *Organic Gardening* has, from time to time, run articles about the luffa (June 1974, for example) for those who desire more information.

PLATE 446

PLATE 447

AFTERWORD

by Richard M. Dorson

In the past Eliot Wigginton and I have had our differences. I have criticized the *Foxfire* books for dealing with the materials of folklore and folklife in an incomplete way. "Wig" retorted that he had no intention of training folklore scholars but wanted to arouse his bored students and get them interested and aware and alive to their surroundings and their people. He was a journalism teacher, and had never heard of folklore during his college years at Cornell. As a university professor of folklore and director of Indiana University's Folklore Institute, I felt that he had an obligation to his students and his large reading public to acquaint himself with the methods, collections, and studies of the folklorist and use them selectively for the enrichment of his materials. To which Wig queried, why didn't the Ph.D. folklorists go outside in the mud to find the people and get their diplomas dirty instead of sniping at little folks from the safety of their certificate-lined walls? At the end of this exchange in the pages of the *North Carolina Folklore Journal* Wig invited me to Rabun Gap and I invited him to Indiana University to continue our dialogue.

In June 1976 Wig did come to Bloomington, and he and I held what was billed "The Great Debate" before the graduate students and faculty of the Folklore Institute. I attacked him for presenting a nostalgic, romanticized picture of mountain folk and their ways. He asserted that the *Foxfire* books portrayed with complete accuracy the people of Nacoochee—and he convinced me. On the conclusion of this duel Eliot Wigginton's eloquence, sincerity, and humanity had won us over and I said as much. He is indeed a brilliant and inspired educator, who has appreciated, and taught his students to appreciate, the values to be learned from a traditional culture in the southern mountains. It is a tribute to his openmindedness that he will give the scholars of traditional cultures a chance to make their point, and has invited me to tender this statement in *Foxfire 4*.

There are two connected thoughts that I as a professional folklorist wish to express about the *Foxfire* books. First, their contents are one hundred percent folklore and folklife. Second, scholars have been collecting and studying folklore and folklife for nearly two hundred years. Neither of these facts has been recognized in the first three *Foxfire* volumes. Readers can enjoy these warmly human books as they stand, but they should know that folklorists have collected similar practices and customs and life experiences for other parts of the country and also quite different traditional lifestyles for other Americans. The Foxfire concept has led students out of the classroom into their community, to speak with their grandparents and neighbors and new friends, and learn their folk wisdom and folk history, and this is admirable. But the logical extension of the Foxfire idea will then be to lead the students into the library, to dig for and locate counterpart items to the folklore they have uncovered, and to develop an interest in other peoples. They will discover with an eerie thrill that a supposedly local incident, told as a gospel true happening, has been reported in distant places and over long stretches of time.

A Maine lobsterman once told me of a "cove about two mile below where I live called Yoho Cove" named for a wild man who lived there years ago and always hollered "Yoho, yoho." When a party of natives went raspberrying by the cove one time, the Yoho ran out of the woods, grabbed a girl from the group and made off with her. A couple of years later this party returned to the cove, and the girl rushed toward them, carrying a year-old baby and screaming for help. The berry pickers lifted the girl into the canoe and pushed off from the shore, when the Yoho ran down to the water, seized the baby, tore it in half, and with a hideous yell threw one part at the retreating canoe. "So it's been called Yoho Cove ever since."

This account sounded real enough, but the folklorist senses that the same gruesome episode may be reported elsewhere. His research discloses that the tale of the Yoho is told in the Kentucky mountains, in French Canada, and in several European and Middle Eastern countries. Foxfire student-interviewers, like all folklore collectors, must learn how to distinguish factual from fictional narratives. The line is not clear, for historical figures, like Jesse James, become embellished by legends, and imaginary heroes, like Paul Bunyan, are given historical roots.

As they read about folklore in the library, students will come to know that traditions thrive in the cities as well as in the hills, among factory and office workers as well as among mountain people. They will learn that folklore reflects the concerns of the present far more than the remembrances of the past, and that the automobile, for example, is a subject of many legends. If they pursue the study of folklore in college and graduate school, they will find themselves looking deeply into the cultural behavior of humankind.

A strong word of caution. Too many writings about so-called folklore may deceive and misinform rather than enlighten and instruct, for the professional folklorists are few and the amateurs and popularizers numerous. Beware of fakelore—a term I coined in 1950 to denote the spurious, synthetic, and syrupy distortions of folklore. The *Foxfire* books contain examples of genuine traditional folklore and folklife, collected and recorded with notebook, tape recorder, and camera, and not invented or "improved" by writers who have never talked with the folk. Part of the educational ideal represented by the Foxfire concept will be fulfilled if teacher, student, and reader recognize the distinction between books of folklore and books of fakelore. Their titles often sound the same. The following list is suggested as an introduction to the subject matter of folklore and folklife.

Bibliography (* indicates volumes are available in paperback):

Without too much apology I will begin with some of my own books. My most recent one is *Folklore and Fakelore* (Harvard University Press, 1976); the first essay recapitulates some of my battles to establish folklore studies on a sound basis, and other essays illustrate the theories and research methods of the folklorist. Two similar volumes of my collected writings are *Folklore, Selected Essays* (Indiana University Press, 1972) and *American Folklore and the Historian* (University of Chicago Press, 1971). A general survey of the discipline on an advanced level is *Folklore and Folklife, an Introduction* (University of Chicago Press, 1972) which I edited, and to which eighteen professionals contributed chapters on their special fields; each chapter contains an annotated select bibliography for further readings. My *American Folklore** (University of Chicago Press, 1959), and *America in Legend** (Pantheon, 1973) discuss the folk traditions of the American people within a historical framework, and *Buying the Wind, Regional Folklore in the United States** (University of Chicago Press, 1964) provides examples with comparative notes of those traditions as collected in seven regions. My field work from the Upper Peninsula of Michigan is presented in *Bloodstoppers and Bearwalkers** (Harvard University Press, 1952, repr. 1972).

A widely used introductory textbook is *The Study of American Folklore* by Jan Harold Brunvand (Norton, 1968), which presents the categories of folklore in the United States. Brunvand has also brought out *Folklore, a Research Guide** (St. Martin's Press, 1976) to orient teachers and students new to the subject. A more advanced work is *The Study of Folklore*, edited by Alan Dundes (Prentice-Hall, 1965), who reprints scholarly essays by a number of folklorists.[1] *American Folklife*, edited by Don Yoder (University

---

[1] A book which we've found extremely useful is *A Manual for Field Workers* by Edward D. Ives (Northeast Archives of Folklore and Oral History, Orono, Maine, 1971). —Ed.

of Texas Press, 1976), contains articles especially written for that volume by specialists on folk crafts and material culture. A symposium devoted to *American Folk Legend* produced an excellent series of papers, published in a book with that title, edited by Wayland Hand (University of California Press, 1971). Dundes has also edited a selection of interpretative essays on Afro-American folklore in *Mother Wit from the Laughing Barrel** (Prentice-Hall, 1973).

Turning to field-work collections and writings, I recommend first an older title that is a model for the regional collector, Emelyn E. Gardner's *Folklore from the Schoharie Hills, New York* (University of Michigan Press, 1937). A notable collection of family saga from Kentucky is Leonard Roberts' *Sang Branch Settlers* (University of Texas Press, 1974). The traditions of fishermen on Maryland's eastern shore are adeptly presented by George Carey in *A Faraway Time and Place* (Luce, 1971). A pioneering work of folk history combining oral and documentary sources to reconstruct the history of a vanished Kentucky settlement is Lynwood Montell's *The Saga of Coe Ridge* (University of Tennessee Press, 1970). How historical events and personalities generate folk legends is demonstrated for the Mormons by Austin and Alta Fife in *Saints of Sage and Saddle* (Indiana University Press, 1956). Immigrant and ethnic folklore has not yet been well collected and studied, but Carla Bianco in *The Two Rosetos* (Indiana University Press, 1974) has made an authoritative contribution, in comparing the folk traditions of Roseto, Italy, and its colony Roseto, Pennsylvania. A fine study of a Mexican ballad and folk hero celebrated in the southwest is by Américo Paredes, *"With His Pistol In His Hand": A Border Ballad and Its Hero* (University of Texas Press, 1958), dealing with Gregorio Cortez. The lore of occupations is also undercollected, but a skillful interpretation of one is Mody C. Boatright's *Folklore of the Oil Industry* (Southern Methodist University Press, 1963).

These titles and their bibliographies can lead readers into the charmed garden of folklore.

INDEX OF PEOPLE

THE KIDS

Russell Arthur
Marie Auten
Claire Bender
Scott Bible
Cam Bond
Scott Bradley
Jan Brown
Laurie Brunson
Juel Butler
Lynn Butler
Craig Carlton
Tom Carlton
Brenda Carpenter
Maybelle Carpenter
Bit Carver
Kay Carver
Phyllis Carver
Mary Chastain
Vicki Chastain
Phil Conner
Doug Cornell
Ping Crawford
Ken Cronic
Debbie Crowell
Wendell Culpepper
Roy Dickerson
Mike Drake
Jack East
Jeff Fears
Dale Ferguson

Joey Fountain
Louise Freeman
Wendy Guyaux
Randall Hardy
Jeff Hay
Keith Head
Jay Holt
Dennis Horton
Debbie James
Doug L. James
Anita Jenkins
Sid Jones
Beverly Justus
Ken Kistner
Tommy Lamb
Jeff Lane
Rusty Leggett
Robbie Letson
Don MacNeil
John Matthies
Dennis Maxwell
Ridg MacArthur
Ray McBride
Melissa McGee
Gena McHugh
Scott McKay
Robert McLanahan
Betsy Moore
Karen Moore
Robert Moore
Susie Nichols
Al Oakes
Bob O'Dwyer

Ford Oliver
Shelley Pace
Richard Page
John Pope
Sharon Pope
Tom Powers
Myra Queen
Peter Reddick
Annette Reems
Jim Renfro
Aline Richards
Alison Rutherford
Stephanie Shuptrine
Dwayne Skenes

Loy Smith
Steve Smith
Cheryl Stocky
Annette Sutherland
Barbara Taylor
Debbie Thomas
Mary Thomas
Terese Turpin
Sue Van Petten
Sheila Vinson
Linda Warfield
Lynnette Williams
Donald Wright
Matt Young

THE CONTACTS

C. M. Arrowood
Joe Arrowood
Garrett Arwood
Burnett Brooks
Florence and Lawton Brooks
Marinda and Harry Brown
Ednie Buchanan
Jack Buchanan
Shirley and Millard Buchanan
Louin Cabe
Thomas Campbell
Mrs. Cecil Cannon
Aunt Lola Cannon
Aunt Arie Carpenter
Carl Carpenter
Mary Carpenter
Buck Carver
Leona T. Carver
Doc Chastain
Mrs. Norman Coleman
Ethel Corn
Imogene Dailey
Fred Darnell
Mack Dickerson
Mimi Dickerson
R. M. Dickerson
Terry Dickerson
Barnard Dillard
Bobbie Dills
Lon Dover
Thad Dowdle
Belle Dryman
Hob Duvall
Charles Earnhardt
Mrs. Thelma Earp
Harriet Echols
Harold Embrey
William Flowers
Adam Foster
Simmie Free

Aunt Nora Garland
Buford Garner
Tom Grist
Blanche Harkins
Lonnie Harkins
Tedra Harmon
Dick Harrison
Etta and Charlie Ross Hartley
Pauline Henson
Stanley Hicks
Mrs. Earl Holt
Mrs. L. D. Hopper
John Houck
Anna Howard
Conway and Park Hughes
Ada Kelly
Mrs. Ray Kelly
Ted Lanich
Mr. Ledbetter
Oma Ledford
C. P. Ligon
Faye Long
Garnett Lovell
Lizzie Lovin
Alex Martin
Pearl Martin
Gay McClain
Jim McCoy
Ulysses McCoy
Myrtle McMahon
Harvey Miller
Belzora Moore
Noel Moore
Rev. A. Rufus Morgan
Mrs. George Nix
Addie Norton
Margaret Norton
Richard Norton
Mrs. Edith Parker
Earl "Preach" Parsons
Laura Patton
Annie Perry

Esco Pitts
Mrs. J. D. Quinn
Tom Ramey
Clarence Rathbone
Harv Reid
Lon Reid
Mrs. Monroe Reese
Harley Rogers
Kenny Runion
Will Seagle
Doug Sheppard
Vina Speed
B. J. Stiles
Lake Stiles
Thomas Stubbs
Gladys Swanson
Mrs. Oren Swanson

Gladys Teague
Cal Thomas
Harley Thomas
Nell Thomas
Jason Townsend
Willie Underwood
Mrs. Birdie Mae Vinson
Ralph Vinson
T. F. Vinson
Mr. and Mrs. Jake Waldroop
Pearl Watts
Grover Webb
Naomi Whitmire
Mrs. Ben Williams
Mrs. Grace Williams
Lee Williams
Will Zoeliner

A SELECTED LISTING OF PERIODICALS
AND RESOURCE MATERIAL
ABOUT THE APPALACHIAN REGION

APPALACHIA

There is no charge for a subscription to this journal, which comes out every other month and deals with the economic and social development of Appalachia. It is published by The Appalachian Regional Commission, the government agency that devotes its attention to the improvement of the quality of life in the Appalachians. Write to: *Appalachia,* The Appalachian Regional Commission, 1666 Connecticut Avenue, Washington, D.C. 20235.

APPALACHIAN HERITAGE

Appalachian Heritage is a quarterly, non-profit journal dedicated to the presentation of the life and culture of the people of Southern Appalachia, both old and new, in a pleasing real-life way by means of stories, sketches, essays, tales, songs, sayings, poems, and pictures. A central aim has always been to correct the stereotype (both unpleasant and untrue) image of the Southern Mountaineer and to reveal his humanness and individuality.

"While concerned with the Appalachian region in terms of history, folklore, crafts, music, etc., this has broad enough appeal to be almost a general magazine in the category of *Yankee,* or in the same area as *Foxfire.* It has an intrinsic honesty, unusual for regional magazines, which are understandably concerned with advertising the area rather than pointing up its defects. (Also, it is a non-profit affair, and the editors are 'desirous of making it stand on its own two hind feet.' Librarians can do everyone a favor by doing their bit in this regard.) It also includes poetry (passable) and some good short stories. It is particularly valuable, entertaining, and highly informative, though, for recollections and local history, e.g. death and burial customs and sketches of the mountain people. This aspect makes it a worthy addition for any library. Good illustrations, too." —B. K. *Library Journal,* April 15, 1974.

For information, write: *Appalachian Heritage,* Box 132, Pippa Passes, Ky. 41844.

APPALACHIAN JOURNAL

This quarterly journal publishes a broad spectrum of cross-disciplinary scholarship and opinion about the entire Appalachian region. Major fields of interest are history, anthropology, folklore, geography, economics, politics, education, sociology, and ecology. Included are poetry, short fiction, book and record reviews.

Subscription rates for one year are $6.50. Write *Appalachian Journal,* 134 Sanford Hall, Appalachian State University, Boone, N.C. 28608.

APPALACHIAN ORAL HISTORY PROJECT

The Appalachian Oral History Project began in 1971 as a co-operative effort of the Alice Lloyd College, Pippa Passes, Kentucky, and Lee's Junior College, Jackson, Kentucky. The Project also includes two other schools, Appalachian State University, Boone, N.C., and Emory and Henry College, Emory, Va. Several of the schools have publications. The two we are most familiar with are listed below:

1) *Mountain Memories* is a bi-annual periodical edited and published by student workers. The subscription rate is $2.50 per year, covering postage. Write to: *Mountain Memories,* Appalachian Oral History Project, Alice Lloyd College, Pippa Passes, Ky. 41844.

2) Issues of *Recollections* include such things as trapping in eastern Kentucky, trading—mountain style and railroad stories. The subscription rate is $2.50 per issue annually. Write to: *Recollections,* Appalachian Oral History Project, Lee's Junior College, Jackson, Ky. 41339.

APPALACHIAN PRESS

From the Appalachian Press catalogue: "Appalachia is a colony. Our wealth is daily stolen from us. Our natural resources and our labor are exploited by giant corporations whose owners do not live here. Not only do these owners not live here, but they make no contribution to the process of production. Our natural resources rightfully belong to all of us, and it is by our labor alone that they are made useful to us in the form of products. Yet today we receive no value from our resources and a mere pittance for our labor. The greatest share of what is produced from our resources and labor goes into the pockets of these corporate owners who do nothing at all to earn it. They live and have become the richest people in America by exploiting us. We at the Appalachian Press are dedicated to putting an end to the exploitation of our land and labor."

The Appalachian Press does not put out a publication on a regular basis; however, a catalogue of offerings, which include publications on coal mining, strip mining, labor unions, freedom movements, etc., is available. Write: Appalachian Press, P. O. Box 8074, Huntington, W. Va. 25705.

APPALSHOP

Appalshop is a non-profit multimedia company that was started in the late 1960s in Whitesburg, Kentucky, with an Office of Economic Opportunity grant. It began as an experiment to record the heritage and struggle for survival of people in the mountain region. Now Appalshop has grown into an independent media center that includes projects of high-quality 16-mm films; still photography; a quarterly magazine, *Mountain Review;* June Appal Recordings; and Roadside Theater—a storytelling group that presents programs of old mountain tales along with music in school classrooms and community festivals.

June Appal Recordings provides an outlet for traditional and contemporary mountain musicians who desire some control of the way their music is produced and marketed. The proximity and openness of the eight-track mixing console and recording machine at the June Appal studio in Whitesburg enables musicians to record at their pleasure.

By late 1976, June Appal had released records such as *Passing Through the Garden* (Nimrod Workman and Phyllis Boyens), *New Wood* (Si Kahn), *How Can I Keep from Singing* (John McCutcheon), and *Brown Lung/Cotton Mill Blues* (Mountain Musicians' Cooperative).

Current catalogues of records and films are available from June Appal or Appalshop, Box 743, Whitesburg, Ky. 41858. (See also listing for *Mountain Review.*)

BROADSIDE

A public television facility, Broadside was founded to produce videotapes for and about the Central Appalachian people—their problems and interests. For a closer look at land use, energy needs, coal mining, regional history, traditional arts and skills, order the Broadside Tape Catalogue, a complete listing of videotapes for sale or rental distribution, from Broadside T.V., Elm and Millard, Johnson City, Tenn. 37601; (615) 926-8191.

FOXFIRE

Foxfire is a quarterly magazine written by students of Rabun Gap High School in northeast Georgia. From these magazines come the articles for the *Foxfire* books. The subscription rate for the magazine is $8.00 per year.

Using royalties from sales of the *Foxfire* books, the organization has also started a publishing house (Foxfire Press, which recently released its first book, a history of the small railroad that served the area—the Tallulah Falls Railroad) and has begun a recording company, the first albums from which are now available. For announcements of offerings, send your name to be placed on our mailing list. Write: *Foxfire,* Rabun Gap, Ga. 30568.

GOLDENSEAL

This quarterly publication, distributed without charge, is a forum for documenting West Virginia's traditional way of life. Included in it are articles about farmers, musicians, and craftsmen who are familiar with the older customs and ways of this state. Write: The State of West Virginia, c/o Science and Culture Center, State Capitol, Charleston, W. Va. 25308.

MOUNTAIN CALL, THE

The Mountain Call is a young monthly publication for and about the mountains, the people, the culture. Now in its third year of publishing from the heart of the Mingo County hills in southwestern West Virginia, *The Mountain Call* is a unique, new-day approach to Appalachia and Mother Earth. Designed as a mountain magazine, it is a coming-together of old and young mountain people and life-styles. Its Mountaineer-of-the-Month interviews provide an intimate life experience with hill people.

A sample copy can be purchased for $.35, or a twelve-issue subscription is available for $5.00. Write: *The Mountain Call,* The Knob, Kermit, W. Va. 25674.

MOUNTAIN LIFE AND WORK

Mountain Life and Work is the official monthly publication of the Council of the Southern Mountains. Since 1925 it has consistently led the way for periodicals in the Appalachian Region. Today, *ML&W* provides the only on-going and firsthand coverage of political actions and struggles occurring throughout the region. According to noted author Harry Caudill, *ML&W* "has become a real fighting publication that takes up and deals with issues of great and pressing importance to the rank and file people of the Appalachian hills." The magazine also continues its perennial coverage of culture. For a year's subscription, send $5.00 to *Mountain Life and Work*, Drawer N, Clintwood, Va. 24228.

The "1976–77 Catalog/Bibliography on the Appalachian South," published by the Council of the Southern Mountains, describes over 1,000 books, records, pamphlets, and films available through its Bookstore in Berea, Ky. The 80-page tabloid includes material indexed into 17 categories: Coal, History/Bibliography, Sociology/Non-fiction, Mountain Women, Health, Pamphlets, Photo Essay, Films, Camping/Hiking, Nature Studies, Crafts and Cooking, Fiction, Children, Folklore, Poetry, Music, and Records. It also includes a history of the Council and biographical information of authors and artists whose works are indigenous to the mountains. The Bookstore offers the largest collection of books and records on the Appalachian South available to the general public. The Catalog can be obtained for $1.00 from: CSM Bookstore, CPO 2307, Berea, Ky. 40403.

West Virginia University has recently begun a book club specifically for readers interested in Appalachian materials. They send a bi-monthly catalogue of available materials to members. For information, write WVU Regional Book Club, WVU Book Store, College Avenue, Morgantown, W. Va. 26505.

MOUNTAIN REVIEW

Mountain Review is for Appalachians of all ages and backgrounds, and others interested in life in the mountains. This 48-page large-format quarterly publishes articles, short fiction, poetry, photography, and artwork by mountain people, which are reflective of life here. It regularly features journalism around special topics, children's stories, student workshop writing, a photo portfolio, and book and movie reviews. *Mountain Review* is not out to glorify the past or rehash worn stereotypes—each issue has new and exciting material by mountain writers resulting in a high-quality magazine for mountain readers. Single issues are $1.50 each, subscriptions are $5.00 a year from *Mountain Review*, Box 660, Whitesburg, Ky. 41858.

PLOW, THE

The Plow is a monthly newsmagazine for the Appalachian Highlands. Published in Abingdon, Virginia, by a non-profit organization, it uses a 32-page tabloid format to deal with the concerns of people throughout the mountains. Each issue combines features about mountain history, traditions, crafts, music, and culture with investigative articles about concerns such as strip-mining, energy production, health care, tourism, and the age-old exploitation of the region by outside interests. Single issue price is $.35; the subscription rate is $4.00 per year. Write: *The Plow,* P. O. Box 1222, Abingdon, Va. 24210.

SOUTHERN APPALACHIAN MINISTRY IN HIGHER EDUCATION

Southern Appalachian Ministry in Higher Education is an organization that sponsors, in part, the publication of booklets concerning Appalachian social issues. One of the most recent offerings is a study of land development in the mountains by Anita Parlow. Another is a catalogue called *Appalachian Issues and Resources.* It's an 88-page listing of just about every resource in the mountains. Write: Southern Appalachian Ministry in Higher Education, 1538 Highland Avenue, Knoxville, Tenn. 37916.

SOUTHERN EXPOSURE

"*Southern Exposure* is a quarterly journal that lets the South speak for itself. Sometimes it's through the voice of a blues singer or the testimonial of a tobacco farmer, or maybe it's through the words of older Southerners, whether miner or minister, who made their contribution long ago to a better South today. In addition to oral history and intimate interviews from Minnie Pearl to Julian Bond, *Southern Exposure* uses investigative journalism to probe behind obvious characteristics of life in this region, to explore the deeper political and economic forces shaping its future. We place Appalachia within the larger context of the South, and crafts and music within the same culture that includes labor unions and anti-strip-mining groups. Previous articles in the journal have ranged from an in-depth oral history of the Davidson-Wilder mining battles of the 1930s and 'Bloody' Harlan County, 1930–74, to a photo essay on the crafts of the Tennessee Valley, from a portrait of Bascom Lamar Lunsford and mountain ballads to an investigation of land ownership and second-home developments in Appalachia. Our regular readers have come to expect almost anything from this quarterly journal. It may be a music book one time or a research report on energy conglomerates the next. What ties it together is our passion for this place and its people, our belief in being rooted in a culture in order to transform it into a new future. We view our culture in its broadest terms, and like the populists of old, we're not afraid to name the culprits who chronically destroy it, nor too meek to recommend a few alternatives for its improvement. If you'd like to know more about the *Southern Exposure,* write for a free brochure describing the issues published or send $8.00 for a year's subscription to P. O. Box 230, Chapel Hill, N.C. 27514." ——From a description submitted by *Southern Exposure.*

SOUTHERN REGIONAL COUNCIL

The Southern Regional Council is a non-partisan privately-funded research and action organization, founded in 1944. Composed of a 120-member governing board drawn from eleven Southern states, the Council is working to eliminate institutional racism and poverty by making the region's own institutions more accountable to all the people they are supposed to serve. The Council accomplishes its work through a small core staff and special-project staffs that analyze issues, monitor governmental responses to these issues, and document and publicize their findings with the goal of increasing citizen awareness of and influence on public policy at the national, state, and local levels.

Publications of this organization deal with education, employment, health, housing, rural and agricultural development, etc. A complete list of specific publications is available on request. Write: Southern Regional Council, 52 Fairlie Street, N.W., Atlanta, Ga. 30303.

UNITED MINE WORKERS JOURNAL

While the *UMW Journal* is partly devoted to educating the union membership on job health and safety problems and contract issues, this unusual union magazine also regularly carries features on the lives and problems of coal miners. Topics range from miners' attempts to improve housing, schools, and health care to what it's like to be a coal miner or a coal miner's wife.

This journal is published every two weeks and the subscription rate is $5.00 per year. Write: *United Mine Workers Journal*, 900 15th Street, N.W., Washington, D.C. 20005.